PEARSON   ALWAYS LEARNING

Stories from the Other Side

Thematic Memoirs

Sixth Edition

Cover art: *Occupy Wall Street, 2011,* by Ray Curran

Francis Edward Crowley, Ph.D.
Editor
Professor in the Humanities Emeritus
Gateway Community College
New Haven, Connecticut

Pearson Learning Solutions, 501 Boylston Street, Suite 900, Boston, MA 02116
A Pearson Education Company
www.pearsoned.com

Printed in the United States of America

3 4 5 6 7 8 9 10 V0ZN 17 16 15 14 13

000200010271292372

TF/NF

 ISBN 10: 1-256-79199-7
ISBN 13: 978-1-256-79199-7

Contents

Section Two—The Green World and the Naturalist's Eye

Section Three—Isolation and Community

Section Four—War and Human History

Section Five—America and the Rest of the World

Section Six—Challenges and Recovery

Dedication

to the 'Occupy Wall Street' Demonstrators
2011-2012

How to Use This Book

Stories from the Other Side challenges all readers to live in a larger world. With the premise that geography is destiny, this text covers exciting, new, international territory. With the understanding that almost everybody has a story to tell about personal renewal through hope in the human spirit, this text showcases some new stories from Nicaragua, Costa Rica, Guinea and Senegal in West Africa. It turns out that for this new edition the metaphor of "...*the other side*" is apt: it celebrates stories and voices not only geographically from the other side of the world, but also ethically and morally from the other side of class, race, gender, culture, economics and ethnic origins. It trumpets the values of diversity, individual enlightenment and inclusion; taken together thematically these stories call upon the collective wisdom from the four corners of the globe. Such a serviceable metaphor as "...the other side" also opens up space in this book for stories from the "other side of the tracks," so to speak, where we meet "Daniel" (name changed) who is homeless in New Haven, HIV-positive, addicted, mentally ill and an ex-offender. The other side, also, connotes "the undiscovered country" (Hamlet's metaphor for the afterlife), and in the early story "Death, Love and Life" by David Berg we meet his favorite aunt on her deathbed who seems to go back and forth in her last hours. The "other side" is a gender-bender in "Transmission"; it is childhood sexual abuse in "Proud to Be Me." Finally, *Stories* speaks to students in some of their own familiar voices and tells of experiences from their side.

1. **The Market**
   - developmental courses; E.S.L.; and college composition; college reading courses; high school writing and reading courses;
   - no prerequisites;
   - non-majors;
   - one semester course;
   - main text;
   - "Role modeling is the most powerful form of teaching, even as it was when Aristotle crystallized the idea for his students in ancient Greece: 'The soul never thinks without a picture,'" Timothy C. Brennan, Jr., "Uneasy Days for School" in *Newsweek* (p. 15), June 29, 1998.

2. **The Pedagogy**
   - each selection has a strong, clear and consistent, first person, narrative voice against which the student can test his/her own developing voice;

   - selections include the following range of narrative writing: essay, poetry, memoir, the new autobiography;

   - after reading these stories, students are encouraged to visit: a local museum, a nursing home, a homeless shelter, a day care and early learning facility, a dramatic production, a symphonic concert, a local library, an AIDS clinic or a local church or newspaper;

   - one semester, two-hour-per-week volunteer commitment to one of the above with the time sheets and interview questions is suggested as part of the curriculum.

3. **Distinguishing Features**
   - high school and college composition students (including under-prepared and marginalized) can find a similar voice to emulate in a text that is directly fitting for the challenges they face;
   - the thematic material of each essay shows an individual with "quiet courage" and common bravery overcoming the odds to become a complete and whole human being in the face of what life's experience has thrown at him/her. The touchstones for measuring success tend to be spiritual/ethical/moral;
   - current offerings tend to be disconnected from the actual lives and interests of this market, so telling stories of personal growth in an international setting and in a multi-cultural context challenges the new and diverse community college student of the new century to identify, question and pursue personal growth through writing—first in a journal/notebook and then for publication.

Acknowledgments

The editor wishes to gratefully acknowledge the contributions to STORIES from:

students, writers, poets,
photographers,
professors and adjunct faculty
represented in our new edition.

Thank you—one and all.
Francis Edward Crowley, Ph.D.
March 1, 2012

Section One

Family and Memory

Mother Tongue

Amy Tan

I am not a scholar of English or literature. I cannot give you much more than personal opinions on the English language and its variations in this country or others.

I am a writer. And by that definition, I am someone who has always loved language. I am fascinated by language in daily life. I spend a great deal of my time thinking about the power of language—the way it can evoke an emotion, a visual image, a complex idea, or a simple truth. Language is the tool of my trade. And I use them all—all the Englishes I grew up with.

Recently, I was made keenly aware of the different Englishes I do use. I was giving a talk to a large group of people, the same talk I had already given to half a dozen other groups. The nature of the talk was about my writing, my life, and my book, *The Joy Luck Club*. The talk was going along well enough, until I remembered one major difference that made the whole talk sound wrong. My mother was in the room. And it was perhaps the first time she had heard me give a lengthy speech, using the kind of English I have never used with her. I was saying things like, "The intersection of memory upon imagination" and "There is an aspect of my fiction that relates to thus-and-thus"—a speech filled with carefully wrought grammatical phrases, burdened, it suddenly seemed to me, with nominalized forms, past perfect tenses, conditional phrases, all the forms of standard English that I had learned in school and through books, the forms of English I did not use at home with my mother.

Just last week, I was walking down the street with my mother, and I again found myself conscious of the English I was using, the English I do use with her. We were talking about the price of new and used furniture and I heard myself saying this: "Not waste money that way." My husband was with us as well, and he didn't notice any switch in my English. And then I realized why. It's because over the twenty years we've been together I've often used that same kind of English with him, and sometimes he even uses it with me. It has become our language of intimacy, a different sort of English that relates to family talk, the language I grew up with.

So you'll have some idea of what this family talk I heard sounds like, I'll quote what my mother said during a recent conversation which I videotaped and then transcribed. During this conversation, my mother was talking about a political gangster in Shanghai who had the same last name as her family's, Du, and how the gangster in his early years wanted to be adopted by her family, which was rich by comparison. Later, the gangster became more powerful, far richer than my mother's family, and one day showed up at my mother's wedding to pay his respects. Here's what she said in part: "Du Yusong having business like fruit stand. Like off the street kind. He is Du like Du Zong—but not Tsung-ming Island people. The local people call putong, the river east side, he belong to that side local people. That man want to ask Du Zong father take him in like become own family. Du Zong father wasn't look down on him, but didn't take seriously, until that man big like become a mafia. Now important person, very hard to inviting him. Chinese way, came only to show respect, don't stay for dinner. Respect for making big celebration, he shows up. Mean gives lots of respect. Chinese custom. Chinese social life that way. If too important won't have to stay too long. He come to my wedding. I didn't see, I heard it. I gone to boy's side, they have YMCA dinner. Chinese age I was nineteen."

You should know that my mother's expressive command of English belies how much she actually understands. She reads the Forbes report, listens to Wall Street Week, converses daily with her stockbroker, reads all of Shirley MacLaine's books with ease—all kinds of things I can't begin to understand. Yet some of my friends tell me they understand 50 percent of what my mother says. Some say they understand 80 to 90 percent. Some say they understand none of it, as if she were speaking pure Chinese. But to me, my mother's English is perfectly clear, perfectly natural. It's my mother tongue. Her language, as I hear it, is vivid, direct, full of observation and imagery. That was the language that helped shape the way I saw things, expressed things, made sense of the world.

Lately, I've been giving more thought to the kind of English my mother speaks. Like others, I have described it to people as "broken" or "fractured" English. But I wince when I say that. It has always bothered me that I can think of no way to describe it other than "broken," as if it were damaged and needed to be fixed, as if it lacked a certain wholeness and soundness. I've heard other terms used, "limited English," for example. But they seem just as bad, as if everything is limited, including people's perceptions of the limited English speaker.

I know this for a fact, because when I was growing up, my mother's "limited" English limited my perception of her. I was ashamed of her English. I believed that her English reflected the quality of what she had to say. That is, because she expressed them imperfectly, her thoughts were imperfect. And I had plenty of empirical evidence to support me: the fact that people in department stores, at banks, and at restaurants did not take her seriously, did not give her good service, pretended not to understand her, or even acted as if they did not hear her.

My mother has long realized the limitations of her English as well. When I was fifteen, she used to have me call people on the phone to pretend I was she. In this guise, I was forced to ask for information or even to complain and yell at people who had been rude to her. One time it was a call to her stockbroker in New York. She had cashed out her small portfolio and it just so happened we were going to go to New York the next week, our very first trip outside California. I had to get on the phone and say in an adolescent voice that was not very convincing, "This is Mrs. Tan."

And my mother was standing in the back whispering loudly, "Why he don't send me check, already two weeks late. So mad he lie to me, losing me money."

And then I said in perfect English, "Yes, I'm getting rather concerned. You had agreed to send the check two weeks ago, but it hasn't arrived."

Then she began to talk more loudly. "What he want, I come to New York tell him front of his boss, you cheating me?" And I was trying to calm her down, make her be quiet, while telling the stockbroker, "I can't tolerate any more excuses. If I don't receive the check immediately, I am going to have to speak to your manager when I'm in New York next week." And sure enough, the following week there we were in front of this astonished stockbroker, and I was sitting there red-faced and quiet, and my mother, the real Mrs. Tan, was shouting at his boss in her impeccable broken English.

We used a similar routine just five days ago, for a situation that was far less humorous. My mother had gone to the hospital for an appointment, to find out about a benign brain tumor a CAT scan had revealed a month ago. She said she had spoken very good English, her best English, no mistakes. Still, she said, the hospital did not apologize when they said they had lost the CAT scan and she had come for nothing. She said they did not seem to have any sympathy when she told them she was anxious to know the exact diagnosis, since her husband and son had both died of brain tumors. She said they would not give her any more information until the next time and she would have to make another appointment for that. So she said she would not leave until the doctor called her daughter. She wouldn't budge. And when the doctor finally called her daughter, me, who spoke in perfect English—lo and behold—we had assurances the CAT scan would be found, promises that a conference call on Monday would be held, and apologies for any suffering my mother had gone through for a most regrettable mistake.

I think my mother's English almost had an effect on limiting my possibilities in life as well. Sociologists and linguists probably will tell you that a person's developing language skills are more influenced by peers. But I do think that the language spoken in the family, especially in immigrant families which are more insular, plays a large role in shaping the language of the child. And I believe that it affected my results on achievement tests, I.Q. tests, and the SAT. While my English skills were never judged as poor, compared to math, English could not be considered my strong suit. In grade school I did moderately well, getting perhaps B's, sometimes B-pluses, in English and scoring perhaps in the sixtieth or seventieth percentile on achievement tests. But those scores were not good enough to override the opinion that my true abilities lay in math and science, because in those areas I achieved A's and scored in the ninetieth percentile or higher.

This was understandable. Math is precise; there is only one correct answer. Whereas, for me at least, the answers on English tests were always a judgment call, a matter of opinion and personal experience. Those tests were constructed around items like fill-in-the-blank sentence completion, such as, "Even though Tom was, Mary thought he was—." And the correct answer always seemed to be the most bland combinations of thoughts, for example, "Even though Tom was shy, Mary thought he was charming": with the grammatical structure "even though" limiting the correct answer to some sort of semantic opposites, so you

wouldn't get answers like, "Even though Tom was foolish, Mary thought he was ridiculous." Well, according to my mother, there were very few limitations as to what Tom could have been and what Mary might have thought of him. So I never did well on tests like that.

The same was true with word analogies, pairs of words in which you were supposed to find some sort of logical, semantic relationship—for example, "Sunset is to nightfall as ___ is to ___." And here you would be presented with a list of four possible pairs, one of which showed the same kind of relationship: red is to stoplight, bus is to arrival, chills is to fever, yawn is to boring. Well, I could never think that way. I knew what the tests were asking, but I could not block out of my mind the images already created by the first pair, "sunset is to nightfall"—and I would see a burst of colors against a darkening sky, the moon rising, the lowering of a curtain of stars. And all the other pairs of words—red, bus, stoplight, boring—just threw up a mass of confusing images, making it impossible for me to sort out something as logical as saying: "A sunset precedes nightfall" is the same as "a chill precedes a fever." The only way I would have gotten that answer right would have been to imagine an associative situation, for example, my being disobedient and staying out past sunset, catching a chill at night, which turns into feverish pneumonia as punishment, which indeed did happen to me.

I have been thinking about all this lately, about my mother's English, about achievement tests. Because lately I've been asked, as a writer, why there are not more Asian Americans represented in American literature. Why are there few Asian Americans enrolled in creative writing programs? Why do so many Chinese students go into engineering! Well, these are broad sociological questions I can't begin to answer. But I have noticed in surveys—in fact, just last week—that Asian students, as a whole, always do significantly better on math achievement tests than in English. And this makes me think that there are other Asian-American students whose English spoken in the home might also be described as "broken" or "limited." And perhaps they also have teachers who are steering them away from writing and into math and science, which is what happened to me.

Fortunately, I happen to be rebellious in nature and enjoy the challenge of disproving assumptions made about me. I became an English major my first year in college, after being enrolled as premed. I started writing nonfiction as a freelancer the week after I was told by my former boss that writing was my worst skill and I should hone my talents toward account management.

But it wasn't until 1985 that I finally began to write fiction. And at first I wrote using what I thought to be wittily crafted sentences, sentences that would finally prove I had mastery over the English language. Here's an example from the first draft of a story that later made its way into The Joy Luck Club, but without this line: "That was my mental quandary in its nascent state." A terrible line, which I can barely pronounce.

Fortunately, for reasons I won't get into today, I later decided I should envision a reader for the stories I would write. And the reader I decided upon was my mother, because these were stories about mothers. So with this reader in mind—and in fact she did read my early drafts—I began to write stories using all the Englishes I grew up with: the English I spoke to my mother, which for lack of a better term might be described as "simple"; the English she used with me, which for lack of a better term might be described as "broken"; my translation of her Chinese, which could certainly be described as "watered down"; and what I imagined to be her translation of her Chinese if she could speak in perfect English, her internal language, and for that I sought to preserve the essence, but neither an English nor a Chinese structure. I wanted to capture what language ability tests can never reveal: her intent, her passion, her imagery, the rhythms of her speech and the nature of her thoughts.

Apart from what any critic had to say about my writing, I knew I had succeeded where it counted when my mother finished reading my book and gave me her verdict: "So easy to read."

Selected Poems

Martha Hayes

SURFACE ERRORS

"she always had the feeling that it was very, very dangerous to live even one day"
Virginia Woolf

At the first light of a June morning,
I watch my daughter before she wakes,
her figure carved into pink cotton sheets.
Her friend faces her, the inverse
of a similar shape. The space left
between them is just wide enough
for the boys they dream about.

Buried in sleep, their bodies
recover from the rush of the first Friday
night of summer: fast rides on Ferris wheels,
piercing screams of delight, a dark night
colored by flashing carnival lights.

After the phone punctures a perfect
sunrise, I know that I will have to tell them
of an evening that ingested one good friend,
left another still in a wooden stupor, a night
when sirens cried for one bad turn of the wheel.

I picture the survivor, her teenage body
lying stuck in death's posture:
face up, arms and legs arranged
neatly in a hospital bed. I try
this sorrow on my own child's face,
her friend's. Then I silently close
the bedroom door, take their news
downstairs with me, and try to stall
their morning for as long as I can.

ONE HOUSE

One house,
one tiny house
under a huge sky.
Inside a bed, a bare ankle
sticking out of a sheet,
an open mouth,
breathing.

How could one house,
the way it faced the sun,
the way the trees draped
their arms over its roof,
contain such joy?

Never mind what was floating
around in the dark, circling
its roof and preying on us,
such small fairies within,
sound asleep and unaware
of a dark crow's hunger.

NUMBER 11

As I walk toward the field,
a pop fly cracks the chilled October
air. You're playing deep center and my eyes
aren't what they used to be, but I see
you make the catch, hurl the ball
to second for the double play.
As I take my bleacher seat,
I can feel the ball in my throat.

When you're up at bat, you right your hips
And set the bat in the air as you wait for the pitch,
digging a man's foot into home base dirt.
Inning after inning, as you walk out to the field,
And reach for the rim of your cap, you brush
the years away like the umpire dusts home plate clean.
Then you make a play like you always have, carving
the fight to win into your jaw. Nothing
seems changed except the ball is now soft
and your face is rough with a night's
stubborn growth of stubble.

When you've slapped congrats
to the winners, tossed your glove
on the bench, you turn to me:

"So Mom, what are you doing today?"

I watch the catcher break open
a 12-pack, pass out cans of Bud.

"I have loads of work
to do," I lie.

I drive away, see you sitting
with the team. I can't hear
what you are saying, but I can tell
you are laughing by the way
your back jostles the number 11.

1950's Subtext

In the summer of 1957,
my sister was born.
My father got a raise, so
we moved into a new house.
It was red. My mom got
to choose the color.
Lilac flowers floated up
my bedroom walls and
the warm morning air
slipped into my window,
using its breath to lift the ends
of my dotted Swiss curtains.

My parents say it was a great
time: cheap milk and safe streets.

My dad drove us to the beach
in a station wagon with wood
on the sides, and we swam
in clean salt water and freckled
our skin on the hot sand.

The town was building me a new
school with polished floors
and brand new desks.

Everything smelled new,
even the dirt in my backyard.

In the summer of 1957, my mother
stayed home and took care of us.
She had been having a lot of babies.
One a year for awhile. She and my father kissed
in the kitchen and laughed. At dusk,
they drank gin and tonics in their lawn chairs.

In the summer of 1957,
the same summer my sister was born,
the same summer my parents
were planting new shrubs and buying
us savings bonds, Jimmy Wilson,
an African American handyman,
accused of stealing $1.95 was sentenced
to death in an Alabama courtroom.

Martha Hayes, Professor of English at Gateway Community College, has had her poems published in a number of literary journals including *Vermont Literary Review, Freshwater, TYCA Newsletter, Naugatuck River Review,* and *Orpheus 2.* She teaches composition, literature, and creative writing, is a certified yoga teacher, and is an avid traveler. She is the editor of *Insights,* a literary journal that features writing by community college faculty.

The Language of My Father

Dennis Francisco Cabrera

I awoke to see the lush green mountains as our captain announced we would be landing in San José International Airport soon. My sister Gladys was next to me, and she too was awakening after a long slumber. She and I had made all our flight arrangements the night before. We flew first class because there were no other seats left. All night we packed our bags, sent emails to friends and co-workers telling them we were leaving for Costa Rica for a week because our father was dying.

Our mother called, "*Su papa está mal. No va a poder regresar a casa.*" (Your father is not well. He won't be able to return home).

My father knew he had already returned home; perhaps that's why he began to let go of life more quickly. My mother had planned for the two of them to go to Costa Rica to see his family and friends and return to the U.S. for chemotherapy.

Gladys and I made our way off the plane and through customs. Our aunt was there waiting for us. She was happy to see us, but it was clear the circumstances muted our joy. She drove us to my grandparents' house where my mother and father were staying.

When we walked in my father came over towards us, looking bewildered. He looked through us as if searching for something in the distance. Eventually his eyes focused on me.

"Dennis, ¿verdad?" He sounded relieved to be able to place a name with a face. Those were the last words he spoke to me.

Over the next few days his condition grew worse. The doctor came to check on him and wrote a prescription for morphine, as the pain would only continually get worse as the days progressed. My mother had served as my father's nurse over the past few years. He had been diagnosed with prostate cancer, then stomach cancer, diabetes and finally terminal cancer that was everywhere. She was always there with him, so injecting him with morphine was no different.

One of the things the doctor told us, perhaps to comfort us, was that a person's hearing was one of the last things to go, so if there was anything we needed to tell him, he would hear us. Over the next few days my father would always have one of us by his side. Sometimes we'd speak to him. Often times I did what my father and I often did—sit side by side in silence. Many things occurred to me while I sat by his side those days and nights. I thought about arguments we had. I thought about watching soccer matches with him.

As a teenager I thought what most teenagers are so confidently self-assured of. I thought my parents, particularly my father, didn't understand me. Only, I knew I was right because my parents had both grown up in Costa Rica, and they didn't know what it was like to be a teenager in America. It never really occurred to me until much later that it was *I* who didn't really understand *them*. After all, my parents had lived twenty-five years in America whereas I had only spent a few months in their homeland. Looking back, I know even though I spoke in Spanish to him, my father and I didn't really speak the same language.

As I sat next to my father and he slowly faded, I thought about the time when he told me he was proud of me. It was rare for my father to show emotion. My sister and I always found out how my father was feeling through our mother. Your father is upset with you or your father was so thrilled. It didn't much matter if he was happy, angry, or sad, most people couldn't really tell most of the time. So I remember the day very clearly. I was up for a prestigious scholarship, and my parents and I went to a special brunch with the families of other finalists where they would announce the winners. I got second place and was a bit discouraged because winning would have meant not having to worry about how to pay for college. My parents took me to lunch to celebrate my placing well. My father turned to me and said, "*Sabes que estoy muy orgulloso de tí.*" (You know I'm very proud of you).

I responded, "*Sí, yo sé.*" (Yes, I know). I don't think he ever really knew how much it meant to me to hear him say it and not to have my mother come over and say, "you know your father's very proud of you," as usually was the case.

We took turns sitting next to my father day and night for five days. Sometimes he would try to stand, moaning because of the pain. I'm glad I had a chance to tell him I love him, and to say I was sorry for all those times I resented his advice. I often wonder what he would have said to me had he been able to respond.

For a long time I dreaded becoming like my father, the man who so often sat on the couch in silence probably lost in his own thoughts. I find myself often times doing things he did. My girlfriend occasionally gets angry when I brood for too long, not saying a word for what probably seems like an eternity.

The morning of the sixth day my father's heart faded until it was silent and his breath stopped. With his wife, daughter, son, and youngest brother by his side, he died. My uncle Luis Paulo, the priest, gave my father his last rites. At once we all felt a sense of calm at my father's passing. He had suffered in those last days despite being given morphine every few hours.

My father died on the couch in my grandmother's home. I carried his corpse with my uncle into the bedroom. There, we dressed him in one of my grandfather's suits. My mother said it was important because my father liked wearing nice clothing. She had promised my father not to allow anyone to see him nude. Somehow, she managed to put clean underwear on him by herself.

His eyes were open when he died. I tried closing them, but they would open up again. I held them shut with my thumb and index finger for about ten minutes before they remained closed. He began to smell of death even before the life left his body. The smell is unforgettable. My mother said it was the smell of cancer. She knew he had cancer even before the doctors confirmed it; she could smell it. Death in real life is never as nice and neat as it is in the movies.

When it was all over, my sister and I returned home. We had seen our father. We had asked for forgiveness for any wrongs we had committed. We reassured him we would be fine, and it was all right to give in if the pain was unbearable. We thanked him for giving us all he could. And then we buried him and wept for him. We consoled our mother, as he would have wanted. When it was all over, we returned to our lives in the U.S.A.

Sometime afterwards, as I sat with my sister reminiscing about our father, she turned to me and asked, "Do you think dad is here with us?'

She was as much asking about my spiritual beliefs as she was about our father. I know my father lives on through me. I inherited his wiry build, his silent demeanor, his male pattern baldness. He also gave me his incredible sense of honor, loyalty, and dedication to family.

I replied, "He's with us."

She Said "Yes" to Life

David Garnes

When I was a boy growing up in Springfield I liked to leaf through copies of the new magazines that were always stacked on my grandmother's bedside table. My grandmother, Sarah Garnes, had lived with us for as long as I could remember. My mother worked, so it was my grandmother who was always waiting at the door when I came home from school in the afternoon.

After a snack of milk and saltine crackers with Skippy peanut butter, I'd sometimes stretch out and read on her neatly made bed, on top of a white chenille bedspread with raised tufts that left an impression on my bare arms and legs. I much preferred my grandmother's copies of *Collier's, The Saturday Evening Post*, and *The Ladies Home* journal to my elementary school *Weekly Reader*.

I also liked the humor columns in *The Reader's Digest*, as well as a series of first-person articles in that magazine called "My Most Unforgettable Character." Sometimes the subject of the article was famous, but often the unforgettable character was a neighbor, a childhood friend, or a relative.

In the many years that have elapsed since those afternoons, I've frequently thought of the premise of that *Reader's Digest* series. What for those writers constituted "unforgettableness?" A celebrity's glamour ... the eccentric personality of a small-town resident or maybe a connection of a deeper, more profound nature? My own list of unforgettable characters—those people who have most influenced me always begins with my grandmother.

She was born Sarah Rose Tyre Gordon Munro Macaulay in Thurso, Scotland in 1887. She died at 94 of a heart attack in Springfield on a cold and sunny January day in 1981. She was healthy and sharp-minded to the end, and if ever a death could be described as a "good" one, it was hers. I understood this in the days following her funeral, and yet I knew I had experienced a profound loss, the first death of someone who I felt had loved me unconditionally.

Gradually, my grieving turned into something else, a more peaceful remembrance of the person who had been so much a part of my growing up. What has evolved in more recent years is a deep gratitude for having known my grandmother, for having had the chance to learn from the example of how she lived her life.

My earliest memory of my grandmother—Nana—is of evenings sitting together on a deep-cushioned sofa as she read me a bedtime story. As the oldest of her four grandchildren, I was an audience of one. In my memory, it's always just the two of us occupying a far corner of the living room, bathed in the warm glow of a brass floor lamp, oblivious to the rest of the family. Even now, I can feel the back-and-forth movement of her arm over my shoulder as she turned the pages of the book. I can still hear the soothing tones of her Scots burr as she related tales of Uncle Wiggly and Babar the Elephant.

I'm convinced that my lifelong love of reading owes much to this nightly ritual. Invariably, I'd plead "Read one more page, Nana!" Sometimes she'd give in and read not just one more page but a whole extra chapter. Usually, however, my mother would intervene and announce it was time for bed. I think I learned to read at a pre-school age because I wanted to get to that "one more page" on my own.

These story-time sessions also gave me a sense of security. Knowing I'd be read to every night provided a familiar pattern, a kind of routine that I think can be important to a child. I also felt safe and warm in the comfort of my grandmother's arms. And I know I sensed even then that she was a person who cared enough about me to read to me every single night. She even made me feel that Uncle Wiggly was as interesting to her as he was to me.

As I grew older, my grandmother told me different tales: her own true stories from her Scots girlhood. She was born in a small fishing village on the North Sea, close to where the boats leave for the Shetland and Orkney Islands. Her father's income as the local constable was barely adequate to support a family of a dozen children, and in those days jobs of any kind were scarce in that beautiful but desolate part of Scotland. In 1911, when she was 24, my grandmother and her younger sister Leila emigrated to the United States, following in the footsteps of three older brothers and a sister.

That was the last she saw of her parents, and as the years passed I expect she never imagined setting foot in Scotland again. Listening to my grandmother tell her stories, I would ask her, probably with some personal anxiety, "Will you ever go back to the old country?" She doubted she would, she said, because her home was now in America.

"Then I'll take you back for a visit someday—I promise," I'd reply.

And so I did, in 1968, when she was 81 and had been away from Scotland for 57 years. Preparing for the trip included the complicated task of obtaining a passport from the Scottish records office (fiercely proud of her Scots heritage, my grandmother had never given up her British citizenship).

Finally, early one June evening we flew out of JFK, bound for Glasgow and laden with presents for all our Scots relatives. As we cruised over the dark expanse of the ocean, I studied my grandmother, all dressed up and enjoying her British Airways dinner, looking like an elderly American lady headed for an escorted tour of the Highlands. I marvelled at the contrast between our overnight jet flight and her rough North Atlantic crossing in 1911, when she and Leila endured the rigors of tiny, storm-tossed steerage quarters.

What I remember most about that trip to Scotland is seeing all the places my grandmother had told me about in her stories: Castle Mey (now owned by the British Queen Mother), where as a girl she had played with a friend whose father was grounds-keeper for the mostly absent English owner; the coastal village of Wick, whose shops she remembered being draped in black at the death of Queen Victoria in 1901; the small stone school-house with leaded glass windows, now abandoned, where she had been educated in the justly proud tradition of the Scottish public school system; and most of all, the cottage where she had grown up, still occupied by her youngest sister Ella, who was only 9 when my grandmother left for America in 1911.

This trip was important to me in a lot of ways. After a week with my Scots relatives, I felt I had I gained a new family. The ties I established at that time have endured, and we have since enjoyed visits together on both sides of the "big pond." I also felt a real sense of history as I saw evidence of my grandmother's early life. I marvelled at the fact that she had witnessed some of the most tumultuous changes and events of the century—the advent of electricity, the airplane and the automobile; two world wars, and the arrival of the atomic age.

We had three memorable weeks in Scotland. When it came time to board the small prop plane to Glasgow, I knew, as did my grandmother and her sister, that we'd never all be together again. I was dreading this moment, mainly for my grandmother's sake. She was teary when we departed—we all were—and she waved from the window of the plane long after we had taxied down the runway. Soon after we took off, however, she gave me a poke and motioned me to look inside her pocketbook. Wrapped in plastic was a scruffy piece of plant, roots and dirt intact. "Heather," she said. "I hope I can manage to sneak it by the customs men. It's just the thing for my flower bed—back home."

This attitude was typical of my grandmother's character. She somehow managed to face life's difficulties and dark times—including a very young widowhood, the death of her middle-aged son (my father), and the devastating accidental death of a beloved granddaughter—and still continue on, her strength and sense of hope intact.

At my grandmother's funeral, as the minister spoke on the glories of the hereafter, I withdrew into my own musings. I wasn't sure I shared his vision, yet I couldn't help but imagine my grandmother at heaven's gate. No problem for her, I thought, if indeed she's up there awaiting some kind of judgment. To paraphrase the Scots poet Robbie Burns: "If there's another world, she lives in bliss. If there is none, she made the best of this."

Without ever articulating her beliefs—to me or to the world at large—my grandmother simply lived a consistent philosophy of never looking back, of accepting what was, of existing in the moment—in essence, of saying "Yes" to life. In this regard, she was, by example, my wisest teacher.

In my grief following her burial, I couldn't think of my grandmother as really dead. In many ways I still don't, so strongly does her spirit live on in my mind.

I had asked the minister at her funeral to read a passage from Edgar Lee Masters' *Spoon River Anthology*, a long prose-poem that relates the stories of a wide variety of characters in small mid-western town. One of the inhabitants, an old pioneer woman, speaks to her descendents from the grave. "What is this I hear of sorrow and weariness, anger, discontent, and drooping hope?" she asks. "Always remember—it takes life to love life."

Molly and the Metamorphosis of Me

David Garnes

One day as I was looking out my kitchen window I saw something in the shape of a blurry gray ball whiz across the yard and disappear under my neighbor's deck. A rabbit? No, its gait was too smooth. A possum? I'd never seen one around during the day, certainly not travelling at that speed. A mole? Too big. Probably a cat or kitten, I thought, although stray animals are rare in my neighborhood.

The next day I was out on my deck, catching some early summer sun. I lay facedown on my folding lounge chair, listening to the faint strains of music from my living room radio, lulled into that peaceful limbo between drowsiness and light sleep. A while later I could sense that the sun had gone behind a cloud. I opened my eyes, and as I turned to check the sky above me, I realized I was being watched.

About five feet away, at the edge of the deck stairway, perched a small, picture-perfect cat. Its long smoky gray hair framed a round face, and its yellow eyes were open wide and staring intently at me. The cat's somewhat stubby legs were placed together just-so, creating an unbroken row of tufted claws and an impression of both delicacy and strength. I remained motionless, still groggy in my half-awake state, mesmerized by the stare of those yellow eyes.

The sun soon came from behind the cloud, and when I raised my hand to shade my face, the cat turned, bounded down the stairs and disappeared. I lay back. My heart was pounding from the sight of such a beautiful little creature—and also from the mixed feelings I had always had about cats. Allergic all my life, I had always viewed cats with a healthy respect for the damage they could do to my well-being, literally within minutes of our being in the same room. I also regarded them as somewhat slinky prowlers who sneaked up on you unawares—when they felt like it. They were other people's pets, and I kept a comfortable distance.

The day after my encounter with the gray cat, I happened to mention the incident to my neighbor. "Oh, that's Molly," she said, explaining that a family down the street had recently banished Molly from their house because she was "bothering" their new baby. "They figure she'll get used to being outdoors before next winter."

As the summer wore on, Molly became a familiar figure around my deck, although our contact remained tentative. I liked looking at her and actually began to look forward to her daily arrival, but I never encouraged her to come any further. One day, however, I brought out a small saucer of milk, which she sniffed at and eventually drank. After that, she had some milk nearly every day.

As fall arrived and my afternoons on the deck ended, I began to leave Molly's milk on my front porch. One day, on impulse, I tried to coax her into the house, but she balked at stepping through the doorway. The next day, as I was making a sandwich, I decided to leave a little bit of tuna fish for her, in addition to the milk.

One cold and rainy morning at the end of September, I opened my door, food dish and milk saucer in hand. Molly came bounding from across the street, where she had been lying under a neighbor's car. As she approached my door, I beckoned to her, and this time she gingerly stepped into my front hallway. I set her plates down and walked away. A few minutes later she came into the living room, sniffed around a bit, and then proceeded to take a mini-tour of the house. When she headed back to the front door, I opened it and out she ran.

Molly's visits gradually extended to half-hour, then hour sessions, and finally to long afternoons of sleeping on my living room rug. By now, the days were decidedly cool, and my doors and windows were usually closed. I didn't seem to be bothered, however, by any sneezing or wheezing or itching eyes. Was it possible that I was no longer allergic to cats? I went so far as to pat Molly on the head. Once she playfully grabbed my hand, and I ended up with some scratch marks. My skin was red for a little while, but I noticed an absence of the angry bumps I remember from the many allergy tests I had as a kid. Could I consider inviting Molly to come and live with me?

To make things more "official" I talked to her owners, who were relieved at the prospect of relinquishing their claim to her, knowing she'd have a real place to live. I became determined to give it a try, although not without worried thoughts that I might have to banish Molly from yet a second home if things didn't work out.

I read as much as I could about how to cope with pet allergies. I bought an air purifier and learned about ways to control dander with frequent cleaning and brushing of Molly's coat.

One frosty evening in mid-October I decided to keep her in overnight. I waited until she was asleep in the living room before retiring to my bedroom. I quietly closed the door. During the night Molly fussed a bit on the other side, but when I emerged in the morning she was curled up in a living room chair. She meowed and rolled over on her back when she saw me.

Molly quickly adjusted to her new home. She knew exactly what to do in the litter box I installed in the basement, and she took immediately to the scratch post I installed next to my living room sofa. At this point, Molly was still outdoors frequently, but after an hour or so of sniffing around the yard she was always waiting at my front door to be let in.

The day I first held Molly and let her sit in my lap was a big event. Remember, we are talking here about a person who had never picked up a cat before in his entire life. My only concern was that I would have an allergy attack, but miraculously I didn't. Now Molly regularly hops up from the rug and we both enjoy the close contact, although I am still perfecting the art of turning magazine pages fast enough to avoid the swipe of her paw reminding me to get back to petting her. I've also ceased to close my bedroom door at night, and so Molly is a frequent occupant of the foot of my bed.

When I took Molly to the vet for an initial visit I was afraid she would think her long stay with me was over. She cried pitifully and reproachfully all the way in the car but was surprisingly docile with the doctor. Back home, she hopped up on her favorite chair, relieved, as I was, that the visit was over.

Before settling in for a nap, she gazed over at me. I looked back at her, and she fixed on me that intense yellow-eyed stare I remember from that first summer day on my deck. Don't worry, Molly, I thought, you'll always have a home now, and aren't you the lucky cat?

But as she curled into a ball and fell asleep, the thought occurred to me that maybe I had it wrong. Maybe it was the other way around. To be able to provide shelter and comfort for another living being and to be given love in return—now, that's to be lucky indeed.

Writing "Molly and the Metamorphosis of Me"

David Garnes

Beginnings:

I wanted to write a piece that was different from what I usually write about. I do a lot of essays for reference books, and even when I write first-person pieces they are generally about social issues. But the entrance of my cat Molly into my life was an event of great importance to me. I felt the need to clarify some of my own thoughts about it, and to tell others about my experience.

Content:

I did not want this to be one of those "my cute little cat Fluffy" stories. I wanted to convey several things:

*How Molly gradually entered my life, first as a stranger, then as a casual acquaintance, next as an occasional visitor, and finally as a beloved member of my family;

*The obstacles that I faced because of my allergies and how others can deal with these too;

*A picture of Molly: not only of her physical beauty but of her independent, intrepid and loving nature;

*Perhaps most importantly, the significance of companionship and love in our lives.

Method:

I decided that the best way to tell this story was, in effect, simply to tell the story: that is, to recount in what I hoped would be vivid, visual scenes the way that my relationship with Molly evolved. I also hoped that by putting in some practical details, I could give some information to those who, like me, had not been able to have pets because of their allergies.

I was conscious in writing this piece of going from the "beginning" to the "end." A chronological sequence of events may not be necessary to follow in all true accounts, but I felt it was important for this article.

Drafts and Final Version:

Over the course of several days, I made a lot of notes about what I might include in my story. Then, one day, when I felt the time was "right," I sat down with these notes and began to write. I was not concerned about good writing at this point, just to get the story down (it has taken me a long time to be able to do this and not to agonize over every sentence).

After finishing the first draft, I put it aside. Several days later, I read it over, made a lot of edits, and put it aside again. I repeated this at least two more times. I have found that it is important for me to have the time to do this kind of re-reading and editing.

When I felt I had a "final" version, I asked myself if I had achieved at least some, if not most, of the goals I had set out to accomplish. In this case, I did feel that my story had come together. For this piece, by telling the story chronologically and by highlighting some key facts and events, I hope I conveyed to the reader what I intended—a story about how Molly came into my life and, in so doing, transformed me.

Night of the Grunion

Ken Lamberton

I like to remind my three teenage daughters that if they insist on husbands, I'm all for arranged marriages. I would like to spare you the grief of courtship and romance, I tell them. The only reason romance is so attractive is that it invites risks, which heighten the experience and make you feel alive. So why seek romance when you can stand in three feet of dark ocean with millions of swarming, shin-bumping grunion?

Yes, grunion. Fish. But not just any fish. Grunion are the sexiest of fish. My daughters might disagree, but I think a grunion run with Dad is better than any beach with boys.

The girls and I had always chosen Salt Creek Beach near Dana Point, California. And on this particular night, as usual, we followed a long stairway that dropped us through bank-hugging ice plant to spill us onto a narrow beach.

Darkness came as we waited on the sand, backed against a jumble of rocks above the high tide line. White scarves of fog flagged landward. Blue phosphorescence pulsed along the crest of each wave as it curled toward shore. We settled back to watch, pulling blankets over our shoulders and huddling together for warmth. Occasionally, couples walked by, and we could tell by their conversations that they had no idea of our presence.

Suddenly, Kasondra said, "Oh, look!" And there, only twenty yards away, stood a couple, he in a tuxedo and she in a pink chiffon evening gown. They danced slowly, arms around each other, her head on his shoulder, while music played from a portable stereo.

After a few minutes, Melissa became ecstatic: "Look! He's down on his knees! He's holding out something. A box—it's a ring! Oh my God! He's proposing to her!" Now the girls were all atwitter.

I started to say something and Jessica jabbed me in the ribs and covered my mouth. I pulled away from her and shouted "No! Don't do it! Run for your life!" But the words came out garbled as more hands pummeled me.

Then he was back on his feet and holding her. She held the box and had begun to cry.

"She said 'Yes'! She said 'Yes'!" Melissa repeated.

"They're doomed," I said.

After the couple left, we seemed to be the only people on the beach. The girls dashed madly to the surf, daring the breakers to catch them. Jessica rolled her jeans into sodden masses at her knees and raced along the surf line, long blond curls flying behind her. Melissa practiced karate, her movements like a dance set to the music of crashing waves. Kasondra, her long legs kicking against the sand, ran up and down the beach, in and out of the water, twirling and falling, dragging around seaweed in a wild frenzy matched only by the grunion massing offshore.

Then, our lights started reflecting quick slips of silver shooting along each wave front. Melissa yelled and darted into the waves to scoop up one in her hands, but the blue-green knife of a fish wriggled out of her fingers as she grappled for it, shouting, "Hey, hey, hey!" Soon, hundreds were streaking over the flat wet sand, congregations of males horseshoeing around each spawning female.

Now grunion are an animal I can admire, I thought. No messing with long courtships, no emotional hang-ups with relationships and their multiple contusions, just one frenetic night of activity to propagate the species and it's back into the wide ocean.

Human love, on the other hand, is treacherous. It invents complete fabrications in your mind. It brings the downfall of civilizations. Love is poison, a venomous snake. . . . and it is the most wonderful thing that can ever happen to you.

I'm the one who was doomed. How many years had I brought my girls to that beach for the summer run? My gift of grunion, I realize now, pales beside the one offered in a small velvet box held by a lover's hand.

That night, their young bodies blurring against the white sand, my daughters were also massing, preparing for lives beyond mine when, according to nature's incomprehensible vastness, some near-future moon would raise tides already surging within them, and draw them to other shores to begin families of their own.

Author Biography

When Ken Lamberton published his first book *Wilderness and Razor Wire* (Mercury House, 2000), the *San Francisco Chronicle* called it an ". . . entirely original: an edgy, ferocious, subtly complex collection of essays. . . ." The book won the 2002 John Burroughs Medal for outstanding nature writing. He has published four books and more than a hundred articles and essays in places like the *Los Angeles Times, Arizona Highways,* the *Gettysburg Review,* and *The Best American Science and Nature Writing 2000.* In 2007, he won a Soros Justice Fellowship for his fourth book, *Time of Grace: Thoughts on Nature, Family, and the Politics of Crime and Punishment* (University of Arizona Press, 2007). Currently, he is finishing a book about Arizona's "Dry River," the Santa Cruz. He holds degrees in biology and creative writing from the University of Arizona and lives with his wife in an 1890s stone cottage near Bisbee.

Process Notes

To begin with, I connect to the landscape, that part of our place that Scott Russell Sanders calls "a stretch of earth overlaid with memory, expectation, and thought." I may spend days in one spot, sitting on a rocky outcrop, sleeping in a sand-drenched riverbed. I take notes, adding to my journal not so much what I see and hear but what I feel, what I believe about the place. It's only much later when I sit at my computer, notebook in hand, and revisit that landscape in my mind that I can really write about it.

Amazingly, if I'm very lucky, after many drafts, false starts, and dead ends, the writing begins to tell me what it wants to be about. I always let it have its way.

Selected Poems

Chester H. Schnepf

HAPPY BIRTHDAY

Aging—growing older
Appears a queer thing
Wrinkles—countless wrinkles
To each and every crannie of
The flesh—except
Only not the brain
It alone must feel slighted
Never gaining any new convolutions
Only losing!
Our mind with all its secrets
Dreams and Fears
All fade—empty away
Aging—growing older
Only yields
countless countless wrinkles
To our skin
And as for wisdom It bolts and
flies in countless minute moments
Aging—growing dead such a
curious, queer and peculiar thing.

EASTER DINNER

A smile in everyone's eye floated across
The wide table
Through the crystal wine glasses,
Bouncing off bone china dishes
Reflecting in pepper and salt shakers
Crystallized over crushed ice olive platters
Flickering captive in butane candle dance
Passed on up the cream napkin resting
On lace linen handed down from the dead,
Caressing the edge
To the eyes of the beholder
across the table smiling back.

TOTALLY MELODRAMIC YET TRUE

There's something about a forsaken
lighthouse chalk white decaying desolate
jutting out from craggy mica incrusted
primordial rock cliffs constantly bombarded
by greenish waves stretching its spray
up toward around the man made walls ever
reaching to grab
dark blue black rain clouds descending
downward

There's something about a forsaken
lighthouse which can revive—give a second
Chance even to the dullest man.

We go to the movies to sometimes momentarily escape our own movie! William Carlos Williams was absolutely correct—the images which we allow to enter our camera (mind) are the most essential to our sense of self and our relationship to the world.

GOING TO THE MOVIES

Heading to New Haven with my
daughter—six years old and full of
life—driving I notice parked a
police car complete two officers
reading from clip boards
Busy they pay not attention between
them—a young adult say seventeen
handcuffed lost
Stares blank ahead confused

Heading to New Haven home of Yale
with my six year old daughter full
of life and laughter—driving I see
parked on benches sitting in a row
all too young adults say seventeen
blue and green haired kids not
students just staring blank and
confused armed with roller boards
skin tattoos pierced body parts
all into death before living life

Heading to New Haven with my daughter just six
years old so full
of talking—driving I spy an old woman dressed in
rags screaming
her head and arms shaking the humid
air is thick surrounding all
head and arms are shaking demanding
her voice worn out from screaming
be heard
While shoppers/students pass her
pass her by
Staring to the sky she
screams
a confusion no one hears

Heading to New Haven with my
six year old full of smiles and
teeth—driving I view a flower man
with cart hawking his hand raised high
with a single rose—target for a pair of
lovers
he stares confused with flower unnoticed

Heading to New Haven to the
movies with my little girl we
enter the theatre to see and hear
color visions projected largely
sounds and sights and colors flood
our minds
and my little girl and I enjoy
the show
and I rest from the rest of us
outside where the sights and sounds
and colors of the human melodrama
never end.

Every family, I believe, has a "wise one"—a Shaman who can stand back from day to day family events, conflicts—and speak from love and wisdom. My aunt was one of those "old souls."

Aunt Bea

I dreamt of you last night
How many years has it been since
Since last we spoke and laughed
and discussed all those discussions
my upcoming graduation
the War which waited for me like
a cat—I the bird nervously
sitting in the sights
You listened and spoke of family
and honor and what it would do
to my father if I just said
"up yours" to the draft
We spoke of many things
of family and of Life and
discussed all those discussions
which I had no answers to

I dreamt of you last night
How thirty years have vanished
Since last we spoke and laughed
and discussed all those discussions
and then suddenly you had to
leave and I placed a yellow
rose between your folded hands
and spoke some words of sorrow
which only we could hear

I dreamt of you last night
I saw you in my room
and we did talk of many things
and laugh and cry together
of War which only the old
remember now of my father and of Life
Dear God how many years has thirty
years been
since last we saw each other
and I placed the yellow rose upon
your chest and whispered in your ear.

I dreamt of you last night.

TOWERS AND STAIRS

towers and stairs
and circles
ascending descending
whirling gyres always spinning
encompass envelop each of us and
send us in orbits
towers and stairs
and circles
ascending   descending
we climb a few steps
fall back a few more
Yeats knew this well
yet was his own prisoner
life doesn't
march on
but spins
towers and stairs
and circles unending

Jewelry Does Make the Person

Highlighted by ceiling lights
the museum mummy stared
upward transfixed speechless
presenting a very sad sight

An ancient prince now lay here
a lump of rags and clay
an unnerving sight except
for his beetle gold necklace
Lapis deep blue bright-stunning
even more impressive under today's museum
ceiling lights

How his jewelry caught my
eyes and spoke of who
he was and
and I thought
when I am dead
I'll go out wearing my
jewelry my best jewelry
in case I am cased and
highlighted by museum ceiling
Lights a thousand years from now
I want to make a statement.

THE FORCES OF GOOD AND EVIL

A blade of grass
A spinning blade
An unending battle

STAR TRAVELERS ARE FEW

If I were you and yet not
Thirty
I'd break the spell of sameness and
Make a new accommodation
In short I'd vamoose and soar
To the upper regions
Or
You can wait until you are me.

FATHER

My father was an artist
Complex to the core
He was a giver who never stopped
Giving
Except his thoughts they were his
And when he fought with creative stuff
You knew to walk away
My father was an artist
Complex as heaven and hell
And when he had the pencil
The brush the chalk in hand
His expression was limitless
A man of very few words
His were talents and visions and
Dreams within
He was a giver who never stopped
Giving
Except his thoughts were his.

THE PARK

I fled to the park to hide from them:
>>the sad eyed fifteen year old girl borrow
>>>a quarter
>I fled to the park
>>passing gloria who affirms her love to him
>>>through
>>hallmark picture quotes (mr. sweet thoughts)
>>>both

>>throwing slices of bread on the saturated pond
>I fled to the park
>>hear the faintly warbles of fujica nikon
>>>yashica
>I fled to the park
>>seeing young promising drawers who can't
>>>sketch
>>sketching
>I fled to the park
>>coming face to face to faceless goggled love
>>>children
>>slinging crude mouthed guitars walking toward
>>>the shining
>>parking lot stepping on forcing butts to
>>>nuzzle between
>>the toes
>I fled to the park
>>wrinkled faces watching the ripples of bread-
>>>scum pushed by
>>misplaced swans
>I fled to the park
>>a painted whore the rouge red lip virgin for
>>>the city
>>lunch crowd designed to accommodate
>I fled to the park
>>and children graced this park like so many
>>>popsicle sticks
>>stuck on the bottom of shoes

I fled to the park
    watching the planting of a chinese cherry
      tree purchased
    for its oriental poetic grace
I fled to the park
    to face a sign—closed tomorrow
      for painting lot lines
    to hide from them—
I fled.

The Park—written in 1971 Roslyn Park, N.Y. L.I. I would visit this park many times while a student (college). I noticed many students my own age. By the way, I was one of these individuals but did not know it at the time. In the sixties and seventies we were all trying to find ourselves quickly!

Children trying to be adults (accomplished) practice over and over again at being unique.

MISSING IN ACTION WWII

His parents were sent a telegram
Your son is missing in action
Shot down over South China Sea
A nose gunner in a B-24 moving top speed
His cannons were blasting still blasting
When his plane blew up behind him
Jumping into black sky falling too fast
He cut his chute open with his
pocket knife
falling through black sky screaming
falling through black sky crying
and then it opened—a chute that
saved his life
falling falling to earth
he hit the China dirt hard

His parents were sent a telegram
Your son is missing in action
Lost in China for months
he survived.

I now have the telegram
Long ago once sent by him—
My father.

Some memories you have to actually reconstruct from bits of information—2nd hand. You must construct a picture of something you were never actually part of.

RITUAL

Each of us have a
Breakfast place
a special place
Filled with stacks of steamy
Cups and plates
Where magic pancakes
Are made
Where crowds and noise and
Breakfast smells prepare us for
the day
Each of us have a
Breakfast place—a girdled cave
Where we can hide and feed.
The most important moment of
our day.

Each of our days are nothing more than rituals we have fallen into. Yet we make the best of them. Each ritual we perform is a memory established the day before.

My Process of Writing Poetry

Chester H. Schnepf

For me, the process of writing poetry has never been a whimsical undertaking. My poetry is based on revelations which have occurred in my lifetime which are of a joyous and sad nature. Sometimes an image, call it a picture, will come to my mind, and this will then develop into a specific theme which reflects a powerful moment which occurred in my life. This picture, or image, if it is strong enough, will eventually move to becoming words which seem to capture the emotion and meaning for a poem. For example, this process occurred in my poem "Easter Dinner" with the words "Passed on up the cream napkin resting". Once this line was created a flood of memories concerning a young boy's Easter dinner with his family took on a story for this writer. I vividly could see my grandfather and my other family members sharing this time together. The young boy experiences the moment, but fails to realize that as time moves on, many of the individuals seated at the dinner table will pass on and perhaps be remembered through similar objects which are mentioned throughout the poem. In a knave way the young boy is clever enough to at least superficially record this Easter dinner in his memory. This particular poem has been reworked by me over a thirty year period. This is why I say my poetry is not written as a whimsical release. In the poem titled "Happy Birthday", I recently thought about the absurdity of birthday parties, especially one's own as one ages. The words "Aging—growing dead" just appeared in my mind and acted as the generating focus for the rest of the poem. Again, I seem to first have a strong feeling of joy or sadness which then seems to transform itself into a specific event which can either be of my past or present and then the words seem to come from this source. In the poem "Totally Melodramatic Yet True", I remember walking with my little girl at the beach and being somewhat drained of energy from the day's activities. All of a sudden, this Gothic-like lighthouse appeared and I was instantly revived. Nature had overtaken this structure and transformed it into something greater than itself. So with each poem the writing and rewriting seems to never end. One must continually, over a period of time, go back and revisit the poem if only to test for oneself the honesty of one's feelings and truth of one's thoughts.

The process of creativity is a draining one in terms of presenting thoughts which you hope have some universality said in a unique way. The process of writing and rewriting appears to be endless yet so worthwhile.

Patchen's Kitchen

Franz Douskey

Everyone I know who was alive then and now can tell me where they were when John Kennedy was murdered. I was swimming in the Atlantic Ocean, on a sunny, warm November afternoon, in Connecticut, with a friend, David Dannenberg, when a cop we knew drove up and asked if we had heard about Kennedy. We thought he was telling us a joke but there was no punch line. Dave and I walked home. That was the last time I went swimming in an ocean.

I also remember another time, another killing. Dr. Martin Luther King, Jr. I was sitting in the kitchen of Kenneth and Miriam Patchen, in Palo Alto, when a neighbor called and told Miriam. After she got off the phone, she said, "Better stay here tonight. They've killed Dr. King." That was the darkest night of my life. In a lot of our lives. Something was taken away from us and any hope of trust, of any reconciliation with the past was gone.

That night Miriam and I drank the blackest coffee and talked quietly for hours. I was on my way to Oakland. But Oakland was on fire. So was Detroit, Washington, Chicago, and L.A. There was fire everywhere, but they weren't burning cities. That was our innocence being burned. Our belief in the American Dream turned into ashes. And now it was time for us to wake up. I didn't make it to Oakland that night, but stayed at a small motel off Highway 101.

I wish I could tell you where I was the next few days, but I don't remember. There were the usual roads into the desert, the neon cactus motel signs. Desolation radio, and no way back from that grief. Even now.

Several days later I woke up in my place in Sonora. The sky was silver and hot. So bright, I couldn't see unless I squinted. In those days, I slept during the day and wrote at night. And if I was restless I'd take a walk in the desert. Everyone needs a place where the world is quiet, where the stars pour across the sky as though someone has just spilled an enormous bucket of tar filled with luminous fireflies.

I'd write through the night and into the morning. Patchen taught me that. You work when no one is around. Even the people you love, the do-gooders and the hangers-on, they all want a piece of you, so you have to find a way to work. Patchen used to stay up for days. His legs would fall asleep, but he didn't notice until he tried to stand, and then he'd fall over.

Kenneth Patchen had published forty books of poems, plays and novels, and he was one of my early influences. For years he had been living in massive pain due to botched operations on his back. When he tried to sue the doctors, they responded by cutting off his supply of pain killers. So he found various, random drugs wherever he could. His bureau was covered with numerous bottles of pain killers, supplied primarily through underground sources. By the time I met him he was a huge, bearlike man with circles under his eyes struggling around his home on two canes.

Miriam said I was the only person allowed in their home on Sierra Court other than Kenneth's dentist. Allen Ginsberg and Lawrence Ferlinghetti had tried to visit, but couldn't get in. This prompted Larry to write Jon Webb of Loujon Press that "… someone was sitting on Patchen and ought to get off."

It was not easy being around Kenneth. He had trouble sleeping, and his stomach was ruined from years of taking various pain killers. Whenever I was in town I'd buy a couple of cases of Similac, a dietary product that was easy to digest. And let me say this. Kenneth was not always happy to see me. Once Miriam and I had gone shopping (she didn't drive, and they didn't own a car), and we stopped for coffee. When we got back home there was a vicious note on the kitchen table. In his thick scrawl, Kenneth wanted to know where we were and what we had been up to. These notes were a signal for me to leave, to keep whatever peace there could be.

He was totally dependent on and in love with Miriam. I would head for Frisco, or Seattle. I'd often head to Spirit Lake, my favorite place on the planet until Mount St. Helens erupted and filled it in. In those days, in the words of Galway Kinnell, I "floated freely."

Miriam would write and tell me what was going on and I treasure those beautiful, fearful letters. Kenneth had found one of a kind in her, and she stayed with him through the long struggle.

I'd visit from time to time, write letters that said nothing because I feared that anything warm or loving might arrive when Kenneth's chemicals were going bad, and he'd take his pain out on Miriam, the source of courage and love, the way lovers will sometimes do.

In the spring of 1970, I was at the University of Arizona Poetry Center. I stopped in to visit with Lois Shelton, the poetry center director and wife of Richard Shelton, great teacher, poet and essayist. Lois and I were casually talking when, out of the blue, she asked if I'd like to be a part of the Kenneth Patchen Memorial poetry reading she was scheduling.

The words didn't fit. I was underwater. What was she saying? She thought I knew. I walked into the library and cried for awhile. Now logically there was nothing to cry about. Kenneth was out of pain and Miriam was free from the years of struggle and fear. But what has logic to do with it. I'm a poet, damn it.

I called Miriam. She was okay. She had good neighbors who had looked after her for years. I told her I'd see her in a few days. So instead of being a part of the memorial reading, I was in Miriam's kitchen again. We sat and talked. The door bell rang. It was Al Young, a young poet and novelist Miriam thought the world of. He didn't come in. He was dropping some papers off. Notices of a memorial reading maybe. There were so many.

Miriam told me about the night Kenneth died. He was having a hard time. He had banged his head in the bathroom, and fell asleep on the floor.

She said he often collapsed on the floor and slept because it relaxed his body and he wasn't in as much pain, so she let him lie there.

Early the next morning he was still on the floor. She noticed his color wasn't right. She phoned a neighbor who happened to be a policeman. He tried to revive Kenneth, called an ambulance, but it was over. She told me this not with tears, although I know she missed Kenneth, but with a sense of relief, and knowing her, the relief she felt was for the end of Kenneth's two decades of unending, irreversible pain.

So after forty books, several plays, the famous picture books, the man who pioneered poetry to jazz before the Beats, before Kerouac, before Ginsberg, had quietly slipped away in his sleep.

I do not know how old Miriam was, but she was absolutely beautiful, ageless. And that was the last time I saw her. You know how one road leads to another. Families make us serious. We find our own Miriams. If we're lucky.

A few weeks later I was in Santa Cruz. I was sitting in the home of George Hitchcock, one of America's three great poetry editors. We were sifting through submissions for his magazine, *kayak*. He told me he was heading to San Francisco in a few days. There was going to be a large Kenneth Patchen memorial community reading with Lawrence Ferlinghetti, and maybe Gary Snyder and Philip Whelan. George asked if I was going. I said I wasn't. Probably head back to Tucson. Which I did. Then back east, to Connecticut, where Kenneth and Miriam started out. Not far from Norfolk where Kenneth's publisher, James Laughlin started New Directions Books.

New Directions was quite a publishing house. Laughlin published Henry Miller, Patchen, Nabokov, Rimbaud, Gary Snyder, Richard Eberhart, and Djuna Barnes, Celine, Dylan Thomas, Pound, Levertov, and Neruda. When I was teaching myself how to write, I learned from them. If New Directions published a book, I bought it.

What was unique about New Directions' writers was that they were all outsiders. Miller's books were banned. Celine and Neruda were exiles. Pound was put into an asylum. Rimbaud was dead at twenty-one after a life of chaos. Patchen's novels were impossible to read without a sense of delirium. There isn't a publisher around today who would have the insight and the guts that Laughlin had.

James Laughlin died just last week. He was eighty-three. In his final years he received praise for his own poetry that had been neglected for five decades. I understand there's going to be a big memorial reading. I won't be there. I can't stand to be around the crowd of literary ghouls that is always ready to pay homage to the dead, but never to the living. You'll find me miles away from the dead, standing hip deep in a river, or hip deep inside someone capable of love.

Fuck the dead! My place is with the living.

One Last Time

Gary Soto

Yesterday I saw the movie *Gándhi*[1] and recognized a few of the people—not in the theater but in the film. I saw my relatives, dusty and thin as sparrows, returning from the fields with hoes balanced on their shoulders. The workers were squinting, eyes small and veined, and were using their hands to say what there was to say to those in the audience with popcorn and Cokes. I didn't have anything, though. I sat thinking of my family and their years in the fields, beginning with Grandmother who came to the United States after the Mexican revolution to settle in Fresno where she met her husband and bore children, many of them. She worked in the fields around Fresno, picking grapes, oranges, plums, peaches, and cotton, dragging a large white sack like a sled. She worked in the packing houses, Bonner and Sun-Maid Raisin, where she stood at a conveyor belt passing her hand over streams of raisins to pluck out leaves and pebbles. For over twenty years she worked at a machine that boxed raisins until she retired at sixty-five.

Grandfather worked in the fields, as did his children. Mother also found herself out there when she separated from Father for three weeks. I remember her coming home, dusty and so tired that she had to rest on the porch before she trudged inside to wash and start dinner. I didn't understand the complaints about her ankles or the small of her back, even though I had been in the grape fields watching her work. With my brother and sister I ran in and out of the rows; we enjoyed ourselves and pretended not to hear Mother scolding us to sit down and behave ourselves. A few years later,

however, I caught on when I went to pick grapes rather than play in the rows.

Mother and I got up before dawn and ate quick bowls of cereal. She drove in silence while I rambled on how everything was now solved, how I was going to make enough money to end our misery and even buy her a beautiful copper tea pot, the one I had shown her in Long's Drugs. When we arrived I was frisky and ready to go, self-consciously aware of my grape knife dangling at my wrist. I almost ran to the row the foreman had pointed out, but I returned to help Mother with the grape pans and jug of water. She told me to settle down and reminded me not to lose my knife. I walked at her side and listened to her explain how to cut grapes; bent down, hands on knees, I watched her demonstrate by cutting a few bunches into my pan. She stood over me as I tried it myself, tugging at a bunch of grapes that pulled loose like beads from a necklace. "Cut the stem all the way," she told me as last advice before she walked away, her shoes sinking in the loose dirt, to begin work on her own row.

I cut another bunch, then another, fighting the snap and whip of vines. After ten minutes of groping for grapes, my first pan brimmed with bunches. I poured them on the paper tray, which was bordered by a wooden frame that kept the grapes from rolling off, and they spilled like jewels from a pirate's chest. The tray was only half filled, so I hurried to jump under the vines and begin groping, cutting, and tugging at the grapes again. I emptied the pan, raked the grapes with my hands to make them look like they filled the tray, and

---

[1]The 1982 film biography of the nonviolent revolutionary Mohandas Gandhi (known as Mahatma), which was set in part among the peasants of India. [Eds.]

jumped back under the vine on my knees. I tried to cut faster because Mother, in the next row, was slowly moving ahead. I peeked into her row and saw five trays gleaming in the early morning. I cut, pulled hard, and stopped to gather the grapes that missed the pan; already bored, I spat on a few to wash them before tossing them like popcorn into my mouth.

So it went. Two pans equaled one tray—or six cents. By lunchtime I had a trail of thirty-seven trays behind me while mother had sixty or more. We met about halfway from our last trays, and I sat down with a grunt, knees wet from kneeling on dropped grapes. I washed my hands with the water from the jug, drying them on the inside of my shirt sleeve before I opened the paper bag for the first sandwich, which I gave to Mother. I dipped my hand in again to unwrap a sandwich without looking at it. I took a first bite and chewed it slowly for the tang of mustard. Eating in silence I looked straight ahead at the vines, and only when we were finished with cookies did we talk.

"Are you tired?" she asked.

"No, but I got a sliver from the frame," I told her. I showed her the web of skin between my thumb and index finger. She wrinkled her forehead but said it was nothing.

"How many trays did you do?"

I looked straight ahead, not answering at first. I recounted in my mind the whole morning of bend, cut, pour again and again, before answering a feeble "thirty-seven." No elaboration, no detail. Without looking at me she told me how she had done field work in Texas and Michigan as a child. But I had a difficult time listening to her stories. I played with my grape knife, stabbing it into the ground, but stopped when Mother reminded me that I had better not lose it. I left the knife sticking up like a small, leafless plant. She then talked about school, the junior high I would be going to that fall, and then about Rick and Debra, how sorry they would be that they hadn't come out to pick grapes because they'd have no new clothes for the school year. She stopped talking when she peeked at her watch, a bandless one she kept in her pocket. She got up with an "*Ay, Dios,*" and told me that we'd work until three, leaving me cutting figures in the sand with my knife and dreading the return to work.

Finally I rose and walked slowly back to where I had left off, again kneeling under the vine and fixing the pan under bunches of grapes. By that time, 11:30, the sun was over my shoulder and made me squint and think of the pool at the Y.M.C.A. where I was a summer member. I saw myself diving face first into the water and loving it. I saw myself gleaming like something new, at the edge of the pool. I had to daydream and keep my mind busy because boredom was a terror almost as awful as the work itself. My mind went dumb with stupid things, and I had to keep it moving with dreams of baseball and would-be girlfriends. I even sang, however softly, to keep my mind moving, my hands moving.

I worked less hurriedly and with less vision. I no longer saw that copper pot sitting squat on our stove or Mother waiting for it to whistle. The wardrobe that I imagined, crisp and bright in the closet, numbered only one pair of jeans and two shirts because, in half a day, six cents times thirty-seven trays was two dollars and twenty-two cents. It became clear to me. If I worked eight hours, I might make four dollars. I'd take this, even gladly, and walk downtown to look into store windows on the mall and long for the bright madras shirts from Walter Smith or Coffee's, but settling for two imitation ones from Penney's.

That first day I laid down seventy-three trays while Mother had a hundred and twenty behind her. On the back of an old envelope, she wrote out our numbers and hours. We washed at the pump behind the farm house and walked slowly to our car for the drive back to town in the afternoon heat. That evening after dinner I sat in a lawn chair listening to music from a transistor radio while Rick and David King played catch. I joined them in a game of pickle, but there was little joy in trying to avoid their tags because I couldn't get the fields out of my mind: I saw myself dropping on my knees under a vine to tug at a branch that wouldn't come off. In bed, when I closed my eyes, I saw the fields, yellow with kicked up dust and a crooked trail of trays rotting behind me.

The next day I woke tired and started picking tired. The grapes rained into the pan, slowly filling like a belly, until I had my first tray and started my second. So it went all day, and the next, and all through the following week, so that by the end of thirteen days the foreman counted out, in tens mostly, my pay of fifty-three dollars. Mother earned one hundred and forty-eight dollars. She wrote this on her envelope, with a message I didn't bother to ask her about.

The next day I walked with my friend Scott to the downtown mall where we drooled over the clothes behind fancy windows, bought popcorn, and sat at a tier of outdoor fountains to talk about girls. Finally we went into Penney's for more popcorn, which we ate walking around, before we returned home without buying anything. It wasn't until a few days before school that I let my fifty-three dollars slip quietly from my hands, buying a pair of pants, two shirts, and a maroon T-shirt, the kind that was in style. At home I tried them on while Rick looked on enviously; later, the day before school started, I tried them on again wondering not so much if they were worth it as who would see me first in those clothes.

Along with my brother and sister I picked grapes until I was fifteen, before giving up and saying that I'd rather wear old clothes than stoop like a Mexican. Mother thought I was being stuck-up, even stupid, because there would be no clothes for me in the fall. I told her I didn't care, but when Rick and Debra rose at five in the morning, I lay awake in bed feeling that perhaps I had made a mistake but unwilling to change my mind. That fall Mother bought me two pairs of socks, a packet of colored T-shirts, and underwear. The T-shirts would help, I thought, but who would see that I had new underwear and socks? I wore a new T-shirt on the first day of school, then an old shirt on Tuesday, then another T-shirt on Wednesday, and on Thursday an old Nehru shirt that was embarrassingly out of style. On Friday I changed into the corduroy pants my brother had handed down to me and slipped into my last new T-shirt. I worked like a magician, blinding my classmates, who were all clothes conscious and small-time social climbers, by arranging my wardrobe to make it seem larger than it really was. But by spring I had to do something—my blue jeans were almost silver and my shoes had lost their form, puddling like black ice around my feet. That spring of my sixteenth year, Rick and I decided to take a labor bus to chop cotton. In his old Volkswagen, which was more noise than power, we drove on a Saturday morning to West Fresno—or Chinatown as some call it—parked, walked slowly toward a bus, and stood gawking at the winos, toothy blacks, Okies, *Tejanos* with gold teeth, whores, Mexican families, and labor contractors shouting "Cotton" or "Beets," the work of spring.

We boarded the "Cotton" bus without looking at the contractor who stood almost blocking the entrance because he didn't want winos. We boarded scared and then were more scared because two blacks in the rear were drunk and arguing loudly about what was better, a two-barrel or four-barrel Ford carburetor. We sat far from them, looking straight ahead, and only glanced briefly at the others who boarded, almost all of them broken and poorly dressed in loudly mismatched clothes. Finally when the contractor banged his palm against the side of the bus, the young man at the wheel, smiling and talking in Spanish, started the engine, idled it for a moment while he adjusted the mirrors, and started off in slow chugs. Except for the windshield there was no glass in the windows, so as soon as we were on the rural roads outside Fresno, the dust and sand began to be sucked into the bus, whipping about like irate wasps as the gravel ticked about us. We closed our eyes, clotted up our mouths that wanted to open with embarrassed laughter because we couldn't believe we were on that bus with those people and the dust attacking us for no reason.

When we arrived at a field we followed the others to a pickup where we each took a hoe and marched to stand before a row. Rick and I, self-conscious and unsure, looked around at the others who leaned on their hoes or squatted in front of the rows, almost all talking in Spanish, joking, lighting cigarettes—all waiting for the foreman's whistle to begin work. Mother had explained how to chop cotton by showing us with a broom in the backyard.

"Like this," she said, her broom swishing down weeds. "Leave one plant and cut four—and cut them! Don't leave them standing or the foreman will get mad."

The foreman whistled and we started up the row stealing glances at other workers to see if we were doing it right. But after awhile we worked like we knew what we were doing, neither of us hurrying or falling behind. But slowly the clot of men, women, and kids began to spread and loosen. Even Rick pulled away. I didn't hurry, though. I cut smoothly and cleanly as I walked at a slow pace, in a sort of funeral march. My eyes measured each space of cotton plants before I cut. If I missed the plants, I swished again. I worked intently, seldom looking up, so when I did I was amazed to see the sun, like a broken orange coin, in the east. It looked blurry, unbelievable, like something not of this world. I looked around in amazement, scanning the eastern horizon that was a taut line jutted with an occasional mountain. The horizon was beautiful, like a snapshot of the moon, in the early light of morning, in the quiet of no cars and few people.

The foreman trudged in boots in my direction, stepping awkwardly over the plants, to inspect the work. No one around me looked up. We all worked steadily while we waited for him to leave. When he did leave, with a feeble complaint addressed to no one in particular, we looked up smiling under straw hats and bandanas.

By 11:00, our lunch time, my ankles were hurting from walking on clods the size of hardballs. My arms ached and my face was dusted by a wind that was perpetual, always busy whipping about. But the work was not bad, I thought. It was better, so much better, than picking grapes, especially with the hourly wage of a dollar twenty-five instead of piece work. Rick and I walked sorely toward the bus where we washed and drank water. Instead of eating in the bus or in the shade of the bus, we kept to ourselves by walking down to the irrigation canal that ran the length of the field, to open our lunch of sandwiches and crackers. We laughed at the crackers, which seemed like a cruel joke from our Mother, because we were working under the sun and the last thing we wanted was a salty dessert. We ate them anyway and drank more water before we returned to the field, both of us limping in exaggeration. Working side by side, we talked and laughed at our predicament because our Mother had warned us year after year that if we didn't get on track in school we'd have to work in the fields and then we would see. We mimicked Mother's whining voice and smirked at her smoky view of the future in which we'd be trapped by marriage and screaming kids. We'd eat beans and then we'd see.

Rick pulled slowly away to the rhythm of his hoe falling faster and smoother. It was better that way, to work alone. I could hum made-up songs or songs from the radio and think to myself about school and friends. At the time I was doing badly in my classes, mainly because of a difficult stepfather, but also because I didn't care anymore. All through junior high and into my first year of high school there were those who said I would never do anything, be anyone. They said I'd work like a donkey and marry the first Mexican girl that came along. I was reminded so often, verbally and in the way I was treated at home, that I began to believe that chopping cotton might be a lifetime job for me. If not chopping cotton, then I might get lucky and find myself in a car wash or restaurant or junkyard. But it was clear; I'd work, and work hard.

I cleared my mind by humming and looking about. The sun was directly above with a few soft blades of clouds against a sky that seemed bluer and more beautiful than our sky in the city. Occasionally the breeze flurried and picked up dust so that I had to cover my eyes and screw up my face. The workers were hunched, brown as the clods under our feet, and spread across the field that ran without end—fields that were owned by corporations, not families.

I hoed trying to keep my mind busy with scenes from school and pretend girlfriends until finally my brain turned off and my thinking went fuzzy with boredom. I looked about, no longer mesmerized by the beauty of the landscape, no longer wondering if the winos in the fields could hold out for eight hours, no longer dreaming of the clothes I'd buy with my pay. My eyes followed my chopping as the plants, thin as their shadows, fell with each strike. I worked slowly with ankles and arms hurting, neck stiff, and eyes stinging from the dust and the sun that glanced off the field like a mirror.

By quitting time, 3:00, there was such an excruciating pain in my ankles that I walked as if I were wearing snowshoes. Rick laughed at me and I laughed too, embarrassed that most of the men were walking normally and I was among the first timers who had to get used to this work. "And what about you, wino," I came back at Rick. His eyes were meshed red and his long hippie hair was flecked with dust and gnats and bits of leaves. We placed our hoes in the back of a pickup and stood in line for our pay, which was twelve fifty. I was amazed at the pay, which was the most I had ever earned in one day, and thought that I'd come back the next day, Sunday. This was too good.

Instead of joining the others in the labor bus, we jumped in the back of a pickup when the driver said we'd get to town sooner and were welcome to

join him. We scrambled into the truck bed to be joined by a heavy-set and laughing *Tejano* whose head was shaped like an egg, particularly so because the bandana he wore ended in a point on the top of his head. He laughed almost demonically as the pickup roared up the dirt path, a gray cape of dust rising behind us. On the highway, with the wind in our faces, we squinted at the fields as if we were looking for someone. The *Tejano* had quit laughing but was smiling broadly, occasionally chortling tunes he never finished. I was scared of him, though Rick, two years older and five inches taller, wasn't. If the *Tejano* looked at him, Rick stared back for a second or two before he looked away to the fields.

I felt like a soldier coming home from war when we rattled into Chinatown. People leaning against car hoods stared, their necks following us, owl-like; prostitutes chewed gum more ferociously and showed us their teeth; Chinese grocers stopped brooming their storefronts to raise their cadaverous faces at us. We stopped in front of the Chi Chi Club where Mexican music blared from the juke box and cue balls cracked like dull ice. The *Tejano*, who was dirty as we were, stepped awkwardly over the side rail, dusted himself off with his bandana, and sauntered into the club.

Rick and I jumped from the back, thanked the driver who said *de nada* and popped his clutch, so that the pickup jerked and coughed blue smoke. We returned smiling to our car, happy with the money we had made and pleased that we had, in a small way, proved ourselves to be tough; that we worked as well as other men and earned the same pay.

We returned the next day and the next week until the season was over and there was nothing to do. I told myself that I wouldn't pick grapes that summer, saying all through June and July that it was for Mexicans, not me. When August came around and I still had not found a summer job, I ate my words, sharpened my knife, and joined Mother, Rick, and Debra for one last time.

Gary Soto (1952–) was raised in the San Joaquin valley of California, where he worked for a time as a migrant laborer. He studied geography in college but then turned to poetry, often using his childhood locale in poems about poverty and desolation among Mexican-Americans. His lean, simple prose shows his characters' struggles to rise above their difficult situations. In 1985, Soto won the American Book Award for his autobiographical prose work *Living Up the Street: Narrative Recollections.* In an unpublished interview about this book, Soto says, "I would rather show and not tell about certain levels of poverty, of childhood; I made a conscious effort not to tell anything but just present the stories and let the reader come up with assumptions." His most recent books have been novels and poetry collections for children and young adults, as well as the poetry collection *A Native Man* (1999). The essay about picking grapes for a raisin company is from *Living Up the Street.*

Excerpt from *The Glass Castle*

Jeannette Walls

"Bad news," Lori said one day when I got home from exploring. "Dad lost his job."

Dad had kept this job for nearly six months—longer than any other. I figured we were through with Battle Mountain and that within a few days, we'd be on the move again.

"I wonder where we'll live next," I said.

Lori shook her head. "We're staying here," she said. Dad insisted he hadn't exactly lost his job. He had arranged to have himself fired because he wanted to spend more time looking for gold. He had all sorts of plans to make money, she added, inventions he was working on, odd jobs he had lined up. But for the time being, things might get a little tight around the house. "We all have to help out," Lori said.

I thought of what I could do to contribute, besides collecting bottles and scrap metal. "I'll cut the prices on my rocks," I said.

Lori paused and looked down. "I don't think that will be enough," she said.

"I guess we can eat less," I said.

"We have before," Lori said.

We did eat less. Once we lost our credit at the commissary, we quickly ran out of food. Sometimes one of Dad's odd jobs would come through, or he'd win some money gambling, and we'd eat for a few days. Then the money would be gone and the refrigerator would be empty again.

Before, whenever we were out of food, Dad was always there, full of ideas and ingenuity. He'd find a can of tomatoes on the back of a shelf that everyone else had missed, or he'd go off for an hour and come back with an armful of vegetables—never telling us where he got them—and whip up a stew. But now he began disappearing a lot.

"Where Dad?" Maureen asked all the time. She was a year and a half old, and these were almost her first words.

"He's out finding us food and looking for work," I'd say. But I wondered if he didn't really want to be around us unless he could provide for us. I tried to never complain.

If we asked Mom about food—in a casual way, because we didn't want to cause any trouble—she'd simply shrug and say she couldn't make something out of nothing. We kids usually kept our hunger to ourselves, but we were always thinking of food and how to get our hands on it. During recess at school, I'd slip back into the classroom and find something in some other kid's lunch bag that wouldn't be missed—a package of crackers, an apple—and I'd gulp it down so quickly I would barely be able to taste it. If I was playing in a friend's yard, I'd ask if I could use the bathroom, and if no one was in the kitchen, I'd grab something out of the refrigerator or cupboard and take it into the bathroom and eat it there, always making a point of flushing the toilet before leaving.

Brian was scavenging, too. One day I discovered him upchucking behind our house. I wanted to know how he could be spewing like that when we hadn't eaten in days. He told me he had broken into a neighbor's house and stolen a gallon jar of pickles. The neighbor had caught him, but instead of reporting him to the cops, he made Brian eat the entire jarful as punishment. I had to swear I wouldn't tell Dad.

A couple of months after Dad lost his job, he came home with a bag of groceries: a can of corn, a half gallon of milk, a loaf of bread, two tins of deviled ham, a sack of sugar, and a stick of margarine. The can of corn disappeared within minutes. Somebody in the family had stolen it, and no one except the thief knew who. But Dad was too busy making deviled-ham sandwiches to launch an investigation. We ate our fill that night, washing down the sandwiches with big glasses of milk. When I got back from school the next day, I found Lori in the kitchen eating something out of a cup with a spoon. I looked in the refrigerator. There was nothing inside but a half-gone stick of margarine.

"Lori, what are you eating?"

"Margarine," she said.

I wrinkled my nose. "Really?"

"Yeah," she said. "Mix it with sugar. Tastes just like frosting."

I made some. It didn't taste like frosting. It was sort of crunchy, because the sugar didn't dissolve, and it was greasy and left a filmy coat in my mouth. But I ate it all anyway.

When Mom got home that evening, she looked in the refrigerator. "What happened to the stick of margarine?" she asked.

"We ate it," I said.

Mom got angry. She was saving it, she said, to butter the bread. We already ate all the bread, I said. Mom said she was thinking of baking some bread if a neighbor would loan us some flour. I pointed out that the gas company had turned off our gas.

"Well," Mom said. "We should have saved the margarine just in case the gas gets turned back on. Miracles happen, you know." It was because of my and Lori's selfishness, she said, that if we had any bread, we'd have to eat it without butter.

Mom wasn't making any sense to me. I wondered if she had been looking forward to eating the margarine herself. And that made me wonder if she was the one who'd stolen the can of corn the night before, which got me a little mad. "It was the only thing to eat in the whole house," I said. Raising my voice, I added, "I was *hungry*."

Mom gave me a startled look. I'd broken one of our unspoken rules: We were always supposed to pretend our life was one long and incredibly fun adventure. She raised her hand, and I thought she was going to hit me, but then she sat down at the spool table and rested her head on her arms. Her shoulders started shaking. I went over and touched her arm. "Mom?" I said.

She shook off my hand, and when she raised her head, her face was swollen and red. "It's not my fault if you're hungry!" she shouted. "Don't blame me. Do you think I like living like this? Do you?"

That night when Dad came home, he and Mom got into a big fight. Mom was screaming that she was tired of getting all the blame for everything that went wrong. "How did this become my problem?" she shouted. "Why aren't you helping? You spend your whole day at the Owl Club. You act like it's not your responsibility."

Dad explained that he was out trying to earn money. He had all sorts of prospects that he was on the brink of realizing. Problem was, he needed cash to make them happen. There was a lot of gold in Battle Mountain, but it was trapped in the ore. It was not like there were gold nuggets lying around for the Prospector to sort through. He was perfecting a technique by which the gold could be leached out of the rock by processing it with a cyanide solution. But that took money. Dad told Mom she needed to ask her mother for the money to fund the cyanide-leaching process he was developing.

"You want me to beg from my mother again?" Mom asked.

"Goddammit, Rose Mary! It's not like we're asking for a handout," he yelled. "She'd be making an *investment*."

Grandma was always lending us money, Mom said, and she was sick of it. Mom told Dad that Grandma had said if we couldn't take care of ourselves, we could go live in Phoenix, in her house.

"Maybe we should," Mom said.

That got Dad really angry. "Are you saying I can't take care of my own family?"

"Ask them," Mom snapped.

We kids were sitting on the old passenger benches. Dad turned to me. I studied the scuff marks on the floor.

Their argument continued the next morning. We kids were downstairs lying in our boxes, listening to them fighting upstairs. Mom was carrying on about how things had gotten so desperate around the house that we didn't have anything to eat except margarine, and now that was gone, too. She was sick, she said, of Dad's ridiculous dreams and his stupid plans and his empty promises.

I turned to Lori, who was reading a book. "Tell them that we like eating margarine," I said. "Then maybe they'll stop fighting."

Lori shook her head. "That'll make Mom think we're taking Dad's side," she said. "It would only make it worse. Let them work it out."

I knew Lori was right. The only thing to do when Mom and Dad fought was to pretend it wasn't happening or act like it didn't matter. Pretty soon they'd be friends again, kissing and dancing in each other's arms. But this particular argument just would not stop. After going on about the margarine, they started fighting about whether or not some painting Mom had done was ugly. Then they argued about whose fault it was that we lived like we did. Mom told Dad he should get another job. Dad said that if Mom wanted someone in the family to be punching a time clock, then she could get a job. She had a teaching degree, he pointed out. She could work instead of sitting around on her butt all day painting pictures no one ever wanted to buy.

"Van Gogh didn't sell any paintings, either," Mom said. "I'm an artist!"

"Fine," Dad said. "Then quit your damned bellyaching. Or go peddle your ass at the Green Lantern."

Mom and Dad's shouting was so loud that you could hear it throughout the neighborhood. Lori, Brian, and I looked at one another. Brian nodded at the front door, and we all went outside and started making sand castles for scorpions. We figured that if we were all in the yard acting like the fighting was no big deal, maybe the neighbors would feel the same way.

But as the screaming continued, neighbors started gathering on the street. Some were simply curious. Moms and dads got into arguments all the time in Battle Mountain, so it didn't seem that big a deal, but this fight was raucous even by local

standards, and some people thought they should step in and break it up. "Aw, let 'em work out their differences," one of the men said. "No one's got a right to interfere." So they leaned back against car fenders and fence posts, or sat on pickup tailgates, as if they were at a rodeo.

Suddenly, one of Mom's oil paintings came flying through an upstairs window. Next came her easel. The crowd below scurried back to avoid getting hit. Then Mom's feet appeared in the window, followed by the rest of her body. She was dangling from the second floor, her legs swinging wildly. Dad was holding her by the arms while she tried to hit him in the face.

"Help!" Mom screamed. "He's trying to kill me!"

"Goddammit, Rose Mary, get back in here!" Dad said.

"Don't hurt her!" Lori yelled.

Mom was swinging back and forth. Her yellow cotton dress had gotten bunched up around her waist, and the crowd could see her white underwear. They were sort of old and baggy, and I was afraid they might fall off altogether. Some of the grown-ups called out, worried that Mom might fall, but one group of kids thought Mom looked like a chimpanzee swinging from a tree, and they began making monkey noises and scratching their armpits and laughing. Brian's face turned dark and his fists clenched up. I felt like punching them, too, but I pulled Brian back.

Mom was thrashing around so hard that her shoes fell off. It looked like she might slip from Dad's grasp or pull him out the window. Lori turned to Brian and me. "Come on." We ran inside and up the stairs and held on to Dad's legs so that Mom's weight wouldn't drag him through the window as well. Finally, he pulled Mom back inside. She collapsed onto the floor.

"He tried to kill me," Mom sobbed. "Your father wants to watch me die."

"I didn't push her," Dad protested. "I swear to God I didn't. She jumped." He was standing over Mom, holding out his hands, palms up, pleading his innocence.

Lori stroked Mom's hair and dried her tears. Brian leaned against the wall and shook his head.

"Everything's okay now," I said over and over again.

In late August, I was washing clothes in the tin pan in the living room when I heard someone coming up the stairs singing. It was Lori. She burst into the living room, duffel bag over her shoulder, laughing and belting out one of those goofy summer-camp songs kids sing at night around the fire. I'd never heard Lori cut loose like this before. She positively glowed as she told me about the hot meals and the hot showers and all the friends she'd made. She'd even had a boyfriend who kissed her. "Everyone assumed I was a normal person," she said. "It was weird." Then she told me that it had occurred to her that if she got out of Welch, and away from the family, she might have a shot at a happy life. From then on, she began looking forward to the day she'd leave Little Hobart Street and be on her own.

A few days later, Mom came home. She seemed different, too. She had lived in a dorm on the university campus, without four kids to take care of, and she had loved it. She'd attended lectures and she'd painted. She'd read stacks of self-help books, and they had made her realize that she'd been living her life for other people. She intended to quit her teaching job and devote herself to her art. "It's time I did something for myself," she said. "It's time I started living my life for me."

"Mom, you spent the whole summer renewing your certificate."

"If I hadn't done that, I never would have had this breakthrough."

"You can't quit your job," I said. "We need the money."

"Why do I always have to be the one who earns the money?" Mom asked. "You have a job. You can earn money. Lori can earn money, too. I've got more important things to do."

I thought Mom was having another tantrum. I assumed that come opening day, she'd be off in Lucy Jo's Dart to Davy Elementary, even if we had to cajole her. But on that first day of school, Mom refused to get out of bed. Lori, Brian, and I pulled back the covers and tried to drag her out, but she wouldn't budge.

I told her she had responsibilities. I told her child welfare might come down on us again if she wasn't working. She folded her arms across her chest and stared us down. "I'm not going to school," she said.

"Why not?" I asked.

"I'm sick."

"What's wrong?" I asked.

"My mucus is yellow," Mom said.

"If everyone who had yellow mucus stayed home, the schools would be pretty empty," I told her.

Mom's head snapped up. "You can't talk to me like that," she said. "I'm your mother."

"If you want to be treated like a mother," I said, "you should act like one."

Mom rarely got angry. She was usually either singing or crying, but now her face twisted up with fury. We both knew I had crossed a line, but I didn't care. I'd also changed over the summer.

"How dare you?" she shouted. "You're in trouble now—big trouble. I'm telling your dad. Just you wait until he comes home."

Mom's threat didn't worry me. The way I saw it, Dad owed me. I'd looked after his kids all summer, I'd kept him in beer and cigarette money, and I'd helped him fleece that miner Robbie. I figured I had Dad in my back pocket.

When I got home from school that afternoon, Mom was still curled up on the sofa bed, a small pile of paperbacks next to her. Dad was sitting at the drafting table, rolling a cigarette. He beckoned to me to follow him into the kitchen. Mom watched us go.

Dad closed the door and looked at me gravely. "Your mother claims you back-talked her."

"Yes," I said. "It's true."

"Yes, sir," he corrected me, but I didn't say anything.

"I'm disappointed in you," he went on. "You know damn good and well that you are to respect your parents."

"Dad, Mom's not sick, she's playing hooky," I said. "She has to take her obligations more seriously. She has to grow up a little."

"Who do you think you are?" he asked. "She's your mother."

"Then why doesn't she act like one?" I looked at Dad for what felt like a very long moment. Then I blurted out, "And why don't you act like a dad?"

I could see the blood surge into his face. He grabbed me by the arm. "You apologize for that comment!"

"Or what?" I asked.

Dad shoved me up against the wall. "Or by God I'll show you who's boss around here."

His face was inches from mine. "What are you going to do to punish me?" I asked. "Stop taking me to bars?"

Dad drew back his hand as if to smack me. "You watch your mouth, young lady. I can still whip your butt, and don't think I won't."

"You can't be serious," I said.

Dad dropped his hand. He pulled his belt out of the loops on his work pants and wrapped it a couple of times around his knuckles.

"Apologize to me and to your mother," he said. "No."

Dad raised the belt. "Apologize."

"No."

"Then bend over."

Dad was standing between me and the door. There was no way out except through him. But it never occurred to me to either run or fight. The way I saw it, he was in a tighter spot than I was. He had to back down, because if he sided with Mom and gave me a whipping, he would lose me forever.

We stared at each other. Dad seemed to be waiting for me to drop my eyes, to apologize and tell him I was wrong so we could go back to being like we were, but I kept holding his gaze. Finally, to call his bluff, I turned around, bent over slightly, and rested my hands on my knees.

I expected him to turn and walk away, but there were six stinging blows on the backs of my thighs, each accompanied by a whistle of air. I could feel the welts rising even before I straightened up.

I walked out of the kitchen without looking at Dad. Mom was outside the door. She'd been standing there, listening to everything. I didn't look at her, but I could see from the corner of my eye her triumphant expression. I bit my lip so I wouldn't cry.

As soon as I got outside, I ran up into the woods, pushing tree branches and wild grape vines out of my face. I thought I'd start crying now that I was away from the house, but instead, I threw up. I ate some wild mint to get rid of the taste of bile, and I walked for what felt like hours through the silent hills. The air was clear and cool, and the forest floor was thick with leaves that had fallen from the buckeyes and poplars. Late in the afternoon, I sat down on a tree trunk, leaning forward because the backs of my thighs still stung. All through the long walk, the pain had kept me thinking, and by the time I reached the tree trunk, I had made two decisions.

The first was that I'd had my last whipping. No one was ever going to do that to me again. The second was that, like Lori, I was going to get out of Welch. The sooner, the better. Before I finished high school, if I could. I had no idea where I would go, but I did know I was going. I also knew it would not be easy. People got stuck in Welch. I had been counting on Mom and Dad to get us out, but I now knew I had to do it on my own. It would take saving and planning. I decided the next day I'd go to G. C. Murphy and buy a pink plastic piggy bank I'd seen there. I'd put in the seventy-five dollars I had managed to save while working at Becker's Jewel Box. It would be the beginning of my escape fund.

One morning three years after I'd moved to New York, I was getting ready for class and listening to the radio. The announcer reported a terrible traffic jam on the New Jersey Turnpike. A van had broken down, spilling clothes and furniture all over the road and creating a big backup. The police were trying to clear the highway, but a dog had jumped out of the van and was running up and down the turnpike as a couple of officers chased after him. The announcer got a lot of mileage out of the story, going on about the rubes with their clunker of a vehicle and yapping dog who were making thousands of New York commuters late for work.

That night the psychologist told me I had a phone call.

"Jeannettie-kins!" It was Mom. "Guess what?" she asked in a voice brimming with excitement. "Your daddy and I have moved to New York!"

The first thing I thought about was the van that had broken down on the turnpike that morning. When I asked Mom about it, she admitted that yes, she and Dad had a teensy bit of technical difficulty with the van. It had popped a belt on some big, crowded highway, and Tinkle, who was sick and tired of being cooped up, you know how that goes, had gotten loose. The police had shown up, and Dad got into an argument with them, and they threatened to arrest him, and gosh it was quite the drama. "How did you know?" she asked.

"It was on the radio."

"On the radio?" Mom asked. She couldn't believe it. "With everything going on in the world these days, an old van popping a belt is news?" But there was genuine glee in her voice. "We only just got here, and we're already famous!"

After talking to Mom, I looked around my room. It was the maid's room off the kitchen, and it was tiny, with one narrow window and a bathroom that doubled as a closet. But it was mine. I had a room now, and I had a life, too, and there was no place in either one for Mom and Dad.

Still, the next day I went up to Lori's apartment to see them. Everyone was there. Mom and Dad hugged me. Dad pulled a pint of whiskey out of a paper bag while Mom described their various adventures on the trip. They had gone sightseeing earlier that day, and taken their first ride on the subway, which Dad called a goddamn hole in the ground. Mom said the art deco murals at Rockefeller Center were disappointing, not nearly as good as some of her own paintings. None of us kids was doing much to help carry the conversation.

"So what's the plan?" Brian finally asked. "You're moving here?"

"We have moved," Mom said.

"For good?" I asked.

"That's right," Dad said.

"Why?" I asked. The question came out sharply.

Dad looked puzzled, as if the answer should have been obvious. "So we could be a family again." He raised his pint. "To the family," he said.

Mom and Dad found a room in a boardinghouse a few blocks from Lori's apartment. The steely-haired landlady helped them move in, and a couple of months later, when they fell behind on their rent, she put their belongings on the street and padlocked their room. Mom and Dad moved into a six-story flophouse in a more dilapidated neighborhood. They lasted there a few months, but when Dad set their room on fire by falling asleep with a burning cigarette in his hand, they got kicked out. Brian believed that Mom and Dad needed to be forced to be self-sufficient or they'd be dependent on us forever, so he refused to take them in. But Lori had moved out of the South Bronx and into an apartment in the same building as Brian, and she let them come stay with her and Maureen. It would be for just a week or two, Mom and Dad assured her, a month at the most, while they got a kitty together and looked for a new place.

One month at Lori's became two months and then three and four. Each time I visited, the apartment was more jam-packed. Mom hung paintings on the walls and stacked street finds in the living room and put colored bottles in the windows for that stained-glass effect. The stacks reached the ceiling, and then the living room filled up, and Mom's collectibles and found art overflowed into the kitchen.

But it was Dad who was really getting to Lori. While he hadn't found steady work, he always had mysterious ways of hustling up pocket money, and he'd come home at night drunk and gunning for an argument. Brian saw that Lori was on the verge of snapping, so he invited Dad to come live with him. He put a lock on the booze cabinet, but Dad had been there under a week when Brian came home and found that Dad had used a screwdriver to take the door off its hinges and then guzzled down every single bottle.

Brian didn't lose his temper. He told Dad he had made a mistake by leaving liquor in the apartment. He said he'd allow Dad to stay, but Dad had to follow some rules, the first being that he stop drinking as long as he was there. "You're the king of your own castle, and that's the way it should be," Dad replied. "But it'll be a chilly day in hell before I bow to my own son." He and Mom still had the white van they'd driven up from West Virginia, and he started sleeping in that.

Lori, meanwhile, had given Mom a deadline to clean out the apartment. But the deadline came and went, and so did a second and a third. Also, Dad was always dropping by to visit Mom, but then they got into such screeching arguments that the neighbors banged on the walls. Dad started fighting with them, too.

"I can't take it anymore," Lori told me one day.

"Maybe you're just going to have to kick Mom out," I said.

"But she's my mother."

"It doesn't matter. She's driving you crazy."

Lori finally agreed. It almost killed her to tell Mom she would have to leave, and she offered to do whatever it took to help her get reestablished, but Mom insisted she'd be fine.

"Lori's doing the right thing," she said to me. "Sometimes you need a little crisis to get your adrenaline flowing and help you realize your potential."

Mom and Tinkle moved into the van with Dad. They lived there for a few months, but one day they left it in a no-parking zone and it was towed.

Because the van was unregistered, they couldn't get it back. That night, they slept on a park bench. They were homeless.

Mom and Dad called regularly from pay phones to check up on us, and once or twice a month, we'd all get together at Lori's.

"It's not such a bad life," Mom told us after they'd been homeless for a couple of months.

"Don't you worry a lick about us," Dad added. "We've always been able to fend for ourselves."

Mom explained that they'd been busy learning the ropes. They'd visited the various soup kitchens, sampling the cuisines, and had their favorites. They knew which churches passed out sandwiches and when. They'd found the public libraries with good bathrooms where you could wash thoroughly— "We wash as far down as possible and as far up as possible, but we don't wash possible," was how Mom put it—and brush your teeth and shave. They fished newspapers from the trash cans and looked up free events. They went to plays and operas and concerts in the parks, listened to string quartets and piano recitals in office-building lobbies, attended movie screenings, and visited museums. When they first became homeless, it was early summer, and they slept on park benches or in the bushes that lined park paths. Sometimes a cop would wake them up and tell them to move, but they'd just find some other place to sleep. During the day, they'd stash their bedrolls in the underbrush.

"You can't just live like this," I said.

"Why not?" Mom said. "Being homeless is an adventure."

As fall came and the days shortened and the weather cooled, Mom and Dad began spending more time in the libraries, which were warm and comfortable, and some of which remained open well into the evening. Mom was working her way through Balzac. Dad had become interested in chaos theory and was reading *Los Alamos Science* and the *Journal of Statistical Physics*. He said it had already helped his pool game.

"What are you going to do when winter comes?" I asked Mom.

She smiled. "Winter is one of my favorite seasons," she said.

I didn't know what to do. Part of me wanted to do whatever I could to take care of Mom and Dad, and part of me just wanted to wash my hands of them. The cold came early that year, and every time I left the psychologist's apartment, I found myself looking into the faces of the homeless people I passed on the street, wondering each time if one of them would turn out to be Mom or Dad. I usually gave homeless people whatever spare change I had, but I couldn't help feeling like I was trying to ease my conscience about Mom and Dad wandering the streets while I had a steady job and a warm room to come home to.

One day I was walking down Broadway with another student named Carol when I gave some change to a young homeless guy. "You shouldn't do that," Carol said.

"Why?"

"It only encourages them. They're all scam artists."

What do you know? I wanted to ask. I felt like telling Carol that my parents were out there, too, that she had no idea what it was like to be down on your luck, with nowhere to go and nothing to eat. But that would have meant explaining who I really was, and I wasn't about to do that. So at the next street corner, I went my way without saying a thing.

I knew I should have stood up for Mom and Dad. I'd been pretty scrappy as a kid, and our family had always fought for one another, but back then we'd had no choice. The truth was, I was tired of taking on people who ridiculed us for the way we lived. I just didn't have it in me to argue Mom and Dad's case to the world.

That was why I didn't own up to my parents in front of Professor Fuchs. She was one of my favorite teachers, a tiny dark passionate woman with circles under her eyes who taught political science. One day Professor Fuchs asked if homelessness was the result of drug abuse and misguided entitlement programs, as the conservatives claimed, or did it occur, as the liberals argued, because of cuts in social-service programs and the failure to create economic opportunity for the poor? Professor Fuchs called on me.

I hesitated. "Sometimes, I think, it's neither."

"Can you explain yourself?"

"I think that maybe sometimes people get the lives they want."

"Are you saying homeless people want to live on the street?" Professor Fuchs asked. "Are you saying they don't want warm beds and roofs over their heads?"

"Not exactly," I said. I was fumbling for words. "They do. But if some of them were willing to work hard and make compromises, they might not have ideal lives, but they could make ends meet."

Professor Fuchs walked around from behind her lectern. "What do you know about the lives of the underprivileged?" she asked. She was practically trembling with agitation. "What do you know about the hardships and obstacles that the underclass faces?"

The other students were staring at me.

"You have a point," I said.

That January it got so cold you could see chunks of ice the size of cars floating down the Hudson River. On those midwinter nights, the homeless shelters filled up quickly. Mom and Dad hated the shelters. Human cesspools, Dad called them, goddamn vermin pits. Mom and Dad preferred to sleep on the pews of the churches that opened their doors to the homeless, but on some nights every pew in every church was taken. On those nights Dad would end up in a shelter, while Mom would show up at Lori's, Tinkle in tow. At times like that, her cheerful facade would crack, and she'd start crying and confess to Lori that life in the streets could be hard, just really hard.

For a while I considered dropping out of Barnard to help. It felt unbearably selfish, just downright wrong, to be indulging myself with an education in the liberal arts at a fancy private college while Mom and Dad were on the streets. But Lori convinced me that dropping out was a lame-brained idea. It wouldn't do any good, she said, and besides, dropping out would break Dad's heart. He was immensely proud that he had a daughter in college, and an Ivy League college at that. Every time he met someone new, he managed to work it into the first few minutes of conversation.

Mom and Dad, Brian pointed out, had options. They could move back to West Virginia or Phoenix. Mom could work. And she was not destitute. She had her collection of antique Indian jewelry, which she kept in a self-storage locker. There was the two-carat diamond ring that Brian and I had found under the rotten lumber back in Welch; she wore it even when sleeping on the street. She still owned property in Phoenix. And she had the land in Texas, the source of her oil-lease royalties.

Brian was right. Mom did have options. I met her at a coffee shop to discuss them. First off, I suggested that she might think of finding an arrangement like mine: a room in someone's nice apartment in exchange for taking care of children or the elderly.

"I've spent my life taking care of other people," Mom said. "Now it's time to take care of me."

"But you're not taking care of you."

"Do we have to have this conversation?" Mom asked. "I've seen some good movies lately. Can't we talk about the movies?"

I suggested to Mom that she sell her Indian jewelry. She wouldn't consider it. She loved that jewelry. Besides, they were heirlooms and had sentimental value.

I mentioned the land in Texas.

"That land's been in the family for generations," Mom said, "and it's staying in the family. You never sell land like that."

I asked about the property in Phoenix.

"I'm saving that for a rainy day."

"Mom, it's pouring."

"This is just a drizzle," she said. "Monsoons could be ahead!" She sipped her tea. "Things usually work out in the end."

"What if they don't?"

"That just means you haven't come to the end yet."

She looked across the table and smiled at me with the smile you give people when you know you have the answers to all their questions. And so we talked about movies.

Mom and Dad survived the winter, but every time I saw them, they looked a little worse for wear: dirtier, more bruised, their hair more matted.

"Don't you fret a bit," Dad said. "Have you ever known your old man to get himself in a situation he couldn't handle?"

I kept telling myself Dad was right, that they knew how to look after themselves and each other, but in the spring, Mom called me to say Dad had come down with tuberculosis.

Dad almost never got sick. He was always getting banged up and then recovering almost immediately, as if nothing could truly hurt him. A part of me still believed all those childhood stories he'd told us about how invincible he was. Dad had asked that no one visit him, but Mom said she thought he'd be pretty pleased if I dropped by the hospital.

I waited at the nurse's station while an orderly went to tell him he had a visitor. I thought Dad might be under an oxygen tent or lying in a bed coughing up blood into a white handkerchief, but after a minute, he came hurrying down the hall. He was paler and more gaunt than usual, but despite all his years of hard living, he had aged very little. He still had all his hair, and it was still coal black, and his dark eyes twinkled above the paper surgical mask he was wearing.

He wouldn't let me hug him. "Whoa, Nelly, stay back," he said. "You're sure a sight for sore eyes, honey, but I don't want you catching this sonofabitch of a bug."

Dad escorted me back to the TB ward and introduced me to all of his friends. "Believe it or not, ol' Rex Walls did produce something worth bragging about, and here she is," he told them. Then he started coughing.

"Dad, are you going to be okay?" I asked.

"Ain't none of us getting out of this alive, honey," Dad said. It was an expression he used a lot, and now he seemed to find a special satisfaction in it.

Dad led me over to his cot. A neat pile of books was stacked next to it. He said his bout with TB had set him to pondering about mortality and the nature of the cosmos. He'd been stone-cold sober since entering the hospital, and reading a lot more about chaos theory, particularly about the work of Mitchell Feigenbaum, a physicist at Los Alamos who had made a study of the transition between order and turbulence. Dad said he was damned if Feigenbaum didn't make a persuasive case that turbulence was not in fact random but followed a sequential spectrum of varying frequencies. If every action in the universe that we thought was random actually conformed to a rational pattern, Dad said, that implied the existence of a divine creator, and he was beginning to rethink his atheistic creed. "I'm not saying there's a bearded old geezer named Yahweh up in the clouds deciding which football team is going to win the Super Bowl," Dad said. "But if the physics—the quantum physics—suggests that God exists, I'm more than willing to entertain the notion."

Dad showed me some of the calculations he'd been working on. He saw me looking at his trembling fingers and held them up. "Lack of liquor or fear of God—don't know which is causing it," he said. "Maybe both."

"Promise you'll stay here until you get better," I said. "I don't want you doing the skedaddle."

Dad burst into laughter that ended in another fit of coughing.

Seven Wonders of One Woman's Existence

Melissa Resch

1. SURVIVAL

A prize with a high price;
A drugged up momma,
Writhing in pain while her daughter does the same
Because big brother played doctor.
A mistake in kindness,
An honest gift of handfuls,
Endless orange dots to
Ingest, to calm a crying sister.

Lowered from a shelf,
Taken from a bottle
Marked *St Joseph, seek immediate medical attention in case of overdose.*
She grew up to learn of sisters poked in worse places.
She instead, At eighteen months was needled, hosed, IV-ed
While they stood circles
And cooed over her in
A dead-air blur of finger-pointing;
Whispering, *Breathe, Baby, Breathe.*
Survival.
Her first key in the teething ring of
Silence for addiction and depression.

2. MENSTRUATION

Anticipation.
At fifteen she thought she'd be the exception,
Free from a private bleed of a self-conscious teen.

Healthy surviving girls, however,
At moment's notice receive
Involuntary draft into *the war between the organs.*

Her battle cry: *Leave me alone*
Her station: the bathroom
Her uniform: anything loose and comfy
Except white.

This, her new badge to
Wear as comfortably as a diaper under
A womb opened before she knows herself.
Ready, yet unready to birth a miracle of suckles and giggles.

Menstruation.
An ancient frontier into womanhood, discovered anew
And anew,
The world over,
Time upon time.

3. GRANDMAMA

Last time she saw her was the last time.
Flat, stiff under a newly acquired halo.
Waxy and pale through a salt water veil,
Lifeless.

Time-battered skin stretched over prize-winning features,
So still. Lips denied every chance to slap out tired stories with no
morals. *Good*, some say. Grandmama was a talker.
The good listeners left decades ago.

No last chance to be tucked in an ambush of bosom
Nor sealed by sassy lipstick stains,
Wrapped in tight matriarchal hugs.

But in a heart of love,
Grandmama is timeless.
Memory never dies.
The hope of the world was reborn in the comfort of those limbs,
Hope that sought a home for a tired little girl,
Running to feel love beyond walls of Christian confinement.

Peace, dear woman.
Peace in your suffering's end.
Grazi, Grandmama, for a gift of color and confidence you flung
'round her shoulders.

She is learning to wear this robe with outstretched arms,
Ready to embrace the world
In peace, Grandmama, peace.

4. THE ROAD

A pilgrim loves the road. Or rail.
She thinks the train more romantic.
The swing and click spills stories
From a lonely widow about the old days in the kibbutz.
The clack sways theories
From an atheist who glories in logic.
Within hours the universe is settled.
Nowhere to be but here,
Till she's there.
Then it's one foot before the other to
Learn the secrets
Of gondolas that skim canals,
Castles that stand firm on windy moors,
Birthplaces of voices like Dickens and Mozart.
Turbulence rises, though,
It bubbles up a deeper secret:
That mankind is often unkind.
Within wire fences of a puzzling locale
Such as Dachau,
Electrified by her own terror,
She laid to rest her pure trust in goodness.
On the trail again,
When confusion of conundrums
Steals sleep and borrows time,
Some bit of beauty pierces clarity into reality.
Maps are unfolded,
Destinations chosen,
A new journey is begun with wide eyes and curious strains
To seek secrets that please a pilgrim.

5. THE PARTY LINE

She was five years old.
There was nothing but a
Bold, black stain on her heart.
So she slurped down
Blood and bread and echoed prayers.

Dressed up in Sunday best
Beside all the rest of
Banquet day believers,
Ready to don jeweled crowns and
Pass through pearly gates;

Filled with divinity and visions of infinity
She sang *'Tis So Sweet to Trust in Jesus*
With amazing grace.

What a concept, to accept
A coupon for a free trip from Hell.

What a load
Off her mind
To know her soul's not signed
Over,
Since she hung up on the party line
Before it drove her
Under the field bearing crosses
and stones growing mosses
Just off Route 39.

6. Song of Solvent Love

Joyful, joyful she adores
Thy ruby lips, pomegranate hips!
She went down from the garden of nuts to
Taste fruits of the valley;

Found supple haven and a
Feast to feed and gratify a need for
Love so fundamental,
Silence
Is erased,
Lost in a wild arpeggio.

Indeed, she smiles in drunken joy
Satisfied by wine and a shapely toy
Held in kindred fingers,
Bent gently
Like this flea
That sucked her first, and now sucks thee.

7. CONFINES OF CONVENTION

They loved to laugh at her Bohemian wish,
The one that escaped the petri dish;
Her colorful life experiment that
Outgrew the confines
Of convention.
It must have been tough for them to watch her
Wave goodbye to all that jazz,
Such as what makes them feel
Life's worth living.
Oh, her voice tires of explaining to itself
That tomorrow's poor player
Will make the world richer
If only she stays her hour upon the stage.
Today and every tomorrow
Time gives voice to rhythm;
Signals to the sun
The dance of line and color,
Calling a woman
Concerned with what her hair was doing
On a page of yesterday's newspaper
As she toasted to a season's work,
Strewn neatly on walls.
The rhythmic dance of wonder calls louder and
Louder to take a snapshot
From her soul,
Paint it on a web of linen, stretched
Over a frame destined to record
A flawless moment before
It is forgotten, heard no more.
She's rather lucky to be so poor.

Melissa Resch Biography Born in 1965 into a U.S. Navy family, I lived in several coastal states until my family settled in the Midwest in 1975. Following four years of teaching elementary school in Indiana and after residing in the UK, Massachusetts and Korea, I began my creative pursuits at Massachusetts College of Art in Boston, earning a BFA with Distinctive Honors in Painting in 1999. In 2002 I relocated to Provincetown, Massachusetts, and established myself as a professional visual artist and enthusiastic amateur poet. Between 2003 and 2008, I split my time between Provincetown and Australia, and in 2008 I received a master's degree in painting from University of Tasmania. I now reside full-time in Provincetown.

Selected Poems

John Georgette

POEMS FROM THE WILD

Reflections upon my Basement Room of 209 Glenfield Avenue

Reflections... Notes, Flashbacks...

sitting in my basement room
walled in by paint cloths
hung from the ceiling,
bordered by the cellar stairs
and two cold outside walls
north and east,
with one window closed
shut since 1948,
old dis-guarded metal cabinets piled high
on the other wall in 1965
made it my temporary
new york city loft space come alive
for this fifteen year old writer
hiding from his macho sports buddies
tucked away with pens and paper
listening to early dylan
and poetry from the library
without a clue of how to start
or why,
but the pencil did flow with lead
and images marched across the page
a word at a time and instantaneously
like magic
LIFE A RUSH poem
emerged.
but what was it?
it didn't look like Frost or Auden
neatly rhymed with distinct form,
it wasn't a paragraph like a short story,
it didn't even have much punctuation.
that long three page run-on sentence

captured animals, electricity,
parties, booze, music.
it didn't start anywhere or go anywhere.
but it was something.
I didn't have a name for it,
it stayed hidden and I secretly admired
its existence far from the maddening sonnets, haikus and lyrical songs
so aptly put together
since *Beowulf* and *Sir Gawain and the Green Knight*.
by its mere existence it inspired other stuff
also hidden away for some reason
that would come to me eventually.
at sixteen the sparkeling brand new powder blue 66 Lemans with GTO interior
spun its tires effortlessly and attracted attention,
also for no reason, but it was cool
and this new writing somehow mysteriously
connected to some unknown coolness that existed in the universe.

then on that fateful New York City day
after my routine train ride from Stratford (CT)
home of the American Shakespeare Theater
to Grand Central Station
to ride the subway and exit
to some unknown part of the city
I stumbled out in Greenwich Village
and if I hadn't established my room in suburbia
in the basement
that had its cloth walls converted to panels
and the cement floored with wood
perhaps at sixteen
the city would have
permanently lured me to its writers, painters, sex, drugs and lofts.

but on that day I heard unstructured words
that flowed on in long run-on sentences
from guys with baggy frompy pants
and blue jeans and lumber shirts
identical to mine,
and with some moments
of hesitation, fear, shyness after the last reader
I quietly walked to the front and from my
ragged notebook lifted my personal "holy grail"
and commenced ...

LIFE A RUSH POEM
into the air and I heard my own
voice resonate with trembling caution
gain momentum, ears listened
and cheered and clapped and passed me booze
like I was one of them, and the 'them' melted into
oneness, as the poem declares
and I was lifted off my feet
and life was changed forever.

too young to hang effortlessly with
Ginsberg, Orlovsky, Corso
I passed
on the night time activities needing
to catch the evening train back to my reality home
in the basement of 209 Glenfield Avenue
not to sleep for nights with post-performing energy
putting me over the top and
then I found *HOWL*
on book barn shelf
and *ON THE ROAD*
tumbled into my lap
like *ON THE WATERFRONT*
and Jimmy Dean and I switched gears
from macho cross-country and track
into making metal sculptures
out of dis-guarded electrical wires
and threw paint on dis-guarded plywood
and words into notebooks
that began to line my shelves
like basketball trophies from grade school
I still have saved with the same esteem
and pride
and I don't question why...

October 26, 2005 (12:05pm)

POEMS FROM PARADISE GREEN

MY WOOSTER LAGOON
1963,
edited 2012

I
had my own
Walden Pond
devoid of chores
or
family intervention.

Perfectly located
far enough from the neighborhood
for real adventure,
safe enough to be a good dream.

I
built a tree fort
and ground fort
with discarded job site lumber
stolen nails and
borrowed rope and pulleys,

I
maneuvered
the wood
on my Huck Finn raft
through a small channel
landed, unloaded, pulled
my treasure up the tallest oak
using the pulleys and rope
as I'd seen on construction sites.

With
handmade tomahawk
and modern hammer and nails
I united play, kingdom, dream world
with history,
Mark Twain stories,
and television's Swamp Fox hero.

Like Daniel Boone I kept moving
deeper into the woods
building confidence and pride,
relishing solitude
after years of
fearing it like the dark
or the next bend in the creek.

I

had my own
Lewis and Clark explorations,
named rocks and trees after my idols
and talked to
squaws and medicine men
who remained behind to protect their sacred land.

I

made clay pots and buried
my picture of Telstar
and Mickey Mantle baseball cards
with notes and news clippings
for some yet-unborn explorer.

I

wrote:
*"Who are you
peering down with your hands
on my treasure?
What time is it
and what's happened since 1963
when my lagoon time
was as sacred as church to me?
Is
the big oak grove still looming
over the open grass field?
Does the small deer path run
from the channel to the cave by
the high cliff?*

*Does the swamp still smell ancient
and like rattlers
and only totally freeze after bitter winter nights
when Indian shadows glide over the ice?"*

I
wanted to reach past my
Walden Pond
and to share this private territory
and my life
as I knew it.

[Post poem commentary:
Epilog
I never will know if this Walden
captured the imagination
of any other young naturalist,
yet this wild haven
stays with me
inspires me now
as then.]

John Georgette first performed his poetry in 1966 at the St Mark's Poetry Project Church in Greenwich Village at age 16. Since then, he has performed a wide variety of poetry styles including lyrics for punk, rock, rap, and slam poetry, Beat verse, Haiku, Shakespearean-type sonnets, rhymed and un-rhymed, long and short verse from coast to coast and in Europe and South America. He is an artist, playwright, author of nationally-aired political, economic and social commentaries. His plays, radio dramas and monologues have appeared Off-Off Broadway and in Regional Theater.

He hosted a very successful Literary Salon called Last Sunday of the Month for ten years and was director of Creativity at the Center for Creative Learning for 15 years, both in Connecticut. John has enjoyed being a theater director, poetry director, jazz and spoken word radio programmer in Connecticut, (WSHU AND WLNV). His art work is collected throughout the U.S., France, Italy, Slovakia, Uruguay and Argentina.

His most recent radio drama has been SHAGGY JAMES AND MARA LYN DUBOIS, (15 episodes).

Section Two

The Green World and the Naturalist's Eye

Selected Poems

Charles Grindle

FULL SNOW MOON FROM 'THE TOP'

Orange-red, she shyly peeked over the spiked island greens to see if we were watching;

Rising slowly, a half inch/hundred thousand miles at a glance, she gradually lost her blush, and took on the celestial white hue of her neighbors.

There was at first no watery reflection, but as she rose higher in the clear evening sky, a spotlight shown on the gentle waves beneath her face, highlighting the resting fisherboats and cold water sea-dwellers close to the shore of the island.

Gradually, she expanded her reflection in the waters of the harbor and spread her silvery beams over the whole harbor view.

The island hoppers made their skittering way to the shore, creating their own wake of more brilliant wavelets of shimmer.

The safe- way- in lights twinkled like faintly hued stars in the moonlit universe of the water, with the distant stay away beams showing themselves at odd intervals from the mainland.

An economic shell, emptied of its weight, backed into her light from the safety lines of the goodbye shore, and, helped by the little tugs that can, was guided into the safe passage toward the next port.

As the shutters of her Fresnel slipped open, she lit up the homes perched on the edge of heaven, her light matching the fragility of their marks on the stage of waterfront living.

But who, in their lunar madness, would give up the chance to see her rise, to take up her rightful place as queen of the heavens?

This moon that often left the hunters with empty hands fills the present with the beauty of a million years of rising, flying, and setting, with no haste and no question.

May she always give those who would look at her monthly fullness the same sense of universe-joy that is offered to us tonight.

I Won! I Won!

Ten dollars in my pocket that I didn't have before the drawing,

I'm the seventh caller, and I win a gift card to a restaurant beside the harbor,
then unexpected nights of work after a conversation with the manager,

A tank-filling for the mobile green confessional with gas at six cents
less than usual, and only regular maintenance needed at the garage,

A stroll in the blue-skied park, watery sunlight dancing between feathered
swimmers, earnest conversation with a possible beau,

Free cocktails on the top of the moon-lit mountain, and a lovely meal
with open, caring women whom I will probably not see again,

September ocean warm enough to wade in, pants legs rolled up, jacket
oh so casually over the shoulder,

This morning, I opened my eyes, and the sun was shining:

In the great lottery that is life, again today, I won.

April 5, 2009

I heard my first peepers today, trying loudly to outdo each other in their praise of spring.

Their chorus was chanting in a pond that is seasonal at best, and a mud puddle most often.

They were beginning their journey to frog hood among last year's cat-nine tails that were straining to remain upright.

Wind and rain that must sometimes be harsh to clean winter's debris and gravel bent a few stems, but there they were.

The peepers did what they do, paying no attention to the closeness of the busy path of shoppers, hurrying to the bargains that lay ahead, or back to home.

First fresh breeze of spring through open windows brought me the sound, piquant in the low hum of motorized transport.

I was probably the only who noticed their song in the middle of the noisy commercial fly and buy.

How lucky that they will not need to get anywhere that their grown-up frog legs can't take them, no purchase, or barter, or theft to acquire.

I wish I could be as simple in the world as they, ignoring the zoom of gasoline, the want of food not grown in this season, admitting to being a cog in this recently fashioned pattern of life.

But I have passed my peeper, and tadpole stages, and must now find my way as a grown-up frog, hopping where I must go, catching the occasional fly of delight, and enjoying the bright sun that warms our chilly and ponderous bodies.

Zero to 60 in...

... sixty years. Slow acceleration but steady pickup; good body, and clean lines.

But things can go wrong at any speed; you may start to notice chips in the paint,

a creaky suspension, and the chipped windshield.

But you make it to the mark, barely remembering the pit stops, the doubts, and the occasional cheers as you pass a marker.

Sometimes in the barren salt flats, sometimes on a cramped, crooked mountain byroad, but always moving, always in forward motion.

Others may drop out well before the post, but you must keep on toward your personal marker.

You may find yourself sharing the road with others along the way, but you always end up in your own lane.

After you've reached speed, what do you do? When you've passed the post that others may stop at, should you rest and let your engine cool, or charge ahead while things are warm? Without seeing the next post, is there a reason to keep on with the challenge?

You can probably see the next goal if you just drive on a bit farther...

Rev. Charles Grindle. Having earned degrees in the music field, he found himself wanting a way to touch people's lives more deeply. He was ordained as an interfaith minister in 2008, and is finishing his first CPE unit. Charles is now the Music Director at First Parish UU in Kennebunk. He has just begun sharing his thoughts in poetry, hoping to reach that deeper connection.

Woods Work

Alison Hawthorne Deming

A photograph of an empty house. Weathered clapboards, two and a half stories, a simple peaked rectangular box, windows and doors gone, the interior open to the wind. On the roof, a foot of snow; in the dooryard, a three-foot drift. A few weedy blackberry canes poke through the white crust. Worn and leaning cedar fence posts run along the south wall. The neighbor's cows have been grazing where once a clothesline hung, where a garden of purple iris and oriental poppies made an annual spectacle. In the background, ice-blue sky. Two leafless apple trees, which, untended, have lost their shapeliness. The deadwood is tangled with a snarl of overgrown suckers, the bark scarred with woodpecker holes and burly scabs left from limb falls. In the foreground, a narrow dirt road packed hard with snow, overlapping lines of wheel-track where a few cars and the milk truck have passed. I stood across the road and snapped the picture from my yard.

That ruin was so beautiful to me it might have been the statue of a fallen god. I contemplated the varied patina of aging wood, the damaged fancywork under eaves and over the front door. I never walked inside because the floors, rotted through, had caved into the cellarhole. In the rubble one could see the remains of a lost domestic order—broken skeleton of a cast-iron cookstove, crockery shards, barrel staves, zinc-lidded canning jars, rags of clothing and feedsacks, battered sap buckets, and bullet-punctured tin cans. Whoever the ghost neighbors were who had left this junk behind, they called up the America I wanted, a country where everyone was a farmer, no matter what else they did; a country where everyone lived next to nowhere and had to figure out from scratch how to make the land provide; a country where one could shape the future with the ache of one's own labor.

I moved to that borderland just south of the Canadian line in the winter of 1969, when my daughter was three years old and I was twenty-two. Vermont, until then, had meant playland to me. I skied there, often with free passes my father had gotten from advertisers on his radio or television shows. At one mountain I'd walk into the manager's office, tell him whose daughter I was, and walk out with a weekend pass for myself and my boyfriend of the moment. Our family had driven north to a Vermont resort one summer. I don't remember much about the trip. We must have gone swimming and played tennis and taken walks in the woods. What I do remember is that the owners had a dog who had just come home from the animal hospital. They'd made an entertaining joke out of the dog's experience; they'd ask him about his operation, coaxing a little, until he began to bay and whine. Then everyone would laugh at how smart the dog was, understanding so many words; how cute that he remembered his pain. Again and again, as new guests arrived, the loving owners put the little canine through his performance. Again and again, everyone laughed lovingly, exchanging knowing looks. That was the summer when the adult world began to look a bit perverse to me. And once, several years later, during the Summer of Love I had come to Vermont for a weekend with members of my tribe for a planned acid trip in the fern meadows of an isolated section of woods near Killington. That was the summer that planted some seed in my mind that grew into my moving north.

By then I had scandalized my family by dropping out of college, five months pregnant. I had endured and escaped a short and dismal forced marriage, committing myself to an extent I did not yet understand to an experimental life. Much of the experiment had to do with sex. I was unconvinced by fifties propriety in sexual matters—that Doris Day dream of feminine resistance against the Rock Hudson hounding of male seduction. I'd read enough great literature, seen enough Gilbert and Sullivan, Shakespeare and O'Neill—books and theater bestowed on me by parents who hoped to protect me from the evils of popular culture—to know that human passion was a mystery too complicated to be understood by ignoring it. In fumbling teenage attempts at intimacy, I learned fast that the body's responses are not contingent upon the heart or the head. That seemed good—a capacity to celebrate, not curtail. Erich Fromm's book *The Art of Loving* was passing among students like the flu. From it I got the idea that the shame of Adam and Eve was caused not by sex, but by their separateness, by the man and the woman remaining strangers to each other. One thing the sexes had in common was desire. It seemed a place to meet. In high school I admired an older couple (they must have been nineteen) who were openly sexual. Driving around with them one day, I was stunned to see her nestle her hand into his crotch and keep it there even though she knew I had noticed. That openness seemed a thing to strive for. I vowed to myself that the first time I went all the way would be intentional, loving, and unashamed—not a back-seat fumble in which the lamb succumbed to the wolf.

But sex, like death, is hard to plan for, no matter what one wants or knows. I stumbled into what I hadn't planned on, got lost in the headlong sensations that a certain good-time boy could bring me to. We were seventeen and the only thing serious about the time we spent together was our passion. We may not have been particularly intelligent, or even in love, but at least we taught each other a thing or two about the pleasure our bodies were capable of. For that, I'm grateful. Our daughter was born on March 21, 1965, the spring after I had graduated from high school.

We spent a few years in Cambridge before the teenage marriage came apart; my husband and brother were students at Boston University. I had everything to prove about being a parent and I knew

it. The guys got into psychedelics. Leary and Alpert had just been fired from Harvard. Before that no one had heard of hallucinogens. The drug talk was everywhere—"a structural regression of the ego . . . more in line with Zen thinking . . . mystic states as the function of a flexible ego." People tried blotter, buttons, and speed, as if each were a new album by the Stones. The streets were boiling. There was a cadre of us by then—a circle of tight friends, the circumference as permeable as a cell membrane. Many circles like that. Tribal parties of long-hairs, we met and trusted each other by signs. Weed, hair, clothes weren't fashion, but code to identify cultural revolutionaries working to make life our religion and our art. I read *Summerhill: A Radical Approach to Child Rearing* and began to take motherhood seriously. To love well, for fallible creatures, was a radical act. I felt frightened and exhilarated by the challenge.

My daughter and I ended up settling near the Cold Hollow Mountains, the largest unbroken range in Vermont, situated twenty miles south of the Canadian border. Dairy farm and maple syrup country. Some logging. Much poverty. I worked as a dishwasher at a ski resort—no longer the manager's darling. But there I began to meet other urban refugees who had settled in the hills. Our arrival predated the back-to-the-land movement: more farms were abandoned than working. Land could be bought for two hundred dollars an acre. I owned one savings bond worth a thousand dollars, which my grandmother had given me. With it I made the down payment on a house, barn, and three and a half acres of cleared land on a dirt road. In one direction, I looked out at the forested bowl of mountains where snow could last until July; in the other, at the large empty clapboard house gone to ruin. Our house, not a ruin, was just a dump. In the cellar snored a dinosaur of an old wood furnace used for central heat. There was no bathroom to speak of, a toilet in a closet when we started out; no insulation, no television, no phone. But families had lived this way for decades and I figured so could we.

The first frost came by Labor Day, the last at the end of May. In winter, weeks passed when the mercury didn't climb over zero—the snow and wind grew fierce. Nights fell to twenty, thirty below. In the deepest cold, nothing moved but smoke from the chimneys. Snow packed on the dirt road creaked under foot or wheels. In the gone-by orchard the trees were frozen stiff, icy twig tips clicking in the wind, chimes made of bones. The air itself seemed frozen. In the neighbor's barn, steam heat rose off the backs of stanchioned cows, their breath making warm clouds as they nuzzled in their grain—animals large enough, and enough of them, to keep their own space warm. I worked hard at it—splitting and hauling wood, wearing heavy woolen socks to bed. When pipes froze, I learned to use a blowtorch. Outside the bedroom window, the moon ran its light through giant icicles hanging from the roof. I thought they looked like glass teeth, as if I were trying to sleep inside the mouth of a beast.

In the miserably short summer, I grew gorgeous gardens—never perfectly tended, but productive nonetheless. I froze and canned vegetables, made cider and sauerkraut, dried herbs, raised hens and pigs. Like a cover photo for *Organic Gardening* magazine, I stood beaming knee-deep in comfrey, showing off a cabbage two feet wide, my cheeks as smooth as a butternut squash. I was home. Nothing makes one feel at home, and stay at home, like keeping animals and growing gardens. I was happy in my hardship. I built a desk out of barnboards in the living room, stripped the walls to find, under the plaster and lath, planking three feet wide. I brushed the rough-cut surface with linseed oil to heighten the grain. My daughter Lucinda's room was sprawled with Leggos, Tonkas, Playdoh, broken Crayolas, stuffed and plastic animals, a dripping easel and scattered sheets torn from jumbo newsprint pads. The gone-wild territory of her playing became a sovereign nation with a culture so ingrained it could not be suppressed with my cheerful colonizing dictum, "Time to clean up your room." There was much I could not give her. Yet I felt certain that she'd be all right if I gave her love as bedrock and the skill to deal with change. Nights I'd lie awake in bed, listening to the deep clarity and

silence of the north. I'd listen to my heart and wonder if it was all right. When a lady from the church brought us a gift basket of fruit and nuts for Thanksgiving, I realized that we were poor.

I had come for the woods, not merely to live with a view of green felted hills, but to be nestled into that leafy profusion. The northeast woods, not grand, not intimidating like in the West, are comforting—the mountains old and worn, thickly green with second-growth forest. A century ago the Vermont hills had been a solid patchwork quilt of farms, houses dotting the tended pastures and meadows, hedgerows and a few marker trees growing along the fencelines. When I lived there, the forest had claimed back the majority of the farmland; stone walls marked former boundary lines even in the densest woods; weedy roadbeds once used for logging and sugaring made the backcountry accessible. A mile in, one might find an overgrown cellarhole, the yard marked by huge maples and a single black walnut tree, a rose garden taken over by ragweed, daylilies tangled with timothy. In my own neighborhood there had been a sawmill, tannery, schoolhouse, and a Poor Farm with a barracks-like dormitory—all now vacant and ramshackle. The town had started in 1800, population thirty-six, and by 1859 had peaked at fifteen hundred. Much of the land was clear-cut during those sixty years, white pine six feet across logged off. The tallest and straightest trees went to ship builders; much of the rest were cut in segments and smoldered underground to make charcoal for industrial England. "The Iron Age was necessarily a Wood Age too," wrote Eric Sloane, "for our forests were stripped to make charcoal, then the only smelting fuel." What lumber remained was used for local building, or burned for potash, which was leached out and rendered into soap. French Canadians and Irish refugees had come to settle, raised turkeys and cows, banded together to drive them two hundred miles to market in Boston. And almost just as quickly the population had drained away. Many left to join the gold rush in the West; many died in the Civil War. In 1970, the population just over six hundred, someone painted on the broad side of a barn,

BAKERSFIELD CLOSED DUE TO LACK OF INTEREST. Those who remained were either families who had accumulated land wealth by working a farm for several generations or those too poor and discouraged to try again somewhere else.

The maple trees generally fared better than the evergreens, since they produced a lucrative cash crop while alive. For two months of backbreaking woods work in the spring, a family could earn a large portion of its annual income from selling maple syrup. Without that crop, most of the farms would have long since gone the way of the sawmill and tannery. A tended sugarbush makes elegant woods; competing trees thinned out, the crowns of maple spread wide into the open space, making a canopy that shelters the ground. Underneath, islands of shoulder-high ferns proliferate and the leaf mold sends forth a scattering of trout lilies, trillium, and spring beauties— ephemeral blooms always a gift in rough terrain.

What I hadn't planned on during the quiet first years of that decade was community. Musicians, artists, writers, and scientists who'd left college or careers to strip down to essentials were setting up homesteads back in the hills. They bought up ramshackle places, cleared backlots, threw work parties and pig roasts when they needed help raising beams and walls. They turned barns into houses and houses into barns. They jammed, playing blues and bluegrass with the locals, got hired on farms, or a few with the means did the hiring. One musician, a high-school band director, had been fired because he taught the students to play "Sergeant Pepper's Lonely Hearts Club Band." A zoologist kept seagulls in his haybarn, thinking he might get around to completing his dissertation—something about how the red spot on a herring gull's beak is a code telling their babies where to peck for food. There were other children being raised in free-spirited households and communes. One group called themselves the Dreamers. They used to visit the local family planning clinic to get free condoms, which they used for air locks on jugs of home-brew. There were the ones we called "the bad hippies" who stole the firewood out of our yard; a Catholic priest who'd left the church to marry a Cherokee social worker; a woman who'd lived in an urban feminist collective and left to marry a leftist pediatrician who had worked the medical tents at the Democratic Convention in Chicago. Dreamers all, and we kept dreaming. We started a parent cooperative school, a natural foods co-op, a madrigal group, a sitting meditation circle; jug bands, jazz bands, and farming collectives. And there was visiting, lots of laid-back unannounced visiting over coffee and joints, while the children and the music played on. There were games of hide-and-seek in the woods, adults and children playing together; there were love affairs and domestic rearrangements. Everyone seemed to have time for this sociability, though most of us had no money. No one had moved there for a job. That was the point. To take time into our own hands, to rethink our lives right down to their family and economic basis.

In the early seventies, War on Poverty money began to flow into the county and a number of us found work on the public dollar. After having done time as a dishwasher, waitress, farm worker, linotype operator, and free-school teacher, I got hired to be a family planning worker for the clinic opening in the county seat. We set up shop once a month in the hallway and emergency room of a small hospital. The doctors and staff were volunteers. Not until 1972 were unmarried women legally eligible for contraception. Abortion was available only in New York. The clinic was controversial, but Christian fundamentalists had not yet started picketing, harassing patients, or bombing medical facilities. Much of the clinic's public rhetoric spoke of poverty and "family planning." We were morally defensive, citing the neediest case histories—a Catholic woman who'd had fourteen pregnancies by the age of twenty-nine, who had nine living children, an unemployed farm worker for a husband, and a physician ethically opposed to contraception. But the majority of the patients were single women and many were teenagers. Though we couldn't say so publicly, most of the clinic workers believed these women were entitled to a good sex life.

Seeing

Ken Lamberton

This September morning, to my surprise, the Santa Cruz River roars past me where last night I walked a dry, rock-studded arroyo of sand. Now, apparently due to an overnight thunderstorm somewhere south of me, the river is a corrugated gray torrent forty feet wide.

I push through a bank of desert broom and amaranth. The channel of the Santa Cruz sweeps across an open, stony floodplain, punctuated occasionally with twenty-foot cottonwoods and Mexican elder. The river's cottonwood-willow forest, one of the rarest forests in the world and inhabiting less than two percent of the Southwest, has dwindled to scattered trees. Somewhere, a gray hawk screams. It may be the last one I'll encounter on my way north across southern Arizona.

By midday, humidity and sweat soak my khaki shirt, brightening letters reading, "Same shirt. Different day." The river has drawn down from a muddy flood to six thin fingers of foam grasping at sand. Ahead, the channel becomes a straight, narrow ditch, lined with seep willow and yellow snakeweed, its banks woven together with tangles of Bermuda grass. Flocks of common sulphur butterflies siphon moisture and salts from patches of mud, looking like tiny yellow sails on a chocolate sea.

Beneath Elephant Head Road bridge, the clay pots of swallow nests cling to the concrete supports as if slung there like spit wads. I smell something familiar: the rich aroma of bat guano. In the mud at my feet, ridges of tiny oblong pellets rise directly under the bridge's concrete expansion joints. I twist my head to peer into a seam and the darkness begins speaking to me in pitched whispers. I drop my pack and pull out my flashlight. Hundreds of tiny faces look back. Pin-prick eyes and Shar-pei noses, ears like seraphim wings. I stand in the Sistine Chapel surrounded by angels.

Mexican free-tailed bats (*Tadarida brasiliensis*) are the most common bat in the Southwest. In the old mining town of Bisbee, Arizona, Mexican freetails leak from one-hundred-year-old buildings like the one above Café La Roca, emerging from a hidden joint in pulses like escaping bubbles. In the ghost town of Ruby, Arizona, freetails plume out of a deep mineshaft like smoke. And, all over Tucson, the bats drop from their roosts under bridges and stadiums to wheel across a crepuscular sky.

Mexican freetails usually migrate to Arizona in March, returning to Mexico in October. These bats will be leaving soon, ending their all-summer, sunset to sunrise, 150-mile insect-feeding forays during which no moth, beetle, or mosquito is safe.

***

There's a kind of *seeing* that goes beyond what I do with my eyes, involving all of the senses, and more. This kind of seeing is more a participation, a penetration. To see the world in a grain of sand—to see its dimensions so clearly—that I am part of the picture. There are days when I don't get it right, when my sight is dimmed, when I allow my mind to form a patina over my view of the world and lose the wonder of the simplest things, like membraned-faced bats under a bridge. Days when I'm looking but not seeing.

Seeing the bats reminds me of the approaching departure of another summer migrant from Mexico. Nighthawks, members of the weak-footed, dirt-sitting clan called goatsuckers, also feed after dark on insects.

Once, in the evening post-storm quiet following a monsoon thunderstorm, the windstain smell of wet creosote drew me outside my home. Crunching over the washed gravel of my street, I noticed the boomerang wings and languid maneuvering of a nighthawk sculling through bug-rich cones of light. The bird continued dipping between the streetlights as I approached and crossed into its airspace. It was feeding on winged insects, protean clouds of them vibrating in the air. I sat on the curb to watch and discovered a termite hatch. As if gravity were unwinding, silken chutes sprayed out of the bare ground. The nighthawk was insatiable. For fifteen minutes I trailed the owl-like bird with my eyes as it sifted the air with its wide-mouthed, whiskered beak. I was participating in something intimate, silent yet potent: termite nuptials and nighthawk gluttony; the ecstasy of consummation and consumption.

***

Gloaming comes on this quiet, hot evening as a setting sun casts its longer, redder wavelengths into a reef of clouds and the moon pulls away from the opposite horizon. I'm walking the river when suddenly something out of place catches my eye. A great blue heron shakes out its gray cassock of feathers and lifts itself out of the channel on monastic wings. The bird is huge, prehistoric, reptilian, with bent wings that lean into a Cretaceous sky as it drifts, circles, and slips out of view. It could be an animal cobbled to my imagination, all beak and neck and dangling feet, but it's real.

Here, in a desert that scours you down to essences like hunger and hope, one great blue heron is an excess. Sprays of termites and nighthawk ballets and even a squealing colony of free-tailed bats are extravagances.

***

Digging Mars

Ken Lamberton

Where my steps uncloak a brace of grasshoppers and knock clods of sandy silt into the shining channel, I notice how whole sections of the river bank have broken into puzzle fragments. My youngest daughter Melissa could probably tell me all about the nature of the sediments, whether they're classified as loam or silt or loamy silt or sandy loam. She knows about dirt. She's wanted to be a geologist since before she could spell the word.

The Santa Cruz River near Tucson has played a significant part in our lives, living as we do on a small tributary arroyo of the co-called "dry river." Today, I'm following the deep channel to wherever it might take me and here, at the confluence of the river and San Juan Wash, I'm struck by the emotion I feel, being so simply connected to my home, although I'm miles away. Even the sand beneath my feet carries a special significance. How long ago did I or one of my three girls stand on this same earth? I look for something I might recognize—stranded Pooh-sticks, a forgotten shoe, maybe a cracked graduated cylinder from some long-ago science fair experiment.

I'm not surprised when my cell phone suddenly rings and it's Melissa. "We have photos from the HiRISE showing Phoenix with chutes open descending to the surface!" she tells me.

Melissa is working today in the "PIT," the University of Arizona's Lunar and Planetary Lab's, "Payload Interoperability Testbed" where researchers practice on a full-scale engineering model of the Phoenix lander before they send commands to the craft on Mars.

Yesterday, my wife Karen and I joined Melissa and several hundred scientists, their families, and media people in the PIT for the historic landing. Now moving into her fourth year at the U of A,

Melissa has been involved with the Lunar and Planetary Lab (LPL) since high school. In fact, her senior year science fair project lined her up perfectly with this current Mar's mission. After the previous year's project when she successfully grew cold-loving "psychrophilic" bacteria from the dry valleys of Antarctica in Martian-like temperatures and soil, she decided to raise the bar. This time she would attempt to grow bacteria in complete Martian conditions, not just soil and temperature but atmospheric as well—in the bitterly cold, dry, carbon-dioxide-laden near-vacuum of the polar regions. And not just any resilient bacteria, but those germs she would swab from the Phoenix lander itself.

She didn't require me to dig holes in the Santa Cruz River like previous experiments. She wanted "Martian chambers." What we came up with, after abandoning the offerings from a scientific equipment store and turning instead to a plumbing supply shop, were three heavy, eight-inch metal containers that, except for the valves and pressure gauges sticking out of them, looked a lot like pipe bombs.

The bacteria from the lander bloomed in her chambers, better even than the bacteria from Antarctica, which got the attention of LPL scientists working on the Phoenix mission. Melissa's project became one more of "Planetary Protection," finding ways to protect Mars from Earth microorganisms that may be riding along on a spacecraft, something NASA officials had recently become interested in. Melissa began telling them that if life is discovered on Mars, we should pick up our trash.

Since her first years at the U of A, Melissa has worked with the Phoenix mission, sitting in the clean room calibrating the camera on the robotic arm with its digging tool and lately visiting schools and giving tours in the PIT as the mission's educational coordinator. (I tell people that she could be the next Carl Sagan.) She has also become, with the help of a NASA space grant, the LPL's "historian," interviewing scientists involved with the lab since the 1960s and recording their stories.

Karen and I met several of these scientists yesterday, as they hugged our daughter and swung her around the room in celebration of what the LPL has striven for for decades—the complete management of a spacecraft. It would begin as soon as the Jet Propulsion Laboratory (JPL) in Pasadena delivered Phoenix to the Red Planet.

At 5:39 PM, the first indication of Phoenix's landing came as a JPL technician relayed to the crowd that the cruise stage separation had occurred. One screen began to show a computer simulation of the landing, while another pictured the climbing red line of a Doppler radar. The room fell silent as the voice announced atmospheric entry and peak heating, the beginning of the so-called "seven minutes of terror." Minutes went by. Then, "parachute detected," followed by a burst of cheers and "we have data lockup." People were holding their breath, holding on to each other. I turned to look at Melissa and she held the fingers of both hands between her teeth. This was the point at which the previous Mars polar lander had failed, crashing to the frozen surface of the southern polar region on December 3, 1999 (and thus giving rise to this mission's name). The tension grew as the announcer called out the lander's separation from the backshell and chute, the throttle-up of its engines, and then began reading elevations: "six hundred meters . . . five hundred . . . two-fifty . . . eighty meters . . . sixty meters . . . forty meters . . . twenty . . . Stand by for touch-down signal . . ." Then silence, a very long silence, until suddenly, "Touchdown signal detected!"

The room erupted. People (including me) had tears streaming down their faces. I hugged Melissa, saying, "Your spaceship is on Mars!"

Today, I still feel the weakness in my knees. I once told Melissa that she could be the first woman geologist on Mars if she wanted to. She corrected me, however, saying, "Dad, I could be the first *person* on Mars."

Melissa has been cruising on a trajectory in her life as certain as the path of her spacecraft. What began years ago with digging holes in the dry sand of the Santa Cruz River has led to digging holes in the red dirt of Mars.

The Road Not Taken

Walker Thomas

One rainy and still balmy Friday night in October 1979, I drove west on a dirt road across the northernmost ridge of the Tucson Mountains to Avra Valley. When I last drove that stretch in 1965, the abundant life drawn out by rain had free range onto the less traveled corridor, a passage easily observed on that swath we'd cut through their environment. But fourteen years had passed, and traffic had become heavy, the wildlife reduced to bumps on the road.

Outdoor enthusiasts perched above oversized wheels roared past as I stopped for an injured tiger rattlesnake, a small-headed, dusty gray rattler with tapered bands of faded, tiger-orange. Its head listed to one side, its skull partially crushed by a preceding vehicle. I maneuvered it into a pillowcase and returned home.

In a terrarium, the rattlesnake yawned in an effort to reposition bone in a remarkably flexible skull. Jaws agape, it erected its fangs. One was broken, but a series of new fangs stood in a graduated row behind it, the next largest ready to take its place. The next meal would have to be postponed, but since rattlesnakes eat infrequently, it might rest long enough for bone and cartilage to heal.

Next morning, after I released the tiger rattlesnake in the rocks well above the road, I drove down into Avra Valley. The packed-sand road was still wet, still attractive to wildlife. To my left, a dead roadrunner, long dark-green feathers rustling in a slight breeze, was an exotic-looking heap. A battered, beadwork purse in pink and black on the right had been a Gila monster. Broken under a resilient covering of fur, a dead coyote lay like any dog asleep beside the road.

Among the dead, I found a still living sidewinder. Avra Valley is the easternmost extent of the sidewinder's range. Its unique side-winding locomotion, where it advances over loose sand like a rolling corkscrew, confines the small, salmon-pink and paint-spatter white rattlesnake with a hornlike awning over each eye, to areas of shifting, fine-grained sand west of Tucson. This one was pressed into the somewhat forgiving surface, stunned and sluggish, but still alive. I carried it across the desert far from the road to the shade of an ironwood tree.

As I returned home on paved roads through Gates Pass, I overlooked a city that seemed a mirage on the desert expanse between three mountain ranges: a ghostly Tucson viewed through a smudge of haze rising from the cars of the many who, like me, took to the roads to enjoy the day. One element of that haze has been used over the past century as the suicide of choice for those who would willingly pass through lethargy to a mind-numbing sleep and on to death.

When I drove an ambulance in Scottsdale, we answered a call to an attempted suicide. Passersby were worried about a pair of legs protruding in front of an idling car parked half in and half out of a garage. Instead of closing himself in with the fumes, the man had backed the car up so that its tailpipes emptied outside. He then sprawled in front of the car to await an unlikely death.

In his madness was a metaphor for the slow suicide of us all. The fumes that he so carefully avoided in the staging of his personal drama emptied into what we once thought of as an infinite atmosphere. By the nineteen-seventies we had altered its color and clarity, tinted the firmament with our waste until we could see this vast atmosphere to be finite, like the space within a garage.

An alien visitor to one of our planet's bigger cities that year might think our atmosphere was formed of a dingy, pungent medium that obscured distant objects and burned the throat when taken in excess. That we could visibly alter the chemistry of a planet's atmosphere in a century or two shows the scope of our industry, but little of our humanity (our visible effects in 1979—the browning by sulfur dioxide, the acid rain, the irritation of inhaled particulates, the just visible haze of ground-level ozone—though significant, will prove to be the smaller part of the problem. We will learn that an imbalance of the less visible carbon dioxide will so alter the composition of our atmosphere that our weather, our fresh water reserves, the size of our land masses, and so the structure of the planet as we know it and life itself is at risk). We are small fish to so foul our pond.

We dicker over the magnitude of the problem, see our individual contributions as negligible and continue to heap on abuse, each of us doing our small part. We demand that government put a stop to planetary abuse when it is we who will not be stopped. We, who first see how wrong our effect, must be the first to stop.

Ninety percent of our calls on the ambulance were traffic related. Siren wailing, I raced traffic to get to traffic's victims. Drunk drivers whined that the fault rested on the sober bodies in the cars they struck. Driving began to seem an absurd occupation, the cost exceeding benefits.

That dirt road through Avra Valley, three years later, offered a microcosm of highway slaughter in a naïve environment. We tend to see nature as a powerful mother whose scorn is to be feared, but before our technology she is as vulnerable, as easily compromised, as a child entrusted to our care.

We move on roads carved into mountains, on swaths cut through forests, gravel beds dumped on marshes. What seemed immeasurable land is measured by roads and cut into parcels on a grid of crossroads. The grid isolates and compromises interdependent ecosystems. Pedestrian wildlife must dash through traffic from one square of a checkerboard to another. As we have gained in mobility, we have lost more of the planet to ourselves.

When I stopped for gas in Tucson on that October day in 1979, I discovered my wallet missing. I must have dropped it when I moved the sidewinder. I replaced my University I.D. right away and wrote to get my Social Security card replaced. But I put off the trip to the Department of Motor Vehicles for a new driver's license. When I did go, I stood in line for a while and then left. To continue to drive was out of sync with my concept of human responsibility, my responsibility. The line was too long, I told myself; but the simple truth was that I couldn't bring myself to request another license. I sold the car, a VW Beetle I picked up when I drove ambulances. A driving enthusiast, my two previous cars were Porsches, but I had felt like a hypocrite when, as freeway speed limits were lowered to conserve fuel in 1972, I found myself cruising in a lower gear, wasting fuel.

With the profits from the Beetle, I paid some bills and bought a bicycle. With no more insurance premiums to pay, no fuel and maintenance costs, no more traffic angst, I felt instead of loss, a sense of relief. More than that, I felt a glimmer of pride. I also felt a bit of embarrassment that I was so long in seeing the light, and wonder that I was among so few who had.

Like a newly saved Christian, I grew impatient with those who hadn't seen the light, who still sinned in the same ways as I once did. I became a bore on the subject. Edward Abbey invited me to an EarthFirst! meeting where he and Doug Peacock—template for his Hayduke character in *The Monkey Wrench Gang*—were featured speakers.

"What do you think?" Ed asked on the church parking lot afterward.

I had hiked down from the mountains and walked to the meeting, and I was especially full of myself.

"Look at all these cars,' I said, "What sense is there to pollute the planet on the way to rail against planetary pollution?"

"You need to shake that 'holier than thou' attitude," Ed said as he turned to autograph a book.

He caught me on U of A campus a couple weeks later.

"I've got something to show you," he said, "You're gonna love this."

He led a quick pace off campus and over to Euclid, where he had parked the vintage, '60s Cadillac he'd just bought.

"Nice, huh?"

I reread his first book, *The Lonesome Cowboy*, to put his sentiments in the proper perspective, to remind myself how, in the quiet, opening pages of that novel, he shared my skeptical view of, and distress at, technology's place. But more the skeptic, he must have sought then a better way to express that skepticism to a Pollyanna world, and was happy to set himself up as bad example, to stir the pot. Ed was always stirring pots. That's my take on it. I hope that vulture soaring overhead—Ed's self-proclaimed alter ego—agrees.

Walker Thomas spent nearly eight years living in and around a mountain wilderness cave, photographing nature and contemplating the life that led him there. His four pieces in this edition of *Stories from the Other Side* are taken from a recently completed book manuscript of that material, now in search of a publisher. Other excerpts from that book manuscript have been published in *Outside* and *Natural History* magazines.

Excerpt from *The Outermost House*

Henry Beston

Late August, and day by day, I see more shore birds and see them oftener. All summer long there have been sandpipers and ringnecks on the beach, but earlier in the season the birds are elusive and may disappear for days. The first great flocks to return from the Northern breeding grounds arrived here about the middle of July. I remember their coming. For four interminable days a strong and tireless southwest wind had billowed across the lagoon and off to a smoky sea; on the morning of the fifth day, just before sunrise, this wind had died; then had come dullness and quiet, and, between nine and ten o'clock, a breath of easterly air. All that fifth afternoon the beach had been black with birds, most of them ringnecks or semipalmated plovers. The long southwester had apparently dammed up a great migrational stream. These first flocks were vagrant mobs. Walking to Nauset between two and three o'clock, I must have put up between two and three thousand birds. As I drew near, mob after mob after mob crowded the air and sought feeding grounds ahead. The smaller autumnal flocks had flown in psychic unity, rising and falling, wheeling and alighting together; these mobs scattered and divided into wandering companies.

Late August, and my wild ducks, having raised their families, are returning by hundreds to the marsh. During May and June and early July, when I wandered about this region in the night, I heard no sound from the flats. Now, when I get out to signal to the first coast guardsman coming south at half-past nine, I heard from the dark levels a sentinel quack, a call. The marsh fills with life again; the great sun goes south along green treetops and moorlands fruiting and burned brown.

The quality of life, which in the ardour of spring was personal and sexual, becomes social in midsummer. Stirred by the vernal fire, a group psychically dissolves, for every creature in a flock is intent upon the use and the offering of his own awakened flesh. Even creatures who are of the flocking or herding habit emerge as individuals. With the rearing of the young, and their integration into the reestablished group, life becomes again a social rhythm. The body has been given and sacrificially broken, its own gods and all gods obeyed.

The other day I saw a young swimmer in the surf. He was, I judged, about twenty-two years old and a little less than six feet tall, splendidly built, and as he stripped I saw that he must have been swimming since the season began, for he was sunburned and brown. Standing naked on the steep beach, his feet in the climbing seethe, he gathered himself for a swimmer's crouching spring, watched his opportunity, and suddenly leaped headfirst through a long arc of air into the wall of a towering and enormous wave. Again and again he repeated his jest, emerging each time beyond the breaker with a stare of salty eyes, a shake of the head, and a smile. It was all a beautiful thing to see: the surf thundering across the great natural world, the beautiful and compact body in its naked strength and symmetry, the astounding plunge across the air, arms extended ahead, legs and feet together, the emerging stroke of the flat hands, and the alternate rhythms of the sunburned and powerful shoulders.

Watching this picture of a fine human being free for the moment of everything save his own humanity and framed in a scene of nature, I could not help musing on the mystery of the human

Excerpt from "The Year at High Tide" and "Orion Rises on the Dunes" from The Outermost House by Henry Beston. Copyright 1928, 1949, 1956, © 1977 by Elizabeth Beston. Reprinted by permission of Henry Holt and Company, LLC.

body and of how nothing can equal its rich and rhythmic beauty when it is beautiful or approach its forlorn and pathetic ugliness when beauty has not been mingled in or has withdrawn. Poor body, time and the long years were the first tailors to teach you the merciful use of clothes! Though some scold to-day because you are too much seen, to my mind, you are not seen fully enough or often enough when you are beautiful. All my life it has given me pleasure to see beautiful human beings. To see beautiful young men and women gives one a kind of reverence for humanity (alas, of how few experiences may this be said), and surely there are few moods of the spirit more worthy of our care than those in which we reverence, even for a moment, our tragic and bewildered kind.

My swimmer having gone his way, out of a chance curiosity I picked the top of a dune gold-enrod, and found at the very bottom of a cocoon of twisted leaves the embryo head of the late autumnal flower.

So came August to its close, ending its last day with a night so luminous and still that a mood came over me to sleep out on the open beach under the stars. There are nights in the summer when darkness and ebbing tide quiet the universal wind, and this August night was full of that quiet of absence, and the sky was clear. South of my house, between the bold fan of a dune and the wall of a plateau, a sheltered hollow opens seaward, and to this nook I went, shouldering my blankets sailorwise. In the star-shine the hollow was darker than the immense and solitary beach, and its floor was still pleasantly warm with the overflow of day.

I fell asleep uneasily, and woke again as one wakes out-of-doors. The vague walls about me breathed a pleasant smell of sand, there was no sound, and the broken circle of grass above was as motionless as something in a house. Waking again, hours afterward, I felt the air grown colder and heard a little advancing noise of waves. It was still night. Sleep gone and past recapture, I drew on my clothes and went to the beach. In the luminous east, two great stars aslant were rising clear of the exhalations of darkness gathered at the rim of night and ocean—Betelgeuse and Bellatrix, the shoulders of Orion. Autumn had come, and the Giant stood again at the horizon of day and the ebbing year, his belt still hidden in the bank of cloud, his feet in the deeps of space and the far surges of the sea.

My year upon the beach had come full circle; it was time to close my door. Seeing the great suns, I thought of the last time I marked them in the spring, in the April west above the moors, dying into the light and sinking. I saw them of old above the iron waves of black December, sparkling afar. Now, once again, the Hunter rose to drive summer south before him, once again autumn followed on his steps. I had seen the ritual of the sun; I had shared the elemental world. Wraiths of memories began to take shape. I saw the sleet of the great storm slanting down again into the grass under the thin seepage of moon, the blue-white spill of an immense billow on the outer bar, the swans in the high October sky, the sunset madness and splendour of the year's terns over the dunes, the clouds of beach birds arriving, the eagle solitary in the blue. And because I had known this outer and secret world, and been able to live as I had lived, reverence and gratitude greater and deeper than ever possessed me, sweeping every emotion else aside, and space and silence an instant closed together over life. Then time gathered again like a cloud, and presently the stars began to pale over an ocean still dark with remembered night.

During the months that have passed since that September morning some have asked me what understanding of Nature one shapes from so strange a year? I would answer that one's first appreciation is a sense that the creation is still going on, that the creative forces are as great and as active to-day as they have ever been, and that to-morrow's morning will be as heroic as any of the world. *Creation is here and now.* So near is man to the creative pageant, so much a part is he of the endless and incredible experiment, that any glimpse he may have will be but the revelation of a moment, a solitary note heard in a symphony thundering through debatable existences of time. Poetry is as necessary to comprehension as science. It is as impossible to live without reverence as it is without joy.

And what of Nature itself, you say—that callous and cruel engine, red in tooth and fang? Well, it is not so much of an engine as you think. As for "red in tooth and fang," whenever I hear the phrase or its intellectual echoes I know that some passer-by has been getting life from books. It is true that there are grim arrangements. Beware of judging them by whatever human values are in style. As well expect Nature to answer to your human values as to come into your house and sit in a chair. The economy of nature, its checks and balances, its measurements of competing life—all this is its great marvel and has an ethic of its own. Live in Nature, and you will soon see that for all its non-human rhythm, it is no cave of pain. As I write I think of my beloved birds of the great beach, and of their beauty and their zest of living. And if there are fears, know also that Nature has its unexpected and unappreciated mercies.

Whatever attitude to human existence you fashion for yourself, know that it is valid only if it be the shadow of an attitude to Nature. A human life, so often likened to a spectacle upon a stage, is more justly a ritual. The ancient values of dignity, beauty, and poetry which sustain it are of Nature's inspiration; they are born of the mystery and beauty of the world. Do no dishonour to the earth lest you dishonour the spirit of man. Hold your hands out over the earth as over a flame. To all who love her, who open to her the doors of their veins, she gives of her strength, sustaining them with her own measureless tremor of dark life. Touch the earth, love the earth, honour the earth, her plains, her valleys, her hills, and her seas; rest your spirit in her solitary places. For the gifts of life are the earth's and they are given to all, and they are the songs of birds at daybreak, Orion and the Bear, and dawn seen over ocean from the beach.

Selected Poems

Charlie Rossiter

THE NIGHT I SLEPT IN THE LEAVES

The idea was
to spend the night outdoors
and wake cleansed
of soul sickness
tests, deadlines,
cleared
from the cramped feeling
of day in, day out

It was a great plan   but
have you ever slept in the leaves?

I woke at three
stiff, damp, cold
disheartened.
There was a lot of dew
in those leaves.

Cursing my stupidity
I stumbled inside
to bed.

Looking back
I could see
I was not
completely stupid.
I was wrong
about the comfort
of leaves
but I needed something
out of the ordinary
that night
and in the morning
I did feel a little bit
cleansed.

SNOW BLIND IN NEBRASKA

The light was blinding white
from oncoming headlights
and our own
reflected back
as I pushed it at fifty
driving through the night
radio tuned to K-O-M-A
across the flatlands
of Nebraska
from the coast
to Colorado
for a long weekend
with my buddy Craig.

Around two, Mike woke
in the back seat
and almost yelled out in terror,
snow blind,
he later told me,
but just then
guys being guys
all he said was,

how's it going?

and crawled
into the front seat
to keep me company
and awake
as we plowed through
the prairie night,
hearts set
on adventure,
the mountains,
the coming dawn.

Charlie Rossiter, NEA Fellowship recipient and three-time Pushcart Prize nominee, hosts the audio website *poetrypoetry.com*. His work has been featured on NPR and numerous statewide public radio networks. During the '90s he hosted the *Poetry Motel* TV program, still seen on cable stations in some parts of the Northeast. His recent co-authored book *Back Beat*, a memoir with poetry, has been praised by Lawrence Ferlinghetti. His chapbook, *What Men Talk About*, won the first Red Wheel Barrow Prize from Pudding House Press. He has performed at the Geraldine R. Dodge Poetry Festival in NJ; and was among a handful of poets chosen to perform at the Chicago Blues Festival in 2005. His latest book The Night We Danced With the Raelettes (2007) is available at www.FoothillsPublishing.com

Alex

Walker Thomas

At first Alex aggressively chewed my fingers. When I began to feed her insects, she learned to be gentler to the fingers that offered them. My ninth grade biology teacher gave me a *Scientific American* article by zoologist, Ernest P. Walker, on his theory that physical warmth was the way to a bat's heart. Even in a summer sleep, a bat's pulse and respirations slow to hibernation levels with a dramatic drop in body temperature. Professor Walker felt that a bat bonded with him as to a maternal surrogate when he took it from its roost and warmed it in his hands. I'd read a later study that showed how orphaned monkey babies more quickly and completely bonded with heated monkey dolls, as surrogate mothers, than to identical dolls left at room temperature. Coincidentally, scientists will later say that certain bat species—the larger, fox-faced, fruit-eating types—developed as an offshoot of the same primates from which the monkeys and we evolved.

I took Alex from the curtains where she slept and held her until she warmed, and she did seem to warm to me. Alex's flights around the room lost the erratic quality of fearful escape. She soared, taking my thoughts on her back.

By the second day, she learned to fly to me when I called. She sought the sound of my voice and flew straight to my face. I'd see her coming in, her face suspended between the knife-edge line of spread wings. She'd tumble in air and, in the next instant, come to rest like an autumn leaf hanging from my lower lip. She took me from my world into hers, thrilled me with the grace of her flight, the look of her, the smell of her like a kidskin glove beneath my nose.

In the nights that followed I'd hear a soft rustle from within a fold of the window curtains as Alex stirred. Soon she would fly from the curtains and glide in low over my feet to skim the length of me. Musty-scented wings fluttered, fanning my face, as she swerved to avoid hitting the headboard.

The first pass was a signal for me to sit up, to act as a pylon for her to circle in order to land. I'd pick her from the sheets then and warm her in my hands. When warm, she'd sit on my open palm, propped on folded wings, as if on crutches, and preen her fur with her tongue. She had lice in the wild and her fur was matted, dusty and disheveled, but away from the close quarters of her colony, she had eaten her lice and groomed her fur to a soft sheen.

Her fur was brown, her rubbery wings a crinkled black. In her borderline human face her nose and muzzle were bare brown flesh, while her black eyes were set under a were-wolfish widow's peak of fur.

She'd take a beetle or a crumb of the moon-white cheese I kept in a headboard compartment, spread her wings and flap from my hand to vanish into the dark, the course of her flight revealed in the crunch of beetle shell or lip-smacking sounds she made with the cheese. She'd make a pass over the tropical fish to skim off a drink of water, swooping beneath the aquarium rim. Sometimes her wings would catch on the sides, and she'd fall in. I'd hear her splashing, fish her out and hang her in the curtains to dry.

She flew every twenty minutes from nine p.m. until two in the morning. One night, I decided to ignore her in the last hour, to teach her what I considered a more realistic schedule. When I failed to sit up, she returned to her curtain, and I gloated over how easily I had adjusted her life to suit my own.

In a while, though, she flew again, so close I could feel the touch of her wings through the sheets. She delivered a feathery flurry of slaps to my face before she returned to her curtain to roost.

A few minutes later, she flew directly to the bed and crawled across the sheets, a small soldier under the wrinkled black poncho of her wings. Arms of folded wing reached out in a stiff, hand-over-hand motion as, with remnant thumbs, hooks where the wings fold back, she pulled herself to my exposed hand. She took a finger in her teeth, spread her wings and flapped with all her might. I allowed my hand to rise. When hand and bat were a foot off the bed, she bit down hard. Her tiny teeth did not break skin, but the sudden, sharp pain surprised me. With a reflexive jerk, I slung her across the room. She just managed to brake her headlong rush into the wall with furious strokes of her wings.

She circled the room and came to rest on the sheets beside me as I sat nursing my finger. I had so succeeded in gaining her trust and dependence that provider had become servant. She better understood our roles than I and would tolerate no variation.

My ninth grade biology teacher and I caught the bat as it emerged from the eves of a log building at a camp in the New Jersey Pine Barrens. He was unsure of its gender, so I chose a neutral *Alex* as its name. Later, I'd learn that such a large gathering of big-brown bats would be a brood colony of females. The males live alone or in groups of two or three in trees. Later that summer, babies were born to Alex's colony. Several times I'd find one that had lost its grip on its mother's breast—a naked, hammer-headed creature; a tiny, winged piglet—mewing silently in the grass, its mouth moving rhythmically as if emitting a hypersonic cry for help.

When I took Alex from a bug-filled, Pine Barrens sky to confine her in a suburban bedroom as a pet, my father expressed disgust with another of my intrusions on the natural world. I knew he was right. Not content to observe nature, I had to hold it captive in my world, while my father's major redeeming quality was in the way he walked through the woods to see, to hear, to smell, but never to touch. He struggled to instill the same respect in me, but he compromised because Alex was an educational project encouraged by Mr. S, my ninth grade biology teacher, whom both parents agreed was a positive though eccentric influence as mentor.

At fifteen, I couldn't be hired outright, but Mr. S convinced my father—excessively frugal in the way of many who grew up during the Great Depression—that if he'd spring for me to spend a week at camp, he could get me hired on as his assistant for room and board. My father, who would save money in the long run, liked the idea.

On the Monday nature hike at Camp Columbus I saw a flick of gray in the periphery of my vision and caught a fence lizard that had dashed under a woodchip beside the trail. Mr. S began to invent my legend, lauding my sharp eyes and quick reflexes to the dozen campers gathered in the woods. Tuesday, I tried the felled-cedar catwalks, grabbed a water snake and held onto it even as I fell into the swamp. I caught a spotted turtle on Wednesday, a flying squirrel Thursday.

Flying squirrels had taken over a purple martin house in the junior village clearing. The thirty-foot post had a wrap of sheet metal at the base to prevent mice and standard-issue squirrels from climbing to the scaled-down, two-story white colonial birdhouse on top, but the flyers were able to glide in from taller trees on the lake margin. Snakeman had watched their evening flights back into the woods from the birdhouse all week. He knew their favorite trees and where their glide paths ended on the trunks before they scampered up into the crowns for further flights along the lakefront.

Thursday afternoon, he arranged campers in a wide circle around the martin house. Only a few of us stood in front of trees, while the rest were backed by treeless clearing and cabins. I stood alone in front of a distant tree that Mr. S had observed to be a popular target for the squirrels.

"They hit the trunk low here," he told me as he gave me a pair of thick gloves to wear. Already tagged as a Frank Buck among campers, I was the only one given gloves.

With full swings of a sledgehammer, Snakeman sent vibrations up the pole until the house on top swayed like a tall building in an earthquake. Squirrels popped out of bird holes, ran across balconies and onto the roof. Hammer thuds echoed across the lake. Squirrels launched themselves and sailed above extended arms toward the trees. Two that were jarred loose fell short, to be caught on the ground in a tangle of pillowcases. I reached high overhead and made a lucky catch as one sailed toward my tree.

Within a few nights flying squirrels retook the martin house. Our three never adjusted to captivity and died.

I volunteered to prepare the weekend campfire, a large, square-based pyramid of split logs. Campers dressed in Indian attire would light the fire. First they'd strike a spark from a stone flint against a steel file into a square of scorched t-shirt. The t-shirt ash was inserted into a hand-spun bird's nest of cedar bark fiber, infused by nature with a volatile dust. The spark would create a glowing ring in the ash, and a galaxy of cedar-dust particles would sparkle like tiny stars living brief lives. One of the boys would blow gently into the nest cupped in his hands until it burst into flame. He then placed it within the pyramid. Both boys would add increasingly larger twigs to build a bonfire that grew to consume the pyramid over the course of the night's program.

As I split logs for that Friday's campfire, Mr. S fed me facts about each day's catch so I could field questions when I showed the critter between reels of the evening movie.

As my wildlife show-and-tell became a popular bit, Mr. S told camp administrators that I'd become irreplaceable to his nature program. At the end of the week, I was offered room and board and a refund of camp fees already paid to stay on as woodcutter and Snakeman's assistant. I was to perform an Indian dance around the Friday night campfire to celebrate the honor before a crowd of counselors, campers and visiting parents.

I wore feathers and a stiff plastic loincloth with a snakeskin motif and held a corn snake in each hand. Campers cheered for the snakes, each doing its own serpentine dance from my hands. I coiled one on my head. Its tail made a spit curl between my eyes. As I did my clumsy dance, I smelled musk and felt a warm ooze on my face.

Alex spent that first week in a cage in the rec-hall captive to the sounds and smells of her home roost. Her freedom was overdue, and necessary since I wouldn't be going home to a bedroom we could share. I showed her Sunday evening and then released her in the rec-hall. She made several passes through campers' up-thrusting hands, zigzagging nimbly around and between them before settling in the rafters. I secretly hoped she would fly back to me, or later, outside, flutter around my head to show she shared my inflated view of our friendship. I feared that our friendship was little more than a bond of forced dependence.

During the movie, Alex hunted bugs in the projector's beam, a flittering presence in my world, completely absorbed in her own. After the campers went to bed, Snakeman and I opened the doors wide. Two other bats came to her when she flew out, and the three careened and tumbled together as they fluttered out of sight.

Monday, campers found a dead bat a hundred yards from the rec-hall. It was shrunken in death, and I could not find Alex in its unanimated face, but our having found the corpse of an otherwise identical bat seemed an unlikely coincidence. I guessed that the welcoming sisters were instead attacking the reek of humanity emanating from her fur, or that she fell exhausted, too weakened by her confinement to keep up. Mr. S assured me that it was some other bat, dead of natural causes. We should expect a degree of mortality from any large colony, he told me. He said that the campers were just more alert to the presence of bats after seeing Alex.

As he injected his embalmer's solution into the body, Mr. S seemed shrunken too. He was determined to see us as innocents in the service of science, the death as a normal event in the natural world. We see ourselves above nature, though unable to fully assess our effects on that complex world. Claiming scientific interest, I ran with S through the woods. Like boys in pursuit of trophies, we wreaked havoc. Innocence is no excuse. The innocent are as responsible for nature's plight as are its profiteers.

Buzz

Walker Thomas

When school resumed, I remained on the mountain and commuted from my camp at Crow's Foot to the University of Arizona. I took a tennis class so I'd be issued a tall locker in McHale Center, where I could shower. Tall lockers were issued only to football players and students taking tennis or golf. Anyone else got one just big enough to hold a duffle bag. One morning, my locker started a great buzz among the U of A football players gathered for a workout.

A couple hours earlier, I had penned an assignment for a nonfiction workshop with Edward Abbey:

I see a diamondback as I come down this morning. It is stretched out in the open: four and a half feet, and a long tail with broad base: typical male. I walk around to where I can get a good, full-length shot. Photography is a great medium for communication with rattlesnakes.

He is still as I circle to find the best angle for a shot. Only his tongue moves. Its forked ends spread and flick once, twice, picking up my scent from the air. He draws back into a defensive coil, rattles raised to the side, neck pulled into a tight "S" behind and above the head. His tongue flicks out again. He is cautious, but not alarmed. The rattles are still.

I stretch out on my belly, looking up through the lens at the white of his chin. I inch toward him on my belly until most of the frame is filled with head and rattles. We remain motionless as I wait for another flick of his tongue to complete the pose. No tongue. I click off a shot of that static pose and wriggle back a bit to elicit a flick. Out comes the tongue, and I get a shot with tongue and eye in focus. I rise to move away. He uncoils and slides slowly, straight as an arrow, into the shelter of a mesquite. He has not rattled, nor struck, though I've been within reach.

I went on to describe the stop at the ranch for the bike, where:

One of the ranch dogs becomes excited about something near where I'm doing repairs on my bicycle before heading in to school. A big diamondback is crossing a pile of lumber. It is much larger than the one I photographed this morning and more silver in overall coloration. By size alone, approaching the maximum for the species, it too is most likely a male. It is still unaware of being observed, and moves with confidence into the open.

John hears his dog barking.

"Diamondback," I say.

"Rattler?" he yells.

His wife Mollie and their daughter Kari call from the house for the dog to get inside. Instead, another dog runs out from between Mollie's legs to add to the confusion. Mollie and Kari run out, too.

The diamondback extends his tongue and flicks it through air filled with the scent of six frantic mammals. At the same time, infrared sensors located in pits in the rattler's face pick up our heat. He draws into a defensive coil and loudly, furiously, sounds his rattles at the hot-blooded creatures rushing about.

"Kill it, John!" Mollie shrieks several times.

I convince John to let me relocate the rattler (later studies indicate that relocated reptiles are unlikely to survive, but at the time, it seemed my best course of action). *I take the head off a mop I find beside the house and approach the rattler. John brings a grain sack out from the shed.*

The rattler is acting like its Hollywood counterpart, a vision of vicious serpent rearing and striking amid a ceaseless roar of rattles.

Vicious is in the diamondback's scientific name, Crotalus atrox. Atrox means vicious. I have seen little viciousness in these animals. Diamondbacks watch coiled as I pass them on the desert distant from human passage, rarely raising a ruckus. Their behavior is different near heavily used trails, where a defensive pose is taken up immediately upon sensing me. At those times, only a fool would step too close.

The dogs join in the clamor, along with an occasional shriek from sidelined humans, as I spread the grain sack open on the ground near the rattler. John watches silent, intent.

"The trick", I explain, "is to lift the snake on the end of the stick, with its weight distributed so that it prefers to balance there than to fall off. I'll maneuver it into the open mouth of the sack, catch a fold of the sack with the stick and pull the sack up around the snake."

This is not usually difficult, but the rattler is terrified, agitated into continual motion of its unmanageably large body, always with that loud blare of rattles ringing in my ears. By the time he is finally in the sack and the sack tied, I am exhausted.

"You've got some kind of nerve," says John.

"I don't want that thing set loose nowhere near here!" says Mollie.

I've never seen a rattlesnake so riled up as that one, as it responded to the mood conveyed by dogs and people.

I was late, so I packed my books as a barrier between the grain sack of rattlesnake and me, loaded it on my back—*I need to get panniers*, I thought—and bicycled to school. I'd leave the snake with Cecil in environmental biology for the day, but first I put it in my locker at McHale while I took a shower. When I returned, towel around my waist, half a dozen players back from a morning workout, were standing around my blaring, vibrating locker.

One insisted, "I grew up in Louisiana swamps, and what I'm hearing in that locker is a rattlesnake."

The banging of locker doors when they came in must have set it off. I pressed through the line sheepishly, opened my locker and brought out the buzzing grain sack.

I heard, "It *is* a rattler!"

I said, "Yeah."

Several players took advantage of the opportunity to practice wind sprints. I opened the sack for the remaining players to peer in.

"Damn! It *is* a rattlesnake! It's huge," one called to the others laughing in the next row of lockers.

The man in the window of the equipment room at the end of my row took it well.

"Don't worry," he said, "Stranger things have happened here."

I dressed and headed over to a quiet back room full of cages and specimen jars in the Environmental Biology building where Cecil Schwalbe, with long sun-bleached hair, the light, nimble physique of a surfer and a hint of Southern California in his voice—herpetologist to Chuck Lowell, a professor touted as foremost authority on Southwest deserts—was pleased to see the, by then, calm and quiet, rattler.

A Carnivore's Dilemma

Ken Lamberton

"I've found our Thanksgiving dinner," I told my wife Karen last April after I located her among all the wandering hippy throwbacks at our farmer's market in Bisbee.

I led her through the vendors selling killer bee honey, grass-fed beef, tamales and salsas, garden vegetables and fresh-baked breads, past the woman who claims her poop doesn't stink because she only eats a wheat substitute she grows herself.

"Here," I said, pointing to a table of wire cages. Inside the largest, a dozen or so baby turkeys scattered and ricocheted like billiard balls at opening break.

"Which are the males?" I asked the woman behind the table.

"Hard to tell," she said. "Maybe the big ones?"

I selected the largest and darkest chick and she placed it in a box for me while I counted out six dollars.

"You don't really want to do this, do you?" Karen said. It was more of a statement than a question. "You realize what it involves…"

"Yes, I'm sure," I assured her. "And I know just what to name him," I added, purposely ignoring the warning Barbara Kingsolver gives about naming your food. "We'll call him 'Butterball.'"

***

Last Thanksgiving, our oldest daughter's boyfriend, an avid sportsman who works for the Arizona Game and Fish Department, spent the morning at nearby Whitewater Draw hunting wintering sandhill crane. Before the 1950s the birds were unheard of in the Sulphur Springs Valley, although the area had much to offer a four-foot tall, russet-capped, gray-feathered migrant that's all legs and neck and beak: a mild climate and shallow standing water. Then farmers began planting corn. In 1960, a few cranes ventured into the valley from a population in New Mexico. The following year more cranes arrived. The first survey in 1970 counted 750 birds. In the winter of 1978-79, they numbered more than 5000. Today, farmers continue to plant mostly corn and chilies—the stubble-fields of which the cranes relish. Also, the Arizona Game and Fish Department pumps water into protected ponds at places like Whitewater Draw that the cranes can use for roosting regardless of weather conditions. Since 1996, the yearly census of sandhills at Whitewater has numbered better than 20,000 birds; wildlife officials are confident enough about the population that they've opened it to hunting.

"If you get one," I told Eddie, after he and Jessica arrived for the weekend, "we'll cook it for dinner." That afternoon, he returned with a pair of deep, blood-red breasts the size of his open hands.

"Rib eye in the sky," he called them, and they were, their flavor straight from the grill unmistakably like steak. That corn-fed sandhill crane was the best steak I'd ever eaten.

***

Carrying that young turkey home from the Farmer's Market, I knew Eddie would agree to guillotine Butterball for us when the time came.

***

Butterball soon began visiting our neighbors, taking handouts if they were offered but mostly just to be friendly (a nuisance). He would hear voices across the creek and want to join in the conversation, calling with a particular squeaky nasal, "Qwerrrt, qwerrrt, qwerrrt" as if asking "Do you wanna play? Can I make a mess?"

He needed to be caged with our chickens. Instead, I bought a blue harness for him (our neighbor Shelly called it a "pretty bra") and began taking him on walks.

Once, another neighbor, Charlie, was waxing his gorgeous 1958 Dodge Pickup. Butterball decided he should supervise and flew onto the shiny black hood to watch the progress. Charlie said he didn't mind.

But I did. Too often I've had to wipe up the turkey crap on Charlie's front porch. Have you ever seen the size of a turkey dropping? It's criminal. It's as big as a tennis ball, large enough to track through an entire 1700-square-foot house.

It seemed that Butterball got along better with the neighbors than with me. I think he had issues with his rising hormones and was trying to exert his authority and position in some turkey-brain-imagined pecking order. When I came near him, he would assume what I called the "Thanksgiving position," cocking back his head, fluffing his feathers, and dropping his wings, to which I responded, "Sure, Butterball. Remind me of *that day* on your horizon." This behavior became more aggressive and he started screeching, drumming his feet, and attacking my shoelaces. Of course, he never displayed this way toward Karen.

I ended his challenges by asking him if he needed a hug, then grabbed him and lifted him into my arms.

***

As the fall approached, Butterball grew tall and lanky, the chocolate feathers along his back and tail lengthening and his head and neck becoming more vulture-like with their red tubercles and short, stiff tufts of down. He was the striking image of our native Gould's turkey, a Mexican subspecies of the more common Merriam's turkey that has only recently repopulated the mountains of southeastern Arizona. We began to wonder if someone at the farmer's market hadn't sold us a wild turkey.

I regularly encounter wild turkeys in just about all of southern Arizona's mountains, all except the Mule Mountains where Karen and I live. As a child, I chased them down forested hillsides in the Catalinas north of Tucson. At Cave Creek of the Chiricahuas, I might encounter flocks of wild turkeys searching for insects and grass shoots on quiet afternoons at the Southwestern Research Station. From the Huachuca Mountains on my western horizon, wild turkeys may be spreading as far as the San Pedro River. I keep hoping these birds will eventually find Banning Creek, a tributary to the river, and follow it high into this oak-draped canyon in the Mules and to my home.

***

"You don't want any turkeys in your canyon," Richard said after I asked him about how I might relocate a few from his flock in the Santa Rita Mountains. I felt a sudden pang of guilt. Years ago, Madera Canyon had only one wild turkey, a female that lived around Richard and Cora's Bed and Breakfast called "Madera Kubo." One day while I was visiting with my family, an Arizona Game and Fish officer was talking with them and mentioned finding a mate for the turkey if he could determine her species. "We need to get some DNA," he said.

"I know where she roosts," I offered, and quickly collected a few feathers while he waited.

Today, Madera Canyon has dozens of wild Gould's turkeys, a feathered mob that regularly stops traffic along the road or roosts in sycamore trees at night to drop like bombs on cabin roofs at first light—or perches in yards to drop bombs of another sort.

Richard threatens to serve turkey dinners to his Kubo guests. "I believe that you should know where your food comes from," I say over a couple of beers.

I say it often.

The previous Christmas, I had prepared a traditional rib roast with young potatoes and Yorkshire pudding. Karen's parents joined us, along with our three daughters and their partners.

I rubbed the fat with a mixture of olive oil, flour, salt and pepper before placing the roast on a bed of potatoes, onions and carrots. The meat roasted for two hours, and during its cooking I faithfully basted it and the vegetables with drippings from the bottom of the pan, removing some for the pudding.

When I sliced the roast, Karen's dad was horrified. This is a man who always orders his steak well done. Thick red slabs rolled away from the knife and bloody juices spread across the platter. "It's still alive!" he said.

"Yes, just as it should be," I answered. "We should know we're eating cow."

While planning this dinner, Karen and I had discussed the virtues of purchasing locally raised, grass-fed beef. In the end we settled on the convenience of our local Safeway. It's always about convenience, it seems. I'm all for getting as close as possible to the food we consume, and I often tell Karen—an unrepentant meat-eater—that if we're going to be carnivorous, we should at least participate in the full act, the killing and butchering as well as the eating. She's sympathetic, and she agrees with my sensibilities. "However," she says. "What I like about living in the 21st century is the separation. I want my meat packaged in plastic wrap and Styrofoam. I don't want to hear the sounds of the slaughterhouse every time I pick out a T-bone steak."

***

So it was with the sounds of the slaughterhouse in mind that "The Fattening" began as November approached. I figured turkey goes well with cranberries and apples, so I fed Butterball cranberries and apples. He got tomatoes—until he began stealing them straight off my vines. He deserved bread and water, but I treated him to seasoned breadcrumbs, celery, and fresh rosemary. He would come running at the sound of my voice.

"You aren't really going to eat Butterball?" my vegetarian neighbor, Hayley, would ask every time she visited, offering to buy me a "tofurkey" if I would spare him.

"Only if Obama himself pardons him," I would reply, wondering what was more barbaric than a society making a public display of pardoning a Thanksgiving centerpiece while at the same time so easily sending a human being of serious questionable guilt to the death chamber.

Since Butterball was a free-ranging turkey, used to an open yard, I tried caging him in a small enclosure, hoping he would gain weight and perhaps change his ways as well, becoming fat, tame, and tasty. This was a miserable failure, since Butterball detested his confinement, refused to eat, and struggled constantly against the wire. He sorely missed roosting in our backyard apple tree. And, he missed flying to the ledge of our bedroom window at first light, where he would remain, pecking at the glass, until I rolled out of bed and released the chickens from their coop. I soon turned him loose again.

Then, exactly one week before Thanksgiving, he disappeared.

I thought: *Someone has stolen my turkey for their Thanksgiving dinner!* But Karen and my neighbors believed Butterball was smarter than I gave him credit for, that he'd escaped into hiding for the holidays. Maybe. He was an intelligent bird, wary of foxes and skunks and dark silhouettes against the sky. This was no domestic fowl that stared at the rain until drowning, if the myth were even true. When Butterball cocked an eye on the sky and began cooing in a minor key, I knew he was concerned about a raven or red-tailed hawk overhead and wanted to warn me. "It's okay, Butterball," I would reassure him. "I see it, too."

There was also the possibility of larger predators, and I thought about this as I searched for him. Recently, I had captured on film several mountain lions, a mother and cubs and at least two juveniles, only a mile upcanyon from our home.

***

I picked out another Butterball for Thanksgiving dinner, this one at fourteen pounds, plucked, gutted, frozen solid, and wrapped in clean white plastic (Safeway, again). After thawing, and in preparation for brining—with fresh rosemary—I removed the small package of innards and unwrapped the neck. I ran my fingers along the tapered S-curve, feeling the warm, pink flesh and knobby vertebrae from nape to throat. It felt the same as if I were holding Butterball in my arms.

The week following Thanksgiving I was watering some new lettuce in the yard and when I looked up Butterball was standing there, watching me. "Where have you been?" I asked him. As he started in on the chicken feed, I ran inside to get him a crust of bread, but by the time I returned—less than a minute—he was gone.

The next day, at about the same time in the afternoon, it happened again. Only this time I followed him down the road to the creek where he disappeared into a dense patch of dry grasses and didn't reappear again. *Had I missed him? Was he roosting in the trees or under our neighbor's shed?* I told Karen and we searched for him at dusk along the creek and among the oak trees, but we could find no trace, not even a feather. He was weirdly silent to our calls.

A few days passed without seeing Butterball again. Then, late one afternoon, he reappeared just as before but ran back down the road toward the creek as soon as he saw me. I chased him in a wide loop, across Charlie's porch, over his redwood bridge to Leon's place, then up the hill to our house, finally cornering him in a side yard. "Butterball," I said, as I picked him up, "why are you being like this? You've turned wild."

When I released him, he headed straight for the creek and the tall grasses. *Something is up*, I thought. This time I followed his path through the stiff clumps of broom straw and there, tucked into a shallow depression among the stems sat Butterball.

I moved closer. He watched me with one dark eye as I reached beneath him—eggs! A nest of eggs! Butterball is a girl!

***

"Wait a minute. You were going to eat Butterball and now you're worried about her being depressed?" This was Barbara's reaction after I told

my writing workshop that I had to do something, that Butterball would freeze or starve herself on a nest of infertile eggs and I couldn't just take them from her or she would freak. I told the group on that Thursday night in Tucson that I had decided to replace her eggs with baby chickens, two half-fledged Marans that I had just bought at a local feed store and were right now peeping in a cardboard box on the front seat of my car. "Tonight," I explained, "Karen and I will take flashlights down to the creek and make the swap."

Afterward, as we walked up the road to our house with seven warm turkey eggs, we heard Butterball in the grasses, quietly cooing to her new family.

In a week, she would lead her brood up the hill and into the yard, tucking her chicks beneath her wings on freezing nights, her dark feathers glistening with frost each bright morning.

***

"We the living take every step in tandem with death," says Barbara Kingsolver matter-of-factly after a long day of butchering nameless chickens and turkeys on her Virginia farm. "Harvest day," she calls it, a nice euphemism for slaughter, though the blood-soaked t-shirts of her family express perfectly what the day means. (At one point she has her arm all the way to her elbow inside the private parts of a turkey.)

I can't see myself becoming fruitarian, or vegan, or even vegetarian. Kingsolver seems to have made her peace with killing animals, but I wonder how comfortable I could be with it? Or even worse, in a kind of self-imposed blindness, how comfortable I could become with allowing others to do the killing for me?

No one enjoys the smell of the slaughterhouse any more than the stink of the execution chamber.

Out of sight, out of mind. It's how civilized people deal with the unpleasantness of killing. But perhaps it isn't the unpleasantness we fear. Maybe we're afraid we'll recognize what *we've already become* in the act of it.

"The first to surface was this powerful upwelling of pride," Michael Pollan writes about his feelings in *The Omnivore's Dilemma* after killing a pig he intended to eat. Posed with his quarry, one hand holding a rifle and the other laying on the dead animal, Pollan feels "absolutely terrific—unambiguously *happy*." Only later, when he sees the photographs of the hunter with his fallen prey and his own wild grin, does the disgust and shame come crashing down on him. "I realize it isn't the killing they record that I felt ashamed of, not exactly, but the manifest joy I seemed to be feeling about what I had done."

In his book about the private life of the American death penalty, *The Last Face You'll Ever See*, Ivan Solotaroff crushes the myth that even state-sanctioned killing is a detached, "medicalized" procedure, and shows how we are just as complicit in the act as the person pulling the switch. "In a state of nature," he concludes, "there is nothing random, cruel, or unusual about killing…an execution is in the deepest weave of the social contract."

There is no escaping our profound connection with killing. We are all killers, whether we bloody ourselves to the elbow in indifference, insulate ourselves with distance, or stand aghast at our own obscene grins.

When **Ken Lamberton** published his first book *Wilderness and Razor Wire: A Naturalist's Observations from Prison* (Mercury House, 2000), the *San Francisco Chronicle* called it an "…entirely original: an edgy, ferocious, subtly complex collection of essays…" The book won the 2002 John Burroughs Medal for outstanding nature writing. He has published five books and more than a hundred articles and essays in places like the *Los Angeles Times, Arizona Highways*, the *Gettysburg Review*, and *The Best American Science and Nature Writing 2000*. In 2007, he won a Soros Justice Fellowship for his fourth book, *Time of Grace: Thoughts on Nature, Family, and the Politics of Crime and Punishment* (University of Arizona Press, 2007). His latest book, *Dry River: Stories of Life, Death, and Redemption on the Santa Cruz* has just been released by the U of A Press (2011). He holds degrees in biology and creative writing from the University of Arizona and lives with his wife in an 1890s stone cottage near Bisbee. Visit the author's website at: www.kenlamberton.com.

Selected Poems

Bill Earls

WANTING THE BIRDS

After planting dogwood, weigela and viburnum
And tacking the small house – O-shaped door,
Slanted roof and no porch – to a pine,
We await the sight and sound of birds.
It annoys – their not coming instantly, a cacophony of twitter
Chirp and song at suddenly-arrived public housing,
With its westerly view toward the deck
Where strangely nocturnal creatures walk upright and loud
In the shroud of meat-flavored smoke
And wink of citronella.
We want bird chatter, flutter and skitter:
Cardinals' neon, shadow-smoke of junco on snow,
Finches flinging peanut hearts over purple shoulders
And chickadee's ceaseless whacking of talon-clutched seed.
It is a small thing – wanting the birds:
This land is our land: so many rods east and west
From a steel pipe adjacent land of or formerly of
S.D. Simpson et ux – both long dead – but it is not, too:
Blue jays acknowledge no boundary lines, sparrows no tax stamps,
And genetic memory ignores survey stakes and land grants:
Finches understand evergreens and pines, thrashers
The understory of the backyard; in laurel and dogwood
Chickadees stake claims and wrens say, "Mine, mine"
In the voice of a high-pitched king. It is their land, too,
Where lounge chair, gas grill and picnic table
Are temporary obstruction, shelter or perch
In a place that goes from green to winter and back
Shuttling residents with season change:
November comes on junco wings, in drift of January
Grosbeaks are sunshine and if this is April it must be warblers,
As redwings seek waterview apartments in nearby marsh and
Early spring's precocious chickadees are May's serious parents.
We watch their coming and going – high-pitched trills
Of avian imperialism and defiance, sexual conquest and infidelity,
Warnings and beckonings, finch's flash in shrubbery shadow,

Graying November's junco convocation – and work toward it:
Filling feeders, moving brush, planting cover and shelter,
Food and nesting material, hoping for an acceptance
That will never be granted and an awareness that may never exist,
As the empty birdhouse on the old pine will testify.

SPRING ON THE FARM

Winter was tough: the three-day blizzard followed
The two-day blizzard and it took a payloader to dig through to the barn
Where the sheep were grumpy and new lambs whimpered in the cold – two died.
The wood stove smoked – the house smells like we'd had a fire –
And the den needs washing and painting;
Some of the stuff we canned went bad –
No one got sick, but I dumped 40 quarts of tomatoes suddenly turned gray.
Now spring is here – blossoms, grass and croci – and things aren't much better:
Ice buildup ruined gutters and the roof leaks
Just about where the squirrels are nesting
And running around at three in the morning.
The driveway's muddy and potholed, the town snowplow
Wiped out 100 yards of windbreak, and the upper orchard,
After the ice storm, needs four days of pruning.
The lower orchard is worse
Except we can't get there: snowmelt
Pooled for three days and washed the access road into Cable Brook.
It'll take twenty loads of gravel, Charlie thinks,
"When I can get to it," which is probably August.
Cows flattened a fence, trampled
The raspberries and got sick on new growth in the pasture;
Three lambs are missing – the neighbor's dog, I think – and the
Tractor flywheel just busted. There's none in stock,
The dealer says, "A week . . . if you're lucky . . . they're made in China now,"
Like it's my fault farm equipment went overseas with software
And fabrics. Not enough I got planting to do, shearing to do, fencing to erect:
Now the balance of payments is my fault. Spring put a mischief in somebody
Besides Robert Frost, I think. All of a sudden January's lookin' good again.

THE DEATHS OF MALE RACCOONS

(News item: Wildlife biologists say that 90 percent of all raccoon deaths on Interstate highways are adult males. Biologists are not sure why.)

Male raccoons suicide on summer nights.
It's too much for them:
Suburbia encroaches and the streams they fished are gone –
No fat trout or tender clams in iris gardens or manicured lawns.
Orchards go and fresh apples vanish,
Bulldozers and golf courses consume pastures, hedges and wood lots
And the birds' eggs, field mice and fresh food with them.
What's left – flecks from backyard birdfeeders,
Cookout fragments, litter on ball fields,
Compost and backyard mulch – is garbage, and male raccoons know it.
There's no future in garbage cans,
Not for self-respecting masked men,
And besides, the kids are bitching and whining –
"I wanna stay up past sunrise . . . all the fox kits do it,"
And, "Orange peels again? I want a bird's egg . . ."
But there are no birds eggs or young fish
And the wife is talking about the new den her sister has,
How her brother-in-law finds fresh fruit every day,
(Behind the grocery, pawing through dumpsters)
"And maybe if you got up before sunset once in a while . . ."
It's too much for them: the pressures, the futility, the loneliness,
The world they trusted downsized
To parking lots, ladies tees and foundation plantings.
Which is why, on summer nights with the shrill of crickets
Around them, male raccoons walk to the interstate
And dreaming of slow fish in clear streams,
Endless orchards and a million sparrow nests,
They saunter, past all caring and pain,
Into the middle lane to meet the buses and trailer trucks.

POEM FOR A FARAWAY GRANDSON

When I tried to call you yesterday,
The phone line stayed busy and I felt increasingly sad,
Wanting your falsetto, "Hello, Grandpa,"
To come across the fiber optic, copper
And too many miles of prairies and forest,
Highways and rivers – and 57 years – between us:
Your laugh, stories of Frances, Curious George and Pooh
And the so-real people of your untrammeled imagination,
Your world that knows no boundaries,
And sees unlimited possibilities in
The underside of a dining room table that becomes,
Because you wish it – and I do too –
The cab of a bumping garbage truck; and a stack of Lego blocks
A cloud-scraping chimney to a bug
House where purple crickets and orange grasshoppers
Play soccer with gumdrops,
And where awareness increases geometrically.
And I wanted desperately to tell you what I cannot tell you:
That because I love you in a special way, and am not
Responsible for your manners, diet, clothing,
I can show you what your mom and dad cannot . . . dare not:
Adventure, acceptance and a stretching of boundaries.
Grandpas can share Coke for breakfast,
Wear stripes with plaids, walk a whole block backwards,
Skip church or peel an orange with a teaspoon.
Grandpas do not have to eat their vegetables,
And small boys in diners with grandpas can eat ice cream first,
And then bacon and eggs,
And mop the eggs up with lots of toast
And then have another ice cream for dessert.
Grandpas talk to firemen so small boys can sit on firetrucks
And maybe wear a too-big fire hat, and grandpas
Know how to skip stones on the water and shoot a .22
If Mama says it's all right. Grandpas also know
A flatbed from a stake truck and a tank truck
And where to find crayfish under rocks,
How to throw a slider, and funny poems about animals.
These are all good things to know,
And someday we will do them, but not today,
Because the telephone is busy and I wish you were here

Bill Earls: U.S. Navy journalist, 1961–65. (Have called myself a professional writer ever since)

BS Sec Ed/English, Worcester (MA) State College 1971

MA English, University of South Dakota 1972

MALS Wesleyan University 1997

Science fiction stories in *Analog, Galaxy, Isaac Asimov's Science Fiction Magazine*; anthologized in Best SF: 1970, Best from Analog, others

The Gladiator, "future fiction" novel, Dell Publishing 1981

Corporate speechwriter for several firms, 1979–1995

Daily columnist, *Daily Journal* Elizabeth, NJ 1974–79; numerous awards

Freelance columnist, writer 1979–present: publications from *American Legion Magazine* and *Runner's World* to *New York Times, Wall Street Journal* and numerous others

Adjunct faculty, Middlesex Community College, Albertus Magnus College; 1995–present

Section Three

Isolation and Community

"A Passion for Poetry"

Richard Shelton

On a Saturday night in late January, Mark Menlove and I arrive at the Santa Rita Unit of the Arizona State Prison, Tucson, as usual. Mark is carrying my heavy crate of books and writing pads. He refers to himself as "the mule." We are eager to meet the 15 members of the Creative Writing Workshop who provide the high-point of my week. I have been working with several of these men for years, watching them grow and develop. Their energy and eagerness always make the two-hour workshop exciting.

John is undoubtedly the star at present. He has published more than 20 poems in journals in the past year. I have seen his work progress from bad to spectacular. He is dogged, taking criticism on the chin without flinching. He's a big redhead, and only his coloring changes when we come down hard on something he has written. Then he comes back the following week with an excellent revision. Nothing can stop him and nothing will.

Ray has also become one of the leading poets in the Workshop. His work is lyrical, beautiful, and imagistic. He too is starting to publish. And right behind him, Matthew is moving up the ladder, struggling but succeeding—each poem is better than the last—with the encouragement of everybody in the group. And Ken, a black man of great presence and dignity, has made remarkable progress recently. His work deals with his childhood and family. Steve writes both prose and poetry, exploring some dark places in what must have been a bleak childhood. John C. provides the comic relief we need, writing savage but hilarious light verse. Nothing is safe from his zany wit, not even himself.

Tom and Ed are somewhat older than most of the others, and both write prose. Tom writes gentle, thoughtful essays that are being published in many places. "Uncle" Ed, as everybody calls him, is writing a memoir. When he finishes it, if he dares to publish it, it will be one of the most remarkable memoirs I have ever seen. It will show exactly how a professional criminal is made, and it will do so without self-dramatization or self-pity. It is factual, straight-forward, beautifully written and devastating.

Mark and I are looking forward to the Workshop session with these men and the others in the group. A female correctional officer unlocks the classroom for us, and we begin to move furniture as we always do, arranging the tables into one long table big enough for everyone to gather around. Just as we finish, the men arrive like a tornado of energy. They are all wearing orange jump suits. (John, the big redhead, refers to himself as "the orange pumpkin.") Instead of sitting down immediately, as they usually do, some of them surround us and some of them stand tentatively around the table. Something is terribly wrong. The electricity in the air is palpable. I can tell even before I see John, and when I see him (that ruddy face can never hide any emotion) I know it's bad, bad. He's carrying a large plastic garbage bag full of books over his shoulder, and it makes him look like a young Santa Claus.

"We gathered up as many of the books as we could," he says, looking away from me. "I think I got most of them. Except the ones Ray had. They took him yesterday. We're all being transferred. Nobody knows where we're going for sure. The yard is going to be all Mexican Nationals. I'm sure glad Mark came tonight. I was worried about you carrying all these books out by yourself." He says all this in a great rush.

I'm in shock. Where will they go? Will they be able to stay together?

"We're going to be scattered all over the state," Uncle Ed says in his quiet way. I have never known him to say anything that wasn't accurate. "Some to Florence, some to Buckeye, maybe some to Safford or Douglas or Yuma."

It's the end of the Workshop. The end, for these men, of a program that gave them back their humanity and some hope of rehabilitation. For me, it means starting over in some other facility, starting from scratch again, as I have done so many times in the past. Each time it gets harder. It's never been harder than this sudden, unexpected blow.

Next year it will be 30 years since I established the Creative Writing Workshop in the Arizona State Prison System, and if I have learned anything in those 30 years, it is not to ask "why" in regard to any policy of the Arizona Department of Corrections. I have become fatalistic, like the inmates I deal with. I obey the rules. I take what comes. I know it is useless and a waste of energy to question any Department of Correction's policy, no matter how ridiculous the particular policy may seem. One always gets the same answer: *Security*. And I know it is useless to expect the upper administration of the Department to take into account any program of rehabilitation, no matter how good a track record that program has over however many years, just as it is useless to expect the Department to take into account the concept of rehabilitation at all.

I have had to abandon workshops in the past, but in most cases it was because the facility was falling apart or degenerating into a riot zone and I no longer had access to the inmates. In one case, I moved from Florence to the new facility near Tucson because the 140-mile drive each week was wearing me down. Over the years, I have conducted Workshops in 10 different correctional facilities in Arizona.

On this January night I can see that the men are distraught. It's my job to channel their energy into constructive work. I pass out the worksheets and we go to work at once, making use of these last two hours we have. I make arrangements for them to send their work to the magazine for editorial consideration, and to me for comments. We work frantically until it is time to break up.

Then we have to say goodbye, the thing we have all dreaded. I try not to look at John. Big, tough John is in trouble. Matthew too. Several others. Steve looks like he's at a funeral. I'm having more trouble than anybody, and I know I must not show it or some of them will break down. You don't cry in prison because it will make you look weak. You don't cry when you get word that your mother has died. You don't cry when your wife writes that she is filing for divorce. You don't cry when your parole is denied. You don't cry in prison. So we shake hands and say goodbye. I see tears in several eyes. I look the other way.

Since that night I have started another Workshop in the Manzanita Unit, where I have the cooperation and encouragement of the Deputy Warden. I have also received letters from most of the men in the old Santa Rita Workshop. Uncle Ed was right. They have been scattered all over the state. Not only was the Workshop suddenly and effectively terminated by these transfers, but any classes the men might have been taking were discontinued. Ray, who will be getting out soon, was about halfway through two computer courses he needed for employment on the outside. He will now have to take his chances out there without them. He will be released into the free world not only without the two classes he needs for employment, but as an embittered young man. His chances of making it on the outside have been seriously curtailed.

For the most part, the men from the Santa Rita Workshop are picking up the pieces as best they can. They write to me from Florence, Safford, Buckeye, Winchester and other facilities around the state. They are trying to continue to write. It's difficult without the weekly dose of encouragement and criticism the workshop provides. But most of them continue.

Tom, in a recent letter, said: "It seems that these constant moves have the purpose of keeping the prisoner from forming any bonds or having any sense of dignity. Yet, when we remember that we carry our dignity within ourselves, nobody can defile us."

While there have been and still are a few wardens at various levels who have encouraged the Creative Writing Workshop and seem aware of its potential for rehabilitation, it receives no consideration nor encouragement from the higher levels of the prison administration. This has not always been the case. Dr. Ellis MacDougal, when he was Director of the Arizona Department of Corrections in the early 1980's, appeared on television saying that the Creative Writing Workshop, then functioning in two of the Florence facilities, was "the most effective tool for rehabilitation" he had ever encountered.

It is no wonder that mid-level administrators of the Department of Corrections hesitate to encourage such a program when they know they will not have the support of the upper administration. They will not have the support of the upper administration because the program is educational and rehabilitative, and upper administration apparently cares about neither of these goals. I speak from almost 30-years experience as a volunteer in the Arizona prisons. Administrators have come and gone during those years. Some who were children when I began in 1972 are now in positions of the highest authority. Yet the policy remains the same. Nor can these administrators suggest that they cannot afford such programs because of chronic underfunding. Such underfunding is a very real problem, but I work as a volunteer and my program is fully funded by the Lannan Foundation.

Each time some debacle like the sudden transfer of all the men out of the Santa Rita Workshop occurs, I want to take the considerable amount of grant money the Lannan Foundation has provided for the prison Workshop and walk away. But I can't do that. The Foundation believes in rehabilitation and so do I. I believe in it, even if the prison administration doesn't, because I have seen it happening year after year. I am not going away.

I have a new workshop in the Manzanita Unit made up of talented and enthusiastic men. I am attempting to establish at the new Women's Facility in Perryville, a workshop under the direction of Ms. Joni Wallace, a highly trained professional writer with a Master of Fine Arts Degree in creative writing. I cannot help but think it is significant that starting this program has now been delayed more than four months by the prison administration, in spite of the cooperation and encouragement of the Educational Programs Manager at Perryville. This Workshop will also be fully funded by the Lannan Foundation.

Today I received a letter from Ray. In an earlier letter he talked about how he hated the prison unit to which he had been transferred, and how unhappy he was since leaving Santa Rita and the Workshop. In today's letter, he sounds much more positive. "I'm just trying to write through my unhappiness the best I can," he says. He speaks of "this absolute hunger for poetry within me." He isn't talking about a hunger for drugs or booze or illegal sex. He's talking about poetry, the love of which and the writing of which can save his life. He, like many others over the years, has come to realize this fact, and it is a knowledge no prison policy can take away from him, now or ever.

From the *Walking Rain Review VII*
Richard Shelton
Regents Professor
University of Arizona

About the Author

Richard Shelton is a Regents Professor in the English Department at the University of Arizona, where he was director of the Creative Writing Program from 1979 to 1981. His poetry and prose have appeared in more than 200 magazines and journals, including *The New Yorker, The Atlantic,* and *Paris Review.* His first book, *The Tattooed Desert,* won the International Poetry Forum's United States Award, and *The Bus to Veracruz* was nominated for the Pulitzer Prize and the National Book Award. Shelton's most recent book, Going Back to Bisbee, won the Western States Book Award for Creative Nonfiction. He is the recipient of two fellowships from the National Endowment for the Arts and a prestigious Completion Grant from the Lannan Foundation. In 1972 Richard Shelton established the Writer's Workshop at the Arizona State Prison, out of which have come eight books of poetry and prose. He continues to direct workshops at the Arizona State Prison Complex in Tucson, Arizona and various Arizona Correctional Facilities. In 2006, Richard and his wife Lois were honored with the first annual Arizona Literary Treasure Award. This award recognizes an individual or individuals who've made a significant contribution to the literary fabric of Arizona.

A service of the Arizona State Library, Archives and Public Records.

The Warrior

Gillian Haines

The first morning I met him, I dressed as if for a lover. I stood at my dressing table. No altar to beauty, it secreted no potions and balms, but I fingered dozens of earrings dangling from their wrought iron stand. I held up two glistening pearls. These? I pushed up my hair, flirting with my reflection in the mirror. No, too staid. I then chose a French pair of coral-colored, ceramic flowers. I raised my hair and admired bejeweled earlobes. Playful. Yes, these ones. Opening the green door of my wardrobe, I sighed. It was bereft; it grieved for clothes recently thrown out in a temper because they no longer fit. I could see the walls between limp offerings on white plastic hangers. What could I possibly wear? I had so little and the list of forbidden items was intimidating: nothing red, khaki, or orange; nothing skimpy, short, or revealing. No watch or necklace. It was May and hot outside but open-toed shoes were a no-no. I sighed. I wanted the mere sight of me to please and delight the senses, and yet the thought of our meeting filled my stomach with fear.

He moved proud like a Viking, broad-shouldered and powerful. The coarse beard that hung to his chest looked as if it were steeped in blood; his shaven head shone with health in the harsh, florescent light. Blue eyes inherited from the fjords of Norway assessed the room, gauging its threats. When our hands met, mine was engulfed in warmth. Tattooed, indigo symbols sheathed his forearm beyond where it disappeared into a baggy sleeve. Casey wore the forbidden khaki, the modern equivalent of convict stripes. The loose coveralls were several sizes too big; the elasticized waist drooped to his hips and he had rolled the pant cuffs so as not to trip. None of this hid his strength; not just of muscle and sinew, but of attention. I felt myself observed and considered.

"Hey, Casey." I gave my warmest smile. "I'm Gillian. Let's sit over here." I led him far from the raised platform where the guards sat. I was nervous. The crimes and personalities of the men in the visiting room were unknown to me. I felt grateful for the guards' diligent watch but didn't want them to hear us. We sat on grey chairs molded from hard plastic and connected one to another to form rows. My seat was on the side designated for visitors and Casey sat opposite me. The seats were arranged so that visitors were back to back with other visitors: contraband could not easily be passed from outsiders to insiders.

"Thanks for coming." Casey broke the ice and I was grateful because it felt awkward.

"You're welcome." I smiled again. My role was to provide a whiff of outside air, news of the humdrum free, and a conversation without agenda. Now I was there, I had no clue what to say. I glanced at him. He was sitting with hands clasped and elbows on his spread knees, waiting for me. His lightly freckled face seemed studiously neutral. I said, "Where do you come from?"

He raised his head and spoke quietly, "Ohio." I leaned forward. Prisoners speak quietly; privacy is precious in a place where it is stripped away. Keeping conversations to themselves maintains a semblance of control and independence.

I replied, "I used to live next door, in Michigan. I hated it. No wonder, it was the first place I went to from Australia. I couldn't believe the cold. In autumn, I cocooned myself in all the warm clothing I possessed until I could barely move my arms. When I told my friends how cold it was, they grinned." I chuckled, my eyes connecting with Casey's, "They were laughing at me! They said, *Gillian, this is not cold*, I felt truly frightened. I didn't know if I could take it."

Casey gave me the beginnings of a smile. "Yeah," he said nodding, "It's cold. As a boy I used to hang out in the winter woods. Test myself. See if I could build shelter, shoot squirrels: survive."

Oh, no, I thought. He's a backwoods hunter. "And could you? What was that like?"

"Uh huh. That's where I learned to shoot. I learned to take care of myself. All Midwest guys love guns and hunting, That's why it's prime recruiting ground for the Army. Guys like me jumped at the chance to join up."

I held prejudices against the military. If I had a flagpole in my yard, a slender spire, an oversized grey-metal knitting needle visible from the furthest adobe house in the city of Tucson, I would run up a striped beach towel. Its gay stripes would sing of the sting of salt water on my wounds and bronzed Aussie life guards, not bugles or battles or bloodbaths. My heart brims for my sunburned Australia, and increasingly, for the desiccated town where I now live, but I'm not patriotic. I tried to push these thoughts away; judgments and pre-conceptions would close my ears to Casey's story.

"Huh," I said to give myself time. "I never knew that." What could I say? What options did he have? Ask questions, Gillian, it's the only way to understand. I said "Is that what you were doing before you came here?" I didn't say the word, prison.

He nodded and leaned back, placing one arm along the top of the neighboring chair. With his raised ankle on his knee, he allowed his other hand to hang cupped, in front of his genitals. The gesture seemed overtly masculine and I didn't like it.

"I did a couple of tours but nope. I was in special ops." I could hardly hear him although I leaned as far forward as my seat would allow. My back was beginning to ache. The vast, white, windowless room was built of cement blocks and the acoustics were terrible. I was right to wear colorful clothes, to over-decorate with earrings. The place was sterile except for the clusters of visitors. There were families with kids. A small kids' playroom opened off from the visiting room and we could hear the TV and the clatter of toys.

"What does special ops mean?"

He said something I couldn't quite hear. "What was that?" He said it again but I still didn't get it. I thought he might have said he worked for a private organization. The newspapers were full of nefarious reports about Blackwater at the time, and inwardly, I grimaced and changed the subject.

"Where were you stationed?"

"Iraq, Afghanistan, Bosnia."

I nodded.

Casey directed his eyes at mine. "What's in this for you?"

I paused. "I don't really know. I'm curious. Prison is like a country unknown; I thought it might be like visiting an exotic culture." I shrugged. I didn't say that my travels have always taken me off the beaten path, to Rajasthan, Pagan, the Tanami Track, and the Atacama Desert. In far, foreign places where I moved without true understanding, without a support network to back me up; these far-flung destinations always took me, paradoxically, to the depths of my own heart. "I guess I'm interested in people who live at the edges. I'm a migrant, I'm not a citizen: my green card calls me a resident alien." I put wiggling fingers to my forehead, imitating antennae. "I live at the edges, too. I don't buy the whole package."

"What do you mean?"

I leaned my head to the side, considering. "I don't watch TV, hate malls and shopping; I loathe the hypocrisy of politics. It's hard to put into words."

He looked at me for a moment. "You know, when I'd come home from a tour, strangers would come up and thank me. I'd despise them."

I jerked up my head. A soldier who didn't fit the mould. "Why?"

"They don't have any idea. They don't know what I had to do and they don't want to know. They live in denial."

"You mean that as a soldier you have to kill people?"

He nodded. "When we were first in Afghanistan, kids would run out on the road in front of our vehicles, chasing balls. We stopped for them. Then later, some of our guys were ambushed for doing that. Killed. We stopped stopping."

I pressed my lips together. "I think anyone who believes in the glories of war or the precision of killing is naïve. War is brutal. It makes people do awful things. That's what war means."

Casey said, "I don't want to be thanked for doing that."

We were silent for a long moment.

"All prisoners stand! Go to the back wall." The loud command made me jump.

Casey didn't exactly saunter, but neither did he hurry, he walked on the edge of insolence to join the ragged line of khaki. All the visitors stared. The prisoners clasped hands in front or behind. I knew that feeling: where to put hands? I looked at Casey. He stood at military ease, hands together and feet shoulder width apart. A crisp, white-shirted guard in navy pants and black boots moved along the row listening as each man recited his eight-digit prison number and checking them against those listed on his clipboard. It was count: the whole prison stops until everyone is accounted for. I had hurried to arrive before it began knowing that I would be forced to wait for over an hour if I were late. There was nowhere to look in the barren room except at the people. So I watched the prisoners too. I watched for clues. What was the tone of interactions between jailer and jailed? Every man standing looked bored; they had done this many times. Some looked resigned. All of a sudden, I felt guilty. Gawking humiliates.

When Casey rejoined me, I glanced at my clear plastic, prison purse heavy with quarters and remembered to offer him a drink from the vending machine. "Coke, please."

The cold, plastic bottle passed from my hand to his and I asked, "Are you angry?"

The color disappeared from his face. "I'm fucked." He replied so softly, I barely heard. "I am so fucking angry."

The naked admission chilled me. In a voice as gentle as I could manage I asked, "Casey, how long are you in for?"

His lips thinned with rage. "Forty-five years." Once again, he whispered but the number slammed me in the chest.

"How many have you done?"

"Two."

I swallowed and met his gaze. A long recognition passed between us. My stomach lurched and I felt uneasy. We don't stare into stranger's eyes. Long, unblinking looks are reserved for lovers. I felt like squirming in my seat but didn't. It felt like we were both naked. Weeks later, the power of that visual connection still troubled me. Surely I wasn't susceptible to infatuation in such circumstances? Were my feelings inappropriate? And then I realized: it was my humanity seeing his.

There was nothing I could say but I wanted to give an acknowledgement; to recognize the enormity of his sentence. Without looking away from his eyes, I said, "That's a long time."

A loud, rhythmic jingling came up behind me and Casey stopped talking. Puzzled, I turned to see a guard drawing near. A heavy collection of large keys hung from a massive chain clipped in two places on his belt. With every step of his thick-soled boots, the keys slapped against his thigh and rang like a tambourine.

After the guard passed, Casey nodded in the guard's direction, "He's a good one. An ex-marine; a lot of them are ex-military. They're the best. They just do the job and don't cop an attitude." He shrugged, "Not like some."

I wondered what stories he could tell but a glance at the clock showed me that Casey and I had talked for an hour and a half. It was time to end. I stood and held out my hand, my skin dry and scaly because of my eczema. "I'll be back next month."

"Thanks for coming," he said again as our open palms met. He walked to the blue-grey door and waited for a guard to escort him. I knew that to see me, he had to strip off and change his clothes before and after the visit. I wondered what it was like. To stand before a guard who held the key to your cell, a man who could punish you. To take off your clothing observed by a man who wore the insignias of power. To feel the goose-bumps on your chest in the silent, chill air. To slide your underwear down from your hips; stepping out of their empty warmth. To bend over; knowing that the guard crouched to his haunches to better see you. "Spread 'em and cough!" the guard would say. You would release the harsh sound from your throat, feeling the guard's stare fixed on the eye of your arse.

How long would I go without conversation and a handshake before it was worth that to me?

Gillian Haines lives in Tucson.

Teaching at Gateway

Margaret Hall Dunn

In 2004 I began teaching part-time (two classes a semester) at Gateway Community College. Although I had been a teacher all my life, I had never experienced any teaching so exhilarating (and sometimes frustrating) as my teaching at Gateway. I have taught basic composition, advanced composition, public speaking, and literature and composition, and all of it has been joyful. It is true that teaching part-time in an urban community college is battling in the trenches of higher education: you never know what is going to land on you. But teaching at Gateway has opened me up to new kinds of students and new classroom experiences, and I wouldn't trade my teaching there for any other teaching I have ever done.

So. What's so great about teaching at Gateway? Why do I love it so much? How has it contraverted all my complacent expectations of my classroom life? I think the best way to tell the story is to give you a few facts and then introduce you to some of the classes and students I have met over the years. Fact One: The maximum enrollment for most of the classes I teach at Gateway is 26, and usually when I print out my roster before the first class, the class is full. Fact Two: Of the students on the roster, not all will show up for the first class. Some may come a few classes late, but there are always one or two who never appear, even though at the end of the semester they have not withdrawn from the class, and I therefore have to give them a grade for a course they paid for and never took. Fact Three: Of the ones who do show up for the first class or in the first couple of weeks, five or six will disappear before the semester ends, usually when the first written assignment is due. Again, they do not usually withdraw, so I am forced to give them a grade at the end

of the semester. The result of the disappearances and no-shows is that I am usually teaching a class of about seventeen, a highly manageable class size.

Before the first class I print up 35 copies of the syllabus (26 for the students on my roster, one for me, two for the academic dean's office, one for the chair of the humanities department, five for the students who will have lost their copy just before the first assignment is due). On the syllabus I list due dates for all the assignments for the semester and a number of stern warnings about the results of plagiarism, excess absences, use of cell phones in class, and penalties for late work (which will not be enforced because in the end I take what I can get). In the first class I go over all this material and then give a brief writing assignment so that I can form some idea of what I am up against for the coming semester. Come along and meet some of my students.

Evan

When I saw Evan's name on the roster for an afternoon composition class, I groaned. I had already had Evan in a public speaking class the semester before, and I remembered him all too well. In his mid-twenties, smart, and always eager to show off, he loved to come to class and talk, whether or not anyone else was talking at the same time. In public speaking the students give speeches, and he gave all of his about Rap musicians I had never heard of or about the pleasures of smoking weed. He good-spiritedly and loudly complained about the low grades that I awarded these performances, and he never failed to turn in the required written copies of his speeches. I gave him a C- and thought I was well rid of him.

But there he was, sitting in the back row of the classroom on the first day of the composition class, dressed for the warm Fall weather in a sweatshirt and heavy jacket. "Dr. Dunn!" he yelled when I came in. "Are you gonna give me a better grade in this class?" Straight-faced and stern, I told him that depended on him as I do not "give" grades. He wrote his "How I spent my summer vacation" first day essay on his trip to Martha's Vineyard and what a great time he had there smoking weed. The essay was not broken into paragraphs, but the sentence structure was sophisticated. I hoped he would develop some skills in this class.

Evan continued to come to all the classes for the whole semester, and he spent most of his time sitting in the back row talking to other students. He paid enough attention to what I was doing to complain about it loudly, especially when what I was doing was grammar. "Why do we have to know this? What good is it gonna do us?" I got tired of telling him to be quiet and give the other students a chance, but nobody seemed to mind his verbosity. Finally one day he got to me. I announced a writing assignment, and he hollered "Why do you make us do all this writing all the time?" "Because it's a composition class, you jackass!" I blurted out. For once there was silence in the classroom. I sat down and thought. Then I said "Evan, I apologize. You are not a jackass. You are a very smart young man, and I love having you in my class, but someday you are going to go too far." I resumed the lesson, the noise in the classroom picked up, and I felt that things were back to normal. At the end of the class, when Evan left the room, he came over and kissed me lightly on the cheek.

Despite his resistance to order and to orders, Evan was a sensitive young man who liked to write. When asked to write a memoir, he produced two pages of stream-of-consciousness about his mother, mentioning along the way that "she was a crack addict, but she quit it before she lost her looks" and concluding "she is a rose in concrete." He got a C in the class, and I have no idea what became of him after, but I'm not worried about him.

Johanna

Johanna was a returning student (she claimed to be over fifty) in one of the liveliest composition classes I have ever taught at Gateway. Filled with a boisterous mix of olders and youngers of all shades of the racial spectrum, the class was never quiet. Students were eager to talk, to read their poetry, to answer questions, to argue about the interpretations of assigned readings. I gave up on strict decorum early on. Throughout, Johanna sat tense and silent in the front row, staring at me, holding up her hand in hopes of attention. When she talked to me after class one day, Johanna explained that she was returning to college to learn to write well enough to write a book about her Italian aunt, who had died the preceding summer. She was terrified because papers had to be word processed, and she had never touched a computer (it's amazing how many students I get who graduated from high school before 1990 and have never touched a computer). Despite her terror and her difficulties, Johanna wrote an exquisite memoir about her beloved aunt, divided into sections by time and separated by carefully chosen passages from Scripture. I thought her well-deserved A would calm her down, but trouble lay ahead.

The trouble that lay ahead was grammar. One problem I have never resolved in teaching at Gateway is how much grammar to teach and how to teach it. My problems in this matter are compounded by the fact that I love teaching grammar and I am never sure when to stop, or how to convey the main points (do not write fragments; avoid run-on sentences; commas are not conjunctions) without going into more detail than I have time for in a class that meets twice a week for thirteen weeks and is filled with people who have long since forgotten how to find the subject and the verb in a sentence, if they ever knew.

In the class Johanna was in, with so many capable students, I decided to plow forward into the complexities of grammar. I introduced modifiers and thought I was doing well, so I tried participles and gerunds. I thought everyone was with me until Johanna wailed "What is this?" I know when it's time to stop. "OK," I said. "Where did you get lost?" "Just tell me one thing," she implored. "What is this *predicate* business?" Take a breath. Back ten. Ask another member of the class to explain. Go over some examples. Ultimately, acknowledge defeat. Cut to the basics and say "All you really have to do is be able to find the verb in the sentence and identify its subject." I gave a quiz that everybody passed and left the fine points for another day.

Grammar was not the end of Johanna's difficulties. The final assignment in my English composition class is a four-page library research paper. We go to the library for an introduction to its resources, including online databases that make vast amounts of information available to any enrolled student. Johanna was scared to death. She couldn't think of a topic. She would follow me out of class and into the parking lot, asking if she could write about this, if she could write about that. Yes, yes, I would say. Just choose. Time is passing. One day she said "I guess I could always write about the Second Coming of Christ. I mean, we know it's going to happen and I could research when." No. There is a limit. This is not a possible topic for a four-page library research paper. I forget what she wrote about, but it wasn't religious and it was fine, but, worried to the end, she begged me to mail the paper back to her with comments as soon as possible.

Johanna got an A- in my class, and she signed up for a class in literature for the following semester. She asked me if I knew the teacher. I did. Was he nice? Yes. Was he a hard grader? Did he accept late work? Would she be all right? I could not predict the future. I am sure she did fine, but I never inquired.

That Saturday Class

The first time I took on a class that met on Saturday afternoon, I was a little nervous. Who would the students be? Would they actually attend from 12:15 to 4 p.m. on Saturdays? How could I keep my own energy up for such a long session? I needn't have worried. The class was fascinating, and from beginning to end a joy to teach. It was one of the most diverse classes I have seen at Gateway. There were a woman and a man from different parts of Africa, a man from India, and most vividly Rosa, a native speaker of Spanish whose country of origin I never did find out. There were several African-Americans and, in addition to a few less vibrant students, one Italian-American man, Marco, who by size and intellect quickly became a leader in the group. From the beginning, the energy of our meetings derived from Marco, who announced on the first day that the books were too expensive, that he was just trying college out, that he might not stay the term, and from Rosa, who addressed me as "esMeeses Dr. Dunn", and who could not hold back from comments on every topic that came up. Despite his protestations, Marco took hold immediately: he got an A on his first paper, quickly mastered the details of MLA documentation of sources, and generously served as a second instructor for students who were having problems with their citations, going around to look at everyone's drafts, pointing out errors, and saying sternly "You just have to follow the directions in the book."

Things didn't come quite so easily for Rosa. She was bright and interested in her work, but her Spanish spilled into her English in her writing: she had trouble with verb tenses and her spelling was often more imaginative than accurate. Nevertheless, she was determined to succeed. She chose good topics to write about, drawing on her experience as an aide at Yale-New Haven hospital to describe her present and her hoped-for future. She sat in front of the other women of color, who formed a chorus behind her in class meetings. On the days when I returned papers, she could barely control herself until she got hers back, praying aloud "Oh, please God, an A," and when she saw the grade (usually a B) she would moan "Oh, esMeeses Dr. Dunn you are so *hard*." Behind her the more timid but equally eager others would repeat "Oh, yes, *so hard*." These lamentations went on until the day I returned their vocabulary lists.

The vocabulary list is an assignment I give to drive myself crazy. Students have to find fifty new words in their reading, list them with part of speech and dictionary definition and use them correctly in a sentence of their own. As I tell them at the beginning of the semester, if they start at once and work on it every week, it is an easy assignment. If they leave it for the last minute, they are not even going to succeed. Most of them actually keep up, although the list doesn't count a large percentage of their final average. It takes me forever to grade them (checking for parts of speech and correct use in a sentence). When I handed the lists back in that Saturday class, most of them had As and A+s and Rosa cried out "Oh, thank you Jesus," followed by shouts of "Praise God" and "Yes to Jesus" from the chorus behind her. For once I couldn't say a word.

Our final meeting of that class was in every way memorable. All the work was done, and we knew we wouldn't be taking the full three hours. I handed back their last papers, and then there was a muttering and a whispering. Marco and Rosa approached me carrying a large paper bag. They handed it to me, everyone murmuring in anticipation, and when I opened it I found a small wooden plaque with a brass plate engraved to me in thanks for my dedication and hard work, and hoping that God would continue to bless me always. (There was also a box of chocolates, which I shared around.) I hope that God will continue to bless them all, always.

(It's unusual at Gateway to see your former students after the semester is over, but I have continued to run into Rosa. She comes up and rubs my arm and says "Oh, esMeeses Dr. Dunn, I thank you so much for all you teach me." She is on course to graduate and transfer to a full-time nursing program, and I am sure she will bring joy to all her teachers, as she brought joy to me.)

Mike

Some tales are short and sad. Mike was doomed from the beginning. Appearing about two weeks after the opening of class, he explained that his cousin had been shot and his best friend had died of an overdose. I asked him to do a diagnostic writing, and he couldn't write a sentence. Tall and strong, he explained to me that he wanted to pass the class so he could stay on the basketball team. I told him that I didn't see much hope, but if he worked, and if he took his papers to the writing center for extra help, he just might pass. He missed more classes, reappeared with the report that another friend had been shot, and begged to be allowed to turn in his work late. He never turned in the work and I gave him an F. At the beginning of the following semester, I found a short note from Mike in my mailbox. Couldn't I please change his grade to a C so that he could transfer to another state and get out of "this killing New Haven." Compassion has its limits. I ignored the note, but I have never forgotten Mike.

Lucas

Quiet, punctual, bespectacled, Lucas did not at first attract much of my attention at the outset of a large afternoon composition class, but when I read his memoir, I knew that I had a writer in my hands. The memoir was a short but moving story of his relationship with his father, beginning with his childhood longing to know his father, tracing his father's re-entry into his life when he was about ten, and then the loss of his father when he married and had three more children. Paralleled with the story of the loss of his father was the story of his developing relationship with his mother, beginning with his early blaming her for the disappearance of his father and ending with his gradual realization that she was the one who had loved and supported him throughout his childhood and adolescence. The memoir was carefully written, including the kinds of evocative details that student writers often leave out. When I returned the paper, I talked to Lucas about his skill, and told him that I thought eventually he should be able to earn an MFA in creative writing.

Later in the semester, Lucas had a surprise for me. He and a friend (not a Gateway student) had gotten together and published privately a collection of their poetry. The book was arranged so that two poems by the same title, one by each poet, were on facing pages. Lucas was selling the book for fifteen dollars a copy. Of course I bought one, and I arranged for the library to buy a copy as well. The poetry showed in its rhythmic structure the influence of the Rap music the young men had been listening to, but much of the imagery was original and the poems, though highly personal, made compelling reading. Of course, I congratulated Lucas on his work and his enterprising spirit, and I advised him to go forward, reading as much poetry as he could to increase his sense of what a poet can do with language. I never saw him again after that semester, but I have hopes that some day I will see his name in print somewhere.

A Bad Day at North Haven

My afternoon composition class at North Haven began badly. No matter how I tried to get their attention, the students sat in clusters and carried on private conversations. Finally one day I shouted "Everybody Shut Up!" For once there was silence, so I continued quietly: "Is there anyone in this room who is under the delusion that this is high school? Because if I'm teaching high school, then I expect to have to constantly remind you to be quiet and pay attention. But if you think this is college, then it is time to grow up and behave like adults in the classroom." That was Monday, and on Wednesday two of the biggest talkers moved conspicuously to the front row and from then on gave me full cooperation. After the normal number of drop-outs, I thought I was teaching a good class. It went along quite happily for several weeks.

Then one Monday late in the semester, everything fell apart. Difficulty began when Tim arrived early and asked if he could talk to me in private. I was worried about Tim. He had a good attendance record, and he was a lively participant in discussions, but the semester was more than two-thirds over and he had turned in no written work. We went into the hall, and he looked at me and started to cry. "I can't afford to fail this class. My father says if I fail this class he's going to throw me out of the house, and I don't have any money. I don't know what to do. Is there any way I can get a D?" I told him that I couldn't give him a passing grade if he didn't do the work, but I would accept his papers late if only he would write them. Could he work on at least two of the three papers that had been due so far? I pointed out that he was smart and he would get some credit for class participation, but he had to do the work. He nodded and sniffled a little, then forced a smile and said "I'll try," but I had a premonition that I would not be seeing Tim again.

When class began, I knew I was headed for more difficulty. I was returning papers, and two students were getting grades they would not be happy about. I returned the papers, and for a while ignored the muted thunder of indignation from one side of the room. When I return papers, I usually take time to visit around with individual students, answering questions about my comments, making suggestions, touching base. That day I started out with Frankie, who had done very well but had a question about documentation. I checked in with Jasmine to explain that if she cites a short story as evidence for an argument, she must make it clear that she is citing a work of fiction. A few more visits, then I headed for Edward: he was waiting for me. Edward was my favorite student in the class. He was not the best writer, but he was the most passionate about his work. Aggressive, argumentative, energetic, quick to engage in any activity, he always brought life to the room. I sat next to him and he started right in. "I never got a C on a paper in my life." "There's a first time for everything." "What's wrong with it? I showed it to my girlfriend and she said it was my best piece of writing." Stifling the temptation to inquire into his girlfriend's credentials as a critic, I turned to the paper and pointed out problems of grammar and organization. I complained about wordy sentences. He argued valiantly. His errors were not errors, they were his way of writing. Great writers write wordy sentences. "No. Great writers may write long sentences, they may write complex sentences, but they do not write wordy sentences. They make every word count." He was silent for a moment, then he said, "Can I write it over?" This of course was why I loved Edward. He fought for his version of his work, but in the end he wanted to learn, and he wanted to improve. "Of course," I said. "Give me the revision next week."

Sitting next to Edward looking as if she had been shot was Justine. She had an F on her paper, and I could see that she was close to tears. She had worked hard on the paper, but it was a mess: impossible to follow, mixing history and religion without clear transitions between the two, filled with errors of spelling and punctuation. I moved over to her and asked if she had time to meet me after class. She nodded, and I said that we could go to the library and sit down and really talk about her paper. Unlike Edward, she was not a performer, and our discussion would go better in private. (It did, and I encouraged her to rewrite and straighten out the problems.)

After these encounters, I had only about twenty minutes left for class proper, and I spent the time discussing their next assignment, the research paper; but when I left that day after meeting Justine I was tired and worried, and it seemed like a long way home.

Steven

Steven was a student in a Saturday afternoon composition class. At the end of the first day, he came up and introduced himself and told me a little about himself. He was 48 years old; he lived in a halfway house in Bridgeport (I didn't ask what kind); he had never used a computer but he had a friend who would type his papers; this was his first college experience; he was nervous, but he would try. As the class moved on, I got a better sense of Steven. He always came, always sat in the back, always did his work. His first paper was handed in with three-inch left and right margins. What remained wasn't much of a paper, and I gave him a D. Two weeks later I got his second paper; though the margins were impeccable the paper was disappointing. Asked to write about some aspect of social service in his home town, he had produced a laundry list of public housing projects in Bridgeport. There was no thesis, no argument, no point. I gave him a D+ and spent some time explaining to him where he had gone wrong.

Three weeks passed and I saw no more of Steven. I felt guilty. Oh God, I thought, I discouraged him too badly with that D+. He's given up. I felt terrible. Then at the final meeting of the class, Steven appeared. I practically hugged him I was so glad to see him back. He asked if he could talk to me later. Of course. When he came up after class he told me that he had had an allergic reaction to high blood pressure medication, and to get the medication adjusted he had to go "back to corrections," and hadn't been able to come to school. But he was fine now, and he had with him all the work that he had missed during the weeks he was away. Then he asked me tentatively "Am I going to pass this class?" I replied "Steven, you are definitely going to pass this class." He broke into a broad grin and said "Well then, you're going to see me around, because I'M GOING TO COLLEGE!"

And these are a few of the reasons I love teaching at Gateway.

PS: One evening not too long ago I was having dinner in a Yale College dining hall with two distinguished members of Yale's English Department. As we were carrying our trays to our table, a loud voice rang out "Professor!" and racing up to me came a vaguely familiar-looking woman in a dining hall uniform, "Remember me? From your 101 class at Gateway?" Well I didn't, but of course I said I did; I asked her if she had graduated and got her whole life's story including details of her illnesses over the last few years. She was so happy to see me, to see someone who considered her a valuable person, a *student*, and not just a dining hall cashier that I wanted to embrace her. When you teach at Gateway, you are teaching people.

© Margaret Hall Dunn, Dec. 2010

Margaret Hall Dunn was born and raised in Philadelphia. She received her Ph.D. from Yale University and teaches at Gateway Community College and Southern Connecticut State University. She lives in New Haven, CT, with her husband and her cat.

My Buddy, Daniel

Francis E. Crowley

Sunday, January 5, 1992

Daniel is 25 years old (b. 5/11/66); he is HIV positive, and he lives at Columbus House Shelter for homeless people on a quasi-permanent basis. I met Daniel through the Buddy Committee of APNH (AIDS Project New Haven) where I am a sometime buddy. Daniel is about the fourth buddy I have taken on, and by far, he is the most needy.

Daniel told me he has been on the streets since he was 15 years old. That was the year his younger brother committed suicide with a gun that Daniel's older brother had given to him. Daniel has not seen or spoken with his older brother since then. He doesn't seem to have any contact with any members of his family, which is of Italian/Portuguese background. He told me that he grew up in the old neighborhood of Columbus Avenue and Portsea Street in the Hill section of New Haven under the shadows of the Columbus House steeple where he now lives. He remembers the little park for kids behind Columbus House where he used to play until he and a small friend were beaten up by a gang. He pointed out the spot to me as we drove by.

On the streets since age 15, he has had to fend for himself. He has struggled during this time with visions, voices, and hallucinations; he has been diagnosed as schizophrenic at CMHC. Last Thursday, January 2, as we crossed the New Haven Green during our second meeting, his step slowed and he hesitated for a moment. He said he was seeing things. As we approached a park bench, I asked Daniel if he wanted to sit for a moment, but he waved it off, saying his hallucination passed. He had his bi-weekly shot that morning at Connecticut Mental Health Center where he is an out-patient and he showed me his collection of pills.

A little further along on our walk, Daniel said that Diane (Richter), his case worker at Columbus House, wanted him to start a program to stop smoking. I noticed that Daniel lights up one cigarette after another, even while we are walking, but especially in Dunkin' Donuts across from Macy's in downtown New Haven.

"Not cigarettes," he says, cutting short my half-formed question.

"For drugs?" I ask. "... do you feel that you want it?"

Silence. He's not sure.

We talk about school, reading, a high school diploma. He doesn't have one, he says, because he has always had trouble reading. All the while, Daniel impresses me as much more than street smart; far more than just the "lost kid" image that he presents. I sense an active intelligence in our conversations, a maturity, an understanding of people and the world.

"What's the worst thing in your life?" he asks abruptly as we round one of the stone walls around the Yale campus.

"That's a deep question," I say, thinking fast on my feet.

Struggling for the truth, I survey my life: all blessings. I feel a rush of empathy in my heart, and then I know the true answer to his question. "Too few friends ... I was not available to people," I offer.

"Too many friends," he says, answering the question for himself.

"Friends?" I question.

"Yes, the kind of friends that take advantage, that use you for what you've got."

I notice that Daniel is a soft-touch to a short man on crutches who has lost the lower half of his right leg. He hands out some of his remaining cigarettes one at a time. He explains that the man had been in prison for manslaughter, for killing a man over a bottle of vodka. We spot him again during a stroll through the Chapel Square Mall.

It's approaching 3 p.m. as we head for the bus stop in front of the Federal courthouse. I had bought Daniel a large coffee with my last change; he had declined the donut in favor of the 75¢ bus fare which cleaned me out. It's not payday, I explain. He had a pair of pink tights stuffed in his coat pocket for his girlfriend whom he was going to see.

I leave him on the courthouse steps, lumbering from concrete pillar to pillar, shuffling like an imprisoned bear, his grey New Haven Register hat visible above the crowd (he sells street corner newspapers most days from 5 a.m. 'til noon), and I think of my own son, John, who has just turned 15 on December 27. What if … ?

Wednesday, January 8, 1992

Yesterday, Tuesday, January 7, I went in to visit Diane, Daniel's caseworker at the shelter. Diane is a 38-year-old Ph.D. candidate in sports theory, feminism, etc., and she is a member of MCC. We hit it off, and she told me a lot more about Daniel. What a reverence I feel in my heart for Daniel's pain and suffering from earliest childhood. Yes, it's true that his 15-year-old brother committed suicide. Diane confirmed that he comes from a multiply dysfunctional family (alcohol, drugs), and that he probably formed no binding attachments in his primary relationships so disconnected, dysfunctional, and destructive was his childhood environment. He has no primary relationships now, except for Diane (one year) and a distant aunt. I am so moved by Daniel's alienation that I would like to help him change his life if he wants to.

Daniel was sexually abused as a child and, more recently, in jail. He has spent time in CVH as a chronic mentally ill patient; in fact, Diane says, it has been about a year since his last hospitalization which reflects a long period of relative mental stability. The hospitalizations have been needed to stabilize him, periodically, and they may recur again, as needed, for Daniel has a dual diagnosis: he is both schizophrenic and a chronic drug abuser. This means that behavior may be caused either by his mental conditions or his drug abuse. He has visions and hears voices, probably hallucinates regularly, but keeps these in check through medication and his own adjustment. Diane confirmed that these symptoms probably will not lead to a psychotic break, although with a dual diagnosis, the case is complex. He is on AZT.

Daniel is a drug abuser but only when he has the cash (at the first of the month) to support this behavior. He consequently lets money slip through his fingers like water every month until he is broke. Diane reports that he will use some money to buy clothes and other personal items if someone takes the time to accompany him to stores and outlets, but otherwise, he will spend, "loan," and lose it very quickly. He doesn't appear to crave drugs the remainder of the month, and he cannot afford a continuous habit anyway, but he does smoke crack cocaine, marijuana, and other substances whenever he can. He told me last visit that he "fell off the wagon" and drank for New Year's after an abstinence of six months.

Daniel has sex, probably with women in the crack houses, certainly with a girlfriend he is now seeing. Moreover, he gives some of his cash away to them. Diane says that Daniel may think that by having sex, he is having relationships. He understands that as an HIV positive person, he must take precautions; he seems to understand that he needs to be protective of others. He has come a long way from his initial reaction to being HIV positive when he was afraid to touch or to hug another person for fear of giving someone else the disease. He and Diane have had a series of frank discussions about sex, and he seems to be following through, according to Diane.

Daniel talks of suicide with Diane, and he has bad dreams. Some days are worse than others for him, but he seems to be able to accommodate these bad spells within a larger pattern of slow improvement. He has a short attention span, and he cannot consistently commit himself to a drug treatment program, in part because of his inability to sit through a discussion; however, as long as he takes drugs for his schizophrenia, he cannot enter a drug rehabilitation program. He has lived independently at times but has proved unable to plan ahead for regular payment of rent out of his monthly check. For Daniel homelessness, drug abuse, and lack of primary relationships are long-established intertwined patterns. He seems to be just beginning a slow, steady ascent into an adult world where personal responsibility is the norm. At 25, he is still very much an adult/child and the responsibilities of independent living are still beyond his grasp. He is behaving at the level of a 15-year-old who is just beginning to find out what adolescence, within caring relationships, feels like.

Saturday, January 25, 1992

The Trip to the Yale Art Gallery
Yesterday, Friday afternoon, I drove into New Haven to see Daniel. I went in relaxed and open. As I drove up to Columbus House, I could see his lumbering figure shifting feet in the bright sunlight. The world looked new, bright and clean from a rainstorm the day before—even the world of Columbus Avenue. The temperature had risen with the rain, and the day had the feel of false spring-time. Daniel smiled from across the street as he saw me pull up in front of Columbus House and roll down my window to wave. He crossed to my side of the street after waving on the car behind me. I wonder how Daniel has managed to live to the ripe age of 25

the way he crosses streets, dodging and staring down cars in his way.

He jumps into my car and giggles, "Do you notice anything different about me?" We shake hands.

As I drive off, he says, "I used my last $10 on a haircut instead of buying drugs."

"Looks good. Congratulations! That's a good move!"

That shows a change in his sense of himself. Maybe, he's showing me this as we round the corner of Portsea Street.

"I like that little kids' park," I tell him.

"Yea, it had big swings and basketball hoops when we played there."

As we drove downtown for lunch, I noticed that Daniel seems happier to see me this time or, perhaps, just happier about himself. He sports his new short haircut, a flannel shirt, and short scarf tied in a dapper fashion around his neck and he's smiling. (Long scarves are for girls, he explains.) I'm glad he seems so relaxed and happy; I want to begin to develop the relationship slowly and steadily.

I offer to buy lunch for us as payday was yesterday. He agrees. We head for the Copper Kettle downtown—POPC, Cedar Street, Macy's, the corner of Church and Chapel.

"This is where my wife cracked up her Escort. A 65-year-old lady ran a red light and plowed into her back end."

"You've got to watch that," he explains. "Some times of the day are better for running red lights."

Daniel has an explosive giggle for every street-smart observation he makes, and he has lot of them. I like his style.

Lunch at the Copper Kitchen is easy for us. I find a comfortable table in the back as he searches for a bathroom. We settle, and I explain that this is on me. He doesn't quite catch the idiom.

"Are you paying?" he asks, double checking.

"Yes, it's on me. That means I'm paying so order what you want."

"O.K. The hot roast beef sandwich @ $5.95, a coke." He hesitates, "and a chicken salad."

"You can have one," I explain with a smile.

"O.K." He laughs, and tells the waitress.

It was payday, but I'm down to $14 anyway after Finast. Hot roast beef, french fries, and mixed vegetables with lima beans. A free lunch—he's happy.

I give him my $14 as the bill is something like $13.23. He keeps the change.

Outside, I mention that I accept his offer to show me around the Yale Art Gallery from two weeks before. It's cool. We enter. He asks which floor. We go up to the third floor to the new exhibit of American mirrors (a metaphor for American life of 18th, 19th and 20th century *wealthy* life). I love the new section of the gallery, too, along with the exhibits. He feels my enthusiasm and my gratitude as we move from room to room.

Daniel explains that this art museum is a second home to him, and the security guards know him. On cold, rainy days, he seeks refuge in the museum.

"That's good," I say.

"Yea, but the guards ask me to leave sometimes."

"That's not very nice."

We skip coffee as I'm out of funds; he smiles at my explanation. We head back to the car, across Chapel, down York.

"They brought a man to Columbus House yesterday in an ambulance. They turned him away, and I told him to come back later," Daniel gloats.

"He should be able to make it on his own."

I drop Daniel off at the train station so he can make a few phone calls. I pull up; he gets out.

"I enjoyed the day," he smiles. "Thanks for the lunch."

Sunday, February 2, 1992

Yesterday, Saturday, I drove into New Haven to see Daniel. I brought a garbage bag filled with some of my old clothes to him, and he seemed pleased. He checked through the selection, and he gave away a few sweaters to some of his friends. I told him that was generous of him. He doesn't like sweaters, he said.

Diane was out on an errand so we drove over to the Chapel Square area, and I parked behind Atticus on the street parallel to Chapel. Daniel doesn't like Atticus, "too fancy," he said, so we went down Chapel toward College. We stopped awhile in the Copper Kettle, and I handed him a new $5 bill. He brightened up when I asked him if he had lunch. The place was packed.

"No, I'll have a steak and cheese sandwich."

Daniel is very careful about trying to keep his cool. I'm feeling that he's warming up to me slowly. This second lunch on me helps, I'm sure. He seems more open this time. As he was chowing down his sandwich (he offered me half), he said that his mother and father had abandoned him, given him up when he was only a baby.

"My aunt took me in," he explained.

He sees her now and helps her out buying her food stamps with his money. She is the only family he has in New Haven.

"My grandmother went to court, and then she took me in when I was two," he went on.

His grandparents kept him until they died. He went back out on the streets when he was 15. Daniel explained these facts without any visible emotion. He seemed to be recounting somebody else's history.

He ate quickly as I sipped a tall cup of coffee. He asked if I wanted a refill. I did, and some water. He called the waitress like the man-in-charge.

Daniel is a strange combination of little uncertain boy and macho man who lives by his wits. As we walked slowly down Chapel in the cold wind toward the mall, he stopped at a storefront (empty) window and noticed an ad for karate classes—black belt. He carefully peeled the masking tape holding the notice from its borders and pocketed the ad. "Karate classes," I observed.

"Yes," he succinctly answered.

In the mall, we strolled the upper deck and returned on the lower.

"Can I ask you a question?" Daniel looks at me.

"Yes, of course, anything!"

"Have you ever heard of Amway?"

"Yes, I have," I replied, knowing now what Diane had been talking about when she said she was concerned about Daniel's preoccupation with some promotional and motivational tapes he now has.

"They've been growing for 30 years," I said, indicating that I thought that they are a successful company.

"Meet me Wednesday," he says.

"I can't. I've got to teach."

He looks disappointed but from his look, after I repeat myself, I think he gets a glimmer of the difference in our life styles. Daniel seems to think and act from minute to minute. I don't think it enters his mind to consider what he might be doing five minutes, five days, or five years from the present moment. Occasionally I have to guide him back to what we've been talking about. He willingly rejoins, but I can tell from our conversations that his thought patterns are disconnected, and he wanders mentally much in the same way that he wanders the city as a homeless person.

As we return up Chapel toward the Yale Center for British Arts for the 2 p.m. free Alfred Hitchcock movie, *The Lady Vanishes,* we cross College Street again. I venture to say: "That's where the APNH (AIDS Project New Haven) office is, where we have our buddy meetings."

"PLEASE, don't mention that word to me ever again!"

We continue quickly up to the Yale Center, and settle into seats in the back row. ("So I can rest my weary head on the back wall," I say.) He smiles. He suggests that there's room behind any seat for hat, gloves, coat, "but not your valuables," he cautions.

"I thought I lost $300 in a movie theater once," he explains, "but it was in my pocket all the time."

I excuse myself and wander up to the 4th floor to the real splendor of the British collection. Delight! When I return, the hall is packed with elderly folks here to see Michael Redgrave and the glories of English acting. It's Hitchcock, 1939, just before he moved to America.

"Let's make a pact: if either of us gets bored before the movie's over, please let the other one know, and we can leave." I feel this film may tax Daniel's powers of concentration. He smiles.

"O.K.," he laughs.

I show him the playbill for today. I read to him. I point out a Long Wharf Theater trip to London and Dublin next summer for $3,400 for 11 days. Steep!

"If you had money and time," he asks, "where would you go?"

Daniel is a man of good, imaginative questions.

"Europe for three months—for six months."

"Paris for me," he says, "the women."

He loves the movie and squeezes his chuckle/giggle into an explosive laugh like a little kid when the house is silent. He coughs explosively, too, in the silence of the theater. He is silent when everyone else laughs at Hitchcock's subtle, humorous portrayal of the unflappable, droll British character. But, he guffaws when everyone else is quiet. I attempt to slide down in my seat. Most of the time, he covers his mouth with his hand when he coughs, and I wonder if the gentleman in front of him feels anything on his bald pate.

"You're like a little kid," Daniel says to me, turning to smile that street-smart smile.

He claps generously at the end of the movie. I could tell he was captivated.

"And it's old," he says.

I enjoy his enjoyment. We move out with the crowd, use the facilities, and return to the car.

"No parking ticket," I gloat. I had only one quarter for the meter today.

"The meter maid doesn't have PMS today," he says with a laugh, "and sometimes, it's a man."

We return to Columbus House, and he asks me in since we had planned to meet together with Diane.

"She's there," he says, and he points to her jeep.

Diane gives me a big hug after we negotiate the crowd on the front steps. It's 3:40, and there is a short but determined line of homeless people with all their worldly possessions blocking the front door. Daniel shouts to clear the stairs. He meets resistance.

Diane, Daniel, and I agree to meet next Friday at 3 p.m.

Wednesday, February 26, 1992

I've been in twice to New Haven to see Daniel since my last entry, and we are beginning to establish a relationship of trust. On the first of these, I took my son, John, in with me. We went to the front door of Columbus House to call for Daniel. I could see him through the glass coming down the hallway. John and I went into the waiting room/office. Daniel grabbed his dark police coat after trying on another one. We walked down the front steps after I introduced Daniel to John.

John looked anxious at first, the few moments we were waiting for Daniel to appear, and even more nervous when they were face to face. After John got in the back seat and we began talking, he seemed to relax a little. As we drove downtown to the Copper Kitchen, John initiated a conversation with Daniel who struck the pose of a knowledgeable, older brother. It was fun to see them interact. At the Copper (Kettle) Kitchen, we sat down at a three-man table, and I ordered coffee only for the three of us, as that's all the money I had to my name. Daniel wanted a second cup, but the waitress explained that a second cup is free only if food is ordered. Daniel nodded but he looked a little disappointed. John asked Daniel a lot of questions, which he brushed off a little with the air of that experienced, older brother.

"So, Daniel, what's up in your life?"

Daniel hesitated with a mischievous twinkle in his eye and then he answered, "My erection," and then he giggled.

I think that finally broke the ice between them.

After coffee, we went on to the Yale Center for British Art for the free movie, *Those Magnificent Men in Their Flying Machines* (1965) with Terry Thomas. We sat in the back row, and I left them

to go up to the 4th floor to look at the early British collection. That gave John and Daniel a chance to get acquainted. I peeked in a little later, and I noticed a lively conversation. (On the way back home, John told me about the scar Daniel has on his wrist from a suicide attempt. John said with sadness in his voice that Daniel never had a chance, that he was discarded in a wastebasket after birth. He was a throw-away kid. John took all of this in.)

The movie was fun with lots of laughs and guffaws from Daniel; John was a little embarrassed. It was a long movie, and John became a little bored toward the end, but not Daniel. He seemed happy to be hanging out with us. After the film, we dropped Daniel off back at Columbus House.

(Daniel, what does it mean to lack nurturant love at an early age, from birth actually? What does it feel like to know that your parents abandoned you at birth and never claimed you after that? How does that hole in your heart get filled up? Why do I feel connected to you in this way? How do you make up for such a loss? Why do I feel that I want to help you, Daniel, make up for that loss? All the injustice of the world is rolled up in that loss of love, of parental nurturant love; it is the greatest injustice of all in my heart.)

My second trip in, I went alone—with some money this time. I took Daniel out to lunch. At first, he suggested Burger King, but I told him that I couldn't eat meat.

"Rice and beans," he said.

"Yes," I said, "yes!"

He directed me off to Fair Haven, to Grand Avenue and a Spanish restaurant. We went in and sat down after ordering at the counter. Daniel spoke in Spanish to the proprietor. He ordered his own, and then he helped me say that I couldn't eat meat even though the owner understood English. Daniel was a little embarrassed that he spoke up for his own food first, I think, although I'm not sure.

We took our huge pile of rice and beans, and Daniel had a pork chop to go along with it. We sat and ate and talked sparingly. Daniel was into his food. He looked up from time to time to smile and to check on how I was enjoying my rice and beans. They were good, and I told him so. He seemed pleased that I liked his choice of food. We connected over food, and it was a good sharing time.

We walked out onto Blatchley, I think, and back to Grand. When we drove off, I told Daniel I'd like to sightsee in the neighborhood, and he directed me down toward the canal. We parked and walked down along the water's edge. There was a path and sidewalk and several sitting spots, which Daniel intimated were possible drug hangouts. We walked the full length watching people feed the swans and the other birds. I noted a grandfather and a small girl bending down to the water's edge to feed a pair of swans. I mentioned that swans mate for life; that's the reason you always see them in pairs. Daniel seemed interested in my observations. It was damp and raw and overcast, but we talked about the coming spring, and Daniel observed that the little canalside park would be filled to overflowing as soon as the weather turned warmer. The flowers, like the people, will gather along the water's edge.

As we walked, we established an easy familiarity through shared impressions and observations. I noted again that all the former foundry buildings which were set back from the parallel street had been converted to luxury apartments. Daniel assented. He pointed out the two bridges at either end of our view: one he called a swing bridge, and the other, a lift. As we reached the end of the walk, we spied a tug coming up the canal. We wondered whether or not the lift bridge would need to come up for the small tug with no mast. It didn't look so at first, but sure enough, the bridge broke in half as it lifted. Sharp observer that he is, Daniel thought that was unnecessary. We watched the tug work its way slowly up the canal as we turned and retraced our steps. We talked about life. Daniel seemed relaxed and more at peace with himself and his surroundings. The

tug stopped and turned before the second swing bridge and came to berth across the canal from where we stood. We strolled back to the car. I told Daniel I loved the place and thanked him for showing it to me. It was a lucky find. Daniel told me that I could come back the next day, Sunday, to buy a New Haven Register from him on Grand and Blatchley as he was going to try a new selling spot.

We drove back to New Haven and up Chapel Street. He asked if I wanted to stop in the comic book shop.

"Not really," I answered too soon, and I regretted saying that as soon as it was out of my mouth.

"O.K., we'll go when John is with us," he said, a little disappointed.

I had told Daniel I was going to see Nurse Nancy in St. Raphael's Hospital later in the day. I had a red rose and a card to give her. He suggested that he come along. I hated to discourage him, but I had to. We stopped at a card shop and shared laughs and good jokes looking at the cards; I bought two. I bought Daniel a St. Patrick's Day pin to wear. He said he had a friend who is half German/half Irish.

"I'm half Irish myself," I said.

Walking back to the car, Daniel asked if I wanted to go up to the top of the York Street parking garage to see the city from the heights. I declined. I had to get along to the hospital, I explained. He told me visiting hours were until 8:30 p.m. I regretted not going to both the comic book store and to the top of the parking garage.

"Yes, Yes," I'm going to answer next visit. We'll hit both, I told myself. I also regretted not taking Daniel to *Star Trek VI* yet; he had asked to see it several weeks ago.

"*Radio-flyer,*" he said. "I want to see that one now. I've heard some things about it, and I'm curious."

I need to follow through more positively on Daniel's spontaneous suggestions. They are innocent and free kids' things to do. I can be a kid again, for him, with him, together.

Monday, April 20, 1992

Cooked Goose—9:45 a.m.

I went in to see Daniel on Saturday. Good Friday was such a special day in giving Easter love—to Jerry, my folks—that I wanted to continue the run. I had called him earlier, about 10 a.m., so he was ready and waiting for me when I rang the front bell at Columbus House around 1 p.m.

"You're five minutes late," he laughed.

"Yeah," I chuckled. "I'm always five minutes late." But in actuality, I thought I was about five minutes early.

Daniel is sometimes a stickler for details; he's got a good memory, too. I'm always surprised and happy when he flashes that sense of authority and control over his own life, tenuous though it is, for it gives him and me a sense of hope that things could get better if he continues to make an effort.

As we walked out the front door, I turned around and shook his hand. He smiled, and he seemed genuinely happy to see me. I was brimming with the gift of a bag of shirts, a pair of casual pants, three sports jackets and my prize—a used, green spring suit from my brother-in-law, Mike. I was hoping it would fit without the need for alterations as Mike is a good couple of inches broader and wider than I am. It was a little big on me, with wider lapels and an ample waist, but Daniel is broad shouldered and bulky, and at least six feet, so I hoped he would try it on before the day was over.

A friend at the Buddy Committee at the last meeting (she is the costume designer at the Yale Repertory Theater) had offered to do any sewing should Daniel need it.

We stood there for a moment admiring the look and color of the suit and the green club matching tie.

"I can wear it to my cousin's wedding next month," he beamed as he jumped into the car.

"And you can sell Amway Products in it, too," I said as we drove off.

"I don't know if all this will fit in my locker," he said.

"Where do you want to go to lunch?"

"I thought the Copper Kitchen," I offered, very careful to correctly say "kitchen" and not "kettle," which is my usual slip. Daniel always corrects me.

"I'd prefer rice and beans," he smiled knowingly.

"Yea, rice and beans," I willingly agreed.

As I had only $7 and some change on me, I realized that this was the better choice.

I missed my right-hand turn to Fair Haven, preoccupied with last week's upsetting event at Southern and pensive about Daniel's future. Like a plutocrat gently admonishing his chauffeur who has taken a wrong turn, Daniel guided me gently past all those one-way streets in the Tower/Chapel area that kept me from correcting my mistake. (Finally, we reached Olive Street heading east, and I asked Daniel's advice on each further turn.)

While we were still lost in the maze trying to find our way, Daniel told me that Diane was encouraging him to go into a 90-day drug treatment program at Front Street (a federal "grant" through Yale). He seemed uncertain about it, searching for my advice. He seemed lost in the face of the commitment it would mean for him—the loss of personal freedom to come and go at will.

"I don't want to go in," he said confiding in me; his fears flew across his face.

"Oh, Daniel, it's a chance, an opportunity for you to change things, turn things around."

"I could come out on furlough; I could see you." He brightened a little. "Diane's pushing for it."

"I want to strongly encourage you to do it," I said supporting him without seeming forceful in any way.

(The next day at MCC, Diane told me that this was the first big step in getting Daniel into a permanent placement in a mental health half-way house arrangement. The stipulation, of course, is that he must be drug free first to qualify. She explained that she had pulled some strings through a Yale connection to get him a bed. It would be tough the first couple of days, cold turkey, in a lock-up, but then it would get easier for him, and he could come out on breaks. She added that this past month had been the pits as Daniel had blown his monthly check on drugs, and he had exhibited a lot of anger, even toward her, which was a first. He had been a bear [which is the closest approximate physical description of him—a brown bear] at the House; angry and fighting with everyone including Diane. It was also the very first time he had kissed her on the cheek affectionately in a year and a half of working together. She cautioned that Daniel is dealing with a lot of anger generally from earlier times; prison, abuse [emotional and sexual]. I offered to be a member of his treatment team when he goes in.)

As we entered the Spanish cafe, I handed Daniel a $5 bill, which he quickly pocketed. I had $2 left and change. I explained that he had to cover his lunch out of the $5 as that was my last. He took the news evenly, not at all showing if he was crestfallen after having asked if he was free to order anything he wanted!

I ordered only beans @ $1.50, and he did the same, paying for his out of the $5. He spoke with an elderly Puerto Rican lady who had a full plate of food, and he wistfully looked over at the table next to us which was empty except for a half-finished plate of rice, chicken, and beans. When he looked over at the remaining food on the plate again, I wondered if he was about to claim it. Instead, he followed my lead and sprinkled some hot red pepper sauce (tobasco) on his beans and savored them, eating rather more slowly than he was wont.

"I have only two meals a day because I don't like to go to the food kitchens," he explained proudly.

"Don't you like the potatoes?" he followed up.

"Yes, I do." I had been eating more slowly than he. "I like them in the beans this way," I added.

"I eat only Puerto Rican beans; they are the best," he coolly commented.

We finished, got up slowly, and walked out past the incoming lunch crowd of Hispanic faces. Daniel had the look of the mayor of the city grandly exiting after a particularly satisfactory banquet.

"Want to explore?" he asked, meaning the neighborhood.

"Yes, I'd like that."

"It's been a tough month for me financially," I explained, a little embarrassed, sad, and defensive that I couldn't splurge on lunch for him. I continued to feebly explain that my daughter's college tuition payment this month of $315 broke me and that I had lived for a week on the leftovers in the cupboard.

"Do you want to stop at the food kitchen?" he asked compassionately. This took me aback.

"Yes," I answered. "For you?"

"No, for you. You can get a 20 lb. hunk of cheese, loaves of bread, popcorn. When I was 16 years old, I lived in an abandoned building through the winter. The windows were broken. I came out only for food. I lived for two weeks on the cheese. The next week, I lived on popcorn. Once, when I left, someone took my stuff and hid it. I came back with friends and found it. Then, I went to the Grant Street shelter. Then, when the Columbus Annex opened, I stood in line. I lied about my age; I told them I was eighteen to get in, but I was only seventeen. After a while, I moved from the Annex into Columbus House."

"Thanks," I said, touched that he would be concerned. "Thanks for thinking of me, but not today because I bought a turkey. I have a turkey at home to cook for the weekend, so I'll pass on the soup kitchen today, but I'll keep the cheese and bread in mind when things get tight. You can show me where to go."

"My birthday is coming up," he reminded me.

"I know," I smiled. "Let me guess. May ... yes, May 11th," I guessed.

"Yes!" he beamed.

"You're 25 now," I said.

"Yea, another day older," he said.

As we walked down Grand Avenue toward the car, we stopped in an Hispanic all-purpose bodega that sold religious, music, and toiletry articles. We walked over to the shelves of large religious candles after checking out the cologne, perfume and music tapes. $1.80 per candles, I noticed, but I had only about $1.30 left.

"I don't have it," I said to Daniel.

He reached in his pocket for 50¢ and gave it to me for a large St. Joseph candle with a prayer written on the glass. As yet, I wasn't exactly sure who it was for, but I knew I wanted the candle for someone. (I gave it as a gift to Shawn later that day.)

I paid, we left the store both satisfied and pleased with our purchase, and we drove toward the canal. Daniel pointed out an abandoned storefront across the street from where the car had been parked that was used to sell antiques. Ever the observant one, he had a sense of proprietorship about the neighborhood around Grand and Blatchley.

"You lived here as a kid," I observed.

"Yea, one of my many neighborhoods as a kid."

The area around the canal was deserted this overcast, damp, drizzly, raw and cold spring day. It felt like Good Friday should feel. In contrast to our last walk along the promenade at the canal's edge, this time there were no swans, no kids, no boats to cause the bridge to go up and down.

"Wait 'til it's warm," he said, "wait 'til summer. There'll be lots of people hanging out."

"A park?" I asked.

"A park. Flowers, people."

"Let's go," he suggested.

"O.K."

Wednesday, April 29, 1992

10 a.m.—Hidden

Tuesday, Daniel called me at noon. He had received my call and message on Saturday, so lines of communication were working. It felt good to know that he could and would pick up a phone. I was about to hit the Westwoods trail when he called, so I went for a shorter walk on the Green. I told him 1:30 or 2:00, and I didn't want to be late as he badgers me about that.

After that happy trail walk on newly formed paths, I changed for church and tooled into New Haven. The weather was changeable with dappled sunlight and patches of rain. It was windy, blustery even, and cold when the sun went behind a cloud.

I pulled into Columbus House as the sun came out about 1:30, and I rang the bell. I noticed that the place was deserted, but people were arriving for church next door. Paul answered the door, and we introduced ourselves. I told him I was Daniel's buddy, and he explained that he was the director. With a wry smile, he told me that Daniel wasn't there but that he would probably be back by 2:00 or 2:30. I decided that "he also serves who only stands and waits."

I am standing beside my car, the sun is out, and I am feeling patient and understanding. Sunday strollers and churchgoers begin to crowd the scene. I drift in and out of a pleasant reverie when I notice two figures rounding the building in animated discussion.

It takes me a moment to recognize Daniel. He looks shorter, and a little more hunched. He's aware of me and twirls away to take leave of his companion, a short, stocky, homeless man younger-looking even than Daniel. Daniel looks as if he is up to something; not guilt, exactly, but half-hiding something. He's cocksure and jaunty. He's smiling that Daniel smile, that worldly-wise grin and he's spaced. As he approaches, I see his eyes, and I suspect that he is on something. I'm a little disconcerted as I realize that he had asked me to come to see him, and he has distanced himself from me at the same time. We get into my battered Buick, and Daniel notices the bag of clothes I brought for him.

"The suit fits," he exclaims, "but the shirts are too tight in the collar."

"Wow, the suit fits!" I echo with joy.

"You can go to your cousin's wedding," I add.

"No, he didn't invite me. I knew he wouldn't."

"Well, you can sell Amway in your new green suit. Where do you want to go for lunch?" I ask gingerly.

"Burger King," he smiles.

"I can't eat beef!" I remind him. "Copper Kitchen."

"Rice and beans," he counters.

"O.K. We'll go to Grand Avenue. Yeah, rice and beans," I agree.

This time, I let go and unconsciously I take a right turn without thinking. We head for Grand Avenue, pass Olive, and I'm relaxed and easy. It feels good to be tooling around with Daniel.

"I'm high," he explains.

The old, explosive giggle is back. It's as if he's playing a trick, a practical joke on me.

"Marijuana," he says.

"How long does it last?"

"Two or three hours."

The Hispanic restaurant is closed on Sundays. We drive down to the wharf, and Daniel jokes about seeing some tugboats this time and the bridges that don't go up and down.

"What are we heading this way for?" he seems to forget.

"I want to see the wharf," I explain.

Saturday, May 2, 1992

The Visit

It's about 2:30 p.m., and I'm having a carwash at Mobil. I think about Daniel and his options as I prepare myself emotionally to drive in to New Haven. It's really the first warm, sunny day of Spring; I'm feeling light and airy.

I had called Columbus House earlier and left a message for Daniel that I wouldn't be in until after two. I arrive about three, fearing he is long gone, but I ring the bell in hopes he's there. The desk clerk goes into the TV room, and he comes out quiet and subdued.

"I'm sorry about yesterday," he says sheepishly.

"What? No problem; I didn't have any plans to come in," I answer. I wonder if he had planned on my coming in because he had asked me to keep some money for him when he got his check on May 1. I'm puzzled but let it go.

"Can I smoke?"

"Not in the car."

"Where are we going?" he asks.

"My place. Would you like to see Guilford?"

He says not one word all the way to Guilford, and I wonder what he's thinking. He's pensive even, deep in his own thoughts as he notices the new scenery. It's breezy and warm in the car. My eyes keep filling up with tears. We pull into 90 Fair Street, the driveway to my Hollywood-style garage apartment way in the back between the 1850 Edwin Leete Octagonal House and my landlord's c. 1830's place.

"You live here?" he asks incredulously.

"Not in the big house, in the garage."

"You live in a garage?"

"Not in the garage; above it—a garage apartment."

We pull in all the way down the drive. I park the car underneath, and I live above.

"See my rabbit in the window!"

"Nice," he offers as he gets out somewhat uncertainly.

We walk around the back amid the full flora of springtime. Tulips are everywhere, reflecting on all the garage windows. Suddenly, Daniel is a kid again by the expression of his face. We sit in the back. He settled into Jane's hand-me-down patio chair, and I on the yellow card table chair. Daniel looks like a little boy, my son when he was 7 or 8.

"Want something to drink?" I ask.

"Yes."

I open my door and leave it wide open as I walk upstairs. As I get the soda and ice cubes, I hear Daniel climbing the stairs.

"Coke without caffeine?" I ask.

"No."

"Sprite?"

"Yes."

"This is my daughter," I say, showing a graduation picture from high school. We settle down.

"My T-cell count is below 300," he suddenly breaks out.

As I look Daniel in the eye, I see that he has let down his guard. He looks back at me.

"Are you feeling okay?" I ask after a moment. "Do you have any symptoms?"

"No, no diarrhea—nothing."

"Are you still on AZT?"

"Yes, the doctor gave me a prescription so I could take it more often. I have it in my pocket."

I suspect that Daniel doesn't take his medications regularly. He sees my serious concern. Silence. My mind races. Suddenly, the reality of Daniel's becoming sick flashes before my eyes. The years I'd imagined we'd had ahead of us begin to evaporate as we sit during a moment of silence.

He moves on to other topics. I get up to use the bathroom.

"I'll be out in a minute."

"The bathroom?"

"Yes," I answer. I come out. He's waiting.

I walk into my bedroom and pick up John's oil painting from Foundation School days.

"This is John's work. An oil! Here's his photo/montage on the wall."

Daniel tentatively enters my bedroom and looks around. Does he see the cross, I wonder. What strikes him? He looks closely at John's oil painting, my furnishings.

"That's a watercolor of California," I point to the far wall, "from when I was there two years ago."

We re-enter the living room, and I reach for my watercolor of the gazebo outside.

"Watercolor," he says knowingly. "That's pretty good."

"Yeah, I'm happy with it. The first thing I've ever done in my life. Can you believe it?"

We walk back to the kitchen.

"Can I have some more soda?"

"Sure."

We settle into separate seats, he on the couch, I in the orange chair. At some point, I take my rabbit out of his cage.

"He doesn't want to come out," Daniel says.

"He's okay!" I say kissing the rabbit on his snout.

"I get to see the town?"

"Sure."

"Let's go."

"O.K."

"Here's a copy of *Boy's Life* for you. John left a copy here. I want you to have it."

"What for?" he asks, unsure of himself.

I take it with me, and we go out. It's warmer. A day for the beach.

"Want to see the dock?" I ask.

"Not really; I try to stay away from bodies of water."

I'm puzzled. "O.K., we'll see the Green and the downtown."

"Is it 'bigger' than New Haven's?" My inner ear hears "different."

"No, smaller, but it's special in its way."

"Do you have to be back by four?" I ask.

"No."

We sit for a lingering moment outside again. I spy John's old bubble bottle from last summer, and I open it. I blow some feeble bubbles into the air and the child in Daniel comes alive again. He smiles at my efforts. After he plays with some floating uncertainly in the light breeze, I hand him the bottle and he tries.

"You have to try to detach faster from them before they burst," ever the expert, he says, smiling.

I love his boyish quality, like my son's, unconsciously free, happy, and open to the world. All barriers down, all fears washed away, all past troubles and hurts dissolved in the soapy liquid in the small plastic bottle. And out of this sad, old mixture, the dreams of childhood rise into the lifting breeze. They catch the sunlight and twinkle, suspended between the past and the future; they wait for the next chance breeze to carry them aloft in the hopes of making it through the branches and into the open air, rising higher into the sky on a wing and a prayer.

He's pleased with his prowess. His bubbles are many, like the dreams of his lost childhood, and they take off successfully into space. Funny, I think to myself, that I'm usually skillful at this, but I could manage only one or two bubbles per breath. Daniel, on the other hand, lets loose a string of them in gleeful success. He tires of it, but the magic of that moment was not lost on either of us.

We drive down Fair Street, the historic houses preening themselves in new paint in the sunshine.

Guilford has a Newport look on this one street, my street, in town.

"That's the library. I use the Congregational Church," as we round into Park Street, past the town hall to Broad, right on Broad, left on Whitfield, down to the Old Stone House (1639).

"The oldest house in Connecticut that's still standing," I say.

Daniel's impressed. I take a left on New Whitfield to the town dock. Both restaurants are out of commission. The Dock House is undergoing extensive renovations.

"Let's head back to New Haven," he asks.

"I thought you wanted lunch," I say.

"We'll pick some up in New Haven."

It's close to 5 p.m., and I think about getting Daniel back by 6 p.m. so he won't get into trouble with *the man*. It's the height of the calm and peaceful afternoon, and the full light, diffused over all the roof tops, has not yet begun to wane. I drive up #77 to I-95, and Daniel falls back into his silence. The mellow afternoon is flooding in the car windows, and Daniel can't take his eyes off the passing scene: fruit trees in blossom-pinks, -whites, -purples—new houses spring up like plants along the highway—new life everywhere.

"Rice and beans?" I ask.

"No, Burger King," he says emphatically. "It's been a long time since I've had one."

We park on Church Street after a fruitless search around the block, and we stroll over to the Burger King at the corner of Church and Chapel. The New Haven police are in the middle of a search-and-seizure drug bust on the southeast corner with two vehicles involved—kids, a van, a sedan, and much posturing. We're in the window facing the scene, and Daniel waits impatiently for his double burger. He wolfs it down, and we saunter out.

As I pull up in front of Columbus House, he mentions that he's going to the pharmacy for something. I hope in my private thoughts that it is the AZT. We shake hands solidly after a little

confusion, as he gets out, and he says he'll call me during the week. I think of his birthday coming up on the 11th as I drive off. In my rearview mirror, I see his lumbering bear-walk following me. He fades, turns, and I let go.

Monday, May 18, 1992

Daniel calls me early to ask if we can get together. He's excited about the trip he took on a bus to Washington, D.C. over the weekend, and he's just back.

"Sure," I say, "I'm coming in to New Haven today to drop off student grades at South Central. How about noon?"

It's good timing, I think to myself, and I'm anxious to see Daniel after missing him over the past 3-day weekend. The previous Saturday, I had called and talked with a helpful lady at the desk. She had explained that Diane had been fired and that Daniel was away for a few days and wouldn't be back. I had dropped off a birthday card and homemade brownies on Monday, May 11, but he was still away. I was very disappointed not to get to see him on his birthday, but I felt good about leaving the card and the brownies which he'd subsequently gotten, as he later told me. When I'd stopped on May 11, I'd wondered if he had a blow-up with the night supervisor again and been evicted or whether he'd had a psychotic break precipitated by losing Diane—his one, true, stable relationship in his life—or whether he'd just gone off to be by himself. What relief on Saturday, May 16, when I'd called again to learn that he had not been at Columbus House because he had joined a group of homeless people, three busloads full, and had gone to demonstrate in D.C. From worry to wonder, my emotions ranged at the resilience of this guy (but I also wondered whether the organizers just herded them like cattle onto the buses to go south for a show of force).

"Around noon?" he asks.

"Yeah, around noon, I'll be there after I drop off my grades."

At 12:10 I pulled up in front of Columbus House, and I could see Daniel through the chain-link fence sitting on the grass like an impatient bear.

"You're ten minutes late again," he repeats.

"Yes, I'm ten minutes late, again," I apologize. "You know how hard I try to be on time," I say. "I'm sorry."

"It's okay," he jokes.

I notice that Daniel seems relaxed and carefree. He looks like that kid again—that carefree kid in my backyard blowing bubbles and laughing at his own skill. He's free again, I say to myself.

"Congratulate me," he beams, "I'm drug free—for the past week. No alcohol or anything," he says proudly.

"Wonderful!"

"I'm in a program. They pay $5 for each urine test."

"How often?"

"Whenever. Let's go to Riverside Park this summer," he suggests.

"Okay, that sounds like fun; we'll bring John. I used to go there as a kid. Lunch?" I ask, "Copper Kitchen?"

"How about Burger King?" Daniel asks tentatively.

"No meat," I answer. "Besides, we went to Burger King last time. It's my turn this time."

"Okay, since you're driving."

I find a lucky parking spot one street over from Chapel, and I chuckle as I squeeze into a 2-for-1 with a meter. I have the 25¢. We saunter down Chapel in the sunshine. Flower vendors are outside the Yale Center for British Art. Daniel says, "Hello," to some street friends. I've never seen him fail to greet his fellow homeless friends. He's cocksure of himself.

"Let's sit in 'the booth,'" I motion after Daniel points to a small table. The booth hasn't been cleaned yet, but our favorite, friendly waitress banters with us already. She knows who we are; hungry and ready.

"Sausage and peppers special, and coffee," Daniel orders after some indecision. I have the feeling that he wants all three or four of the specials for the day.

"And I'll have hot turkey, no coffee," I smile, "and water."

"You can get refills if you have a meal," Daniel reminds me.

"I'll have coffee after all," I wink at the waitress as she comes back.

I notice a familiar face in the corner where three younger fellows are sitting. I can't place him—school, I think. He waves. I wave back tentatively; South Central Community College? He waves and flashes his hand like a fan with the fingers separated. I'm puzzled. Daniel gets up to go to the bathroom. The stranger walks over. "I've been waving at you for five minutes," he says.

I feign near sightedness as I reach for my glasses, but I really still can't place him. Now, I see. "Mike, from church," he says, indicating with a surprised look that I'm with Daniel who hasn't yet washed clothes this month. (He tells me later that he needs to do his laundry.) I wave enthusiastically, Daniel comes back, and Mike and his buddies get up to leave. I extend a hand to Mike as he passes; he seems to want to avoid stopping at our table.

"Yes, from church," I say, shaking hands, "and this is my friend, Daniel."

"I've got to get somewhere," Mike says, noticeably cooler. I wonder to myself what Mike's earlier odd hand gestures were supposed to mean. They depart.

Daniel is famished. "I don't eat breakfast when I eat lunch," he explains, "and I don't eat lunch when I've had breakfast. It's the pills."

Walking over to Chapel Street earlier, Daniel showed me his pills. Sinegran, I looked at the labels but the drug names were different from those he had told me about. Can he read, I think to myself? He's taking a lot of medication, and perhaps he gets the pills mixed up.

"And AZT?" I ask.

"I've got to refill the prescription," he says. "I get 60 days supply at a time."

"That's a lot," I offer.

I take the birthday card, which Daniel had looked at in the car, and which had nothing in it. "Nothing?" he commented with a smile.

I reach for my wallet, and I carefully place $26 in the card in which I had signed John's name. I hand the card back to Daniel. He noticed that I had put some money in, but he doesn't open the card again. He puts it carefully into the breast pocket of his sports jacket. Like most homeless, Daniel was over-dressed, even though it was a warm summer-like day. He wore a sweater, sports jacket, and he carried his lined, winter jacket. He did not, however, wear a hat. His pants were summer pajama pants. This combination looks bizarre to me.

"Do you know how much money is in the card?" I quiz him.

"Money?" He pretends ignorance and disinterest. I like this delicacy even though I know he's waiting to count it.

"Twenty-six dollars!" I affirm. "One for each year."

"Wow," he's pleased. "I wish I was 50 years old."

"Like me," I laugh. "It's not worth the 50 bucks," I kid. (And next year, you'll get $27, I affirm to myself.) I know that he's thinking to himself that he can do laundry now. I wonder to myself if he's thinking about next year.

"I told my doctor that I might buy a gun." I remain silent. "… to shoot myself."

I think of the $26 I just gave him—not enough.

"… or maybe to shoot somebody else."

"I don't want to have to travel to Enfield, Connecticut to visit you," I say, looking Daniel straight in the eye. I do not blink. He smiles back at me like a cheshire cat. He continues to enjoy his sausage and peppers.

"You want my bread?" he offers.

"Yes, I do," I say as I reach over for it, suddenly aware that he hasn't coughed on it yet, which he usually does. I enjoy my turkey and whipped potatoes.

"I ran an education program up there once," I add, "in Enfield at the Correctional Facility. I taught, tutored, counseled, and arranged for teachers to go into the classrooms. I have the sense that Daniel is listening carefully to what I have to say.

"By the way, I thought your shrink was a man."

"Yes, but he's in the hospital for a month with a hernia operation … and he's doing okay. I told her I may buy a gun. She said that would not be a solution."

"It wouldn't," I affirm. "I'll bet it's difficult sometimes," I offer, as I think of his low blood count.

"Yes, it's hard!" He looks dejected.

"I want you to call me first," I say, seriously concerned. He picks up on that and smiles as if he's been relieved of a burden.

"Okay," he says, looking directly into my eyes. "More coffee?" he offers indicating the waitress nearby.

"No, thanks."

I sit for a moment savoring the meal. Daniel stands up, always ready to move on in a moment as if unconsciously rehearsing his peripatetic life patterns. I remain seated, and he cracks a few jokes, good ones that draw on higher cognitive skills with word-play at the center. He's really bright, I think to myself as I reluctantly get up and reach for my wallet. I see before me that kid again, as he rests one foot provocatively on the seat and poses with a street-smart, happy, kid-look playing over his features. He's satisfied with his joke-telling prowess in the same way he was pleased with himself for blowing bubbles on my back patio. I smile. I pull out my greenbacks.

"Green, my favorite color," I quip.

"Why?"

"I'm Irish! See, green shirt, green car, green jacket. It's my hallmark."

This time I pay; I leave a $2 tip for our $13 check. He eyes my change automatically.

As we walk up Chapel, he spies a gumball machine. "Got a quarter?" he smiles.

"Yes," I answer cheerfully as I hand him the coin.

He stops like a kid in his tracks and turns back. He twists the handle with alacrity. It's as if it's the first time he's going after a gumball.

"Green," he laughs, and pockets it.

He's warming up to the possibilities of a real relationship, I think to myself, one that helps him to feel good about himself as he is. I see the glow on his face as we joke and stop to look in shop windows on the side street on our way back to the car. There's consistency in his warmth toward me, I think to myself. He looks as fresh as the springtime breaking out all around us.

"Who would wear that dress," he laughs, pointing at the funky, ankle-long patterned skirt in the hippie 60's window display near the corner.

"My wife," I answer, smiling.

"Let's take that table," he jokes. It's garbage pick-up day in New Haven. I like his acumen, his humor, his sense of himself as a man on top of his world, no matter what adversities he faces, no matter what his deeper fears and anxieties are. I admire his fortitude.

"I was 6 feet and 230 pounds in school; everyone was afraid of me. I broke my uncle's arm. I didn't want to do that, but he needed it. He hasn't talked to me since then. He just passed by."

"Wow."

"I've lost 30 pounds. I'm watching my diet," he adds delicately raising himself in his shoes.

I have the sense that Daniel's life story will fill many books. He has given me the gift of intimacy, and this is only Chapter One! He has taken me into his world, his street-life existence, and in so doing, he has exploded all my stereotypical biases and myths about homelessness that I have carried with me. He has put a face on courage and resilience in the midst of despair by letting me see his private pain and terror. He has given me hope.

"Where to?"

"Columbus House. I have a son who's about five or six now. I don't talk to his mother. I'd like to see him sometime."

I am suddenly shocked trying to see Daniel as a father, too; a walking oxymoron.

"I want to go to Riverside Park this summer and ride the rollercoaster. It's been a while."

"We'll do it. How about the third or fourth week of June after John gets out of school? He'll be out the 16th, so we'll go on a Tuesday or Wednesday."

"I like the weekends … the crowds."

Oh, oh, I think to myself; the traffic, the parking lots. "It's been a long time since I've been there."

"Wednesday's okay," he adds.

"We'll go the third Wednesday in June," I assure him, "and we'll ride the rollercoaster—you, John, and I."

"I'd like to ride with a girl in the back seat," he fantasizes. "That's a ride. That would be fun."

We pull up in front of Columbus House.

"I love you," Daniel says as he struggles to get his frame out of the front seat of my car. We shake hands warmly.

"I love you, too," I say, looking him in the eye.

He forgets his winter jacket in the back seat.

Sunday, May 31, 1992

Daniel calls me around noon—just as I was deciding whether to drive up to East Hartford to see my folks. My mother is back home from the hospital as of yesterday morning, and I'd like to see her, but Daniel's call makes the decision for me.

"Hey, Frank?"

"Hi, Daniel! I'm glad to hear from you."

"I'd like to get together."

"Lucky you called. You're on today! My Buick crapped out on me Friday. Fire! I had it towed, and it is not driveable any more. I was without wheels, like you, for two days. I walked."

"So you know what it feels like."

"Yeah, I'm 'wheelless,' and if I don't pay my rent, I'll be homeless, too."

Daniel explodes in his characteristic giggle.

"I'll be in around 3 o'clock. No, let's make it around 1:30. Okay?"

"Sure, between 1:30 to 1:45." Daniel is accommodating.

I drive in after putting a chicken in the oven. I arrive at 1:45 and spot Daniel on the front steps of

Columbus House talking, shouting and wildly gesticulating with some homeless friends who are camped out early on the steps waiting for the line to form for the evening's shelter. One of these is a strange-looking adult/child, a dwarf sitting on another's lap for comfort and consolation like those maternally deprived children who take care of another child even though theirs is the greater need. The front steps of Columbus House are not only a roosting place but also a nurture center where the hapless and homeless commiserate and support one another.

I walk up to the sidewalk entrance and Daniel greets me with a loud "Halloo." He introduces me to the adult/children on the steps. I wave a greeting and a look of sympathy which is returned. Daniel acts like the social director.

It's Sunday, and I'm planning on the Metropolitan Community Church at 4 p.m. so we have a couple of hours. I also only have a couple of bucks, so lunch is going to be lean. As we drive down Howard Avenue toward Yale-New Haven, I fess up.

"I've got two bucks, Daniel."

"Two coffees," he says cheerfully.

I round York Street and take another right on George Street.

"Dunkin' Donuts," he suggests.

I park in front of Ma Bell's (SNET).

"Some clunker of a car, huh?" I say. "My wife took pity on me."

"Nice hat," he suggests looking at the 3-foot sombrero in the back seat. "Did you get that in Texas?"

"No, man, Guilford, the week after I got back from California two years ago in June. John loves it."

We walk east to Church Street and go into Dunkin' Donuts. I offer my other dollar for a donut for Daniel, and I take water. Daniel orders a Big One and a round bun.

"Not even coffee?" he asks.

"No, already had my breakfast."

We sit in our familiar spot and Daniel lights up a cigarette. He looks sober.

"Tomorrow's pay day," he says anxiously. "It's hard to wait," he groans, and I wonder if it's just the money (He gets $422 from Uncle Sam as it turns out). He's itchy for the cash, I think to myself.

"You also get $20 from the drug counseling sessions and $5 for the urine tests," I say.

"$20 every two weeks and sessions are every Tuesday and Thursday," he corrects me.

"Oh, I see." He's out of cash—bone dry.

"My counselor held up the test results and said, 'See, drug free.' She really got a charge out of that."

"And you, too?" I ask, wondering about the equation.

He smiles in assent and then grows more serious than ever. Then, he opens up. "I've got a girlfriend, Louise, I saw last week."

"How long have you known her?" I ask.

"I've known her about three years. She has a temper. She gets mad real quick."

"How old is your son? Five? You mentioned him last week."

"Six or seven. I had him before I got the virus. I saw his mother, too, a couple of weeks ago. She didn't talk to me."

I wanted to ask him if he'd like to see his son, but didn't.

Daniel grows more serious. "He'll go on after me." He seems somber. "At least, I've got that to leave." He lights up again.

"Want to walk? Are you taking your pills?"

"Retro, yes," he answers. He means AZT.

We walk through the Chapel Square Mall, and I suggest a rainy walk under my umbrella up Chapel. We pass the umbrella back and forth to cover both of us. It's a huge one my sister gave me, red and white, and Daniel sports his British expression as we walk up to the Yale Center for British Art.

"Shall we go in?" he asks.

"How about the one across the street?"

First, we enter our favorite card shop adjacent to the Atticus Book Store. I notice the shoplifting warning sign on the window. "These bracelets are yours if you shoplift," and it shows a pair of hand-cuffs. I have a tight feeling in my abdomen as

Daniel fingers some of the trinkets and the proprietor watches. We ask about the museums, and he is customer-friendly.

"Yes, both are open," he says cheerfully. "The Yale Art Gallery across the street is open from two to five."

"Let's go across," I say to Daniel.

"Okay," he agrees.

"You'll need to park your umbrella outside in the rack," the guard cautions.

"What do you want to see?" Daniel smiles.

"How about the first floor show?"

We walk around the new (to me) open room on the left into an environment of plastic container repetitions and hanging, macrame-type, spreadsheet, room dividers. Daniel has his chuckle ready as he fingers the material. I cringe as the guard looks gruff and growly, but he doesn't get up. I'm anxious about what Daniel will touch next. It's so natural to want to touch the artworks but such a social blunder, and it can get you thrown out of a museum fast. I'm uncomfortable so I walk out into the balls dipped in tar and suspended in air with macrame. Daniel follows. I chuckle to myself as I see giant scrotums and testicles in my imagination.

As we meander through the rooms, I notice Daniel's interest. We stop and listen to the video on the artist's life.

"She's dead?" he inquires.

"Must be," I nod as testimony to her is recorded by critics and other fellow artists.

We walk through glass doors into a cloistered hall with stained glass windows.

"I love this room," I say to Daniel.

He leans against a vertical steel slab. "Let's knock it over," he says gleefully.

We exit, and Daniel kids me that my umbrella is missing. He laughs as I spy it and take it with us.

It's still raining and only 2:45, so I suggest a walk to the quad to see the tent set up for the Yale 25th reunion, but Daniel prefers to head back to the car.

"When you've seen one, you've seen 'em all," he says. "Drive down Columbus Avenue, would you?"

"Sure."

"Have you been down this far?"

"No, I've never come this far down."

"Stop by that brick building. I'm going to see my real father. Maybe he'll give me $10." Another surprise! I never imagined a continuing relationship with his biological father!

"Don't forget your jacket this time," I say.

"Or my pack. Come by tomorrow, would you, just before 1:00 when the checks come in? Even a little before."

"Sure, I'll be there.

"Thanks, Frank."

"Bye, Daniel. I'll be there."

Monday, June 1, 1992

I park in the Columbus House lot as I don't spot Daniel. It's 12:45, and I've finished my errands at SCCC. I'm perfectly on time. I ring the bell. A skinny, lame man about 35 lets me in.

"Oh, Daniel just left, but he'll be back for his check. You can wait inside if you want."

We talk—about his bone disease, a broken vertebra, ankle, the ailments that come with age.

A young, black woman with all her possessions in two plastic grocery bags comes in after ringing. She's been sent down from Derby for a bed for the night. She's tired, anxious, lonely and downtrodden … in need of a loving home. The man lights up, calls upstairs for arrangements and tries to comfort the girl. He's polite—"excuse me, thank you."

We think it's Daniel at the door because of the heavy walk and banging. It's not.

Daniel rings and spies me through the glass window. (We've changed places.) He's anxious to get his check but they haven't come in yet.

"Let's go outside and wait," he says impatiently.

We sit in the car. I put the key in the ignition. He notices. All his senses are alert.

"Let's go to my credit union so I can get some cash, too," I suggest while we wait.

"Okay," he agrees. "Where?"

"On Whalley Avenue, not too far."

"You're taking the long way," he says, a little irritated.

"I'm slow and pokey," I agree.

I get the impression that Daniel has only one thing on his mind today, and I'm wondering why he had wanted me to be here on check day with him.

"Thanks for coming along with me," I say after getting my $50 cash. While I was in line waiting for a teller, Daniel had gotten up to ask me for a quarter, but I only had pennies in my pocket. He's in need. We walk back to the car.

"Let's take the short way back," he says. "I'm going to give you $20, Frank."

"Thanks, but I can't take it," I say, knowing that he feels bad my car is gone.

"Why?"

"You have your own responsibilities," I answer, feeling that he's grateful to me.

"Well, I want you to hold it for me then."

"Sure," I say, feeling much better about that arrangement as he's sure to be broke before the 1st of next month. "I appreciate your offer of cash, but I'd rather hold it for you when you need it," I say.

"Good."

We're back at Columbus as he directs me quickly down the Boulevard.

"I used to walk to Edgewood Park along the Boulevard to catch frogs when I was a kid."

"That's a long walk for a kid," I offer in sympathy. "What was this street called before?"

"It's always been called the Boulevard."

I picture Daniel, a lonely kid of 12 or 13 walking alone to the park—a long, lonely hike—to catch frogs like any other normal kid. Only Daniel needed some hugs which he never got. Maybe he hugged the frogs, I think to myself, as I used to hug my chickens in the shed when we had no one to return our hugs. I smile as I realize that I'm now hugging my rabbit and Rita, the bird, every morning.

We're back and Daniel hops out quick as a wink. A thin, good-looking black man about 30 comes uncertainly over to the car and asks if he can get in. He explains that he's been Daniel's friend for 5 or 6 years. I ask him to hold off until Daniel's return. We talk.

Daniel scales the fence with the check in his hand. He asks if we can bring Paul along. Sure. Paul gets in the back. I notice he shakes a little and is unsure but pushy at the same time.

"To the check-cashing place," Daniel commands like a millionaire to his chauffeur.

"Sure, show me."

We're on Howard Avenue and he directs me to pull in to a storefront.

"They charge to cash but not for money orders," he explains. "I need a couple for the Amway man, and my father …"

"And for the *Register*," I suggest, since he's under a warrant for keeping about $120 that belongs to the circulation supervisor. He sold papers on the corner of Chapel Street and the Boulevard for many weeks.

He's silent.

"And to open a bank account," I push.

"*What* bank account?" He's in no mood to joke.

Daniel jumps out and asks me to wait. Paul leans forward and begins a monologue for ten minutes on legalizing drugs, the cosmos 666 myth, religion, respect, and responsibility for your fellow man, but he's disjointed, illogical, and incoherent.

I'm genuinely frightened when I realize that I'm staring into the face of a truly lost soul who has no center, no identity, no allegiances, no hope. He is a stream of undifferentiated, unconscious urges, impulses, and needs. He's dangerous—I feel it in my bones.

Daniel returns with an apparition in a long pull-over, a drug pusher ready to make a sale. Daniel hands me a $20 bill and Paul a $10 bill, and says he's got to go. I nod in acceptance. He walks away, hesitates, returns, and says goodbye. I look at him.

"Call me tomorrow?" I ask. He's in a rush.

"Okay, okay. I'll call." He hurries off with the man.

Paul gets out, walks away, and then comes back and wants to get in the passenger seat. I motion him to stay out.

"I'm going back to the college." I push him away.

"So, you got your money," he observes.

"Daniel asked me to hold it for him," I explain.

"I'm going to get high," he offers.

I'm shaken by the transactions, the brutal leave-takings, dealings, desperate needs, losses and escapes from real, human, emotional connection into a solitary world of alienation, loneliness, and detachment.

But, I have $20 for safe-keeping, I say to myself.

December 1, 1992

The Elm City Diner

A couple of Sundays ago, I drove into New Haven on a rainy, dismal day. Even Daniel remarked on the bleakness of a lonely Sunday.

I was late, unconscionably so, as I had been out dancing the night before at Choices. A little hung over, I moved toward getting ready more slowly than usual.

Ring.

"Frank, you're late. How long will it take?"

"I know. I'll be there in 45 minutes. Sorry."

"O.K. See you soon. God bless and God bless your son."

"God bless you, too, Daniel. Soon."

I bustled, packed a gift for a friend (his 40th birthday party was that evening), and trundled off in my blue '79 4th-hand Rabbit. I thought of our friendship, of how much Daniel had been through with his last overdose and his long stay in the hospital in October, his continued stamina, and hope, and yet his helplessness in the face of the terrible algebra of his life and of how I had come to love him like a son.

He had almost killed himself this time, popping junk into every available vein in his hands, arms, and legs. In a feeding frenzy of coke, he kept cracking bag after bag until his check was gone, so by November 1, he was in the hospital on IV for the fungus infection on his hands and arms. He had found a trash bin behind which he had hidden out from the cops and from himself. Hours later, reviving in the cold, he had walked into the E.R. of Yale blasted, bruised from sitting crumpled up so long in one position.

I drove up to the "We the People" Homeless hand-out house on Howe Street, opened one week before by the mayor as a token gesture for the holidays. Daniel was standing like a wet puppy outside. I felt bad I was so late.

"How're ya doing," he asks, jumping in, his smile a boyish, impish grin.

"Good, sorry I'm so late. I'm glad to see you."

"Where to?" he hungrily asks.

"How about here?" I say as we drive a few feet to the Elm City Diner. It's grand opening day. "O.K.," I think to myself as I see the signs for $1.99 complete breakfast. I have only a $5 bill and change in my ash tray and my pockets.

"Sure, it's good! It's the 50's Hollywood style."

I cross Chapel and we park. Daniel is out and across the street before I can get out of the car. A homeless friend with his right eye missing greets us on Chapel as we approach the steps.

"A buddy shot his eye out with an arrow," Daniel explains as we enter. I look warily back as if the same thing could happen to us. "The streets in New Haven are mean," I think to myself.

Daniel wants to wait to be seated. I push onto the wrap-around corner facing the intersection of Howe and Chapel. He faces the corner and I sit across.

"See that parking space?" he points across to a vacant lot on the north side of Chapel and Howe. "That's where the abandoned building was where I lived through one whole winter when I was 17 and 18."

His face grows darker and he scowls as the memories of that winter pass before his eyes. He's a mixture of Hispanic, Black and White; as his moods change, his ethnic look changes. He's a boy-man; big, but not grown up yet.

"I lived on popcorn for a week. The owner chased me with a crowbar. All the windows were broken. I came back and someone had pissed in my water bottle."

A kid, I thought to myself, a kid of 17 with no family, no place to go, no help, terrified, vulnerable, and a man chased him with a crowbar … a lost abandoned kid.

"My mother left me in a trash barrel with a note pinned to me when I was only a few days old. My aunt told me that the rats almost got me, but she pulled me out." He looks directly across the street at the YWCA.

"I got AIDS over there on the top floor."

"When you were doing drugs?"

"Yes, when I ran away from Connecticut Valley Hospital."

"How long had you been there?"

"I was arrested for assault, carrying a dangerous weapon, and resisting arrest. I spent four months at CVH, and then I couldn't take it any more so I ran away—just walked down the road and hitched back to New Haven. Then, I was staying over there at the Y, and we were all shooting up together. I got AIDS. When I woke up next morning, I went to the E.R. because I knew I couldn't make it on the streets no more. They sent me back to CVH for three years—four months in Whiting for the criminally insane. After I got back there, they did some blood tests. I had AIDS. I destroyed two candy machines—picked them up and threw them against a wall. While I was there I met the guy who stabbed that little girl in Middletown. He is crazy!"

Daniel paused, looked over at me, and I could see the desperation in his eyes as he looked at the four corners of his life, trapped by his past at this very spot as we sat and talked. He *was* trapped; his life was circumscribed by the events he was telling me about.

"Down the street behind P.J.'s, I tried to cut my wrists. I did, but my blood clotted up too fast. I couldn't even *bleed* to death." I had noticed the stitch marks before. "I went to the E.R. again."

He leaned over after his fourth cup of coffee, opening up to me even more. A rare moment for Daniel.

"I'm the same. I can't change. I let God down, myself down. I try to start over, but I fall down. I do drugs."

He finishes the remaining home fries on my plate.

"See, it's amazing what you can do on $5," I say, after the bill for two huge breakfasts, and bottomless cups of coffee comes at $4.23. He smiles that kid smile.

"You could have stayed home in the rain," he says, "if all you had was $5."

"Didn't you want to see me?" I ask.

"Sure. Do you have any money for cigarettes?"

"Let's check the ashtray in my car." I nod.

I give him all the change in the car. He notices some spare pennies on the floor and we get them.

"Maybe there's enough," I say.

Thursday, December 3, 1992

The Hidden Kitchen

As we leave the car, I notice the holes in the seat of Daniel's pants.

"Yeah, I need some new pants," he says as he displays his posterior to the world of Chapel Street.

"I've got some large cords for you. I'll bring them in. Sweat shirts, too."

We walk down Chapel to the smoke shop. "Diane says maybe you could hold some money for me. I called her."

"How about a conservator?" I suggest again. "Rebecca says that's a good idea. What do you think?"

"Maybe. It's a half-good idea."

"You could still have some money left toward the end of the month," I add encouragingly, fully looking at him as we reach York. "And, you could save for an apartment."

We stop outside the news shop and Daniel goes in after a two-pack.

"I ripped off a car stereo the other day." he boasts. "I needed some cash."

"Back to square one," I think to myself as we head back up Chapel.

"Get a girlfriend for yourself, Frank."

"What's the worst holiday for you, Daniel?"

"Christmas," he says dejectedly.

I imagine a tree in my apartment over the garage, all decorated and glowing in the warmth of a loving family: Rita, my cockatiel; Ajax, the rabbit; John, my son, and Daniel, as we laugh and open brightly wrapped presents.

As we reach the car, I realize that it's been almost a year since we first got together. Outwardly, nothing has changed in Daniel's life.

He grabs his bag from the back seat and ambles off toward the Crown Street shelter. He turns and looks directly at me.

"Thanks for the talk, Frank," he says, beginning to smile.

"Something has changed," I think to myself as I wave goodbye.

Monday, January 11, 1993—11:50 a.m.

The Cooked Goose

Yesterday, John and I went in to New Haven to meet Daniel at the Copper Kitchen at 2 p.m. He was waiting outside in the cold, and I could see his blue stocking cap—the one I gave him for Christmas—against the dull brown background of a cold winter day.

"Let's go," he said as he walked up toward the car.

"How about a cup of coffee?" I suggested.

"O.K., but not in here," he answered.

"Too crowded," I thought to myself, but I led the way inside the Copper Kitchen. Just then, a few people got up from the counter. I noticed that all the booths were filled. There were just three spots at the counter, and we slid in like three giddy cowboys. I noticed John looking at Daniel out of the corner of his eye. Daniel was between us.

"No menus, just three coffees," Daniel ordered, taking charge in his usual fashion.

"That's good," I thought to myself. I was stone broke, but I knew John had at least $7, so we were free and clear for coffee.

"You're coming home with me," he laughed.

"How's the new place?" I was almost as excited about it as Daniel, and clearly John was very happy, too. We grinned at each other and burst out laughing again. Whenever we are together, we seem oblivious to the other patrons in the place. It was Daniel's

day; he had his own room, finally. It was a happy conclusion to a year's effort to get himself his own place. He couldn't suppress a burst of boyish glee.

Daniel has a way of bubbling over with self-satisfaction. "Sharon came over. She helped me fix the place up a little," Daniel giggled.

"Do you know that a diaphragm is?" Daniel asked, turning to John. He enjoys playing the older brother.

"Yes, I do," John nodded, a little embarrassed, but keeping up his side in response to Daniel's wry smile.

"Sharon and I did some neckin' for 20 minutes. She wants to get a diaphragm first. And she wants me to use a condom. I had to respect that."

I could see that Daniel's new sensitivity was not lost on John.

"She sounds nice," I offered.

"She cleaned up the place a little."

"Does she have a car?" I asked.

"No, she took a bus from Branford. After she cleaned up, we necked. Then, she had to catch the first bus."

"She's quite a woman to come all the way by bus to see you. I like your new girlfriend already."

"Yeah, she wants to improve my grammar."

"Wow!" I say, at the same time observing John taking all this in with a knowing smile.

"Let's go." Daniel gets up. I can see that he can't wait to show us his place. "Do you have the stuff you promised me in the car?"

"Yes, we brought sheets, towels, curtains, a hot pot, instant coffee, tea, and John and Jane brought a bag, too. She's donating the hot pot, a comforter, and some towels, too."

"Can we get the girl who gave us coffee?" Daniel asks at the cash register like the boss of the place.

We walk up Chapel, turn the corner at the Yale Center for British Art, and head for Crown Street.

"The limousine!" Daniel declares, making fun of my beat-up, rusted, tiny, '79 blue Rabbit.

As we tool up Whalley, Daniel plays the radio searching for a rock beat. We jive and jump in the car bouncing it to death on its little springs. We stop for cigarettes at the Chucky's in Westville where Fountain splits from Whalley.

"Sorry you had to walk all the way downtown to meet us in the cold," I said.

"It's O.K. It's away from the drugs, anyway. I had two chances after I got out of the hospital. I didn't take them."

[Flashback]

Daniel had checked himself into the Connecticut Mental Health Center around December 1, 1992. Just after he had received his monthly check, someone had mugged him for about $200. He was at a woman's apartment when he had called November 30, and I was surprised by that. It turned out to be a bust for him; a woman in a wheelchair, a shady friend, and more of the same.

He told Rebecca, his worker at CMHC, that he was suicidal, and he had been admitted. John and I visited him a couple of times while he was in the hospital; John bringing some smokes which were confiscated at the desk. I had brought Daniel some pants and socks to tide him over. He had called several times from the hospital, leaving messages on my tape. He had been worried about his belongings left behind at the Crown Street overflow.

While he was in the hospital Daniel made plans to search for a room and, with the active help of the hospital staff, he would be released once he found his own place to live. He worked with Penny, a real estate agent, whose card he showed me on an earlier visit, and I checked this out with Diane. Penny, it turned out, was legit, so I was relieved when Daniel called to say that he was putting his January check down on a room through Penny. The stage was set: the month's stay at CMHC was ending, his monthly check was due, he had been drug free for 30 days. Moreover, his attitude had changed, and he seemed "up" each time he talked about a new place to live. Through all this, he seemed more self-possessed, keeping control of the decisions, testing his own

powers and ability to make changes in his life under his own steam, happy and self-confident about his own "moves," with support waiting in the wings.

[Flashback—Christmas Eve, 1992— Elm City Diner]

The Hug

I had promised Daniel to take him out of the hospital on a pass, so when he called, I suggested Christmas Eve. The city streets were deserted when I drove in; it was cold and raw with a wind blowing. I had stopped earlier with John to shop for a few last minute gifts at Bradlees in Guilford. I had bought Daniel a blue stocking cap, and John a pair of sweat socks. When I walked to the doors on the fifth floor at CMHC, a guard let me in. Daniel was ready and waiting. I handed him his gift. He tore the paper off and tried on the hat.

"I thought you'd bring me a $100 bill or something," Daniel smiled.

"You'll need this tonight," I retorted.

"Let's go," he said gleefully.

I could tell he was happy as a kid to go out for some real food.

"Where to?" he asked, jumping into my little tin can. He wore the hat down low over his eyes in the bitterly cold wind. "No heat!"

"Not yet. It takes a while."

"Let's try the Elm City Diner," I suggested. "It's probably the only place open tonight."

"O.K."

There was no life on the empty streets. All shops and restaurants had long since closed, so that New Haven resembled a sleeping city more like 4 a.m. or as if it had been transported to the tundra of Alaska. It was only 7:30 or 7:45 p.m.

The new Indian owner was waiting for us—the only lights burning on the corner of Chapel and Howe. We sat along the inner wall. It was festive and warm inside.

"You know, Frank, sometimes I'm afraid that I won't think of anything to say when I'm with you." He settled into his seat.

Daniel had a vulnerable look in his eyes; unusual for him. It was a rare letting down of his guard.

"You've said a lot over the past year. You've told me a lot about yourself."

"It's been about that long, hasn't it?"

"Yes, exactly; it's an anniversary. We got together on December 29 last year. I'll toast to that."

"O.K. Me, too. We made it! A whole year!" he said.

"I'll have the fried fish," he told the waitress after his second cup of coffee.

We were alone in the diner except for two gentlemen in a nearby booth.

"I'll have a bowl of chicken soup. I ate earlier," I explained. I was trying to stay under $15, as I had left my $50 bill at home.

"Yes, Daniel, it's been exactly one year, and we made it," I toasted again, "and we'll go for seven."

"I'll drink to that," he smiled. "Yeah, we'll make seven more. Have a piece of fish," he offered after taking a few bites. I helped myself to a small piece of fish and tartar sauce. My cream of chicken soup was good. Daniel was mellow and pensive and yet happy to be out on Christmas Eve: an old man and a kid at the same time.

"The fish was good," he smiled.

We bundled up. I paid the bill—$13 and change so I just squeezed by with tip.

"Good timing. I've got a Christmas service at 9 p.m.," I said. It was about 8:30 p.m.

We drove back toward the hospital. At George, I took a left. "Let's see the lights on the green," I suggested.

"Yeah, that's nice."

As we drove once around the New Haven green, it was just me and Daniel—no cars, no people, just a hushed silence, and the lights on the huge pine in the center of the green.

"There used to be another tree, larger with lights," he said. I could see he took it all in. Maybe he was remembering the green from his childhood.

As we approached the hospital again, he said he needed cigarettes.

"I'm out of cash, but you're welcome to check the ashtray again."

"O.K. Here's some change," he counted.

"And I've got a dime on the floor," I offered.

We parked; walked over to a corner hole-in-the-wall market. The door was open but the man inside told Daniel it was closed.

"Just cigarettes," Daniel pushed his way in.

He came out smiling. "Just enough," he said.

We stood there a fraction of a second, and then he threw a bear hug at me. I returned it with several pats on the back. We laughed; he turned.

"I'll check myself back in," he said, leaving me standing there.

"Merry Christmas," I yelled across the parking lot. He waved back and disappeared.

[Postscript—Tuesday, January 12, 1993—The Cooked Goose]

A Coincidence

Yesterday, John and I tooled into New Haven to my credit union for some cash. I had promised John breakfast, so after a quick visit to Gateway, I suggested the Elm City Diner. We sat down in the far corner facing Howe. As I turned around, I spotted Daniel and Sharon crossing the street.

"John, it's Daniel and his girlfriend. Quick, run out and let them know we're here."

John came back with Daniel and Sharon in tow, and we sat down for coffee.

"You're perfect for him!"

Daniel held out his palm to be greased, and I slapped his hand with an imaginary five.

"I prefer cash," he smiled. "I'm embarrassed," he said after a moment.

"Why?" I asked smiling across to Sharon.

"Thanks," she said looking across at John and me.

Sharon has a fey and hard-as-nails look to her at the same time. Blond with strawberry tarts hair pulled back, recessed blue eyes with a vacant look. For a moment, I thought she was blind because of the expressionless look, almost as if she were looking inward. A knowing, worldly-wise smile playing across her lips.

"I go for oddballs," she laughed. "He looks Indian, don't you think?" she looked at me, "with a red ruby in his forehead."

"By gosh, yes, an Indian potentate, a maharajah to be sure, with the red ruby," I said.

Daniel smiled his cheshire cat smile and settled into his chair like a buddha.

"How did you meet Dan?" she asked me with an easy intimacy. "I call him Dan," she smiled.

At that moment, Daniel leaned even further back in his chair and motioned me to be cautious and discreet with a gentle flick of both wrists.

"Oh, we became friends about a year ago," I said evasively after a moment's hesitation.

That seemed to satisfy both of them. "And yesterday, Daniel was a big brother to John, my son, advising him to not smoke at his age because his lungs are not fully developed."

"Yeah, Dad," Daniel said holding out his hand for money again.

"You don't mind John's earring?" Sharon looked directly at me. "Most dads can't abide that; you must be very accepting as a father."

"I love the earring; hate the smoking," I said, putting my left arm around John's shoulder.

All the while, John was enjoying the interaction between Sharon and Daniel. I could tell by the smile playing across his face.

"You're educated, too. I can tell," Sharon said, addressing me with closer scrutiny. "I've heard so much about you from Dan. You must be an unusual person. He needs to wash clothes; look at the spots on his pants. Dan, you must have some change for the machines," she said distractedly.

"It's priorities; I need food first," he smiled with the wisdom of the ages in that cat-like grin.

"I'm working on the radio, TV, clothes, etc.," I offered. Sharon smiled, relieved to learn of my genuine concern; she was not alone as a source of support.

"Or I can bring them home to mother … oh, mother," she thought better of it.

Daniel rolled his eyes. It occurred to me in the few moments of embarrassed silence that followed that Daniel had not shared everything about himself with Sharon. Was she as naive and at the same time as worldly-wise as Daniel? His warning gesture not to explain that I was his buddy from APNH made me wonder if he had told her that he was HIV positive. I was glad, then, that she was insisting upon a condom before they even thought about sex.

"You know how Daniel and I met?" Sharon asked, unsure of herself again.

"No," I raised my hands in a question mark. Daniel had told me only that they had met in the hospital, but I wanted to continue to play dumb. I remembered, too, that he had put her on the phone once while in the hospital when she, in an importunate tone, asked for clothes for Daniel. I remembered the sound of her tone—casual and yet insistent, as she was now.

"We met in the hospital," she waved with a vague gesture of her hands. "I'm in the day program now, working on getting it together. I'm with mother in Branford. She doesn't care for any of the men in my life." Daniel rolled his eyes again. And as Sharon had predicted, Daniel was ready to pull this off like some Indian potentate.

Daniel stood up ready to make tracks. We followed. I paid the bill and passed the $2 to Daniel.

"Thanks for the coffee," Sharon smiled.

"Two dollars?" He looked incredulous at the checkout register. John reached into his pocket, pulled out two bits and handed the 50 cents to Daniel.

"I still can't believe the coincidence that brought us together today," I smiled. "Goodbye."

Daniel ushered Sharon down Chapel after shaking hands all around. Neither looked back as we watched them lean into each other talking in confidence.

Monday, January 18, 1993, Martin Luther King Day

The Room

"I used a condom for the first time with a woman," Daniel beamed. He sat down with me on his beat up couch—black leather with holes and patches all over—somewhat like his pants.

"Congratulations!" I smiled. "That's responsible."

We sat for a moment, happy to connect after a whole week. I was worried about him all week, wondering whether he would crash again because he had no money.

"I stopped earlier, right after church, but I didn't see any lights in your room."

"I was here."

"Sleeping?"

"Yeah. I got my uncle to give me a ride back from the soup kitchen. I'm eating dry corn flakes now," Daniel smiled.

"Here's some cheesecake my daughter made today. Huh! She's a cook now!"

"She has a job as a cook?" Daniel asked incredulously, and I realized how circumscribed his life and his thinking was. He was living in one room, mentally.

"No, she's a senior at Fairfield University, but she cooked her first meal on Christmas Day, and now she's trying new things in her condo."

"It's better than the corn flakes," he laughed. He settled back. He looked a little spaced as if his eyes were disconjugate in his head.

"Drugs, medication, schizophrenia," I wondered to myself. "Exhaustion, hunger, and disorientation," I decided, but I had thrown a snowball at his window earlier to get his attention.

He checked out the two bags I had brought in earlier: shaving cream, razors, toothpaste, shampoo, and a large pair of pants, green corduroy from Uncle Mike, and a blue and white striped shirt I had thrown in at the last minute.

Daniel's room now had plaid drapes and some sheets and towels which John and I had brought on our first trip, the Sunday before. His mattress was up against his one window. All his laundry and clothes were thrown into the one closet. He had his toiletries and pills on one shelf. The outer room where he was sitting had the couch, his major piece of furniture. He seemed happy with his place.

"Sorry I was out when you came by on Tuesday. I went to the store."

"I never made it," I said sheepishly. "I was afraid of the weather."

I always feel bad not showing up when he is depending on me. He smiled at me understanding that we both occasionally miss.

"Can you come to family day at St. Raphael's Hospital on Wednesday? Sharon's mother wants to meet you."

"Sure," I said. I felt honored to be considered family by Daniel. I was amused by his formality.

"I'll stop by Wednesday afternoon at the hospital."

"You know where it is?" Daniel asked, wanting to make sure. I thought to myself that Sharon must be an important part of Daniel's life now.

"Where are you off to now?" Daniel asked, still sleepy.

"Home to my rabbit!"

Trans-Mission

John D. Allen

One of the saddest moments of my professional life occurred on Friday, August 17, 2001, at 2:20 p.m. I facilitate a support group for people with intellectual disabilities who identify as gay, lesbian, bisexual and transgender. This group is believed to be the first of its kind in the country. As a community-based organization, the Rainbow Support Group draws many people who either provide professional support to the members or participate in the group simply because they enjoy hearing about the lives of a little-known segment of society.

That day, I had a 2:00 appointment scheduled in my office with Mark (an alias), a public relations consultant who facilitates a cross-dressing support group at the local gay community center. Mark was going to finish a discussion we started in May regarding Ben, a 57-year-old male with a mild intellectual disability, who regularly cross-dresses. Mark and I last spoke in May when we arranged a concluding meeting, so I gave a confirming call in the morning after the three-month absence.

The first time I met Mark was during the New Haven Gay & Lesbian Community Center's (NHGLCC) festive and crowded holiday party in December, 1999. Since he was dressed as his feminine alter ego, Lisa, and was introduced as a member of a local cross-dressing social group, I immediately had Lisa speak with Ben. They hit it off and made plans for Ben to attend one of the upcoming meetings.

During a few subsequent phone calls over the next two years, I came to know Lisa and Mark, as Mark, and for our first visit he came to my office casually dressed as Mark. Additionally, when we spoke just a few hours before this meeting, he continued to speak with me as Mark.

Around 2:15 p.m. that day, I stepped out to the receptionist to ask if Mark had arrived, and since he was late, I returned to my office and became immediately involved in another project. The phone rang five minutes later, and the receptionist said in a forceful and matter-of-fact manner, "Lisa is here to see you."

Flustered and not recognizing the name, I stalled for a moment, and then a sense of horror flushed over me as I realized just who was in the lobby. For all of my desire to be understanding and accepting of transgender people, my true feelings materialized in a flash, and I was immobilized.

"Well, are you coming out or should I send her in," said the receptionist in a somewhat puzzled tone of voice forcing a response after the pause became awkward.

Standing up and straightening my clothes, I began hearing laughter and a buzz of whispers outside my office. My office is on a corner adjacent to a waiting area for client members and their staff which fills up between 2:15 and 2:30, and I noticed the area was packed and all conversation stopped—dead silence! She had started walking down the opposite hallway, which was toward the ladies room.

Lisa had to walk through a gauntlet of staff, who remained silent; they were trying to erase all traces of a smirk from their faces. Closing the door to my office behind us, I fumbled an attempt to begin the discussion.

"Were those people laughing at me?," said Lisa in a question that we both knew was stating the obvious. I explained that the area is a waiting room. Since it was Friday, everyone was excited about starting the weekend. To help her save face and to manage my own discomfort, I told her that they were not laughing at her.

At 200 pounds and 6 feet tall, flat footed, Lisa is a big girl. She does a good job of trying to make an inconspicuous presentation, and on this visit she was appropriately dressed for a Friday afternoon. She wore a plain summer skirt, a brown scoop-neck leotard top covering a large bosom, hoop earrings, a long auburn wig with bangs and 3 inch heels thick enough to support a Lane Bryant frame.

Her make-up was equally appropriate, not garish like so many drag queens ready for a glamorous evening, but subtle with just enough to cover a freshly shaved face and muted lipstick. Even though Mark has obviously practiced his feminine persona and can pass undetected on a first glance, everyone was aware of just who walked through the lobby that afternoon, and, unfortunately, some staff felt justified in making their reaction obvious.

My embarrassed and appalled state, when Lisa asked about the ridicule from staff, was actually three separate simultaneous emotions. I have spent twelve years at an employer with a primary mission to provide support for people with disabilities. The hundreds of people that come to the agency every day are from many different backgrounds and cultures. Some are homeless, mentally ill, profoundly disfigured, or in need of personal care assistance, and not once have I ever witnessed an incident where an individual was ridiculed for his or her appearance when entering the building, and certainly not in the person's presence. What I felt was much more than anger or disappointment toward a group of staff who are all college educated and supposed to display a professional courtesy toward others; I felt emotionally betrayed by the people whom I hold in such high esteem in my role as sales representative for our program to the community. The incident has shaken me to the core!

On further reflection, I am aware that not all of the disappointment was directed toward a few, naïve, young staff. Over the past two years of trying to connect Ben with the cross-dressing social group, Mark and I had several conversations, both on the phone and in person, and I felt relaxed around him. Mark shared with me that he identified as heterosexual,

had a girlfriend and had discovered that he lived a third of the time as Lisa.

I have great empathy for people who try to live an honest and open life. People who are transgender—those that cross the many and complicated gender boundaries—have few legal protections and are among the most maligned individuals, even within the gay community. An ironic fact is that it was primarily transgender people that are credited with starting the modern gay movement during a rebellion against police bias in New York City's Greenwich Village in June 1969 (DeMilio & Freedman, 1997). Cross-dressing, when not intended as comedic, has elicited violent reactions from people that rigidly believe in gender roles.

When I invited Mark to visit, I expected the male persona of Mark, especially after having just confirmed the appointment a few hours earlier. When the receptionist called to announce Lisa, I paused at first to try to recall the name, since we did not have an appointment. I would have paused regardless of who called unexpectedly.

However, I can't help but feel that there was something more to the incident. In fact, I feel that Mark set me up. I can only imagine what the feelings must be for Mark to see the reaction on unsuspecting faces as they figure out Lisa. Additionally, he explained that he wants to write a book similar to John Howard Griffin's "Black Like Me," where a white man undergoes a temporary skin darkening treatment to experience life as a black man. He wants to legally become Lisa for a year, living as Lisa full-time and then write about what is revealed. He would get a job as Lisa, become a non-sexual friend to Mark's girlfriend and would go throughout the community as Lisa during both day and night. Mark was set to go before a judge the following week to discuss changing his name. I believe that in the few hours between my confirming phone conversation with Mark, and Lisa's appearance in my office, that it was not a whimsical change of plans that came over my guest, but rather a deliberate effort to record reactions as preparation for the book. Still, that does not excuse inappropriate behavior from people in a professional setting.

The third set of emotions is directed at my own reaction. Embarrassment and fear are the two thoughts that I believe were present during the incident. I was partly embarrassed because I already knew what to expect of Lisa's appearance. While she makes a good presentation, Lisa is still a *trompe l' oeil** woman, and I knew that the ridicule being directed at her would soon transfer to me by association. Other times when I am aware of being in the presence of transgender people, it has always been in the safety of gay settings where it's "okay" to pretend. The embarrassment I felt was that I, too, would be obligated to uphold a deception that no one believed.

There is also disappointment directed at my own naiveté, for not realizing that there is no sacred space for those that are different. But it was the fear I felt, and what continues to remain, that has come to define the moment for me. The fear is that even with some legal and social protections for the cultural group that I identify with, specifically the gay, lesbian, bisexual and transgender community, that somehow it is still acceptable for co-workers to mock me, and my community members, even in our presence. The incident was a current reminder of being bullied in junior and senior high school, where I was verbally taunted and physically assaulted. The incident robbed me of the comfort to feel emotionally safe in my place of employment and to truly believe that my co-workers have exceptional manners and compassion for people who are different.

In an attempt to seek closure with my own feelings over this incident, I confronted the staff that I knew participated as a crowd. Only one individual apologized for the actions of the group. I accepted the apology, and, surprisingly, it was liberating and allowed me to release some of the anger I felt at the injustice. As for the others that denied being involved, I take comfort in having at least confronted them. The exchange let them know that everyone who enters the agency, regardless of how he or she is dressed, will be regarded with the respect and dignity everyone deserves.

*(*trompe l' oeil* is a style of painting that means "deceive the eye.")

Reference

D'Emilio, J., & Freedman, E.B. (1997). *Intimate matters: A history of sexuality in America.* Chicago: University of Chicago Press.

John D. Allen is a doctoral student in Educational Leadership at Southern Connecticut State University and the author of *Gay, Lesbian, Bisexual and Transgender People with Developmental Disabilities and Mental Retardation: Stories of the Rainbow Support Group* (2003) by Haworth Press.

Tucson Character Sketches

Francis E. Crowley

'ZOOM, ZOOM'

2/6/12 Monday. Slept like a baby—nice bed. A little air pollution over town today, but still blue sky and sunny. At 7:00 a.m. awakened to a hormonal, teenager's yell, "Torsha!" outside my bedroom window. A beanpoll kid, probably, still in school, letting off his animal cry of maturational changes. Then, the start-up roar and growl of a souped-up teen machine ready for the racing wars.

I like it: the deep seclusion, the cactus wren boot in plain sight of daily life. Eight-year-old Sergio and his tiny sister, four, roam the courtyard on his motorized, souped-up, miniature hot-wheels with battery slung under the long frame. He's slowly getting initiated into the outside roar and sweat of the streets—so gradually, subliminally and gently, even, within the protected, enclosed compound, his happy playground.

I speak a few words of greeting in Russian to Sergio each year I return to Tucson. At first he looks puzzled: "WHAT?!"; no smile. *"Zdravstvoite, zdravstvoite; shto novova!"* (Hello, hello; what's new?) I give the sweeping hand gesture with it; and, then, the light, a little sunshine of recognition through the cloud of confusion. He chuckles, and quickly off he goes round the track. He's taller, but his older sister is too, a full head and a half and another beanpole in the making. What a joy to see them grow like my grandson, Nathan, age 14, a skinny stingbean with a pumpkin smile. I'm back.

"LIFE IS, INDEED, IMPROVIZATION"

Sasha caught my ear first and then my eye. As I walked down 4th Ave. to Goodwill, I heard the old, happy sound of accordian, and I plunked some change in his open case.

When I came out with my bag of socks, Sasha was resting, so I put another dollar in his tin cup.

He smiled.

"I love that sound," I said; "it brings back sweet memories."

I walked on, and when I reached the Co-op, he came abreast and nodded.

"I decided to play up here for a while."

I watched him settle; soon a gypsy melody switched to Appalachian Mountain hillbilly. I sat down, and I could feel the strong morning sunshine through my jeans. Across the street a new Tattoo Parlor was opening next door to Cafe Passe'. A sturdy, long-haired fellow with desert brown jeans climbed up and down the tall ladder; so nice to watch him stretch and flex with the loud drill and new sign, "BLACK ROSE TATTOO." Careful, well-heeled tourists stepped among the feeding pigeons on the bread crumbs I had tossed, and the carefree, young co-op crowd—always gorgeous in funky clothes—casually hooked up bicycles and chatted. Kids in strollers, a cantankerous homeless fellow and an occasional man in a dark business suit wander by.

Sasha is a beanpole with a fat accordian strapped to his middle; a pregnant eel and sweet grateful smile on long legs. I love powerfully built men; tall and skinny, too, who are lean and fluid in movement. He's playing New Orleans Jazz now, collecting some more change. I rouse myself from this dreamy meditation on love and music and walk into the Co-op for a sandwich. It's busy; stock clerks bustling about, replenishing vegetable bins and customers getting cold drinks. A pee break and I'm back outside in the shade by the door. Sasha has finished playing and enters the Co-op. I wait and catch him when he comes out, quickly offering him half a turkey and avocado sandwich.

He sits right down at my table and looks me in the eye:

"Got half?"

"Yeah, here," I offer.

He places his tin cup top the accordian case, sits back and turns to the fellows next table; he shakes hands with Ira and Brock who are in their prime 20's, "You are the second person today I've met named 'Ira' and I've never heard it before."

Sasha bends down and greets their pooches, too, "Coot" and "Restful" who wander, circle and come back. They greet me with a sniff and tail shake. Ira, dirty-blond, shoulder-length hair and light blue eyes, gets up and pours water for Coot out of a five-gallon, metal bucket. I shake hands heartily with Ira and Brock, and we relax in easy drifter friendship, offering to share what we have: a bag of food and Ginger Beer. As the dogs settle in the shade, Sasha finishes his sandwich and pulls out a pack of rice cakes; the top one has dust and black flakes covering it. All three fellows call themselves "train-musicians," as they ride box cars from state to state. They migrate to music venues and festivals, mostly jazz and modern fusion, planting some roots in spare rooms at friends' places across the continent. Sasha tells me he has a commune home in Virginia, ala the 70's back-to-the-land-Vermont-style roost, where he retreats in the Spring to plant, cultivate and harvest.

"It feels wonderful to watch vegetables grow," I interject.

"...and to harvest and eat," he adds. He still looks famished to me. He offers to share his large, fruit-nut yogurt with Ira and Brock. They pull out their own from the big bag. Sasha tells me that he'll spend this entire month here playing up and down 4th Ave.: days and evenings around 6:00 p.m. I think to myself that he must relish the change, that contrast to Winter that the Southwest affords, along with the nomadic migration from the East, as I do.

"I bought a ticket for this Friday to a concert at the Congress Hotel!" he says.

"What band," Ira asks.

"Jazz ensemble that I follow; I'm learning new moves from them. Last fall they were in Phoenix."

Mostly, he's solo. He tells me that the accordian goes with most instruments, in answer to my question, "...but not all."

Why jazz? I'm thinking that it goes with the lifestyle: easy, drifting, changeable; after all, life is improvization! Tonight, after playing 4th Ave., Sasha says he's catching a freight to El Paso, and, then, back in the morning to Tucson. Ira and Brock and the pooches have just come in from Yuma today, they say, with no trouble from the heat sensors now installed in railroad boxcars to detect stow-a-ways, but they were chased away earlier from the grounds of the Annual Gem and Mineral Show downtown by Tucson's Finest with the warning that the dogs would be arrested.

"And we don't have the money to get them back," Ira adds, "so we left...

...and we're heading East tonight to New Orleans."

I notice now that Ira has a sweet, sweaty odor combining a cloudy scent of male feromones, unwashed armpits and slept-in soiled clothes. He's a gentle hunk; even white teeth shine through.

Sasha trembles slightly at rest, I notice, while holding his drink. He seems so at ease with our conversations but shakes a little from time to time. I'm wondering if it's lack of protein nutritious food or whether he's coming down off something; I don't know. He's a little jumpy, too, moving frequently to play different spots up and down the Ave., but that may just be for better coinage and cover. After 20 minutes or so with us, he packs his unopened yogurt, looks at me with a smile and says, "...for later...and thank you for the sandwich."

"Where you headed now," Ira asks.

"Back down to the tracks to a spot I know to rest and hang for a while."

Sasha gathers his cup and accordian. We shake hands warmly.

"Catch you here this weekend," I say.

"The Muse of Mexico"

Ahhh, creative well-being! Tucson does it for street musicians and me in February and for all the happy denizens of Fourth Ave. in their funky shops.

A photo show of Frida Kahlo at the TAM: clearly I feel her charismatic power, her great animal magnetism; I see her stunning facial beauty in various flesh tones captured by Nickolas Muray. Her creative ecstasy is shining in her eyes in one close-up; her deep affection for her lover Muray is reflected in another as she stares straight into the lens. Ironically, her persona, as cult figure for us in the late 20th Century, has surpassed our recognition of her as artist and painter in her own right. She was the thoroughly modern woman before anyone else; now for painters and poets she is MUSE.

At the Tucson Art Museum there are 50 art photographs of Frida; most are color with delicate shadings of flesh tones. All were taken between 1938 and 1941, although Muray continued to photograph her until 1948. Many show her in iconic poses, as she is dressed in red and magenta regional, native folk costumes and halo-headdress, which is her signature look. I love her range: lesbian queen; spiritual, suffering virgin; magnificently arrayed earth mother; lover; wife; mostly, MUSE. In some I see her as Madonna in ritual, elaborate, native dress; in black and white she is a peasant goddess and icon for the poor, the lame, the abused, the injured and disfigured. She lived all these roles for sure, and now she reigns in her consummate role in the new century as "post-post-modern" Muse. Which is to say that the down side of this evolution is the commercial replication of a license-plate lovely face on mugs, banners, books, etc.

Frida was German Jew on her father's emigre side and Spanish/Mexican on her mother's. She, herself, as lovingly photographed by Muray, her long-time lover, has that "Mona Lisa smile" when pictured together with Diego Rivera, her husband (x2), twice married. It's a "sadder but wiser" look she has in these black and white, casual and almost candid shots with Diego. Some of these images show an expression that is seductive and sad; others with her distinctive "unibrow" elevate her look of underlying vulnerability from prior physical injury. She has said quippingly that she has met two disasters in her life: one was permanent disability from being struck by a streetcar and the other was Diego Rivera.

As an artist, she was a "surrealist" painter of stunning originality, although she discounted the label:

"...I don't paint my dreams; I paint the reality of my life." Picasso, Miro, et al., admired her work, liked her style, talked about her influence. In the autumn of 1938 she left Diego to open a successful solo show of her paintings in New York at the JULIEN LEVY Gallery; it was during this visit that Muray took many photographs of her. She moved on later that fall and winter to Paris at Breton's invitation for another show and exhibit. Marcel Duchamp came to the rescue, after Breton's lack of follow-through in planning and securing a gallery, and the show was a big draw and success. In New York she had sold over half her paintings. She returned to Mexico in 1939 depressed from the harsh Parisian winter and the gathering signs of impending war; moreover, she missed her home in Mexico. She then painted one of her most famous successes: "The Two Fridas." Most of her work is self-portrait, and in this painting she shows two full-length images facing front: one represents herself with Diego's love and the other shows her bereft.

Always, always she appears in life as in art in full-length elaborate dress which allowed her to cover her deformity. What an inspiration she is and what an inspired show of her life in the photography of Nickolas Muray!!

'THE MEANEST GUY IN TOWN'
#4 Tucson Character Sketches
(2/2/12 first full day in Tucson)

Outside Coronado Courtyard Apts., around 10:30 a.m. on my way to the bus stop at Speedway "mad dog" appears in front of me with a buddy. Slowly, he forms a look of a recognition and cautiously breaks into a smile. I shout his name, and he throws a bear hug at me. Pure synchronicity and delight. I had wondered if he was still breathing, still in the neighborhood?

Ahhh, the gift of the freedom to love and be loved: my cousin, Adele, had written to me the week before a sentence of such emotional valence that I carried it in my heart on the trip to Tucson.

"You are fortunate to have so many to love and who love you!"

I take that deep inside, when I hear it, as I never had that full understanding as a child, however true; later, as a coming-out-gay-man-married-with-children in my 30's, I struggled with it. A couple more bear hugs from "mad dog," and his buddy asks:

"Do you know each other!?"

I chuckled, "Yeah, for the five years I've been coming here winters. I met John..."

"...that's his real name, you know..."

"Yeah, I met John outside the Walgreen's store up there at the corner. He was giving out his faces on the back of envelopes. I loved his drawings and characters: some with teeth missing like him."

Mad Dog John beams with my praise, "He's a poet! Writes about me!!" John puffs out his chest, looks less beaten and downtrodden.

"I wrote a poem about John," I tell his buddy.

"We're heading up to St. Vincent de Paul's Thrift Store for clothes," the buddy says.

"I know the place well, myself," I say. "Here's $7.00," I offer the buddy. John radiates his magnetism and pride, showing me his sore left hand.

"I took on three young toughs last week." John struts his bravado; "it's swollen."

Actually, John has bruised knuckles and a broken left hand from fighting street thugs for money under the bridge; it's Tucson's homeless man's fight club. Spectators bet on John, and he never disappoints. He wears multiple layers of torn, ragged, filthy clothes. We hug, again, and I put my wallet in my back pocket. John is a tortured ghost of himself today: he's lost his concentration, his looks from five years ago when his girlfriend was his companion; his stooped posture, long graying hair and puffy face camouflage his ferocious nature and "brick shithouse build." I'd NEVER confront this man in an alley.

Today, he's a bit wobbly and unsteady on his feet, strung out on street living, weak from no food (he drinks his food), no bed, no home, but always with a friend, a companion, and always, always with a joyful 'HELLO!' for me. He's clearly aged 10 normal years in his face from the last five street years.

"See you fellows later!" I say, walking on to Walgreens up Craycroft.

"Where will you be?" asks the buddy, "...in an hour or so?"

"I'll catch you later up there," I say, walking on, hoping that the friend will buy clothes with $7.00.

Two days later around noon, I finally get moving to catch the bus on Speedway. No sign of "Mad Dog," on Craycroft, but as I approach the bus-waiting-bench and cover, I see two figures sitting there with a shopping cart. It doesn't look at all like John and his friend at first; other passengers are milling around. I slowly approach the bench, and it takes John a while to recognize me. I look twice to make sure it is John under the pullover hood; he looks like a shrunken, old man at a little distance. I notice that the cart is filled with bedding up to the brim. John rises slowly for a hug; we embrace. He's happy to see me. Oooops, I think to myself, I once caught scabies holding babies in Haiti. I hope John doesn't have lice. His smell is overpowering. He's drying his clothes, still on him, in the strong sun. The temps have dropped into the 30's!

"I slept in the drainpipe. It rained."

The old growling laugh and twinkle come out.

"I drank so I could get back to sleep. I kicked heroin, crack-cocaine, pills, all of it. I need drink to sleep."

"Wow!" I say.

"I'm 55!" John says with pride, signaling the accomplishment of still being alive.

"But you have to eat to stay alive," I add.

The bus arrives, and I give John a quick $5.00.

"Bring me your book!" he yells as I step on the bus, "... and the copies of poems about me! I lost mine."

"O.K., I'll get it," I say, turning back to wave. I look out the bus window as I walk down the center aisle, and I see John standing and waving with both arms through the tinted glass.

The next afternoon I catch the #9—"Sabino Canyon"—bus from downtown on my way home instead of the #4 "Harrison Ave." so that I can shop at Safeway at Grant and Craycroft for some supper. It's a long block home to Pima, and my arms are full with groceries. It's now about 4:00 p.m. As I approach the corner of Pima and Craycroft, I notice two bodies sprawled on the sidewalk behind the bus-bench, half-sitting. It, again, doesn't look like John. About 50 feet from them I notice that a stooped-over, homeless man gets up and walks towards me and the back alley; it is John, but he doesn't recognize me at all and passes. As I come abreast of his friend, I see an open pint of Vodka half-empty; he doesn't look up and I continue home. I feel a little guilty and sad that, maybe, the money didn't go for food or clothes. At least I have the memory of John's radiant face.

Selected Poems

Barbara Peabody

AVE MARIA

I have an old tape
Of my son, Peter, singing
A practice tape, scales and exercises
He had a cold, was cranky
Annoyed and impatient
with himself
I listened to it once
A week after he died
Exploded with tears
Salty tears that choked
I could not listen again.

He sang with his chorus
At a high school competition
The judge asked
Who has the chocolate voice?
Everyone looked at Peter
Peter of the chocolate voice
That melted and streamed
From his mouth
And down his shirt
Upsetting the balance
Of the chorus.

He sang for us just once
Schubert's *Ave Maria*
At Christmas, home from New York
Shimmering overtones spangled the room
My spine tingled
My hair stood on end
My eyes filled
I hid my tears
He never knew
That his voice made me cry.

MARTIN

Martin called the Hemlock Society
He was a perfectionist.

Funny little man
Fortyish, maybe thirty-eight
Gray, intelligent eyes
Behind thick-lensed granny glasses
Beige pork pie hat
Squashed atop thinning hair
Red suspenders kept khaki trousers
From obeying gravity
Protected his frailty from pity.

He'd been a waiter in a big Las Vegas hotel
Told me about a wedding there
Where the bridesmaids were naked waist up
Waited till I laughed, then joined me
He always told jokes straight-faced
Funny stories with wry twists
Vignettes of the crazy life in Vegas
Always waited, serious, till I laughed
As if to be sure it was funny.

What did your mother say when you told her
You had AIDS? I asked once
She dropped dead the next day, he said
I laughed cruelly, thinking it was another joke
Then apologized when he didn't laugh
You're all alone, then, I said
He nodded, eyes sad behind
His thick-lensed granny glasses.

The Hemlock Society told him
Take these three drugs, then
Tape a plastic bag tight around your neck
Being a perfectionist
Martin followed instructions
To the letter.

PETER PAN

Wild slashes of color
Red, yellow, lime, cobalt blue, black
Fill the paper, edge to edge
Jagged edges cut into each other
A small, dark figure at the top
In a field of white
"That's me," he pointed with his brush
"All alone. Lonely."

Lonely Michael
Slim, curly black hair, dancing eyes
Charming, wry, restless
Bouncy stride in his Reeboks
Always at a bar
Drinking
Doing drugs
Doing sex
Masking
The black gape inside
That booze, drugs and sex
Couldn't fill.

Peter Pan died
Of AIDS
Alone, in the hospice
The Reebocks quiet
Beneath his bed
Longings forgotten
Desires stilled
Peaceful
Unsatisfied.

SWEET WILLIAM

Sweet William, I called him
An ethereal wisp of a man
An idealist, a dreamer
Sparse, graying beard, thin, eyeglasses
Soft gray eyes, shy grin
Twisted and bent in constant pain
Syphilitic arthritis
Dying of AIDS.

His big paintings were brilliant, abstract
Slashes and puddles of color
Intersecting, writhing
Orange, cobalt blue, yellow, red, purple
Bold affirmations of life
And his love of art
No figures, no images
Always bordered, closed in
Like his life.

His knees wobbled and shook in pain
"Sit down, William," I urged
I wanted him to ration his energy
I wanted him to paint forever
"No," smiling sweetly
"I paint better standing
Makes me forget the pain."
I said no more.

Infections leaked into his brain
Maybe syphilis, the virus, maybe other infections
Maybe all the above
And his paintings slowed down, shrunk in size
Fantasy shapes melted into horizontal lines
Brilliant color dissolved into grays
Pale streaks
Shapeless clouds
As life faded away
Quickly, silently.

His mother came near the end
A small, colorless woman who cleaned and packed
After he died
Smiled, said little
Gave me paintings William wanted me to have
And his sister came then, wiry and electric
Dancing dervishly around the apartment
"I can feel William's spirit everywhere!"
Flinging her arms out, long hair flying
I was angry she hadn't come when he needed her
He wouldn't have begged her to come and so
She waited till he died
A sad, neat package of bones
Wrapped in his soft cloud of dementia.

Sweet William
Your paintings hang on my walls
Splatter their color on my life
Shine brightly in daytime sun
Glow in the night
You wanted me to remember the best of you.

THE PARTY

I saw them in the eighties
On the streets of Greenwich Village
Shuffle-footed, emaciated
Gray splinters of young men
Awkward with canes
Eyes with a death-knowledge
Peculiar to ancients
Blank with dementia
Skin polka-dotted brown
Men who'd danced like dervishes
In the bars and bathhouses
Only yesterday.

Still they danced
Had sex
Took drugs
Laid out buffet-style
On coffee tables
Shared needles
At parties
Or in misty alleys
While a studded cannonball
Slaughtered white cells
Slow
stealthy.

Not a disease
Of polluted water
Not cholera, Ebola
Diphtheria or typhus
But a quiet plague
That took root
In the red blood of youth
And made the act of love
An act of death.

THE SUNDAY MORNING GOLDEN HILLS BREAKFAST CLUB

My eyes sting
I feel the old burn of grief
The hot burn beneath my sternum
I must run away again
Back to the desert
I push my coffee mug away
Grab my purse
Wisp a slow goodby kiss
To my beloved ghosts.
I peer through the dusty windows
Of the Golden Hills Coffee Shop
It's still here, twenty-five years later
I shade the dust-mottled glass with my hand
See the low counter on the right
Scattered chrome and formica tables in the center
Tan vinyl booths looking out at Avenue B
Watch the same grumpy-faced waitress
Zigzag slowly between tables.

My eyes veer to the big corner booth on the left
I see us all sitting there, Tom and Johnny
Michael, Chris, Lana sometimes Joe, myself
Membership involves Golden Hills residence
And an HIV diagnosis
I twist open the tarnished bronze handle, step inside
The air is thick with years of doughy pancakes
And ebony coffee
I slide into the empty booth with care
I don't want to disturb my ghosts.

*   *   *

"You're always late," complains Lana, exhaling smoke
At ninety pounds, she looks like a model, blond ponytail swinging
She's pulled herself out of bed and will rush home to bed
Drugged with sugar, caffeine, nicotine
Better than heroin or cocaine or sex, anything
That blotted out her self-disgust
I look around the table, everyone's here today
TomandJohnny so close they're called by one name
Michael, whose wealthy mother sends money to keep him here

Because his addictions break her heart
And Joe, his partner, HIV-positive but healthy
Fair Chris, his sardonic humor masking the pain of family rejection
He jokes about the gay cowboys whom he used to fool around with
In the parkinglot of a small-town Wyoming bar
And laughs, visualizing the huge painting over his family's mantel
Of his rainbowed ascension to heaven
He painted it on my front porch last week
It is to hang above the urn of his ashes
As directed in his will.

We meet every Sunday morning
Either here or at my house for waffles
I, their art therapist and neighbor
Sometimes a substitute mother
The only one without HIV
And they, my students
Though they are my teachers
And their uninhibited art humbles me
Every new pain or fever reminds them
Of fast-eroding immune systems
Their fears bleed on to paper in brilliant color
But Sunday mornings they only laugh.

Today, they giggle at the illicit romance of two of the AIDS clinicians
No secret now, since someone spotted them smooching in the alley
They roar at the list Lana's sister has sent
Of exotic herbs, brews, diets and potions
Bizarre compounds of hope and weeds
Snort at the foul-tasting wheatgrass elixir a clinic doctor
Is convinced will kill the virus
He comes to your house, blender in hand
They think he's infected, too
They stuff themselves with pancakes and coffee
The smokers snicker at the threat of lung cancer
And inhale, exhale, tap the butts
And fill the ashtrays.

*　　　　*　　　　*

The sad-faced waitress shuffles over to my table
Refills my coffee, shuffles away
Hospitality is still not her strong point
I wonder if she'd known her Sunday guests years ago
All had "the AIDS" and how had she felt about that?
The jacaranda trees are blooming on Avenue B
Tom always admired their lavender snow in April
My eyes drift around the table
TomandJohnny, Michael, Chris, Lana, sometimes Joe.

*   *   *

Johnny died first, Tom and I were with him
Stroking his forehead, turning him, murmuring
I left San Diego before the other deaths
Fled from AIDS and its wreckage
Tom went back to work at a travel agency
Got a new partner, danced across the world on cruise ships
Died ten years later, a longtime survivor
Michael went into hospice, only his brother came
Lana's mother and sister came from Los Angeles and Utah
Found a bigger apartment and moved in with her
But she lived longer than expected, they had to leave
Before her death or lose their jobs
She died in the AIDS hospice, alone
Chris' parents came and left before his death
His Army officer father unforgiving
His mother conflicted
I wonder if the urn is on their mantel
The painting above it
I lost track of Joe, surely he has died.

My eyes sting
I feel the familiar burn of grief
The hot ache beneath my sternum
I must run away again
Back to the desert
I push my coffee mug aside
Grab my purse
Wisp a slow goodby kiss
To my beloved ghosts.

Barbara Peabody. I live in Tucson, Arizona, where I am a professional artist, digital photographer and writer of poetry and short stories. I write about the people and places in my life; the comical absurdities of the human race, especially politicians, and odd fantasies I dream up. I attend Ken Lamberton's weekly writing group at the Poetry Center of the University of Arizona, where I inflict my latest literary efforts on my patient and tolerant colleagues.

Section Four

War and Human History

Emily Hears the War

Stephen Vincent Kobasa

(for Clare and Rachel)

The planes curve in the sky
Over Emily Dickinson's grave,
Shadowing toward Iraq,
Their dark noise trundling
Behind them like a hunchbacked servant.

Snow fingers the headstone's
Curt explanation—
"Called Back."
Death a mother's voice
Cutting across the field

She envied the monuments
To her own day's slaughter.
Now an ashamed ghost,
Her hidden life
Distant as ours from
The sound of dying.

Without irony,
For once clear with the horror,
Her desperate questions hanging
Each mangled body on a word.

Behind the closed curtains
Of what was her room
The sound of breaking glass,
Flowers trampled underfoot.

No gingerbread basket dangles
From the scaffold of her hands
For the children
Dancing below.

January–April, 2003

Stephen Vincent Kobasa is an activist, poet, and contributing writer to the *New Haven Advocate* and the arts web journal *Big, Red and Shiny*.

The Story of a Union Soldier

Anna-Maria Lee

This is the story of Gottlieb Schnepf who was a Union soldier in the American Civil War. It is also the story of a human being who served his country and died an unspeakable death in a Confederate prison camp. It is also, sadly enough, the story of thousands of Americans who died fighting for all of our freedoms.

Courtesy of NARA.

The journey begins with a German farmer from Long Island, New York who enlisted in the Union Army on September 17th, 1862 to fight in Lincoln's Army. He would become part of company B, the 159th Regiment from New York and his journey to his own death would begin. Sadly, he would leave behind his wife named Margaret and his baby named Martin. Gottlieb was 36 years old and an immigrant from Boekingen, Germany. He arrived in New York City around the 1840's. Although he was among the older volunteers, his age was by no means unusual. President Lincoln needed more soldiers. The war was going bad for the Union, and more and more men were being asked to save the Union. Did he join for honor, for duty, or even the sign-up pay which was offered then, one cannot say. What is fact is he did sign-up and he did leave his family to fight in battles. Thousands of men along with Gottlieb would now start a new and deadly chapter in their lives. They would suffer along with their families and friends.

Gottlieb was mustered on November 1st, 1862 and joined the Union Army to begin his training. Things started out badly for his Company. The government issued them rifles which did not work and incomplete supplies in terms of uniforms, boots, and other needed items. His company would say farewell to New York on December 4th, 1862, to leave for New Orleans, Louisiana. They would arrive thirteen days later in Baton Rouge, Louisiana, where the main troops were gathering for this area. Army life was tough and there were severe physical hardships for the soldiers. They were fed food which was not always healthy and their living conditions consisted of poorly equipped tents setup wherever they were. Their blankets were of poor quality, their clothing would fall apart, and their weapons and ammunition did not always work. They would learn quickly soldiering was far from being glorious.

Gottlieb stayed in Baton Rouge until March 18th, 1863, and then participated in the Teche Campaign from April 11th to April 20th, 1863. After fighting battles in this campaign his company was ordered to move to Irish Bend, Louisiana on April 14th where they fought again against the Confederate Army. Over 5,000 Union troops fought in this battle and many were captured. The next time we hear of Gottlieb and his regiment is on July 17th, 1864 when they are returned to Baton Rouge. Their next mission would take them to Bermuda Hundred, Virginia where the regiment arrived on July 25th, 1864. Another battle would take place and his company would lose ten more soldiers to the battle.

Things began to look better for the Union with the next campaign. It was critical to force Confederate General Jubal Early out of the Shenandoah Valley in Virginia. This valley was made up of rich farmland which supplied much of the Virginia Army. Without controlling this important farmland, the Confederate forces could not feed their troops. The Union Army and President Lincoln who soon had to run for re-election needed to gain back this territory badly. The President needed a victory for the Union. The Union Army needed to cut off the enemy's food supply. On September 14th, 1864, the Union Army attacked the Confederates at Winchester, Virginia. General Early with his 16,000 men faced General Sheridan with his 40,000 men. Gottlieb Schnepf and his regiment were part of Sheridan's army. The Confederates opened deadly fire on the Union troops. Soon, the 159th would lose 75 more soldiers during the battle. It would end with General Early being forced to withdraw. On September 22nd, the battle of Fishers Hill took place and would be another Union victory. The Union Army was ecstatic. They would soon not be. After Fishers Hill came the battle of Cedar Creek. Here Gottlieb Schnepf's life would change forever for the worse.

General Early surprised the Union force during an early morning raid. His troops were covered by a low line of mist and he would force the Union troops to break and retreat. It is hard to imagine the amount of suffering and blood which was spilled during this Confederate sneak attack. Over 8,000 men died within an hour or two from the start of the battle. The Union alone lost over 5,000 men. The 159th which was on the front line

which was totally taken by surprise. Two of their men were killed immediately, ten were wounded badly, and five were captured by the Confederates. Private Gottlieb Schnepf was one of the five captured during this battle. The rest of his life would consist of being marched, dragged and beaten from one prison camp to another in the South.

It is hard to say exactly where and when he was taken, since various documents state that he died on three different dates in three different Southern prison camps. Prison camps such as Libby, Salisbury, and Andersionville, were "hell holes" for suffering and death. The most likely scenario is that he was taken to Andersonville camp following his capture at Cedar Creek. He was then taken to Libby and Salisbury Camps at later dates.

Union Captain Willard Glazier, who was also a prisoner described these camps as places of "pain and perfect horror". At Andersonville alone, over 14,000 prisoners died in just 14 months. At Salisbury Camp where Gottlieb would die over 12,000 Union soldiers would be starved to death and then thrown deep dug dirt trenches, each over 240 feet long. The men have no shelters, hardly any clothes, and ate diseased food and drank from water which was polluted from human waste. Vermin such as lice were everywhere. Private Gottlieb Schnepf and the thousands of other prisoners were unable to bathe in clean water or receive anything that might make their life habitable. In fact, Confederate soldiers would charge the prisoners 20 cents a person to have a small amount of clean water for their needs with winter weather upon them, the prisoners would dig holes in the ground to live in. Disease, cold, and beatings, would kill off many of the Union soldiers. Even the hospital at the camps were hellish. Men were left to die on the dirt floors without any help from Confederate doctors. Those who did not die were reduced to mere skin and bones. These poor human souls were so desperate that they would forage through human excrement hoping to find undigested food to eat. Men would take food from the ground and drink from gooey, putrid, human wastewater filled with maggots. The stench of filth and death could be smelled from miles around each of these camps. Gottlieb and his fellow soldiers were forced to live and die in cesspools created by a Confederate Government which neither had the will nor the money to prevent.

Prisoners who survived these camps told of how millions of mosquitoes would feasts upon the dying bodies of these poor soldiers. If conditions were not bad enough as described, the men also faced what was called "dead-line" boundaries which they were not allowed to go beyond. Young and immature guards were allowed to shoot anyone close to these lines. Malaria fever, typhoid, gangrene, diarrhea and starvation, were the main causes of death. Starvation of the prisoners for days was also another method of punishment.

Everyday was a struggle not to go mad. There was no exercise or recreation of any kind. For a macabre form of entertainment prisoners would "hunt" for lice and see if they were strong enough to squash them. This is how weak they were because of the conditions they lived in.

The records show that Gottlieb died on December 27, 1864, at Salisbury prison camp in North Carolina from disease and starvation. Before he died he probably was given one last bit of horrible treatment by the Confederates. It was

their practice to give dying men a little card which said "Good News You Are Being Sent Home." Another trick of false hope and certainly the final insult one human being can play on another. Once dead, Gottlieb and fellow soldiers were taken out of the hospital and thrown in a large trench to be covered when it was filled up with other bodies.

And so, Private Gottlieb Schnepf's journey through hell would end. His wife and his child, Martin would be told by the Army that he died a prisoner of the Confederate Government. They were also told his body would forever remain in an unmarked grave in North Carolina along with thousands of other heroes. For over 141 years, this soldier would not receive an official thank you from the United States Government until his great, great grandson wrote the Department Of The Army to right this wrong. On January 6, 2005, Chester H. Schnepf received a letter awarding Private Gottlieb Schnepf the Civil War Campaign Medal. The letter stated, "We appreciate the late Mr. Schnepf's faithful and dedicated service to our nation."

May his soul and the souls countless other patriots rest in peace. And may we never forget their sacrifices for our freedoms.

Letter Written by Gottlieb Schnepf

A translated letter written by Gottlieb Schnepf to his wife and child. Original was written in German.

Thibodaux, December 12, 1863.

Dear mother and Martin:

The love of my heart is extra strong for you at this time, near Christmas and the coming New Year. So I want you, my dearest wife, to receive my very best wishes. The past year for me was one of the longest, and was filled with sorrow, suffering and endless dangers. The history books will tell coming generations about it, as they see it, how their fathers fought under the banner of the Union, not knowing when a bullet would end their life. –God held his hand over my life through all the dangers. Many dear comrades died with the words on their lips: "For the Union." Nobody knows, how many more will lose their life.

Dear wife, thank God that you and I are still alive. Whatever the New Year will bring, let us carry on, like Jesus did. He will be with us and will change our suffering into joy. This joy will be endless until death shall part us. –Should I, however, not return from this war, it is my wish, that you and Martin live on for many years, healthy and happy. Educate Martin in the fear of the Lord, so that in your life you will have one who takes care of you.

I hope you received my picture and enjoyed it. Thank you also for sending a picture of both of you. With this hope I will close this letter, wishing both of you once more a happy New Year, health, good luck and soon a reunion with you. Farewell and answer soon.

Greetings to you and Martin.
Your loving husband

Gottlieb Schnepf

Many greetings to Mr. Stolz and Schuchmann and children.
Many greetings to Floh and Andreas, Gabriel and Catharina and also to Michael Hoffman.

Translated by John Silvester
January 1975.

Stooping to your ear hear me and understand
I know of your sleep from past memory of living
Hear me, listen — I am your blood
I am the thing on your door step of knowing
You are me as I was your father and his father and his
Father before (my son) cosmic losses upon losses I
Suffered and suffer from endless lands of death time served up by the
Southern Death Camp
Where my body was tossed twisted among other endless twisted
Union just dead.
Now listen to me in your sleep!
Name me to my nameless grave for once did I have breath of air
And feel love of human touch. Name me to my nameless grave
I am the thing on your door step I am your blood
End this oh so empty madness Tell my story
And say it loudly so all the dead know I am released!
Here lies the dust of a man named
Pvt. Gottlieb Schnepf
Give him peace for he has traveled far and suffered much
Stooping to your ear hear me now and understand!

Dec. 1864.
G.S.

PA0271
Sixth Plate Ambrotype Portrait of Gottlieb Schnopf, 159th New York Infantry, wearing a great coat and seated in an arm chair

Warzone Dispatches: First-Hand Accounts of Iraq and Afghanistan, Summer of 2006

Daniel W. Smith

Forward:

Daniel Smith travels to places of violent conflict and extreme poverty to document its effects with photography and writing. His primary focus has been on Iraq and Haiti, and his photography exhibitions have the duel purpose of education about the places he goes, and fundraising for the people he meets there. He has begun on this, his fifth trip to Iraq, to also bring medical equipment to clinics and hospitals in need. Preferring to travel alone and without press crews or armed escorts, he would be best described as "roving" versus "embedded". This approach is very important to him, and direct contact and trust in the people he meets is essential to his process.

-Part Two: Afghanistan-
Warlords, Drugs, and the Taliban
An Update

Afghanistan hasn't been in the news much in the past year. Sure, rioting in downtown Kabul might get mentioned every once in a while, and one can sometimes find stories about the US military (often right out of the Pentagon's press releases), but for the most part, it's surprising how little information gets to us.

The last time there was mass coverage of Afghanistan was nearly a year ago in September, when the election was pronounced a resounding success. This happened in Iraq as well, but we've continued to hear other things about Iraq. The impression given of Afghanistan is that things are running smoothly, burqas are a thing of the past, and that a 'Mission accomplished' sign could be tacked on the country.

Well, the Taliban never left, and their control over many parts of the country is growing. Security is on a downward spiral. Over the past few months, 'Operation Mountain Thrust', (an offensive of US and Afghani forces) has met with mixed reviews so far, and has served to disperse AGEs (Anti Government Elements) from their traditional turf in the South and the East, into provinces that have been relatively safe until now.

Women's rights (and human rights in general) are still in an abysmal state, girls' schools are still being bombed, and there are enough landmines and unexploded ordnance waiting to be stepped on that amputees will be a common sight on the rubble-lined streets of Kabul into the next century.

The Cabinet recently approved reinstating *The Department for the Promotion of Virtue and the Discouragement of Vice*, which was famously active under the Taliban. Much of the support has come from conservative religious leaders that many in Afghanistan are concerned may want to steer the country toward the old days. Support is also fueled by the influx of liquor, pornography, and prostitution, largely introduced by the presence of foreign soldiers and workers. Anti-foreigner sentiment is understandably growing, and people such as aid workers, once fairly safe, are now being killed.

Getting rid of regional warlords in Afghanistan has always been a big part of the rhetoric of the United States government. In its invasion, however, the US made alliances with and supported warlords who would cooperate with them and do the ground fighting. This arguably strengthened much of the system that existed before the Taliban took over.

At controlling the warlords, president Karzai has proven to be ineffectual at best, and in fact, needs to work with them in many areas. Widespread corruption guarantees their continued influence.

This brings up the one business that is booming in Afghanistan (other than contracts for foreign corporations, just like in Iraq), and that is drugs. Despite all the money and effort put into eradicating the poppy fields and the drug runners, every season since the ouster of the Taliban has been a record-setting crop of opium and heroin producing plants. The shipment of flour from aid organizations only serves to drive down the price of wheat, giving even less of a reason for the poor Afghani farmer to grow anything other than poppies.

This pumps money directly into the warlord's pockets. Some of these warlords support the Taliban, and some will just increase their bribes to government officials, allowing next season to be yet another record-breaking bumper crop.

Looking out the window as my plane lands in Kabul International Airport (the airport code is KIA . . . really), I am happy to see that, since my last visit in 2002, they've removed the wreckage of shot-down planes from the sides of the runway.

To be fair, there are new roads, buildings, and other signs of progress, but there is not much to suggest that it is sustainable. In the road being laid in Afghanistan are many potholes that are too big to have been caused by anything but mortars.

The Children of Afghanistan
Bearing the Brunt of War

The first time I went to Afghanistan, I brought little else than my camera and an open mind. It was 2002, and was my first visit to an area of real conflict. I spent several days walking around Kabul or Jalalabad, learning how to function in such a place, and how to take it all in.

I remember being amazed at the smiling children in every neighborhood I walked through. They had known only a life of war and poverty, but they acted just like I did when I was a kid, though they might've been climbing on destroyed tanks near a minefield instead of on swings in a playground.

My return to Afghanistan this summer has offered opportunities to meet children in more intimate settings. I was working for a disability organization called Handicap International, documenting their admirable efforts with photography. Much of the time, I traveled around to different programs supported by them.

In medical clinics, in schools for the deaf, the blind, and the physically disabled, and in homes, I met many children from the country's most vulnerable populations. Of course, in a place like Afghanistan, everyone is vulnerable to the forces of war, but children always bear an unfair percentage of the horrors. Everywhere I went, though, I was still greeted with the same friendly, interested smiles I'd been intrigued by, four years earlier.

Children are the most open and accepting members of any society. It's a shame that in places where life is tough, they aren't spared its toughness.

Not only do land mines blow off children's legs routinely, there are many other dangers that befall Afghanistan's children that parents in America don't have to worry about - polio, cholera, typhoid, meningitis, hemorrhagic fever, leishmaniasis, and the list goes on and on. In the first year of life, over one in ten children die. By age five, over twenty-five percent are dead.

Of those that survive, huge numbers are in some way disabled, and I met countless children with missing limbs, or who had other obvious lifelong problems. It can take some getting used to, seeing a hydrocephalic child with a grotesquely large head (and resulting brain damage) that an operation, routine in developed countries, could've completely alleviated.

In a dark, unsanitary room, I saw an infant who had been severely burned with kerosene when her mother tried to fill an unsafe container with cooking fuel. Her older sister, about eight years old, was burned too, but not as badly, and had bandages stretched over her neck, shoulder, chest, and part of her face. A yellow and brown headscarf was wrapped on top of her head. She often sat with her little sister (who had almost no chance of surviving), but she would surprise me by darting around the room unexpectedly, and I kept seeing her peering at me from behind doorways with curious eyes.

We would smile at each other, and though very quiet, she was playful toward me. Her face showed an unconditional kindness and an eagerness to make connections with others that she had not yet learned to cover up, and that I can't come close to.

This pure childlike strength is part of what makes kids able to deal with things that they shouldn't ever see. It also makes it all the more tragic when you know what this little girl can likely expect to look forward to, growing up in Afghanistan.

Death Underfoot: Part 1
Landmines and Other Remnants of War

It is early morning on the outskirts of Herat, and a black and white bird flies over rolling hills, sparsely populated with tall pine trees. The first thing one might notice about this pastoral scene which would differ from such a rural American scene might be the presence of an old, partially buried military vehicle, peacefully rusting as it has for years. The second would be evenly spaced stones, placed over the landscape.

These are both markers that most people in Afghanistan would recognize, as would be piles of stones, painted stones, crossed sticks or a single stick placed in the ground, branches blocking a path, objects hanging from trees, animal skeletons, destroyed bridges, deserted villages, overgrown areas, farmland not being used; almost anything at all one might encounter. They all can be indicators that there is something designed to kill or maim which will blow up if you go near it.

Afghanistan is one of the world's countries most affected by landmines and unexploded ordnance (UXO). For over 25 years, everybody from the Russians to the Americans have added to the amount

of deadly stock (numbering in at least the tens of millions), and the impact is vast.

The two basic categories of things hiding in or on the ground that can kill you break down into these categories; UXO are military ammunitions such as bombs, shells, mortars, grenades, rockets, etc. that have not yet exploded. Landmines are booby traps, intentionally laid and left to go off when either a person or a vehicle gets close enough to be damaged by them.

I walk down a path with a British landmine removal expert named Aldo Alderson, who points out explosives on either side of us, and can identify several different kinds at a distance. He worked as a de-miner for the military for several years, but now coordinates mine/UXO removal in Herat for the French/Belgian organization Handicap International.

He will be the first one to tell you that he can be gruff and verbally direct to the point of offending people, but he is professional and passionate about his work, and I think it takes a certain toughness to do the kind of work he does well. I find him likable and take note of the fact that he talks about his work mostly in terms of the civilians living nearby that the work is intended to protect.

Afghanistan is a nightmare for a de-miner for all kinds of reasons, not the least of which is the fact that any given area can contain several different kinds of mines/UXO left by several different forces, over a 25 year period.

Some landmines will simply explode, some will blow shrapnel in a particular direction, and there are others such as "bounding mines" which shoot a device about three feet into the air which then detonates, shooting red hot fragments of jagged iron for up to 800 feet in all directions. Some mines are buried; some are dropped by the thousands from helicopters, covering huge tracts of farmland. Some have anti-tilt devices that make them explode when removal is attempted, and some are made mostly of plastic, and won't be noticed by metal detectors.

Removing landmines is a dangerous and time consuming process, and though it can cost as little as $.75 to produce one, it can cost $1000.00 to remove one.

The path we are on has old buried Russian bunkers on either side, still filled with the munitions they were built to store. Piles of everything from grenades to anti-aircraft rockets surround us in piles several feet high, and large patches of the area have been identified as a minefield. We trod along with body armor vests and helmets with face shields. Aldo laughs and points out where he spotted a tripwire attached to an explosive on either side, when he was first scouting the path on foot.

He motions for me to be quiet, and turns a corner suddenly, surprising the Afghani staff of deminers that he is in charge of, to make sure they're doing the work the way they should be. They're on the side of a steep hill, removing corroding UXO from the nineteen-seventies. He starts to talk to some of the workers about what they've been finding while I walk among them, snapping photos. Aldo lets me enter the cave-like entrance of the bunker that they just started excavating the day before. He tells me not to touch the roof, "so the whole goddamn thing doesn't collapse". I try to sidestep anything metal in the loose dirt, and stand on a large rock or a secure metal beam whenever possible.

De-miners prefer to use a backhoe in an area like this, as the huge metal machine affords some protection from explosions. One isn't available today, so they are doing the risky and painstaking work of shuffling dirt around with shovels, and removing mortar after mortar by hand. Sometimes a box of bullets or large shells is found, sometimes a grenade. Directly below us are literally tons of UXO.

As we leave to visit where thousands of tons of removed mines and UXO are stored, Aldo voices his pleasure with how the men were working. He's a tough boss, but he cares about his staff. As he likes to say, "I must be doing something right, 'cause I've been doing this for a lot of years, and I still have all my fingers and toes."

Death Underfoot: Part 2
Controlled Demolition

We sat with the engine running, and waited for the explosion.

A single electric cable lay on the ground, following the dirt road into the distance. Further down, it fed into to a detonator, which was attached to a length of bright orange detonation chord. This led down into a big crater-shaped recess in the desert, in which were piled over five tons of bombs, mortars, and shells.

Several sticks of a highly explosive, tar-like substance called P-3 had been rolled by hand into a ball the size of a large grapefruit and placed on a 1000 pound bomb at the top of the pile. The orange detonation chord ran through the black mound of P-3, and snaked in and out of the various kinds of meticulously stacked unexploded ordnance.

I was in the back seat of a four-wheel drive truck, readying my camera. In the driver's seat sat Aldo the boss, and in the passenger seat was Sascha, an imposing but friendly German whose grandfather worked as a mine clearer in World War II. They were both on edge, and constantly scanned the horizon. They work for Handicap International, an important international organization, and are doing their best to save lives.

The area had been chosen for its remote location so as not to detonate near peoples' homes, but there was another reason, too.

Wherever bombs are dropped and mines are laid, you can bet that the economy isn't thriving, and that poverty is rampant (one example is that farming becomes impossible when the land is littered with explosives). This creates a market for the kind of scrap metal that mines and UXO are made of. In war zones, adults and children alike are routinely killed by digging them up or prying them open.

Afghanistan is certainly no exception. Scrappers come to get anything they can, even recently detonated UXO that can still explode. The going rate for scrap metal in Herat is five Afghanis per kilo, or about ten cents for a little more than two pounds. They have come mostly by foot, across the windy dessert.

Aldo spoke. "They're hiding now, so you can't see them, but as soon as the explosion goes off, they'll appear out of nowhere."

We were at the minimum safe distance from the explosion site. As soon as it went off, we were to drive as fast as we could to try to beat the scrappers to the site, and to keep them away for their own safety. Random explosions usually follow the main one, making it a dangerous job.

This demolition had an added risk. The pile contained white phosphorus (which the US Army has lately been criticized for using in populated areas in Iraq). White phosphorus burns for a very long time and cannot be put out. When it gets on anything, from concrete to skin, it simply keeps burning.

Earlier in the week, I went to the storage facility where the mines and UXO cleared from the ground are taken to await demolition. It was basically a big field with some guards and a fence around it.

Thousands of tons of explosive materials are organized into categories and simply stacked on the ground, many still in the original boxes. Several conflicts are represented, as are several countries that manufacture such materials. Everything from fragmentation mines to anti-tank rockets are piled high in all directions. Some are shiny, some covered with rust. Often, tiny crystals form on the surface of the metal and can make an otherwise stable explosive extremely volatile.

There is a separate section where white phosphorus munitions are kept. They are less predictable than the others, and the pile isn't allowed to get too big. At the demolition I was awaiting, over two tons of the UXO contained white phosphorus.

The clock ticked down, and suddenly a huge black and orange cloud appeared, followed by a deep crashing sound. The truck immediately lunged forward on the bumpy dirt road, and I held on.

Through the windshield, I saw the mushroom cloud growing. Then looking down, I saw the scrappers.

It was hard to tell where they came from. As we passed a group of them getting close to the blast site, we slowed down and Sascha jumped out and ran toward them. Aldo and I continued on until the truck stopped, directly between scattered flaming metal and the poor men who'd come to try to salvage it. We got out, and Aldo started screaming and waving for the men to stay away. I snapped pictures.

Other trucks followed, fanning out, and Afghani mine clearers tried to gather the scrappers into groups and keep them back. Aldo took the truck to another side of the blast. I started aggressively yelling at the ones that are again approaching my position, trying to look like I was in charge of something. Secondary explosions sounded behind me, and I noticed a flaming shell that had been blown close to a mile away. An old man was standing over it.

In Afghanistan, there are many aid workers, both Afghani and foreign, trying to help those affected by mines and UXO. They provide all kinds of much-needed support to the wounded and their families. The problem is that millions of deadly objects are still underfoot, and will continue to maim and kill for decades to come.

What I experienced at the demolition seemed chaotic, but was, in fact, controlled. Given the mine workers' resources and the situation in Afghanistan, they were doing an amazing job, and the important thing is that no one was hurt. Watching these men do their dangerous work, I had a thought that if there were enough people like them, some of the other services wouldn't even be needed.

Under the Burqa: Part 1
Interaction with Women of Afghanistan

As a Western male in Afghanistan, contact with women is limited. I have to be constantly watching others' reactions to me, to know how to act toward different women I meet, and to try to be as sensitive as possible. While some women will make direct eye contact and even shake hands upon meeting, I have to let them take the lead.

Though the wearing of burqas is no longer enforced as it was under the Taliban, and many women don't wear them, it is still the norm to see what looks like multiple ghosts floating down the street. Women often discard them when they arrive at their destination, but when I show up, I often see faces immediately and silently covered. Different women react to my presence in different ways. I try to enter a room without looking directly at anyone, giving them a chance to see me first, and give an indication of what sort of interaction they are comfortable with.

Here's an example: I arrive at the lobby of a health clinic, where several women, many with children, are waiting. Another woman is giving a presentation on disability awareness and landmine safety, which is what I'm there to take photos of. I am accompanied by two females, so I'm a bit less threatening than I would be otherwise. There is a rumble of movement, and many of the women (who are poor and likely to be from more traditional backgrounds) become instantly anonymous, disappearing under the familiar light blue cloth of the burqa. I am introduced to the woman giving the presentation. She smiles and says hello while looking me straight in the eye, but does not extend her hand. I just place mine over my heart, a common gesture of friendliness.

I sit for a little while and try to let the women get used to me. Some nod; some look away. An Afghani woman explains in Dari that I am going to take photographs, and to let me know if they don't want to be included. Some of the women leave. I take out my camera and fumble with it a minute or two, pretending to get it ready and allowing all to see that I am about to use it. At first, I snap photos of the presenter, then the children, and finally some of the women.

I note something I've seen before. There is a woman whose face is covered, but the front of her burqa is open, and she is openly breast feeding a baby in her arms. This might seem like a contradiction to most American readers, but I don't necessarily think it is. Cultural differences are always interesting, but ones that point out insecurities in both cultures are something we can learn from.

That being said, the prospects for most Afghani women are beyond pitiful. Ministries of Women's Affairs have sprouted up in the larger cities in recent years, but they face an uphill battle so steep that it's difficult to know where to start. Women's advocates are still assassinated and girls' schools blown up.

There are many Afghani women and men that risk their lives trying to bring change, and have been for some time. One is Sohwaila Aslami. She directs a school for girls in Kabul that teaches females to read and write, but focuses on vocational training. What's amazing is that she's been doing it for 14 years. During the reign of the Taliban, the building was surrounded by armed Talibs. Before they stormed in, Sohwaila passed out copies of the Koran to all the children. By the time the Taliban men entered the classrooms, the girls were all studying, and Sohwaila was able to convince them that it was a religious school, or madressa. A madressa with girls wasn't approved of, but she was somehow able to keep it from being shut down.

Even now, though, she's in danger for trying to change elements of a culture that are fiercely defended by many. The sad fact is that these days, most women's lives aren't any different from years past.

The younger generations, especially in bigger cities, seem to be trying to change things. A young woman I meet when I am taking pictures at a University radio station in Herat seems to personify a modern, young, progressive Afghani woman. She's outspoken, vivacious, and focused. She laughs louder than most women I've met in Herat, and doesn't hesitate to let others know her opinions.

Four of us are told that a car has arrived. She is to interview people for a live radio broadcast, and we walk toward the entrance of the university. I quickly put my camera into my camera bag, and when I look up, instead of seeing her walking next to me, I see flowing blue cloth.

Out in public, she walks with less boldness, is now quiet, and has completely disappeared from view.

Under the Burqa: Part 2
Hairstyling, Self-Immolation

I am excited as I walk down the dusty alley, and I don't know what to expect. It feels the same as when I've been on my way to hidden guerrilla camps in North Iraq, or to meet with armed gang members in Port-au-Prince, Haiti. I always feel very lucky to see something that most people aren't allowed to see or something that is in some way forbidden.

The alley is in Kabul, Afghanistan, but I'm not about to meet with the Taliban, Al Qaeda operatives, or drug-smuggling warlords. I'm on my way to a beauty salon.

Accompanying me are Mrs. Aziz, a matronly teacher draped head to toe in white, a young male translator, and a Connecticut native named Kimberly Mikenis who has coordinated today's visit for the organization. We arrive at a metal door and knock.

It swings open, and we are welcomed with a broad smile by Mrs. Gulwateh, who runs the beauty salon. She has offered her time to teach young disabled women a trade. It seems an odd trade to have in a country where women rarely show their faces in public, but there is a market for it.

Before long, I am snapping away at two students sitting in front of a big mirror, being worked on by Mrs. Gulwateh and her assistant. Other students quietly observe. One girl's whole face is being made up a stark pale color, with her mouth, eyes and brows contrasting boldly. The other is having her hair done, and it is the first uncovered head of an Afghani female that I've seen.

She hesitates before taking her scarf off in front of me, and I feel intrusive. It's a big deal in a place where, not so long ago, it was illegal for a woman to be outside without a burqa and a male family member (this has not changed in many rural areas, a fact that should be known by those under the impression that women of Afghanistan have been somehow liberated). The girl is prepared as a bride would be, with intricate patterns woven and teased into her hair. Little flowers and fine lines of bright glittery green are added.

For me to witness such a thing is a rarity, and I feel honored. I am told that these photos cannot be distributed to Afghans in the area, for fear of repercussions by those who might violently oppose what is happening in this little salon.

The sheepish girl eventually smiles, and it is one of the high points of my trip. Now I'll write about a low point.

In the Western province of Herat, I see two types of patients at a hospital's burn ward for females, and both categories speak to the progress of women's rights.

First, there are young women who were injured when a school for girls was bombed. Second, there are women of various ages who have taken part in the cultural phenomenon of self-immolation, which has left hundreds killed or disfigured in the past few years. Growing numbers of women in Afghanistan are pouring gasoline on their bodies and setting themselves on fire.

There is an intense isolation that befalls many Afghani women. Often a girl (whose only real contact has been with her family) is married, and immediately cut off from everyone but the family of her new husband. Domestic abuse is rampant in Afghanistan, as is poverty, lack of education, and the many other problems females can face all over the world.

Twenty-five years of multiple conflicts has added to the problems. There is a huge population of war widows, for whom there aren't many prospects of making a living (in Kabul alone has 50,000). Thousands of Afghanis have lived as refugees for several years in Iran, where life for women is less restrictive. The effect on a women returning to Afghanistan can be traumatic.

Women feel they have no escape from their depression and no outlet for any feelings at all, so they burn themselves. For many, self-immolation is seen as the only way to end the pain, and it's the only form of protest available.

There are six such women in the burn ward, but I am told that most who do this never make it to a hospital, and the incident may not even be reported. They either live in rural areas too distant to be transported, cannot not pay for medical treatment, or their families keep them at home to cover up what they've done. As is the case with female victims of almost any sort, a violent act is followed by shame and the social stigma of being associated with the violent act.

I see females from ages 12 to their mid thirties, lying down with bandages covering most of their bodies. A doctor tells me that because of the high rate of infection in burn cases, most of them really have no chance of survival. The ones who live will be horribly scarred, may have lost fingers or limbs, or will perhaps be blind.

After a slow, painful process, and with a burqa covering them, they'll probably appear normal at some point. When removed, though, no amount of makeup or hair styling will allow them to ever forget burning themselves, or the isolation that caused it, and is shared by so many women of Afghanistan.

Final Dispatch
A Few Portraits From Iraq and Afghanistan

After three and a half years since the US invasion of Iraq, and nearly five since that of Afghanistan, things aren't looking very good for the people that live in either place. In my recent return to both countries, I did see some rays of hope, but they were always shadowed by a harsh reality. The systems that have been put into place to run these countries simply do not work. Security is the main issue, and it trumps all others. Without some basic level of stability, nothing functions.

People are why this matters. Yes, our lives can be affected by these conflicts, but most of us have no idea what life is like for Iraqis and Afghanis, who will be dealing with the effects of these conflicts for the rest of their lives. The single most important perspective I gain from my travels is a glimpse into other's experiences, and so I end this series with a few brief portraits of regular people I encountered.

Mohammad Abu Zahara owns a mechanic shop. He is also a member of Muqtada Al-Sadr's militia, the Madhi Army. When there is work for

him, such as fixing my driver's car after it was damaged in a hotel bombing, he can usually be found at the garage. Sometimes, he gets a call from the militia, though, and the doors close. He puts on the all black uniform and face covering, carries an AK-47, and does what he's told to do.

Al-Sadr's support has been steadily increasing since the fall of Saddam, having waged two uprisings against the US military, and emerging more powerful after each one. He now has legitimate political clout in the form of parliament seats, and he is only getting stronger. Like Mr. Abu Zahara, many of the country's Shia majority swear allegiance to Al-Sadr, and many of these are members of Iraq's new army and police force. This blurring of loyalties is a major concern, since the Madhi Army is one of the main players in the sectarian violence, which is responsible for hundreds of bodies found every week.

A woman in Baghdad's Yarmouk Hospital looks on as her husband, severely wounded in a suicide bombing, waits for treatment. It is old news that health care is abysmal in Iraq. In the capital city, there is so much sustained violence that the breaking point has long since been forgotten, and entire hospitals are triage areas. A recent United Nations report puts the death toll from violence in the past two months of writing at 6,599. Emergency rooms and morgues are filled beyond capacity, and there's no end in sight.

A young man plays volleyball in Kabul, a city that is home to more than 800,000 disabled people. After twenty-five years of war in Afghanistan, amputees are visible on nearly every street in every province. Armed attacks and bombings continue, land mines and unexploded ordnance still litter fields and roadsides, and other causes of disability (like unsafe working conditions) all contribute.

Somayeh studied journalism in school and now interns with an aid organization in Herat, Afghanistan. Like many people in Western provinces, she lived for several years in Iran, but has moved back to the land of her family, in hopes of its future stability. She is very quiet, as is not uncommon of Afghani women, but has a silent tenacity about her that is not immediately visible, and is always surprising her superiors, spearheading new projects.

Much difficulty faces almost everyone in Afghanistan, but the path for females is limited and difficult to navigate. Somayeh has struck a balance between tradition and independence that seems to work, at least for her, at least for now.

The Children of both Iraq and Afghanistan have much to face in the coming years. Of the forces that compete in forming their development, violence and poverty will often be prominent. If chil-dren are not protected from the worst of life's horrors in countries where our foreign policy is such a driving force, what excuse do we have?

© Daniel W. Smith, 2006
dwsmithemail@yahoo.com

*Postscript: While writing this, I received a call informing me that another bomb had gone off in the city, killing four and wounding twenty eight.

*Postscript: Three months after this was written, Aldo's right leg was blown to pieces by an Israeli anti-personnel mine in southern Lebanon, while trying to rescue a Lebanese shepherd trapped in a minefield. He was on a UN mission to clear mines, cluster bombs, and UXO laid during the Hezbollah-Israel War.

Selected Poems

Abdennabi Benchehda

THE AMBULANT SHOE SHINER

He tumbled in with his disheveled hair like weed.
His angular body slouched from the heavy bags under
his bleary eyes.
He seemed in need.
Half a filter-less cigarette dangled from his lips
like consumed harlot breasts which had long
surrendered to gravity.
He IS in need.
Grimly trudging through the plaza
between tables upon which were perched blind patrons
tossing bread to pigeons,
he tapped his shoe brush on the wooden shoe shining
box in staccato.
Tap . . . tap tap . . . tap
Tap . . . tap tap . . . tap
Never looking at faces,
just feet.
Looking for leather shoes.
In his shoe shining box, he had polish
for all shoes: brown, black, and transparent,
but none for local shoes.
He avoided the locals like a disease
he didn't have yet.
The locals ignored him like a reality they refused to see.
They know his type.
He sniffed glue and dealt kif to hippie tourists.
He looked at my feet and pointed at them
with the shoe brush insistently, meaning:
Mister, you seem to have come from afar.
I know our dirt when I see it
and what you have on your shoes
is not ours.
I can shine them for you.
I signaled to him that yes,

he can shine my shoes
while I'm drinking my cortado
and reading my paper.
There is nothing wrong
with helping this fella
earn a living.
He squatted down and
put the box before my feet.
The sour stench of stale sweat
filled the air.
I put a leather shoe on the shoe
rest and watched him go at it like a pro.
How's it going? I ask.
Up until this morning, we are stilled mired
in intellectual and economic poverty.
We are on our last leg with one foot in the grave.
And we are only in our teens.
Our feet are shackled by
laconic
hollow
Rhetoric of distant
politicians and
intellectuals who,
from their surreptitious way of life,
amusingly observe
the mass in their morass.
Refuse change.
Change!
Change!
Change!
Change foot, mister.
Students, ordinary government employees, unemployed
university grads, and the likes of me striving in our surviving,
the nose barely jutting out through the surface of an ocean
of shit
generated by decades of fruitless
economic plans upon which we were
to start a family,
build a future,
find happiness and
peace
of mind. We are drowning, mister.
His head did not look up once.

His hand did not stop running the brush once.
He only talked once.
Limpidly.
He tapped the box.
He finished.
I paid.
A light breeze blew.
He rolled with it.
Tap . . . tap tap . . . tap
Tap . . . tap tap . . . tap

I stood up and walked to a trash can.
It was filled with newspapers.
I tossed mine in with the rest of them.
And walked away through the pigeon
turd crusted plaza
in my freshly shined shoes.

Get "Mo"

it quite simply starts with the name.
mine is quite a trip down ethnicity lane.
my hair is black.
my eyes are brown.
it prompts the question:
where are you from?
I was born in Fallbrook, California!
no! no!
where are you REALLY from?
what a shame!
are you naturalized?
because if yes,
then you are one step behind, pal.
I am AMERICAN.
I was born in California.
and your mother?
and your father?
are they citizens?
yes!
of what country?

in those homeland security checkpoints,
it does not make sense.
so they dissect your identity
with a microscopic precision,
an impeccably cold professionalism,
a shallow politeness.

in your eyes,
a terrorist by default I am.
continually suspected.
profoundly humiliated
disrespected.
segregated.
searched.
and then, dismissed.

my ticket is lined with
sssssssssssssssssssssssssssssssssssssssssss.
checked with a red marker
by a Bangladeshi immigrant

stoic in his security costume.
profiled—did I say profiled?
I meant some other politically correct word
that means the same thing, but does not
offend your democratic sensitivities
and your self-proclaimed civility—
by the security officials
who view the law
through a thick layer of prejudices,
who read my American passport
with southern eyes
and with uncle Sam's intrusive index finger,
pull me out of the long line.
"this way please, sir!"

pulled along with me is an eighty-five
years old snow white lady with grey hair
and clear perplexed eyes. she struggles
on her walker, inching forward
to the search area.
"why me?"
"maybe they think
I gave you something,"
I said trying to be comforting, but
there is no one to comfort me.
"why me?"
"it's a random security check, sir!"
I am randomly checked
100% of the time.

a terrorist by default I am.
labeled by the layman
who looks at me through
the front pages of
newspapers,
magazines,
headlines of news channels
broadcasting fears blown
into life by corrupt politicians
and bigoted preachers,
inculcated into your children's
brains by dogmatic teachers.
there is you and then...

these men and women like me
you see as ungodly creatures.
some know it's wrong,
but think not lifting an eye lid
to expunge the self-destructive injustice.
"none of my business," they say.
it's a necessary confusion.
all for a good cause.
just like these long lines.
a petulant nuisance
we all have to go through.
don't we all feel safer now?
you, in your semblance of security.
me, in my stigmatizing exclusion.

so here I am.
have your day.
indulge your delusion and
strip me naked of all my history.
discard my American passport
and focus on my cultural identity.
probe your latex gloved fingers
in all my orifices and defile
my humanity while searching
for the terrorist in me.
but you won't find him.
then baptize me and bless my soul.
let me catch my plane home.

There Has to Be a Child

I walk along
graffiti streaked T-walls
in Baghdad thinking . . .
there has to be a reprieve
for a heart that shuns
the hatred.
there has to be
some crumbs of happiness
leftovers here somewhere.
some love,
some crackling
good-hearted laughter
left here somewhere
to subdue the barking
of the guns
and the stomping
of the boots.

the horrors of war
could not have seeped
into all the cracks
of every wall
and every soul.
a child somewhere
still remembers,
between every
gut wrenching
cry and cry,
how to smile.

but, look here!
you see boot prints
on doors kicked
into broken homes.
these rooms,
their walls are splattered red.
they contained the screams
of agonizing men
and yes! the laughter
of maniac terrorizing men.
it's not the laughter I'm looking for.

it's not the laughter I'm looking for.
within these T-walls
dividing the city
and garroting the life
out of it,
we have achieved peace
and buried the peace
of mind and the sanity,
the innocence,
the laughter,
the love,
the tender smile.
there has to be
a child somewhere
still remembering,
between every
gut wrenching
cry and cry,
how to smile.
there has to be.

© 2008 Abdennabi Benchehda

Abdennabi Benchehda was born in Morocco in 1966. He previously published a **Moroccan phrasebook** with Lonely Planet. His travels took him to Asia, Australia, Africa, and Europe. He extensively traveled in the Middle East and lived in some of its countries for many years. He visited Iraq on numerous occasions working for an NGO. Mr. Benchehda is compiling his poetry in a volume to publish soon and is working on his first novel. He resides in Arizona. Visit his blog at http://cabalamuse.word press.com in which he comments on current events, Morocco, and Moroccan immigrant life in the United States.

Intrusions

Walker Thomas

My father has resented me ever since my first intrusion into his life early in 1945, when a girl he was dating told him she was pregnant with me. Nineteen years later, I saw the last of him in an unconscious heap on our living room floor in Pennsylvania after he had attacked me for revealing some of the perversions that could have sent him to jail. I got out of town.

With no financial help from family, I couldn't afford to start college in Arizona after a fall in the Huachuca Mountains later that year. I volunteered for the draft. I'd get that two-year hitch out of the way and then have the GI Bill to help with tuition. In the course of my draft physical, the doctor asked if I had ever been unconscious and for how long.

"I was out for about seven hours this past summer. I fell near eleven in the morning and came to around sunset."

"Bring us the medical records," the doctor said.

Nobody saw me lying under those cliffs, I thought; hospital records would just quote me saying the same thing to the ER docs that I said to the draft physical doc. I'd seen through the pretensions of parents and relatives and was determined to stop jumping through hoops for those who would claim authority—maybe a bad strategy for someone about to enter the military. I didn't walk the six miles each way to the hospital for the records that I'd later learn would have been a way out of military service. In Korea a year later, my CO talked me into going to the helicopter flight school I had more cautiously turned down after basic training. The doctor at my physical also asked about any recent, prolonged unconsciousness.

"Seven hours?" The flight surgeon put down his pen and shook his head, "You can't fly. You shouldn't even be in the Army."

I can look back now at what were two valuable years of life experience, but at the time of that discovery, I'd have been very happy to forego them, and for the rest of my tour, I mourned the knowledge that my time in the Army was entirely unnecessary.

In Phoenix, I had volunteered for the first Marine draft in a hundred years, but I was twentieth in line when they needed eighteen, so I was bussed to Army Basic Training at Ft. Bliss, under the B-52 flight path, near El Paso, Texas, where a grandfatherly major gave us a pep talk and forms to fill out.

"Boys, you are men now. You've been used to parents making your decisions. No more. With these forms, you'll be making the decisions in your lives."

Maybe the rest were boys, but I felt like I had been a man for a long time already, and I was with the major all the way. I filled out tax forms, insurance forms, release of payments to spouse and dependents—all the forms except the one that was like the fill-in-the-blank letter home on the back of cereal boxes at boys' camps. The letter announced my pleasure at being in the Army, my promise to write home every week, and an invitation for parents to attend my graduation from basic training. We were to add Moms' and Dads' addresses for a clerk to put on an envelope and our Ft. Bliss barracks addresses for parents to write back. I pushed that form aside.

"Private Thomas."

My first day in the Army, and a major called my name out of all the names in a roomful of newly acknowledged men. I snapped to attention and gave my best salute.

"Yes, Sir!" I said.

"At ease," the major said. "Son, we can see you're excited to be in the Army, and we appreciate that.

Oversights are usually frowned upon, but we'll make an exception in this case. You've forgotten to fill out one of the forms."

"Sir, was that the DD-XXX?"

"Why, yes it was."

"That wasn't an oversight, Sir. I chose not to fill that one out. Thank you, Sir." And I sat down, pleased with the rapport so soon established with an officer.

"Who is this man's commanding officer?" the major bellowed.

Capt. Allen called out from the back of the room, "I am, Sir."

"Capt. Allen, take this man out of here. Do whatever you think necessary. If you decide on a courts martial, I'll gladly sign off on that."

I walked sheepishly past other nervous eyes to the back of the room and out into the hall.

Flushing pink, Capt. Allen was a low-keyed ROTC officer just trying to put in his required time after college. Recovered from the initial shock, I seethed.

"I can see you're pretty wrought up right now." He gave his winningest smile, "Why don't you go back to the barracks, get a good night's sleep, and drop by my office after breakfast?"

The next morning, before my hand was halfway up to salute, Captain Allen reached across his desk to shake it.

"So, what's bothering you?" he asked, as if of a college roommate.

"I shouldn't have to tell you this," I said; but after I told all, Capt. Allen agreed that I should avoid the family.

"The military has its regulations," he said, "I can stop it here, but you'll need to tell your every commanding officer along the way, or your information will be released."

A few days later, I got a letter from home.

"That son of a bitch!" Capt. Allen said when I told him, "I told the major that you had good reasons and that I stood behind them." He stared at the floor around his feet a moment, and then raised his eyes. "That's okay. Right now, I'm the only one who can release your next duty station. But go straight to your next commanding officer to keep him from releasing it."

Through tests at Bliss, I'd qualified for flight training. I could go to warrant officer school to learn to fly the helicopters used in Viet Nam, and draw an officer's pay right out of basic training. When I took the test, no helicopter had ever been shot down in Viet Nam. By the time I finished basic, they were going down as fast as they went up. I passed on flight school and was assigned to an electric generator class at Ft. Belvoir, VA.

I didn't go straight to my CO when I got to Belvoir, but the day after I arrived, the guy in the bed above pretended to masturbate. The whole structure shook as I tried to read in my lower bunk. I put my foot into where his buttocks bulged down through the military-grade mattress and lifted him, bed and all, toward the ceiling. I failed to notice that I was lifting the steel frame out of its supports. The steel bed teetered for just a moment as he jumped up. When he next hit the bed, it broke loose from its supports and crashed down on my head. A crossbar creased my skull—a straight line of indentation is still palpable across the front third. Blood poured from a gash in bunched-up scalp, and when I reached into its slick, soft-clotting center, I seemed to be pressing fingers deep into brain. Even the doctor was surprised when x-rays showed no skull fracture.

A junior officer visited me in the hospital the next day and asked me to drop in on the CO when I got out. After Capt. Allen had blocked release of my new assignment, a Pennsylvania senator, acting on behalf of my bereaved parents, demanded the information. Reading between lines, my CO at Belvoir wanted to talk to me before he took any action.

So the process began again. When the CO at Belvoir took my side, the information was released without his permission. Then, like Capt. Allen, he refused to forward my next assignment, but advised me to bring the matter up with my CO as soon as I arrived at my next post. I went straight to my CO of my next station in Korea, but the brass in Washington, tired of headaches, decided to quit relying on CO's who didn't fall into line and released the information on their own. I would have to wait until I was out of the Army to shake off family ties.

While I was waiting at Belvoir for that next assignment, I asked a self-proclaimed genius, a Private Freudlich, how he always got out of the work details on Tuesdays.

"Tuesdays I talk to the psychiatrist. It's easy. I told the CO I was feeling a little weird, like I don't fit in, and he sent me to the psychologist. I talked to the psychologist for a little while and he sent me to the psychiatrist, so now I go in every Tuesday and we talk. Next to me, the psychiatrist is the smartest guy here."

In the barracks a few nights before that talk with Freudlich, I was awakened from a sound sleep by a spray on my face. I tried to bat it away a couple of times before I opened my eyes and saw a drunken soldier in pale-blue boxers, one hand holding onto my wall locker, the other holding his part that was pissing on me.

"Ortiz!" I yelled as I jumped up.

He just kept pissing. I grabbed soap and towel and ran to the showers.

I returned to a barracks still filled with snores. Ortiz snored in his top bunk. A few beds down, my old, impermeable Army mattress still held the puddle of his piss.

I stood at his bedside, eyelevel with his snoring face. "Ortiz, Ortiz."

He slept soundly.

I brought a cup of water back from the latrines and tossed it on his face. It splashed onto the guy in the next bunk, who woke up ready to fight.

"The hell!"

"I gotta wake him up. He pissed all over my bed and now I can't find my glasses."

"So why the hell you pouring water on me?"

"It splashed."

"What's goin' on?" Ortiz was waking up.

"You pissed on me. Where're my glasses?"

Ortiz climbed down from his bunk, now the picture of forced sobriety, and walked over to mine.

"What you talking about, man? Somebody played a trick on you. Poured water on your bed."

"No. You pissed."

"It's water, man." Ortiz scooped some from the still unabsorbed puddle and held it to his nose. "It's just water. Smell it."

"Don't put your face in it. It's piss."

"You threw water on me!" The guy in the next bunk didn't want to let go of his own hurt.

"Just go back to bed," Ortiz said, our calm center, "He's all fucked up."

They returned to their beds, the recipient of errant drops from the cup still grumbling. The puddle remained in my bed. I spent the night sleepless in the latrines.

The next day, Ortiz said, "I remember it now. I did get up to piss. Shit, man, don't tell anybody, I'll look like a fool."

I took that story to the CO, and added that a Pennsylvania psychiatrist had advised me to follow up on my childhood abuse. The CO sent me to a psychologist, an easy-going black man with a master's degree who had refused an officer's commission and was soon to be reassigned as a rifle-bearing grunt in Viet Nam. Wednesdays became my days to talk about the inequities of Army life, but only with the psychologist whose complaints, in a firm foundation of life among bigots and with their threat of death in war, outweighed mine.

"Why don't you send me to the psychiatrist. Freudlich gets to see the psychiatrist."

"But there's nothing wrong with you. Freudlich's crazy."

That had never occurred to me; I mean, that Freudlich was crazy. I never thought there was anything wrong with me. But lately, I've begun to realize that while guys were developing post-traumatic stress disorders in Viet Nam, I came to the Army with a full-blown PTSD already established and never addressed. With my discharge, I was able to shed family ties, but the challenge remains to distance my thoughts from its intrusions.

Selected Poems

Francis E. Crowley

"9/11"

Truth is no whore
although she often gives me a standing ovulation
it is 3:00 a.m.
she is knocking right now on the door of my dreams
with her remarkable sense of metaphor
I was learning how to make rice and beans, again,
with Gwendolyn Brooks in white gloves and gown
James Baldwin in a black sequined stove-pipe hat
I get up, float to the door, invite her in for some love-making
put on the decaf coffee pot she looks me in the eye laser-like

"I need a good man to believe in me, as a husband does a wife
as two gold swans on one great pond in September's pure light,"

"I am not he," I answer, "....believe me!"
"even though you are my best mentor mistress Muse
I do not have your Humility honor hope your defense against
Khadaffy's crooks kooks dictators dupes corruption contagion
those who failed to connect the dots............between the FBI and the CIA
I am a weak soft spiders voice...... in the wwweb..."

"it's true," she answers, " I cannot be bought cajoled stored
for some future brave new generation to face
like your corruptible race I cannot be arrested like Assange
covered up like Khodorkovsky suppressed like Osip Mandelstam
twisted by dictators demagogues demanding adulation:
'mission accomplished'
I am not bemused by those who repeat history every 30 seconds
those who try and fail to fuck me... have premature Iraqulation...
my armies of infinite facts are legion like rogue asteroids
roaming the universe blasting Cant bombast received religion rancid lies!
remember: 'Patience is the highest Praise'

As I reach for her nurturing embrace as a child for his mother
I wake.......ahhh....it is only Abby's sweet whiskered face
....................another dream........................but I think...............................
"the only thing that matters in life as in art is she ..... her beauty
and that THIS TIME................THE FIRE............on the edge of glory!"

"the HADITHA massacre"

Justice is blind as they say
marble hooded impassive grand
she surveys impartially our land
but I fear today She rules with irony
partially frozen atop her tomb
with a dead fetus in Her womb

IRAQ: -115,000 USA: -5,000 (and 40,000 wounded)

Lady Justice is still blind, our kind
this time 24 dead Iraqi women children men
this time unarmed in their homes blown up
by Frank Wuterich and his team of eight

our Connecticut neighbor and friend
on his first day deployed and engaged
by a roadside bomb that killed his comrade
first time in battle and first under fire

IRAQ: -24 USA: -1 (and one wounded)

Frank blindly tossed grenades through the front door
shot indiscriminately the fleeing neighborhood men
his team engaged, enraged by their loss their dead
last night(1/24/12) CBS news covered the eight year trial
Scott Pelley's only interview with Frank, "charges dropped"
for all his men; Frank cops a plea "dereliction of duty"

which carries in military court three months confinement
dropped as well by the military judge; he's exonerated
free to come home to Connecticut, to be neighbor, friend
again

I am as blind as Justice with my blindfold on
walking around every day, complaining, complaining
of food served luke-warm, of tax breaks and steaks
for the rich, of pot holes, abusive priests, pipe lines
......of LIFE? try wearing a grenade in my living room
with kids and wife our benighted Congress last night
with Liberty and "justice" for all listened blissfully
unaware to the State of the Disunion Address and blessed
our armed forces which is right and true with Grace

except for this miscarriage of Lady Justice, aborted
impugned in her womb as I listened last night
I could not help feeling let down as big bailed-out bankers
and corrupt Wall St. brokers go free to blindly dance again
with impunity served no time for deliberate deception
and criminality soldiers who serve no time for excessive
and murderous brutality

I am blind drunk naive inured to lies tattooed
screwed bamboozled betrayed bought without a clue
as the President said with Hope Faith and Trust in us
how about our everyday heroes who serve with Loyalty
to our democratic values and egalitarian ideals
who follow the rules obediently finish school who
still believe in her essential unbiased blind Justice?

'the hat of childhood'

I wore a hat from timbuctoo
with holes loose threads crappy green flaps
it carried me through the flu measles pox collapsed
in snow soggy in rain shrunk in the warm sun
to fit my head again wore it to bed at wakes
football games not on early dates on the job
at Friendly's weekends and yet and yet.....
I slowly grew into another one a turtle shell
straps metallic green echoing bloody yells

now my grandson wears that same hat of childhood
flappy crappy snot-green with holes and history
and string torn at the top fading from a thousand washes
I love to watch him strut and shout commands in it
camp it up pretend to be a cop a pope a lout
a talking cabbage head fireman screaming dairy queen
as he grows through the roles of vampire priest poet like me
changing hats into fluid apparitions of desires to be.....
anything but a small defenseless tyke in grandpa's hat.
I hope he never wears the metal one with holes.

"It was the cold that send us out.......into the night...." THE NEWS.

THE NEWS after an NBC report last night by Brian Williams: (I'm paraphrasing) "General Petraeus in a very rare personal apology said, '...this is a tragedy that never should have happened...'"; he was speaking about the NATO air strike on two pairs of brothers and other children in Afghanistan out gathering firewood." Apparently, all died, but that was the extent of the 40 second report.

"it was the cold that sent us out
into the night for firewood.....
any twigs visible in the light of matches
Ali is near I can hear Shahid scratching
no food without fire the baby is sick
tomorrow comes quick as we wake before dawn
it is no school for us we work in the field
but I have one book from one American...and hope..."

hope died for me
I see boys bodies scattered on the hillside
"bombed back into the stone age"
pieces of flesh flakes of brown skin
like dirty snow falling gently in first light
like red kites floating after the cut
in slow motion down to earth and another day

a roar in the sky rosy-fingered dawn reveals
the fire-spitting beast that kills
suddenly silently at first it comes so fast

Francis E. Crowley, PhD, Professor in the Humanities EMERITUS at Gateway CC is also the author of TIME, PLACE AND PERSON(1997). He writes lyric poetry to share at open-mics in New Haven and in Tucson, AZ, where he finds inspiration during January and February. His poems in this book were written at the Poetry Center of the University of Arizona. He spends July and August with his grandson, Nathan, age 14, at Hammonasset State Beach in Madison, CT.

Section Five

America and the
Rest of the World

To, and from, Bhutan

Richard Alther

Bhutan? Where in the world was it? Indonesia, I thought vaguely. But how could I, so ill-informed, merit the opportunity to visit this tiny Himalayan Bhuddist kingdom? My spiritual development was not that advanced. And there were other places on Earth that had beckoned to me as a watercolor painter for years.

Bhutan is about the size of Switzerland, wedged between Nepal to the west, India to the south, and Tibet, its spiritual ancestor, to the north. The country is totally ringed by the mountains which include Everest on the Nepalese border, so it's really inaccessible. Paved roads were completed in 1970. I learned Bhutan is famously isolated from the modern world, and features spectacular views. Vacations in the past for me have usually been visits to just one restful, beautiful place for a week, a chance to hunker down with my paints. No sight-seeing, no running around.

The possibility to join this particular trek came to my attention via two men nearby who have led more groups to Bhutan than any other Americans. Their passion for this spot was augmented by their being long-standing scholars and practitioners of Bhuddism. My experience with Eastern philosophy had been books and tapes: Thich Nhat Hanh, Sogyal Rinpoyche, Jack Kornfield. To venture to Bhutan struck me as the equivalent of a Moslem traveling to Mecca. Peers who had lived in India in the 1960s to isolate themselves in Ashrams for months never hit a chord of envy in me. I couldn't identify with the relinquishing of one's striving, grasping, achieving Western ego. Especially I could not trust the assignment of responsibility for my soul to a guru let alone a doctrine. I figured if the good Lord had meant me to be composed, and capable of staring heavy-lidded for hours at a Mandala, He or She would have had me born in New Delhi, not New Jersey.

By mid-life, however, and contemplating a trip to Bhutan, to the heart of the unknown, I began to realize how appealing were the ideas of letting go, living in the moment, deep breathing, and eliminating frenzy.

Still, it was a very foreign-sounding place, plus a huge outlay of time and money.

"Will there be a chance for me to paint?" "Absolutely," I was assured. "The rhododendrons are the size of a house! And the snow-capped peaks loom everywhere as dramatic background to the ancient farms and simple monasteries." The tour leaders are also birders; they described wildflowers blanketing the valleys and meadows. "We have travelled the world over and Bhutan is truly the most magnificent landscape we've ever seen."

I was hooked, but there was one hitch: after a year of distress, my intestinal tract was pretty much under control. Pretty much.

I had back-packed in the Sierra Nevadas the prior year, drinking (filtered) water from the streams, and found a month later that my insides weren't right. I was tested and diagnosed every-which-way. "Irritable Bowel Syndrome" was the predominant conclusion. "Just drink Lactaid," said one of several gastroenterologists. "I do, and I'm only 35. Millions can't tolerate milk." The more I researched, the more I learned this condition comes about much earlier in life. I'd been perfectly able before that hiking adventure to eat or drink what I wanted. I tested negative for ghiardia, and the usual course of antibiotics for that parasite resolved nothing. Still, I wasn't convinced that this pump-filter device for hikers could be guaranteed to screen viruses as well as microbes.

Mid-year some friends getting understandably bored by my continuing complaints suggested anti-depression medication, at least a psychiatrist, claiming that this thing had roots more sublime than my alimentary canal.

Courtesy of University of Texas Libraries. The University of Texas at Austin.

I had made it through the year, colonoscopy, acupuncture, barium enemas and all, and decided I was well enough for the trip to Bhutan. It would be mind over matter; it would do me a world of good.

My yoga escalated the weeks preceding the departure. We would be staying in simple accommodations, including guest cottages adjunct to monasteries. I read that the men were either farmers or monks; I wanted to prepare myself as best I could for this cultural leap. I am incapable of sitting still. So when I had taken up yoga, I was delighted to have it described by a teacher as "moving meditation." After two years of faithful practice, I considered yoga as a logical, appropriate place where East meets West. It is action, for the body, but it quiets my mind, with total focus on conscious breathing through the nostrils. It fulfills my yearning for both strenuous exertion and utter calm—quite a feat.

I was to join our leaders and the dozen others in the group in Kathmandu, Nepal, literally half-way around the world. Disembarking briefly in Frankfurt, I found myself striking up the stance in yoga known as The Warrior, off to one side of a lobby. People seemed not to notice, so I proceeded to Sun Salutation, Downward Facing Dog, the Crane on one foot. Only a handful of visitors are permitted into Bhutan annually; I wanted to be as respectful a guest as possible, and yoga was the best preparation I knew for emptying the mind. But just the thought of mingling with humble peasants and devout Bhuddists was making me think of myself more than ever as the Ugly American. Would these people laugh at us? Take offense at our traipsing with cameras to their hillside stupas? There was no "tourism" in Bhutan, so our filthy lucre could not help to make amends. The Bhutanese would not be hawking crafts, and, of course, this was much of the trip's appeal.

A friend who had been in the Peace Corps suggested I pack dozens of balloons to hand out to the children, who would never have seen them. Otherwise, it didn't cross my mind that the Bhutanese, upon whom I'd been projecting a near celestial state of self-containment, would take my presence as anything positive, a source of curiosity or even excitement.

As we packed into the small plane, one of a few flights per week from Kathmandu to Paro, principal town in Bhutan, my own excitement couldn't help but soar. The plane had to thrust up and over the Himalayas. There was Everest in all its 29,000-foot majesty, as high as many planes fly over the Earth. I was stepping back centuries as few souls were ever privileged to do.

The article in *National Geographic* depicted the Bhutanese in typically fantastic costumes for their rituals. But everyday? Here, too, the people were indeed in native dress: the monks in rich burgundy wool wraps, the villagers in yards of brilliantly-patterned silken fabrics, gardening, lugging water, chasing goats. Thoroughly non-erotic winged vaginas and spurting phalluses were painted over and astride the doorways as omens to productivity. The rendering of tigers and pythons and great birds dazzled by comparison to the concrete huts upon which they were so lovingly painted.

Day after day, for two weeks, we hunted down the fortress-monasteries, built in the early 1600s and still in active use. We visited the National Archives, preserving the ancient manuscripts, all readily accessible. We spotted the rare black-billed cranes and other exotic birds of this remote mountain enclave. Bhutan isn't so much steeped in its history as living it, unaware of alternatives beyond. The sun would shine, but it was cold and raw at ten thousand feet. The children were barefoot, with runny noses. We were invited into a few bleak rooms, people huddled on dirt floors and smiling with black spaces for missing teeth, searing bits of raw yak meat over an open fire. The meat was in slabs on a crude platter, with flies and sickly dogs and scrappy chickens poking about, fended off now and then.

We, ourselves, were living like sultans, served indeterminant root vegetables and rice flavored with meat at our little hotel. Sometimes the bath worked, and sometimes the water was hot. This I did not mind. I felt tremendously fortunate, for all the obvious reasons. But day upon day, as our journey progressed, I found myself haunted by the smiles. They represented more than innocence. The smiles were as sweet on the toothless oldsters as on the babes. They were not smiles of gratitude, which implies a prior condition of wanting. They were a permanent aspect of the face; they were a way of life.

The eyes shone. To me, the Westerner, they said wisdom. They held a secret, the opposite of what I know. And then I realized, they simply were; their beauty, alertness, spark of pleasure and deep presence communicated a lack of cluttered overlay: all the stuff that fogs my vision, competes for my mind's attention, prevents my restorative breathing when I'm not practicing yoga. Which, of course, is most of the time.

I was not painting, no time for that, but my plate was full, so to speak.

One afternoon we found ourselves at a school for boys. It was a simple, one-storied building surrounded by ratty grass and dusty patches of dirt. The boys were on the ground in their blue smocks, supported by their hands and elbows and craned over paper. Their fists gripped their pens, their brows locked in furious concentration. They were drawing the most intricate of designs: geometric mandalas, strips of interlocking serpents and animals and birds, every feather elaborately etched in fine line. They paid us no attention. The masters strolled about, pointed to a boy's work, erupted with a curt comment, neither threatening nor overly encouraging. "It's an art school," we were told. I was incredulous. "This is all they do here." These were the boys who were being trained to be craftsmen, to decorate the eaves and cornices and walls of the king's palace, the state library, various public buildings but homes as well.

Decoration is the wrong word. The designs and symbols were an integral part of the architecture. Bhutanese art is not a by-product of affluent patronage, as in our culture; it's deemed an essential craft to complete, in this case, a building.

I stood awestruck at this site. As a boy in kindergarten, I waited breathless until I could dig my hands into the pots of finger paint and get to work. While my family stared at the new TV in 1950, I was on the floor, propped up by my elbows, doubled over my sketchpad, painting a portrait of the dog. In college, between History of Western Civilization and Elizabethan Literature, I stole furtively to an art studio to paint, for no credit of course.

So, Bhutan was a "fourth world" country. Or was it?

At the end of our two weeks' stay, we embarked on a 4-day trek through even higher elevations. Most of my companions chose to ride on tough little ponies, with a native guide. I was among the diehard hikers, savoring this opportunity to sweat, eat even more humbly, sleep on the cold ground in a makeshift tent.

A pitcher of hot milk was offered for the morning cereal. The dinner rice was re-heated for lunch. I switched from bottled water to using the filter-pump device, as were the others who were doing just fine. I'd been told it was a fluke, my invasion of something-or-other on my Sierra Nevada hike the prior year. I seemed to be okay in the gut department, here in the Himalayas. And so I tried the cheese. As we broke camp the first morning, I noticed a herd of wild yak grazing upstream.

Villagers smiled as we descended the final six thousand feet. I figured they thought we were nuts, voluntarily climbing up and down these rocky extremes for no good purposes like collecting wild berries or herding sheep. But they seemed to enjoy our enjoyment; we couldn't communicate via language, but we had forged a link.

The balloons! I'd forgotten them, all the while stored in my pack. Our group leader at the trip's onset requested we not give the Bhutanese gifts. "They'll beg of the next visitors, and set off that negative chain." At this some colleagues, knowing of my balloons, frowned in disapproval.

"Go ahead, Rich. They're not around!" I was egged on when we slipped into a hillside hamlet. I yanked out a balloon and slowly inflated it. Two toddlers gawked in delight. I let the air rush out, and they positively squealed. Other children ran up. I passed out balloons, all colors, and demonstrated, again and again. The rest followed suit, unsuccessfully. A toothless elder appeared, and I handed him a balloon. He tried till he was beet read, the rush of releasing air shooting the balloon sky-high. Then the children tried to do likewise.

The village gathered in full force. I handed out all my stash, showed them how to tie the end, but they were having too much fun relinquishing the partially-filled balloons airborne into their dizzying, whistling corkscrew spirals. The cameras of my American companions were clicking as never before on this trip. The smiles of the toothless grandparents were a mile wide.

It was our final evening. Once again we were to sample the special rum before dinner. I'd been invigorated all day from the trek, but was seized in my room with a flash of midriff pain. I doubled over onto the floor. The pain was so intense I couldn't breathe. And then it passed. I felt nauseous, and weak. My belly was soon bloated to the size of two basketballs. I exploded from both ends of my system, and was left in a heap on the bathroom floor. I managed to drag myself to the others, now at mid-dinner. I waved, and flopped on a nearby bench.

Things worsened that night and during our departure for the airport the next morning. I needed help with my luggage. I didn't have the energy to speak. I folded into silence on the long, bumpy bus-ride. We waited a few hours in the tiny airport, which was unheated. I was freezing, gripped not so much with pain as inertia. It was a repeat of the symptoms I'd experienced during the past year, but all at once and a hundred-fold more intense.

Others made a buzz over some person, someone famous, in the cold, overcrowded room. Ellen Burstyn, the Oscar-winning actress. Of course I knew of her but I had not the slightest interest. And Robert Thurman, a few weeks later to be named by *Time* as one of the 25 most influential Americans, as a Buddhist scholar at Columbia. I sat directly in front of them on the small plane, clutching the air-sickness bag and not even minding that I was missing a most unique opportunity to share with them experiences of Bhutan.

Robert Thurman addressed me while I lay on the floor of the bustling Bangkok airport, our layover en route to Singapore. I don't remember a thing he said; it did, however, register that this man was Uma Thurman's father, and then I retreated into my misery.

Colleagues handled my tickets and visa and papers. I drew more and more into myself, a disbelief I'd become this incapacitated 18,000 miles from home. Even weakness was draining from me, leaving absolutely nothing in its wake.

The following day in Singapore I couldn't function. I had a room to myself, with some colleagues checking in by phone. Neither they nor I knew how seriously ill I'd become.

There were hours, I recall, on my hands and knees on the hotel room floor. Inch by inch, I could crawl from the bathroom to the bed. The room was spinning in slow circles. The pain was so severe I would crumple on the floor and focus on the flow of air in and out of my nostrils.

I remembered a red button on the telephone; "Emergency," it had said. An hour later, I remembered it again, and pushed it.

Hours later, when the doctor arrived, he decided the pain was equivalent to that of a woman in childbirth. He shook his head, he made some calls. He wanted to admit me to the hospital. I thought of my daughter, who hated to fly, coming half-way around the world. We settled on an injection, and various pills for the 30-hour flight to Vermont. Singapore Air would never have permitted me onboard if it was known how sick I was.

Travelling companions literally bundled me into bus seats and vans. They lowered me onto the floor of the airports, and helped me back up again. I could not fall asleep because I needed to keep my lips wet and to swallow.

Heavy-lidded, hour upon hour, I stared at a spot on the plane's ceiling and focused on my breath. My breath was all of me that was alive. The breath was the beginning, the end, the essence. Mandala-like, I envisioned the Emergency Room of the Burlington hospital and the woman, a friend, who is its chief physician. I would make it to this person, that place. I made no movement whatsoever. A stewardess would lift my head so I could sip, swallow another anti-diarrhea tablet. Or was it anti-nausea? It didn't matter. My body was on hold. My body was my breath, thin but steady, lips sealed, flowing calmly through my nostrils. It was yoga; it was quiet meditation after all.

Slumped in a wheelchair, I was whisked unquestioned through customs at JFK. An elderly taxi driver in Burlington brought my bags into the emergency room, declined payment. My friend barely recognized me, twenty pounds lighter. I underwent abdominal surgery a few hours later. No obstruction, no major pathogens, but all twenty-some feet of intestine, ordinarily the diameter of a nickel, were inflamed to two inches. A tube was inserted through my nostrils and down my throat for the next seven days, preventing me from swallowing until my guts were again operational. All that time, too, I could only focus on my breathing, to steady me, to stop me from gagging on the hard plastic tube.

After ten days on IV, flushed with all manner of antibiotics, I knew I was cured. My gut felt perfectly normal for the first time in a year. The best guess was that some insidious parasite eluded testing all the while and then really played havoc, once encouraged with yak curds and mock-meat and the Himalayan altitude. The antibiotics finally did it in. It was no less than a miracle, they said, my survival for several days with no peristaltic movement before and during the long flight home. Gangrene usually takes over well before.

"It was your breathing, Rich," said one physician-friend. "Your good cardiovascular shape. Kept that blood infusing all the tiny capillaries. You were working hard on that plane!"

"No. Really. There was nothing to it."

"Bhutan is a sacred place," said my aunt, a psychotherapist and ardent disciple of the human potential movement. "Perhaps you simply had to go there, to be healed."

Writing "To, and from, Bhutan"

Richard Alther

—I was asked by the editor to submit a piece to one of my favorite journals, *Pilgrimage*, out of North Carolina, focused on psychology, especially the Eastern arts, which invites readers and subscribers to submit their own stories of personal growth or inspiring, transitional events;

—The trip to Bhutan had so many impacts—spiritual, physical, cultural, mental, medical, artistic, athletic—that I thought writing about it would bring some cohesion to the experience for me;

—Writing gave me the chance to review all of my photographs and to re-live the trip by way of "research";

—I read more articles in *National Geographic* and elsewhere to get some more of my facts straight;

—I have no trouble sitting down at the computer and plunging in. First draft was way too wordy, but a printed-out document gives me something concrete to work from;

—It's too long, and I have to pare it down. This is the hardest work: honing in on the path of the story without extraneous details. I wanted to bring two opposites together—anticipation of/participation in this far-flung travel adventure, and the very unexpected outcome, the medical condition I was in upon leaving and going home. They seemed unrelated—two totally different experiences, but the transition from Vermont to this Buddhist kingdom actually did prepare me for having a better chance to save my life;

—The essence of yoga and meditation and Buddhist practice is loss of ego, non-grasping at thoughts and individual desires, all by way of concentrating on the breath. And that is what kept me calm enough to fly home for 30 hours until surgical help was at hand;

—Writing helps to synthesize an experience, break it down into digestible pieces, so it can really sink in, and perhaps be useful to oneself. Others? A bonus. Writing can turn experience into wisdom, something truly learned, whether or not it is published and shared. It's shared with yourself, both as writer and also reader. "The process is the payoff" is what works for me.

Russian Hours, 1961

Francis E. Crowley

Part One

My trip was bedbug and danger-free, although the walls in the old Metropole Hotel in Moscow were bugged. It was just after the debacle of Gary Powers that our group of "religious pilgrims" departed NYC on a KLM Constellation for the 20 hour journey. I had the window seat, looking down at the Atlantic breakers below, and upon suddenly waking from a nap, I panicked with the feeling of free-fall in my body. So, I worked on a poem in my notebook, **"The pilgrimage"** in Spenserian stanza, puffed up like the clouds for my first flight, first trip abroad and first real quest. I aped Byron's "Childe Harold's Pilgrimage" with every word and line, imitated his voice and fragrance. I was on my way.

Yuri Gagarin's first manned flight into space in early April, 1961, was celebrated with gargantuan red-banner parades for three days in Red Square. We walked into the middle of it, snapping color slides right and left. Such bookends to our trip (Gary Powers trial followed by Yuri Gagarin's triumph) cast the CCCP into the international spotlight and our little group, as well. Just after I had returned, my acne-faced photo and news-story of "being there when.." appeared at the top of the FRONT PAGE of the next day's ***HARTFORD COURANT***. I was giddy with the blind, dumb good luck of it and suffering from a swelled ego, but my little poem in the notebook was good and growing with each new city and sensation. My naive, 19 year-old's eyes were popping open to a

larger, political world and to inchoate conflicts in the Soviet soul as my observations and understanding grew.

The Rev. Mohrbacker of the New York-based Eastern Catholic Apostolate had coaxed Fordham University in the Bronx to sponsor the three-week trip. Even in 1961 dollars, $600 was a bargain for a world-class, escorted, exotic, educational tour of dark, dangerous and mysterious Russia. Even I knew that, for it was almost the cost of a year's tuition and fees at Fairfield in 1960. I needed every penny for college, so I asked my Aunt Mary for the trip loan, and she agreed. It was also billed as a religious pilgrimage at Russian Orthodox Easter to a nominally and virulently, aggressively anti-religious society and country that had closed all the churches, banned the priesthood and seminaries and shut down all services but for a few at tourist sites. I was not too young to appreciate the irony of our situation or the absurdest scene of handing out religious cards with colorful icons on the street. None of us was arrested; tourist dollars were desperately needed. What was Rev. Morhbacker thinking?

We stopped at the GREAT GATES OF KIEV, St. Vladimir's Cathedral ("smells and bells"), sunbathed with the early birds on the sandy beaches of the Dneiper River, and the Soviet men were all in Russian speedos. Kiev was in full Spring blossom. We then flew 1800 miles directly north on Aeroflot for the first time to the frigid climate of most of Mother Russia. I couldn't wait to meet Russians in a face-to-face encounter at restaurants, on the streets, in parks...and in the fabulous museums, but as for the gorgeous churches and cathedrals...St. Isaac's massive cathedral in Leningrad was permanently closed with a small ante-room opened as a museum. It was here that my religious eyes, however, began to open.

Today, August 14, 2011, at last, I think I have found her: **anima**, the Russian soul, 50 years later, in the poetry of Anna Ahkmatova. And, ironically, she was still alive back then, during our trip to Leningrad, walking the same streets as we did, feeling the same cold, early April wind blowing along the Fontanka Canal, paying homage, as we did, April 10, 1961 to the new Monument to A. Pushkin. Perhaps, that day she passed close by on the Lomonosov Most (bridge).......while we, completely unaware, almost touched the living spirit of Russia in our very midst. Perhaps, she was writing or hiding in a nearby cafe?? Only now can I fully realize and appreciate the gravity of our inspirational time of spending a few days in Anna's city and the city of Peter, THE GREAT. I remember visiting the State Russian Museum not far from Pushkin. We walked the city; saw the canals. Anna Ahkmatova had five more fruitful years filled with fear to live through in 1961, but also with long-delayed official accolades, even from the earlier ostracizing SOVIET WRITERS' UNION, as well as from international recognition and honors in a trip to Italy and to Oxford.

April 9, 1961, in Leningrad I was in deep sinus pain, suffering from the poor pressurization of the new Russian Aeroflot plane, rocketed from Kiev to Leningrad by some Soviet hot-shot pilot the day before! Shivering in my hotel room, I barely slept in my cold, high, hotel bed above the Neva River; the excruciating headache felt as if my sinus cavities had exploded. The next day, April 10, we were to travel back deep into history through the glories of the **HERITAGE STATE MUSEUM**: *Rembrandts, Titian, centuries of French painting, and* Monet, my favorite. I remember the grand staircase of marble pulling us in to the Royal apartments.

Part Two

Russia has always been a part of European culture and consciousness but not necessarily on the itinerary of the "grand tour"; however, St. Petersburg, as Russia's "window on the west" has a strong and peculiar draw for Americans this year (2011). All my friends, including my college "roomie" are going there. St. Petersburg, the "Venice of the North"; Peter's city, but which Peter is it? The Apostle Peter, *petrus*, "the rock" in a far distant swamp near the Neva River which empties into the

Gulf of Finland in 1700 AD? Or, Czar Peter, who was no saint, Peter the GREAT: who cut off the heads of the praetorian guard, the Streltsy (shooters); who is Pushkin's "Iron Horseman," the monstrous-sized equestrian guarding the city (not yet made of steel like "Stalin" to come, but fearsome at 7 feet tall—his actual height in life!). St. Petersburg is now celebrating 300 years. What an opening opportunity for tourism's rediscovery of Peter's city by the sea and for literary revivals of *Blok, of Ahkmatova, Pasternak, and Brodsky. Even Pushkin recently celebrated his 200th birthday (b.1799).

Let's go back! I want to walk the Nevsky Prospeckt, again; smell the acrid tobacco of Russian cigarettes of the 60's ("Three Bogatiree"); sit in contemporary, smoky, cyber-cafes with Russia's youth of 2011; walk the halls of the Twelve Colleges of St. Petersburg State University, which I missed the first trip; sample new poets at open-mics; and, even hear Voznesensky with 30,000 other fans in the Sport's Stadium just outside the city. Most of all I want to march with my LGBT Russian brothers and sisters in next year's already banned Gay Pride Parade, May 11, 2012, even if it means beatings, persecution, imprisonment, as just happened three months ago; they were locked up in the city jail together in one small cubicle for 24 hours and not allowed to use the bathroom (see *www.gayrussia.com*). One marcher smuggled his iPhone in, took pictures, and sent them out: the story went viral when the Italian news agencies jumped on it! So, some things in Russia never change—persecution of some of the following: political dissidents (see the group "VOINA"); CHECHENS; poets and gays and lesbians, still endangered species. Somehow, though, in my imagination and in the reality of Russian history, it is the poets of Russia like Anna Ahkmatova, Pushkin, Osip Mandelstam, Pasternak and Brodsky ....who will have the last word.

Part Three

We flew from St. Petersburg to Moscow on April 12, and by April 14 my sore head was feeling better. It was our last day of the trip. The weather had turned warm, and the blue skies had puffy white clouds like handkerchiefs waving goodbye in the stiff Spring breeze. We had visited many sites of monasteries and churches, now museums of atheism or with displays seeking to disprove religion. Many are minimally maintained as originally established with aged monks. Sad. Most were in disrepair except for the tourist showplaces. We had been excited about the possibility of a Kremlin visit, and I was eager to see the stunning gold-capped, onion domes of the ancient churches within the Kremlin walls.

Later in the morning we were at last admitted through a main gate into the courtyard—all 79 of us! We were treated to the crown jewels of the Czars and Czarinas and to the crown jewel of Russian history. While touring the Kremlin state rooms, we couldn't understand the clapping and cheering in the halls right in the heart of the Kremlin. When we went out into the streets we were amazed! It seemed like a national holiday to me. The Bolshoy Theatre was decorated with huge red and orange paper flowers, and other surrounding buildings were being painted. Red Square was hung with banners every few feet, and St. Basil's disappeared before our eyes.

All of Moscow turned out for the parades. It was almost impossible to move an inch in the crowds in Red Square. I had longed for direct contact with everyday people, and not just with the circumspect Intourist Guides who encouraged us to take all the pictures we wanted. Of course, we had never strayed from the appointed path, even resisting the temptation to go roaming the gorgeous subway stations, each one a singular work of art. So, now I had

*Alexander Blok was a major Russian poet (1880-1921), a master of the iambic tetrameter form and the greatest Russian poet of the first two decades of the 20th Century, according to V. Nabokov, who should know, even though he was tone deaf!

my physical, sweaty, shouting, singing contact right in the line to visit the Lenin and Stalin Mausoleum. We were ushered to the front of the mile-long line as special guests, and I gazed at Stalin's life-like face* and body with shock and awe: 40 millions dead from his Czardom! The parades continued for hours in bright sunshine and billowing breeze; the day seemed made for "spontaneous" celebrations.

Yuri Gagarin was being honored in Red Square, and the crowds kept coming. The Police seemed to be having a difficult time controlling them.

Late in the afternoon, as we boarded the Intourist buses, people shouted and cheered at us. They were all friendly and handed souvenirs and newspapers with Yuri Gagarin's picture into the buses. When all 79 of us American college and university students, clergy and intrepid tourists were safely on the bus, we waved warm "goodbyes" enthusiastically. We clapped; they returned it! It was time to head to Sheremetevo Airport for the night flight home.

© copyright 2011 Francis E. Crowley, PhD

*Stalin's body was removed shortly after our visit and placed in the Kremlin wall, ironically, near the American, John Reed (TEN DAYS THAT SHOOK THE WORLD).

Impeccably Shanghai Resistant

Marita

Red

Original Sin

China Red

Even on my new scarf,
peaking through black lace along with luminescent dots.
Bought in a store riddled with "Pigeons",
girls courting older men with money,
    for apartments.
Where BMW lip-synchs "Be My Wife".
Called a bird name because they fly away when the rich men return to
Taiwan to visit their wives for a few days.

Buildings molded into non-rectilinear shapes with hope
and the achievement of best lives.
Outlined in the kinetic blue and green neon of new money,
rendering the skyline a glossy color cover of a sci-fi novel.

A self-defined port city of multicolored lights and delights,
where in the past men were selected, tricked and taken out to sea.
 "Shanghaied" for their body labors to support the opium trade.

For contrast, at midday,
I retreat with monks into temple grounds and hold heart with the
Jade Buddha.
A spiritual place that mingles calm goodness with green ginkgo trees and
incense offerings.
When I approach the statue a wave of well-being overwhelms me
and I feel and hear that everything will be all right for me.
Like the serene green Jade Buddha,
not even uncomfortable being jeweled,
I am at peace.

It is here I decide I can finally be brave enough to release my love for you.

That night,
In a bar overlooking the Pudong,
after drinks of a cinnabar red "knock-out-punch",
I kiss my fingertips like you have done,
open my palm in the gesture of the Buddha's pose
and blow my love for you
Out into the Huangpu River,
Out to the East China Sea.

Later, in my hotel room, I enter a narcotic sleep.

But, instead of leaving
you vibrantly, vividly appear in your 23-year-old incarnation
in bed with me, and we kiss all over landing on lips.
The deliciously strong Turkish coffee spirals of your hair imprison my fingers,
Till finally they manage to escape the Medusan aggression of your curls,
Re-emerging delighted, cursed and vexed.

I awake
to a drabber city
With "neons out"
between white 5 star sheets
Alone.

When I return home I email you some photos of my trip.
 "Amazing images", you say.

Marita's poetry has appeared in Long River Run and Mithras, where she also served as a founding editor and an editor of fiction. In addition to her love of poetry she sings the blues, plays classical piano, clavichord and harpsichord and is known as an annoying lyric savant. She maintains a keen interest in scientific discoveries, statistics and bioethics and she has authored and co-authored several manuscripts. Her day jobs include a private practice and teaching.

Becoming a Godmother

Sarah Rachel Moros

"Poverty is a multidimensional problem. Its root causes may differ greatly from one context to the next. . .But wherever poverty is widespread, its universal features——malnutrition, poor health care, crumbling infrastructure, lack of education, unsafe housing, social instability—combine and reinforce each other in a vicious cycle from which it is very difficult to escape once trapped."[1]

First Impressions

I followed Jacob as we picked our way around a virtual maze of greasy puddles, plastic trash and dog feces. He knew where he was going in Barracas and, although he did not feel his own foreignness, his clothes betrayed him as American. A friend, Rebecca, followed behind. She too had come before, and while her bohemian look clearly separated her from the slum-dwellers, she at least could have been Argentine. I was the sorest thumb in our group. Blond, blue-eyed and extremely fair-skinned, I felt unusually wary as Jacob turned off the main street and led us into a narrow dirt alleyway.

Lined by small cement-block houses numbered with red spray paint, and partially paved with jagged slabs of stone, the alley was no wider than three and a half feet. Much to my relief, Jacob stopped twenty feet in and knocked on a grimy door. I could still see the street from where I stood, which slightly allayed my apprehension. I tried not to touch or step in anything as I waited for the door to open, unsure of what to expect. This was my first time seeing poverty firsthand, and I was nervous.

[1] Finca International. *New Horizons.* http://www.villagebanking.org/history.htm

This was Lilia's home, and I was here to meet her and tour her slum. According to Jacob, Lilia was a neighborhood organizer and an active participant in the unemployed autonomous workers movement, *el movimiento piquetero.* She was what is commonly referred to in Argentina as a *piquetera,* an unemployed worker-turned-protester. Jacob had met Lilia at a gathering of such workers and she had invited him to her home in Barracas 2124. Originally Barracas had been composed of four slums-21, 22, 23 and 24–constructed by factory workers in the late 1940s during President Juan Perón's first term. Now it was simply known as Barracas 2124, a tired and impoverished remnant of a bygone era of hope and growth. It was in Barracas 2124 that I first learned that poverty has many faces and physical manifestations, but its experience is universal.

On Jacob's first visit to Barracas 2124 he organized an English class for children, which he taught on his second visit. On his third visit he brought Rebecca along to teach. Also on that third visit, Lilia invited Rebecca and Jacob to be the godparents of her newborn daughter, Diana, and they had accepted. By the fourth visit, I was intrigued enough to accompany Rebecca and Jacob to the slum. However, I was determined not to become as emotionally involved with the family and the slum's inhabitants as Jacob already had. I had previously been "an activist", and, at the time, I was a burned out activist two weeks away from leaving Argentina. For me, this trip was supposed to be an objective, anthropological, dispassionate exploration of poverty. I did not realize that such an experience would ultimately be impossible.

Lilia's husband answered the door. A slim, young man in his late twenties, he had yellowing

teeth, grime-covered skin, and a poof of orange-tinged hair atop his head. He welcomed us into his home as if three foreigners showing up at his door was a non-event and led us to the back room, only five paces from the front entrance. Despite the short distance between the front door and back room, a plethora of images-some surprising, some shocking-instantly drew my attention. Laundry hung from the chicken wire ceiling, beyond which I could see blue winter sky. The cement floor was damp and dirty, and the small wooden table looked slimy and rotted. A room in the back, right corner of the house was filled with construction material, and a rooster stood on top of a plank as if to guard its entrance. The room was not much cleaner than the alleyway, and it seemed to double as both a backyard and a common living space.

Entering Lilia's room I first noticed Lilia herself. However, I did not realize the woman was Lilia. Instead, I again found myself dazed by the photograph-like images my brain was absorbing. Before me I saw a woman who looked to be in her early forties lying on a stained and sagging queen-sized mattress. Next to this woman lay a non-expressive newborn swaddled in pajamas, and a white rabbit, of approximately equal size to the newborn, hopped around the bed. The floor was dirty but dry, although I was thrown by a smattering of wilted lettuce leaves and bird and rabbit droppings on the floor *and* the bed. The bird droppings puzzled me as the bedroom had a roof. Next to the bed was a wooden cabinet filled with basic items such as combs, brushes and select medicines, and next to the door there was a broken baby crib

full of tattered odds-and-ends and a half-empty bottle of soda. There was also a television with grainy reception topped by a crooked antenna. I had read about slum dwellers owning TVs in Brazilian *favelas*, but to actually see a TV in a slum was a surprise nonetheless.

I had known to expect the unexpected. Jacob had told me that the living conditions in Lilia's house were dismal. But although I could mask my emotional reactions under an expressionless gaze, I did not know how to feel about what lay before me. I tried to open myself to what I was seeing and to withhold judgment, pity, discomfort or fear, but the state of astonishment induced by my surroundings was coupled with a state of disbelief induced by Lilia's image.

Lilia did not look like the Argentines I knew. Her skin was dark, wrinkled and sun-stained, and her full, loose belly protruded over her old clothes. Beyond looking noticeably poorer and more indigenous than the Argentines I had previously met, she did not fit the visual image of a gung-ho political activist and passionate neighborhood organizer. I simply could not *believe* that this was Lilia, the slum organizer that Jacob so greatly admired. The image he had painted for me was of a dignified individual who had risen above the worst aspects of her surroundings. At first glance, this woman seemed to embrace, if not cultivate, a stereotypical image of poverty and ignorance. Her home could have easily been featured in one of those TV commercials featuring the poor, and the image played into my preconceived notions of poverty as helpless, desperate and pitiful. Here I was looking poverty in the face, and I was appalled.

I only began to believe that this woman was Lilia and that Lilia actually was what Jacob said she was when I looked into her eyes. She had oval-shaped, brown eyes that exuded both liveliness and intelligence. Her eyes lit up with excitement when we entered her room. Following a quick introduction and hello, Jacob and Lilia began to chat in detail about organizers' meetings, upcoming events and social issues. Their discussion confirmed for me

Lilia's natural intelligence and her inclinations as a social activist. Soon, I loosened up and volunteered some of my own thoughts as well. Meanwhile, I began to forgive Lilia for the lack of hygiene in her home as she explained, unprompted, the lack of basic amenities available to slum-dwellers. She had little running water and no shower in the house, but she was proud to pay her electricity bill and not be one of those who pirated their electricity illegally by running wires to their houses from the main street.

Over the course of the two hours I listened to Jacob and Lilia carefully; nevertheless, I remember the dwelling and the day's events much more clearly than the social and political conversation. I remember watching the white rabbit hop onto and off of the baby's stomach without Lilia so much as batting an eyelash. I remember learning that Lilia was not in her early forties but was actually thirty-two, on her second marriage to a twenty-eight year old man, and had seven children of which the eldest was fifteen. I found out that the pile of building materials in the back room was intended to create a pre-school for the slum's children above her house, and that it would be finished when Lilia was able to collect another few thousand American dollars in donations. I also distinctly remember Lilia mentioning another American student and activist, "just like a daughter" to Lilia, who had raised close to $4,000.00 for the pre-school already. Lilia referenced her closeness to this American daughter frequently.

In another curious incident, a pet pigeon appeared from under the bed and proceeded to attack a black rabbit that was hopping around on the floor. I listened to Lilia laugh mirthfully as she recounted how the pigeon, despite its smaller size, had almost killed the rabbit a week before by attacking its throat, but that the pigeon had been pulled off in time. Then she explained that the animals were not pets but economic and nutritional investments: when in need the family could sell them, eat them or breed them and do the same with their offspring. As there was no backyard in which to house the collection of animals she owned, all but the chickens and rooster had free reign of the house. By the end of the day I counted two rabbits, one pigeon, two hens, one rooster, a cat, three children, two adults and one grandparent living in that tiny squalid house. By the time I left Buenos Aires, a few bubbly black puppies had joined the fray.

The animals reminded me of an old Jewish children's tale. In this tale, a poor farmer goes to his rabbi complaining about his wife and the rabbi advises the farmer to bring one of his animals into his hut. When the farmer complains about this first animal, the rabbi advises him to bring a second animal into the hut. This continues until the farmer is half-mad from bumping into animals and stepping in their messes. Reaching the very depths of his despair, the poor farmer runs to the rabbi begging for relief, and the rabbi advises the farmer to empty his hut of all the animals. The farmer returns the animals to the barn and subsequently finds comfort in his home and makes peace with his wife.

I wondered if Lilia ever felt like the poor Jewish farmer, and I marveled at the presence of so many animals in this tiny home. I thought back to how, as a child, I bypassed the moral of the story—that it could always be worse—and, rather, was struck by the concept of completely sharing one's living space with farm animals. Sharing a home with dogs, cats and caged birds was a concept I was comfortable with as a young American. But horses, sheep, pigs and cows living side-by-side with humans? "People actually live with farm animals?" I had asked my father, and he explained that some people had no choice but to shelter animals in their home to keep them safe and warm. Here, in Lilia's house, a house that was barely on the outskirts of a Europeanized, cosmopolitan city and yet a million miles away, was a real life example of that childhood tale. In remembering it, I was trying to both make sense of and to uncover a positive, familiar association with my surroundings.

Second Impressions

After close to two hours of chatting we left Lilia's house to head to the market. Lilia pulled a black sweater over her T-shirt and pulled her short hair back into a ponytail. These superficial changes made her look significantly more put-together and less like the stereotypical "poor person" an American might imagine. She smiled broadly, as was her way, and led us out of the house to the market to buy food for lunch.

Lilia was warm and caring with us, and she treated the outing as a cultural lesson in a living classroom. She explained what foods were expensive and what foods were affordable for slum families. She showed us what to purchase to make the afternoon meal for the family, and she included us in her hunt for the cheapest pair of shoes that she could find for one of her daughters. She explained the geography of the slum and promised to walk us through it later.

From what I had seen thus far, the slum was a low-lying, whitish-gray concrete monster, composed of dirty buildings and iridescent mud puddles. I would later learn while walking the slum that these concrete buildings represented the oldest and most developed areas of the slum, and that on its rapidly growing outskirts many houses were built with rusted tin roofing stolen from bus stops and half-broken planks of wood. These homes were true huts that lacked running water and electricity. Their floors were still made of the slum's reddish-brown dirt and their inhabitants used a chemically contaminated stream for a toilet.

The colors of the slum contrasted sharply with those of the market, enlivened by a riot of bright colors, from the plastic bags to the piles of orange clementines, yellow bananas and green lettuce heads stacked high. The colors of the market made me happy. I think they made Rebecca happy as well, because the two of us purchased these fruits as a luxury to gift to the family. We also wanted to have something light to enjoy alongside all the starch- and fat-heavy food that Lilia requested we buy for lunch. For the first time in my life I bought eggs individually rather than in a carton and saw bulky bags of pet food—bags that an American family would regularly buy and store in its pantry—open for individuals to serve themselves. People scooped out no more than a few days worth of pet food, which was then weighed, wrapped and taken home. The concept of "not for resale" clearly did not apply to the informal slum economy.

Rebecca and I snickered at how oblivious Jacob was to looking so out-of-place as he walked around with a white T-shirt, jeans, and fanny pack. The crowning glory of his foreignness was the big, black camera that hung around his neck like a bruise. We snapped our pictures of the fruit and the soccer field furtively, kept our cameras hidden, spoke English in low tones, and felt superior to Jacob because we knew how out-of-place we were and "appropriately" felt uncomfortable. Now I feel ashamed of my gossiping and my feelings of superiority. In retrospect, we three were all naïve, and our varied reactions to these new experiences reflected our different methods for coping with the poverty we confronted. Acceptance. Discomfort. Denial. Curiosity. Confusion. Guilt. Distance. Responsibility. Such emotions toyed with us as we learned about the slum firsthand from our most-knowledgeable, warm and accepting guide, Lilia. If we treated her as a cultural lesson or a free anthropological study in poverty, she never once showed resentment. No question was too probing for Lilia. No question seemed to offend.

Upon returning from the market, Lilia prepared deep-fried *carne empanadas* for lunch, and as I watched her I began to sweat with anxiety. Always under foot, the rooster flapped its way around the microscopic kitchen, ate food out of the garbage can, and left feather bits floating in the air. There was barely a trickle of cold water to clean the plates from which we were to eat, and although Rebecca scrubbed hard, the plates remained soiled. The soap had run out and no one washed his or her hands before cooking. If that were not enough to make one's stomach sore for a few days, the *empanada* crust was so saturated with oil that the *empanada* itself looked like a giant French fry. When it came time to eat, I had to remind myself that there was no way I could politely refuse the food. Before opening the Coca-Cola that Jacob had bought for lunch, we all drank the half bottle of flat soda in the broken baby crib. Obviously, in Lilia's house nothing went to waste, and thinking back on that moment, I am reminded of the singsong phrase a friend recites: "Use it up, wear it out, make do or do without." My American friend consciously tries to follow these "usage" principles: Lilia and her family have no choice but to live by them.

Aside from the children, at five feet five inches and 155 pounds I was the slimmest one in the room, and I knew that I was fifteen to twenty pounds overweight by Western medical standards. I was also trying to lose weight. Yet Lilia and her family begged me to eat more, saying that I was too skinny and had to put more weight on my bones. This also happened on my third visit to the slum with another family.

I knew from experience that Argentina was a highly body-conscious society and that skinniness was prized among middle and upper class women. What I had not realized was that Argentina's urban poor favored heavier-set bodies, much the way people still do in impoverished countries worldwide and particularly in Africa. Extra weight in Barracas 2124 continued to indicate wealth and personal comfort. I nonetheless refused a third *empanada* as gracefully as possible, claiming that I was full. I ate a piece of fruit instead. Now I wonder if, in rejecting more food, did I somehow reject my hosts' hospitality and my hosts themselves? Or, alternatively, in refusing their generosity, did I somehow disrespectfully acknowledge their poverty?

On our way out the door after that late lunch, Lilia confirmed the time of the baptism for her youngest the following Sunday, reaffirmed Jacob and Rebecca's commitment to be the baby's godparents, and asked me to be her two-year old Ayde's godmother. I laughed her invitation off with some discomfort, said that I was not sure if I would be able to come the following week, and told her I did not think it would be possible for me

to be a proper godmother anyway. I did not explain that accepting the responsibilities of a godparent made me uncomfortable, given that I was Jewish and scheduled to leave Argentina in two weeks. She persisted with her request as I edged my way out the front door. I felt cornered in the face of Lilia's generosity, and over the course of the week I thought about that invitation a number of times. I asked myself uneasily, "Why would Lilia invite three veritable strangers with no ties to her family to be her children's godparents?" I eventually pushed the thought to the back of my mind.

Third Impressions

The morning of the baptism we three Jewish Americans were running on Argentine time: late. We hustled out the door carrying the gifts that Jacob and Rebecca had bought for all three of Lilia's youngest, ages 4 years, 2 years and 3 months, and ran around the block to the bus stop. There we waited anxiously for thirty minutes hoping for the bus to arrive and debating whether to take a taxi. Our concern was not the cost of the taxi, rather, we did not want to inappropriately flaunt our wealth or brand ourselves as targets for theft. Every other bus I had taken in Buenos Aires generally arrived within fifteen minutes during daylight hours, even to low-traffic destinations. Yet only one bus ran per half hour to Barracas 2124, a slum in which many of Buenos Aires' poorest lived and from which they traveled daily to work in the city's wealthier parts. Their lack of political representation was obvious, and for the first time, I began to understand why Jacob found the *piqueteros'* push for political recognition so fascinating.

Upon arriving at Lilia's home approximately one hour behind schedule, we discovered that the house was in disarray, that none of the children was dressed for church, and that our anxiety about arriving late was mistaken. While Rebecca fished tattered shoes from under the bed for Lilia's barefoot 2-year old, Ayde, I painfully brushed the knots from Brisa's hair, apologizing with every tug.

Brisa, Lilia's 4-year old, had beautiful, waist-length black hair and an infectious smile that was often accompanied by a loud, rich laugh. When she was not laughing or smiling, her eyes projected a calm seriousness befitting of an old soul. To this day, I consider Brisa one of the most photogenic children I have seen in my life, and my photo album is filled with close-ups of her face. Brisa and the cat. Brisa and the rooster. Brisa and the rabbit. Brisa laughing. Brisa standing barefoot by the door. Her capacity for love was genuine, and it shone through when she climbed into our laps without warning or begged jealously for our attention when we were playing with her sisters.

As I let Brisa loose from the comb's punishment and watched her play, I could not help thinking that had Brisa been born in the United States she would have been a child actress. The cruel fact dawned on me that Brisa had been born into a world without opportunities, a world where even becoming a maid might require that she speak broken English. I, on the other had, had been born into a world of the highest privilege. I asked myself, what responsibilities, if any, did I have to a child like Brisa? Could there by any rhyme or reason to my origin of birth, or was it sheer dumb luck that I was born into a well-to-do family in a peaceful, clean American suburb? I also contemplated the universality of childhood, and bemoaned the dawning awareness of her world that would one day accompany Brisa's shift from childhood to adulthood. Would she ever have a chance to be a teenager, or would the transition to adulthood be sudden and direct?

Once I finished with Brisa's hair, Lilia attempted to brush out the knots in Ayde's. After a minute of fighting with the knots, Lilia decided instead to pull Ayde's hair into two adorable pigtails. We then helped Brisa put on a checkered blue prairie dress, buckled a pair of stained, white shoes onto her little feet and pushed her out the door. Putting the shoes on Brisa's feet further highlighted for me how poor Lilia's family was, as her girls typically ran barefoot on the cold, wet concrete floor. But as I once again lamented the world's cruel randomness

regarding distribution of wealth and origin of birth, I noticed the very large, very expensive CD player and speakers in the children's room, shiny, black and new. The CD player could only have arrived in Lilia's house in one of three ways: she bought it with the donations she received to build a second floor for a school, it was a donation itself, or it was stolen. I refrained from consciously drawing this conclusion and analyzing the possibilities, but in that moment my growing allegiance to Lila froze cold.

As we left the house, Lilia sent Ariel, her fifteen-year old, to "find Federico" so that he could be Ayde's godfather. I assumed I had misheard as Jacob had already accepted the role of godfather for Lilia's baby and it was Lilia's baby who was to be baptized. However, upon arriving at the Catholic Church, Lilia handed me a white candle and proceeded to hoist Ayde onto her lap. Brisa sat next to me, and Jacob and Rebecca sat a few aisles before us with their future godchild in their arms.

Once Ayde was comfortably settled on Lilia's knee I whispered quietly, "What is this for?" Lilia whispered back, "That's for you." "Why is this for me?" I responded, guessing the answer. Lilia replied, "It's for you to light as you become Ayde's godmother." "You can baptize two children at once? I thought you would baptize her another day," I feebly protested. "Why not today? You are here now and she's already two years old!" Lilia affirmed with a laugh.

I felt trapped by Lilia's words and actions. Just as had happened the week before with the *empanadas*, I found myself in a no-refuse situation. I—a Jewish girl from New York who had only been to a Catholic Church once prior—was suddenly to become the godmother of a tantrum-throwing two-year old growing up in a marginalized Buenos Aires slum. How could I possibly say no? I felt incredulous to the point of laughter at how Lilia had played upon my reluctance to be direct, lest it be seen as judgment or rejection, to maneuver me into this peculiar situation. I had to give her credit for being clever and to gently chastise myself for being blind.

I weighed my options and responsibilities quickly. Was I going to be responsible in the event that something happened to Lilia? Would I feel obligated to care for her child? No, I decided, there was no binding legal contract behind this verbal commitment, and I barely knew Lilia. Further, if finding an appropriate godparent for Ayde in the event something befell Lilia were a true concern, Lilia would have made someone more proximate to her family, someone more likely to care for her child, the godmother. But as a Jew—although granted not a particularly observant one—did I personally have a problem participating in this ceremony? No, I decided again, I would do no more than go through the motions.

But what was it that Lilia wanted? Had she simply run out of people to ask to be godparents to her children? She did have seven of them . . .

Rather than choose the option that was lurking in the back of my mind, that Lilia was exploiting our desire to be included in her world at least temporarily in order to extract gifts and money from us, I opted to believe that she had run out of her existing supply of potential godparents. Perhaps, I thought, one cannot be a godparent to more than one child per family in order to spread the responsibilities around in the event of the parents' death. I decided that Lilia simply had no one else to ask to be Ayde's godmother, but I vowed not to give any major gift to Lilia or her children. If that were what Lilia was after, I did not want to condone such behavior by falling into a pattern that other Americans, including, perhaps, my two kind-hearted friends, had already fallen into. I also absolved myself of any future responsibility for Ayde's care beyond what I could feasibly give. Within an hour I was one goddaughter and a good story richer.

The day turned out to be quite lovely and interesting. Jacob's parents were in town, and they attended the baptism. My co-godparent, Federico, was a young Argentine from a wealthy family that had (mostly) renounced his birthright to adopt the *piquetero* identity and become a neighborhood organizer. His take on *piqueterismo* was fascinating, and when I chose to write my senior thesis on the movement, he became an invaluable resource for

my primary research and fieldwork. The priest turned out to be a liberation theologist, and when my hosts saw that this interested me, they filled me in on the church's history in organizing Barracas 2124 and the subsequent murder at the hands of the government of hundreds of liberation theology priests during the Dirty War in the 1970s.

Once again we ate lunch in Lilia's house and spent the afternoon together, and I went home feeling good about my friendship with Lilia and satiated in my curiosity about the slum. Although I learned that Federico was actually the godfather of a number of Lilia's children, including Brisa, I managed to put this fact out of my mind, to forget about the shiny new stereo, and to forgive Lilia for forcing me into an uncomfortable situation.

Last Impressions

The following week I returned to Barracas 2124 with Federico and Rebecca, this time visiting the newest area of the slum. While Rebecca gave an English lesson to children in the home of a Paraguayan immigrant, Adriana, Federico gave me a guided factual and geographical tour of Barracas. I learned that the slum was filled with Paraguayan immigrants and, as a result, many people in the slum spoke Guaraní as a first language rather than Spanish. I learned that this influx of immigrants was causing tension among the poor *porteños*, as residents born and raised in Buenos Aires are called. Underprivileged *porteños* accused the Paraguayan immigrants of driving down wages at a time when the economy was already doing poorly, and they made scapegoats of these immigrants for their indigenous heritage. It was our same American immigration debate, displaced a thousand miles south.

Federico took me past the soccer and volleyball courts, nothing more than dusty square playing fields cut into the dirt, but filled to the brim with men playing games while others looked on. From there we followed a set of rusty train tracks to a bridge crossing a river flowing toward the sea. The river was filled with trash and chemical pollutants, and its steep sides were covered by an overgrowth of intertwined bushes, yet there stood a woman washing her cloths in the water and hanging them on the branches to dry. Federico pointed across the way to a series of factories in the distance. He told me that these factories, founded in Perón's day, had once provided the ample employment that had attracted people to build Barracas 2124 in the first place. Only the buildings remained, rundown reminders of what used to be and what might have been.

Later, when researching my senior thesis, I read personal testimonies affirming that when the factories were up-and-running there had existed a feeling of hope in Buenos Aires' slums. Slum inhabitants had believed that their living conditions were temporary and life would soon be better. Now slums like Barracas were places where children became addicted to drugs and joined gangs, where garbage collectors went to sell their plastic bottles and cardboard boxes for a pittance, where squatters sometimes created new shantytowns overnight, and where the water was so contaminated it was dangerous to ingest. To emphasize this last point, Federico recounted how the police had made a petty thief swim across this river below us, and how they had watched the boy from where we were then standing. Slum's residents claim the boy subsequently died.

After this sobering reality check, Federico and I returned to Adriana's home where Rebecca was giving her English lesson. The house, no bigger than Lilia's, surprised me. Every room had a roof, the floor was dry and neatly swept, there was soap available to wash one's hands with, and even the bathroom was fairly clean and well lit. Although the electricity and water was pirated, it functioned decently. There were two couches, obviously rescued from somewhere but moderately comfortable, and no animals lived inside the house. Occasionally the dog ran through the common room, but usually it kept to the small front yard, which nothing more than an expanse of empty dirt, where someone had improvised a doghouse. This home was

further away from the main street and in a newer, poorer area of the slum than was Lilia's. Even more surprising, while Lilia was a healthy woman, Adriana had a degenerative hip disease that prevented her from moving rapidly or doing chores easily. The level of cleanliness and personal hygiene that Adriana was able to maintain was not up to American standards, but it made Lilia's house look downright filthy. "Why the difference in hygiene?" I wondered aloud to Rebecca later that evening.

Spending the afternoon Adriana's home in Barracas 2124 forced me to remember the series of observations and interactions that had made me uncomfortable about Lilia. It was not hard to recast my entire experience with Lilia in a new, unflattering light. Her personal appearance, the way she kept her house, the unsanitary conditions to which she exposed her children, the way she had managed to finagle me into becoming Ayde's godmother, how deftly she convinced us to purchase food supplies for her entire family, how frequently she referenced other generous Americans. I also thought of the building materials sitting unused in her house. They were supposedly purchased with the money Lilia's "American daughter" had raised in order to build a pre-school. I then thought back to the new sound system in Lilia's children's bedroom. It seemed like an extremely luxurious item to have when compared with the fact that the main part of the house had no roof. I thought about how there was no space for the animals and how those building materials occupied an entire room of the house. I thought about how no one in the family had a proper mattress, about the broken and moldy furniture, and about the fact that Lilia had not begun to build the future pre-school. I thought about all these things and more, and I no longer trusted Lilia.

My distrust for Lilia only deepened after I left Buenos Aires. Staying in touch with Federico, I learned that Lilia and he had parted ways over how dirty Lilia kept her house and how poorly she cared for her children. When she and Federico had begun to work together as a team to organize Barracas 2124, they had agreed upon two fundamental tenets: 1) that improved hygiene and schooling would be the keys to progress in the slums, and 2) that any organizer or participant affiliated with their group would practice these principles in order to lead by example. However, in addition to practicing an extreme lack of personal hygiene and imposing that practice on her children, Lilia did not send her children to school. Lilia had also apparently told Federico that she preferred to maintain her home and her children as she did because American students would give more in donations if she fit their image of poverty. Federico disagreed with this strategy and broke ties with Lilia. Instead, he continued his work with other individuals in Barracas 2124, such as Adriana.

A year and a half later, Federico reported that Lilia had begun to prostitute Ariel, her eldest. I remembered Ariel on the day of the baptism, how at Lilia's command she had willingly run off to fetch Federico to be Ayde's godfather. In that moment she had been a happy fifteen-year old who was on the verge of her *quinciniera*, the major party for fifteen-year olds celebrated widely in Latin American cultures. I thought about Brisa's beautiful face and what a gorgeous young woman she would likely turn out to be. Would Brisa befall the same fate? Would she become an adult overnight?

Looking back upon those few days I spent in Barracas 2124, I say to myself, even if Federico exaggerated Lilia's faults and actions, Lilia clearly outsmarted us all. She knew how to find idealistic young college students, how to make them feel like a part of her family and how to use their financial resources for her personal gain. Her openness to probing questions about the slum was, I think, a way of astutely learning about students' expectations of slum-dwellers and slum life, and she was able to tailor herself and her lifestyle to meet these expectations. Her frequent references to what other American students had done for her indicated that we too had to repay her for her kindness. In effect, Lilia had turned her house, her family, her neighborhood and herself into an economically viable tourist attraction for students eager to experience "real poverty". By playing into it, a fresh crop of students reaffirmed for Lilia each semester the lesson that poverty pays and charity comes cheap. Jacob, Rebecca and I, throughout interactions with Lilia in our attempt at alternative tourism, served to further institutionalize the destructive cycle of poverty into which children like Ayde, Brisa and Ariel had the misfortune to be born. The first time I realized this I was overtaken by a powerful sense of guilt.

Afterwards

One day after returning to college, Jacob approached me to ask that I help with a fundraiser for Lilia in order to finish building the pre-school she had started. I asked him how he planned to transfer the money to Lilia, and he said that he would give it to her directly upon a return visit to Buenos Aires. I explained to Jacob that I did not believe that Lilia would actually carry out her education project. I expressed my fear that she would squander the money on personal luxuries. Jacob responded that he did not think that was the case, but if she chose to do so that would be her prerogative. After all, who were we, among the world's richest, to tell her, among the world's poorest, what to do with the money? I responded that if students are going to donate money to a particular project, then that money should go to the cause that it was donated for, or, if that is impossible, it should be directed toward something equally worthy. Furthermore, in this case we would not be raising money to go toward a project we had control over, but rather, a community-driven project designed by Lilia and Federico together. There had to be some way to verify that the money was used in a manner that fulfilled the altruistic intent behind its donation. I told Jacob that if he would actually buy the materials and see to it that the second floor was built, or if he would give the money to a group of people rather than Lilia, then I would help him with the fundraiser. That conversation turned out to be one of the last times that Jacob and I spoke.

Meeting Lilia and her counterparts changed my conception of who the poor are in numerous ways. First and foremost, I learned that the degree of uncleanliness is not necessarily an indicator of poverty, particularly in a country such as Argentina. Certainly it is true that when there is no running water, no soap, no bathroom, no electricity and shoddily constructed walls and roofs, it can be significantly more difficult to keep oneself, one's family and one's home clean. It may, in fact, be nearly impossible. I suppose too, that for people living in poverty, attaining a higher standard of hygiene will likely never be an option as long as they live in slum conditions such as those of Barracas 2124. In such instances, I believe that hygiene is not a reflection of character or knowledge but the environment in which the individual is situated. Thus, just as Lilia's sweater and ponytail changed her appearance in a matter of seconds, so too the face of poverty changes depending on the surroundings in which it is located.

What is poverty defined by then, if not automatically dirt and grime? In my opinion, poverty is defined less by its outward appearance than it is by its inward experience. Poverty is living day-to-day without reliable access to amenities such as food, water and electricity. Poverty is the constant lack of access over generations to an equal playing field, as provided by good primary and secondary schools centrally located in one's neighborhood. Poverty is the feeling of being repeatedly judged by one's outward appearance rather than appreciated for the efforts one is making to care for and improve the circumstances of oneself and one's family. Poverty is to lack political power or recognition, and to therefore be unable to affect one's circumstances through civic participation.

Further, poverty is not necessarily undignified. However, poverty lacks dignity when the wealthy strip the poor of the possibility of maintaining their dignity by treating them like objects to be observed and studied, rather than acting as partners in their struggle to provide a better life for themselves and their families. Poverty also lacks dignity when the wealthy, in an attempt to act as partners, are overly generous with their resources, both emotionally and financially. In such instances, by not expecting a return commitment from the poor, whether that be upholding a promise or contributing personal resources to a particular project, the wealthy may allow the poor to play into their preconceived notions of poverty, which can simultaneously exploit the wealthy and denigrate the poor and their families. In part, finding dignified solutions to poverty requires striking a balance between the extremes of objective academic dispassion and emotional, active involvement. For this lesson I will always have Lilia and Adriana to thank.

Fear and Uncertainty in Caracas:
The Underwear Diaries

Stephen B. Kaplan

Two weeks before leaving to conduct field research in Caracas, I opened the *Saturday New York Times*. Upon reading the Latin American highlights, my heart pounded. "Homicides in Caracas are up 67 percent since 1999." Glancing more closely at the article, I felt that recently familiar "lump in my throat" sensation. "Venezuela has the highest rate of gun-related deaths among 57 countries surveyed in UNECSO study." Did I really need to conduct field research in Caracas? Couldn't I select another country? Perhaps, I could instead work out of a satellite university in Aruba or Margarita Island.

I took comfort in a meeting I had scheduled later that day with Professor Ramon Serrano from a prestigious New England university. He too had conducted research in Venezuela and perhaps he would assuage my growing anxiety. I awaited his sage advice, anticipating that he would vilify the newspapers for being too sensationalistic. To my dismay, however, he genuinely recommended taking refuge in my Caracas apartment for three

months. "Don't leave your home! It's not worth the risk" he exclaimed.

Those words had haunted my thoughts for several weeks, but since arriving in Caracas, I had felt surprisingly secure. I had invested my "dolares" in an apartment share in Altamira, the safest neighborhood in Caracas. Indeed, whenever I uttered Altamira, it would always elicit the same response from taxi drivers, store clerks, and work colleagues. *"Altamira . . . una zona muy segura! Lamas segura en Caracas."*

Basking in an illusory sense of confidence, I overlooked the long chain of rather tenuous links between my roommate, Simon, and my good friend and former band mate Eudald, who arrived a few weeks earlier from Barcelona. Eudald—a stranger to Caracas with a flowing, curly mane and an infectiously amiable personality—had only visited Venezuela because of a conversation he had on a Croatian-bound train from Barcelona six months earlier. Eudald had selflessly worked to help me secure an apartment, but met a dearth of rental opportunities before encountering Manuel Cabrera.

Manuel wore bright red Sally Jesse Rafael glasses, dressed like a swinger from an art-deco Miami salsa club, and frequently claimed his dog was the sister of Latin American pop-idol Julio Iglesias's dog. He also owned a popcorn stand in *Paseo Las Mercedes* mall. Eudald first met Manuel while purchasing a large popcorn movie combo before seeing "The Last King of Scotland" and had been selling black market dollars to him the last few weeks. Manuel happened to have a friend, Simon Ortega, who was willing to rent his apartment.

Simon had an abnormally large head, mostly covered with thin, black hair that was ravaged by various beauty products. He was studying to be a lawyer and loved to use the word "espectacular." Simon claimed he was in his mid-thirties and spoke German, but he appeared to be 47 and responded to "Auf Wiedersehen" with a quizzical look. He also boasted about having an important government job in Guarico, where many people worked for him, but rarely left the apartment.

Initially, before receiving my "dolares," Simon intimated that I would be staying alone in his Plaza Altamira apartment, which was reflected in the lofty (in Venezuelan terms) $600 per-month price tag. I decided to rent the apartment. To my surprise, however, when I arrived with my belongings later that day, I found that Simon intended to stay in the apartment. Additionally, another guy named Raul kept emerging from his room to use the bathroom. Fully clad in tight black leather vest, pants, and cap, Raul had apparently just returned from the South American Village People Reunion Tour. According to Simon, however, Raul was just visiting Caracas for a few days to see a "back specialist," but would soon return to his home in El Tigre.

Instinctively, given the change in terms, I thought that I should run for the hills of Caracas. Logically, however, I didn't want to risk the possibility of entering into a more precarious situation. Rental apartments in safe areas were in short supply, my university had unsuccessfully tried to place me with a family, and available hotels were quite expensive. Moreover, my blond-haired, blue-eyed, non-Spanish speaking wife, Heather, was scheduled to visit me for a month. In light of Caracas's high crime rate, I wanted to ensure that she was in a safe neighborhood. Reason and logic prevailed over instincts.

Simon generally seemed to be harmless, particularly given his gregarious Venezuelan nature. He cooked black bean arepas, beef cachapas, and lasagna. He also cleaned my laundry, prompting me to overlook some other odd developments. Each week, Simon had a new houseguest, who completed different household projects. During the night, they would vanish in to Simon's lair, only to materialize once again during the day to paint the

hallways, fix the bathroom floors, and install new electrical wiring. Ostensibly, the world's oldest system of barter was still functioning today in the Ortega hacienda. Fortunately, I was paying rent in currency and Simon seemed to respect my privacy.

With my wife arriving in two weeks, however, I noticed a distinct change in Simon's demeanor. Initially, I thought his newly brusque conduct reflected law school related stress. However, he was visibly perturbed at the mere mention of Heather's name. Simon soon insisted that I pay more rent money to cover the cost of her visit. I was shocked by his effrontery. Rather than paying for an apartment share, I had been paying a price well above the rental cost of the entire apartment. Simon had long known that Heather was going to visit, but suddenly was insisting on more dollars and breaking the terms of our deal. Once again, I thought I should run for the hills of Caracas, but *logic instead prevailed*. Where else would Heather and I stay? Would she be safe? What if we couldn't find a secure living situation? I had recently inquired about alternatives with friends, but only found one rental option in the barrio of Florida, considered to be unsafe by most middle-class Venezuelans.

I also attempted to rationally evaluate the situation from Simon's perspective. After Chavez's December electoral victory, Venezuela's president was decidedly marching the country toward socialism. This seismic political shift was creating tremendous uncertainty for middle-class Venezuelans. Each week, the government appropriated new private businesses, sparking concerns about the sanctity of private property. Clearly, access to my "dolares" represented an economic opportunity for Simon. While US dollars were technically illegal, they allowed Venezuelans to gain access to a more secure investment. And perhaps, renegotiation was more culturally acceptable in Venezuela than in the United States. Ultimately, I decided to stay, but refused to pay more money given my already lofty rent.

The situation quickly deteriorated. Over the next several weeks, Simon responded to my rebuff with a raft of passive-aggressive strikes. He ceased cooking black bean arepas and beef cachapas; commandeered our common telephone; and blockaded my access to the washing machine. On several occasions, Simon jammed his apartment key into the keyhole, briefly barricading my entrance, only to later politely apologize for his "apparent gaffe." One time, he requested 100,000 bolivares for our shared groceries. I gladly complied, only to discover a vacant refrigerator and bare cabinets. Simon had instead replenished his spice rack and household paint supply. Notwithstanding these annoyances, I remained in the apartment, believing it was safer than other ostensibly more perilous alternatives.

During the few days of Heather's visit, we decided to take the opportunity to wash our clothes while Simon was away for the Carnival holiday. While gathering our laundry, Heather inquired, "Where's all of your underwear? I thought you brought more pairs." I never closely monitored my underwear inventory. I thought I might have been missing a few pairs, but never tallied them.

Upon transferring our first load of laundry from the washer to the dryer, we encountered Simon's laundry. Several pairs of striped, Banana Republic boxer-briefs were scattered among his clothes. First, I reflected upon globalization's homogeneity. "Venezuelans were wearing the same boxer-briefs as Americans . . . the same company . . . the same style . . . the same colors . . . the same 34-inch waist? Wait a minute. . . . Nooooooooooooo!!!!!!!" I exclaimed in utter disbelief.

Simon hadn't done a wash for me in weeks. My poor, pilfered underwear was living a life of involuntary detainment! An even worse thought crossed my mind. Had Simon been wearing my underwear? Posing as the New York Gringo with his barter buddies? Mimicking my North American, broken-castellano accent? Heather joked that perhaps Simon planned to rupture our happy marriage by prancing around the apartment in my jockeys.

The strangest part of these events was that several weeks later, my underwear reappeared in my closet, buried among my other clothes. Had he been smuggling and swapping different pairs of underwear throughout my stay? Was there a pattern of boxer thievery, rather than a one-time underpants siege? Or, did Simon know that we had discovered the contraband underwear, attempting to clandestinely return it. Either way, I clearly had to keep my underwear under "lock and key" along with my money.

Upon learning about these bizarre events, my friend Gertrud graciously offered me refuge during my final weeks in Venezuela: a spare bedroom in her "Parque del Easte" apartment that Eudald had previously occupied before leaving for Margarita Island. Gertrud was a passionate and talented artist, whose paintings hung in the national art gallery. She was good-humored, generous, and highly conversant in politics, religion, and life. She also genially assured me that she would not don any of my underwear.

When Heather departed for the States, I finally listened to my initial intuition. As a doctoral student, I was trained to think *rationally and logically*. But, as a human adapting to a new habitat, I learned the importance of *trusting one's innate instincts*. I fled Simon's apartment, leaving a few pairs of trunks hanging in the closet as a "token of good will." My remaining underwear and I took asylum in Gertrud's safe haven. With Simon, the underwear bandit, out of my life, I more readily perceived the benevolent side of Venezuelan people and culture that the *Times* failed to mention. I went salsa-dancing and climbed the mountains around Caracas with my university friends, I talked Latin American politics and art with Gertrud late into the night, and I watched movies, drank whiskey, and ate tequenos with my amigo Jose. I grew fond of Venezuelans' quirky sense of humor, compassion for friends and family; and most of all, their love of an entertaining story.

Haiti

Patricia Willingham

Sassy Tifi's eyes are the windows to an old soul.

The seven-year-old hangs out on the steps patiently waiting to get the attention of Sister Anna who is busy inside the Haitian store next door to the Center for Hope where foreigners like me go to buy arts and crafts to support fledgling Haitian artists. She has a gigantic personality, but she lives in the body of a four-year old. Before I learn her name, I call her Sassy Tifi (the Haitian Creole word for little girl) because she leaps up to grab my hand and demands to play with the Creole-English dictionary that I haven't even purchased yet. I offer her a piece of gum, and Sassy makes a sticky mess of the book, earning herself a mild scolding from the Sister.

A brilliant ball of energy, this Tifi is a contrast to the one of some months ago—the Tifi who was sick and starving—malnutritioned like 30 percent of the babies in this dark country, the poorest in the Western hemisphere, where most eat merely a meal a day. Her belly once was swollen and poked out like a plump watermelon. Her hair was the reddish color of inadequate food and nutrients. She was old way before her time, caught up in a

despondent story in which people have to survive on a meal of too much rice and not enough protein-rich beans, where they suffer for a lack of basic vitamins and minerals in too little food.

Tifi's arrival at the Center of Hope—a medical and educational clinic built in the village of Jeremie, Haiti, with cash donated from an American whose wife died of cancer—was a rescue mission. We are told that Tifi is about ready to go home.

Mission accomplished. A little miracle. Haiti needs a lot more miracles.

Our plane landed at Haiti's international airport in Port-au-Prince, which looked like a fort being guarded by armed United Nations peacekeepers and Haitian police. Violence and mayhem had increased in Haiti in the weeks before, largely because embattled President Jean Bertrand-Aristide, the nation's only democratically elected leader, had been exiled to Africa. It was the second time Aristide was removed from his presidency; the first was in a brutal coup that overthrew him in 1991.

I later learned that several United Nations peacekeepers were staying at the same place as me and my group, partly on a mission to build up the Haitian police force. I guess they made me feel safe, but I realized that I really had nothing to fear. Unlike the violence and protesters in Haiti's capital, people in the anguished, poverty-stricken town of Jeremie, 140 miles west of the capital, care more about where their next meals will come from.

I am curious about Haiti, which is the reason I come. I'm prepared, though, to roll up my sleeves to help and gain some perspective about a people I can't help feeling that I am somehow connected to. They were, after all, delivered to this island as slaves from Africa in the Atlantic Migration. I don't

Haiti

know for sure, but I can guess that my ancestors were in that same forced migration.

I tag along with a contingent of Connecticut volunteers who work in church missions and have come to visit the Haitian Health Foundation to witness first-hand the fruit of their charitable efforts and gather more ideas for ways they can assist in the massive, often overwhelming task of caring for Jeremie's sick and nutritionally-deprived, educating mothers about family planning and child care, building safe homes for the most destitute and sending children to school.

The Haitian Health Foundation, a Connecticut-based organization started 19 years ago by Norwich orthodontist Dr. Jeremiah Lowney at the behest of Mother Teresa, runs medical clinics serving more than 250,000 people in 135 villages surrounding Jeremie. Several times a year, the organization loads and ships containers stuffed with several tons of donations headed for the ports of Haiti—a voyage that takes several months.

I have four traveling companions: Paul and Cathy are members of Manchester's St. Bridget Catholic Church and are here in Haiti the second time. Gary and Mary are members of Manchester's Assumption Roman Catholic Church and are on the first visit and already are making plans to get their church involved in mission work here—work similar to St. Bridget's where on most Thursday nights, the parish house turns into a factory of workers organizing donations, cutting up old towels to make fresh washcloths, folding "third-world" diapers and sewing baby baptismal gowns that may also double as burial dresses.

I am humbled by their commitment to a people and a country that governments worldwide have largely ignored except for the times when they could pillage its natural resources such as its mahogany. I am told that the French are largely responsible for stripping mahogany trees, exposing the hillsides to erosion and runoff from rain. There is an effort to bring back mahogany trees, we are told. Haitian woodworkers responsibly use the wood to make handsome beds and coffins, a good business in a country where the mortality rate rivals the most impoverished nations of Africa.

I wonder how this can be possible in a country a mere one-and-a-half hours from the southern tip of Florida. I try not to dwell on how unresponsive my country has been to the needs of Haiti or how so-called Haiti boat people escaping unbearable poverty get turned back in the waters before they even reach the U.S. shore. To think too much about it now makes me tense and angry. I feel that I need to stay open-minded and hopeful on this trip.

After we arrive in Port-au-Prince, a driver is waiting to take us to a smaller nearby airport where we will take a charter plane to Jeremie where our host Bette Gebrian-Magloire—a nurse and medical anthropologist who has lived in Haiti for about 17 years, working with the Haitian Health Foundation—will meet us. We whiz through a bustle of activity with people trying to sell odds and ends alongside beggars and people skirmishing to carry our bags, hustling for a little change. I am the only African-American in my group, and people assume I am Haitian. They want to speak to me in Creole, but I don't understand.

About 45 minutes later, we land on a rural stretch of land that doubles as a cow pasture—we are at Jeremie's "airport."

Jeremie is serene and rural. After a bumpy Land Rover drive up crude roads that were former riverbeds, we reach Bette's home, a glorious white mansion on a high cliff overlooking downtown Jeremie and its only port, which, incidentally, was once shut down under the dictatorship of Baby Doc Duvalier who wanted to control all goods shipped to the country through one port in Port-au-Prince, a move that further depressed progress in this town.

Bette's house—one of just a few in town with electricity pumped in by generators and solar panels—is nestled among lush green grounds full of imported Swiss pines and bright, waving flowers overlooking a crystal green Caribbean sea. It's a vision of what Haiti could be if somebody with deep pockets cared, if there ever would be one government in place that wouldn't pillage the country and if peace and democracy every truly reigned here.

Bette's mansion is a severe contrast to the homes of the families below—many of them two-room concrete cartons stuffed with as many as 11 family members or leaning bamboo structures with grass thatch roofs full of dirty, hungry children. The town hasn't had electricity in several months. My group and I eat a hearty meal prepared and served by Bette's small Haitian staff. We watch some news on CNN before readying ourselves for the week that promises to be an awakening.

The members of my group are Catholics as is about 80 percent of the population in Haiti. It is the Catholic Church that has sent many missionaries to work here. And so we stop for Sunday morning service at a small, unadorned chapel on the hill near Bette's house. It was built by Bette's mother-in-law who believed that God miraculously healed her throat cancer. Bette and her husband Edwin, were married here. The singing is a lively infusion of drumming and traditional hymns in Haitian Creole. The priest preaches about justice. "We must have confidence that God knows what's going on in the world," he says. "Justice will come."

God knows Haiti has seen a lot of injustices. It's ironic, I think, that Haitians—brave descendants of Africa who fought off their French colonizers and slave masters 200 years ago, gaining their independence six decades before slaves in America were freed—still must wait for justice. I pray with the priest and the other parishioners, only a handful this morning, and I take communion with them even though I am not Catholic. The usual rituals and formalities are not as important here, it seems.

Later at the market, we barter for rice and beans that will be handed out—properly portioned to ensure a healthy dose of protein—to needy families in the high mountain village of Carrefour Prince. The vendors like to bargain and can go back and forth for as long as 20 minutes; they consider it an insult if you don't haggle at least a little. We learn

that a paint-can size of rice—the elementary unit of measurement for a largely illiterate population—costs a whopping $15 and is imported from the United States, undercutting the price of locally-grown rice, which actually is unbleached and more nutritious. Members of my group have brought about $200 in donations for this purchase.

We make our way through the grimy, crowded marketplace that reeks of goat heads and butchered meat. My group members buy a little from several vendors, making sure to spread the wealth of their purchases until they have filled two sacks—one with beans, one with rice. Bette is a familiar face here, so everyone welcomes her friends. Throngs of curious children follow us through the market, asking us to take pictures of them.

On two separate days, we travel to the rural, high mountain villages of Carrefour Prince and Marie Kerotte. The roads are rugged, and in some places we have to make our own roads—the poor or lacking infrastructure is more evidence of government neglect. I help weigh babies at the village satellite clinics, little more than makeshift, unfinished buildings. Mothers sit, holding their chubby, healthy babies. I want to tell them that their babies are beautiful, but there are many superstitions in this country where an estimated 50 percent of the people mix Vodou with their given religion, Catholicism. I am told that, according to superstition, it is better to tell a mother that the baby is healthy than beautiful because beauty sets the baby up for being cursed.

So I learn to say "bonne santé"—good health.

The babies in Carrefour Prince and Marie Kerotte are plump; the inroads that the Haitian Health Foundation has made in helping the villagers improve their nutrition are apparent. In Carrefour Prince, as members of my group pass out individual sandwich bags of beans and rice, I watch the women stir nutritionally-balanced globs of ground up beans and corn in wide vats on open fires out back.

Other women openly breastfeed their babies. Bette tells us that Haitians were once cut off from the African tradition of breastfeeding. The French slave masters, unlike slave owners in America, wouldn't allow mothers to take their babies to the fields with them. Instead, the babies were left at home, fed diseased animal milk or sometimes not fed at all. The end result was a high infant mortality rate and a lost cultural tradition.

I'm getting tense and angry again, so I try not to think too hard.

The toughest day was in the downtown slums. Here, people openly beg. We are driven here so that my traveling companions can meet the families they had adopted with a $300 annual gift—enough to feed everyone, cover the rent, pay school tuition and buy clothes and shoes for the children. As we make our way through the dusty streets and dank alleyways to reach the dark, crumbling shack where Paul and Cathy's family lives, a mass of children and women follow us.

The left jaw of one girl's face is swollen to the size of a plum. She wants to write her name in my journal—Manoucheka Michel. She opens her mouth to show us, revealing a severe abscess and a row of rotten teeth. She has never seen a dentist.

The sea of children's faces and their outstretched hands make me dizzy. I see the faces of my nieces and nephews, my cousins and kids I know from when I was growing up. All the faces get blurry as I start to cry. I am too overwhelmed to continue, so I go back to the truck and sob. Paul follows me to make sure I am OK, but I am embarrassed. I had been warned to prepare myself to handle the extreme poverty I was guaranteed to see, but I have never felt more helpless as I did at that moment. I was at once confused, outraged and sick.

I can still see their faces, all brown like mine and my father's and my sisters' and brothers'. Our skin tones are the same shades of ebony, mocha and everything in between. But, by a circumstance of fate, we are worlds apart. I understand immediately why Americans—both black and white—often turn our collective eyes away from suffering in the world. To handle the truth often is so tough, so unpleasant, especially when that truth exposes culpability.

There is much hope in Haiti, though. Perhaps no one is more hopeful than Yverose who runs an orphanage for about 40 abandoned children. She manages to get by with a small store she opened at her home and on the generous donations of a few. Yverose's heart is so big that when Hurricane Jeanne ravaged Gonaives some 12 hours away, she wanted to travel there to bring back motherless children. Sister Maryann, one of the workers at the Haitian Health Foundation, had to talk her out of a bad idea. Where could she possibly put more children? How would she care for them? Determined to help, Yverose pleaded with people throughout Jeremie to make donations. In the end, we learn, she collected a boatload and saw that it was sent to Gonaives.

Back at the Center for Hope, we see pregnant women waiting in line for prenatal visits and mothers with newborns coming for their babies' vaccinations and early checkups. Unlike at the government-run hospitals staffed by Cuban doctors, people don't come to the Center of Hope to die or as a last resort. They come to live and to live better.

I meet Dagental, a 47-year-old mother of 11. Dagental said she walked four hours from the mountain village of Dayere with her youngest, 5-month old James. Her main mission, she admits, was to fill up the cans and soda bottles she brought with food the Haitian Health Foundation gives to mothers. But this organization doesn't give handouts; instead, the mothers must faithfully bring their children for checkups and must sit through an educational session about nutrition and family planning before they can get the food.

So Dagental listens as a Center of Hope nurse explains the natural rhythm method, proven to be the most effective method of birth control here. I want to talk to her about her life in Haiti, how she lives in a shack with all of her children and her husband. How she manages on less than $100 a year.

Before she will talk to me, though, she wants to know if I will give her any money. I want to so badly—I have 20 bucks to spare, but I'm reminded that helping the people of Haiti is not about charity or handouts, not about enabling the people to be beggars. Rather, it's about training and empowering them to help themselves despite the misery their government has heaped on them. Better reminds my group of this position more than once.

Rose Melodie, one of the young Haitian women hired to work at the Center of Hope, translates for me. A student at Jeremie's small laws school, she is eager to practice her English. She is young, starry-eyed and filled with hope for her country, just like Jose May and Damony, who both are fluent in Creole, French and Spanish. They dream of a formal education, jobs and money to help their families.

They dream of a better, different Haiti. And so do I.

Here's Your Baby

Patricia Willingham

I've got to stop talking to Americans.

I let the cell phone call drop as the signal fades. I don't bother to call Anna back. If I am going to decide here and now to have this baby in Guinea, then I can't listen to her hysterics. Anna is two weeks more pregnant than I am. She tells me that she will continue working with her company, but when she's further along she will head to the States, the developed world where she can have a proper delivery.

"I mean, my God, they don't even do any genetic testing here!" she cries.

My fourth ultrasound has revealed nothing abnormal. Dr. Diallo seems annoyed that I am at the clinic again asking for another one of these tests. Ever since I decided to give birth in Guinea, I've been using the scanned images to help me gauge my baby's health. To Guineans, pregnancy is as ordinary as a hangnail, not deserving of any fancy medical treatment or of an excuse to take a rest. It's common to see pregnant village women—another infant strapped to their backs and a pail of water or perhaps a pile of fire-

wood balanced on their heads—dutifully trudging everyday to and from a grimy, disordered market so food will be prepared when their husbands get home.

I stop the rushing doctor to ask for a blood pressure check. He's noticeably impatient. There are sick people to attend to upstairs.

Tomorrow, my fiancé, Chaïkou, and I will make the seven-hour taxi ride back to Labé. I want to get back to my English classes at the university. Labé—Guinea's second largest city cradled in the northern hills of the Foutah Djalon—is breezy and low-key. What a shame the locals don't fully appreciate the area's natural abundance, especially the grand waterfalls that slice the hills, splashing into seas of slow-moving rapids. A couple of months back, Chaïkou's mother had scolded me for taking some friends out to visit one of the falls. Didn't I know that jealous evil spirits lurk around the waters, waiting to saddle my unborn child with some hideous deformity?

I remember I had gotten angry with Chaïkou for not backing me up when I reasoned that babies aren't born deformed because some spirit put a curse on them. Isn't there usually a more scientific cause like an extra gene popping up where it shouldn't or something like that? Usually, Chaïkou and I mostly get along because he tolerates so many of my Western ways. But what he said next made me remember how I love that unassuming ability of his to reason my Western mind into tolerating some African legend.

"You guys in the West use your science to explain everything for you," he said. "Well, we're not scientific here, and when we need an explanation we rely on our spirits and our beliefs."

Guinea has for at least two decades proudly been one of the most stable countries in West Africa while civil wars and violent coups d'etat have plagued its neighbors. But the season of discontent is soon to begin. The prices of staple items like rice and gas continue to rise above the means of the average Guinean worker, and political corruption is escalating. Just last week, President Lansana Conté went to the jail himself to release two of the country's biggest crooks, reversing the court ruling that had put them there for embezzling millions of dollars from the public treasury. Days after their release, they paraded around town in shiny Chrysler 300s, fresh off the assembly line. Conté, who not only had appointed himself minister of defense, now in a television address declared himself the justice. It has been 23 years since the former army general first came to power in a violent coup. In the past, he has kept the masses silent with the threat of military cruelty, and he claims that his unending rule over the country is God's will.

On January 10th, Guinea's two powerful labor unions declare a nationwide strike, the third within the last year. "On veut le changement! is the chant on the local French radio station. A few demonstrations have already started to organize. I remember the last strike in June was bloody, but when it ended within two weeks everything had returned to normal as if nothing ever happened. Perhaps this strike will end the same unceremonious way. I mark the calendar–12 more weeks to my due date.

As I enter the school gate, I meet some of my students. The strike had finally been suspended after nineteen days of unrest. More than 60 protestors had been killed nationwide, most shot by security forces. My students tell me that they were among those who had taken to the streets in the name of change. Some snuck out of their houses against their parents' advice, taking their IDs with them just in case their bodies would need to be identified later. I praise them for their bravery.

That day's class would be my last.

Within a week the country is once again brought to chaos. Conté didn't keep the promises he made, and the people are agitated. Demonstrators crowd the streets, but Conté clamps down, declaring a

"state of siege." Within days, the country is placed under military control and a 20-hour curfew imposed. We are now under house arrest as gunfire pierces the skies and looters gut buildings just footsteps away.

My co-worker, Dawn, and her husband, Alfred, are at my house. They had caught a ride from the capital city with my boss for a short visit but are now stuck with us in the country's interior. My boss and his assistant had attempted the seven-hour trip back to the capital, but they were turned back by military roadblocks and angry mobs. They were staying with his relatives a few towns over from Labé. I mark the calendar–nine more weeks to my due date.

Dawn and I send the men out to stock up on food and drinking water. The length of this unrest is unprecedented and who knows how long it could last. I notice that Dawn has started propping up sticks and broom handles around the house and stacking piles of pebbles near my slingshot. Just in case we have to fight off looters, she explains. I half jokingly suggest we gather our important papers and plan an escape route. Two weeks of violence pass. We wake up and fall asleep to the cadence of gunfire. Just seven more weeks to my due date.

I might not make it to the capital city for my planned delivery at the private clinic. The friendly Dr. Traoré at Clinique Bambino–just a five-minute motorbike ride away–is probably my best bet now, even though his sparse office reeks of mildewed books, and he can only do ultrasounds early in the morning before the electricity goes out. When I go into labor, he promises, he'll drive his personal car over to get me if he has gas. The stations have been shut down for days.

Like a lot of Muslim men here, Dr. Traoré has two wives and nine children. I've seen him for at least two checkups, so I trust him. And I like him, especially the way he teases me, joking that the ultrasound shows five babies hiding inside my womb. Funny thing is I worry most that Dr. Traoré doesn't use pain medication for his deliveries, doesn't even believe in it. I'd have to have this baby the "natural" way. I hadn't counted on that.

The cell phone rings at two o'clock in the morning. It's Tosi, my friend who was a health worker with the Peace Corps a few villages away. She's calling from Mali where she has been safely installed since early January when the Peace Corps pulled its 110 volunteers out of the country shortly after the first wave of violence.

"Did you hear that the U.S. Embassy is evacuating people?" she asks. There's too much static on the line. The signal fades. No, I hadn't heard. I roll over on my big belly and sob. I imagine convoys of buses sent to pick up the foreigners just like in the movie Hotel Rwanda. Only they apparently had somehow forgotten to take me.

"Are you all right?" my fiancé sleepily asks.

"Yea," I manage between sniffles. "I'm just hungry. I'm having a craving."

He stumbles out into the darkness and returns with a plate of homemade fries.

Turns out the American Embassy is only helping family members of U.S. government workers evacuate. But civilians are strongly urged to leave the country on their own if they can, says the young, panicky voice of the consular officer on the other end of the phone. But because we're in the country's interior, seven hours away from the airport, the young girl advises us to stay put if we are safe in our house. There are reports of massive gas shortages. Some major airlines have stopped their flights.

I liked my house the minute I moved in. In a village just outside of town, it is considered a luxury villa by locals' standards. Spacious with three bedrooms, it has all the amenities of Western life—solar panels that guarantee electricity when the government lines fail, a chateau d'eau that pumps water through the faucets so we don't have to draw it from an outside well and hot water heaters so our showers are always warm. Jasmine, wild flowers and mint leaves bloom inside the property's tall cement gate. Today, it feels like the walls of this house want to squeeze me to death. We have been shut in for too long, protecting ourselves from the turmoil outside.

Dawn's cell phone rings. Eric from the Embassy has been trying to reach me but hasn't been able to get through on my number. Eric heard I was pregnant and it's possible he can get us all on a World Food Program charter plane headed to Dakar, Senegal, if we can get to the capital city. I take a deep breath.

We stuff our bags into my company's oversized Toyota Landcruiser. I worry that the big truck will attract too much attention, inviting looters or perhaps corrupt soldiers who think we have money and things to steal. We're rushing. My boss wants to make it to the capital before the curfew starts again. I've stuffed only the essentials into my big canvas sack—a week's worth of clothes for me and Chaïkou and the big plastic bag of baby supplies that had for months been stored in the bottom of the wardrobe.

The town this morning is quiet. I realize that it's my first time outside the village since the latest unrest began. At every military roadblock the soldiers circle the truck like vultures, demanding to see our papers and to know what mission we are on. My boss tells them that he has been commissioned to get a pregnant American to the capital city. His hand trembles as he passes our IDs to the imposing soldier blocking the driver's window. I have never seen him so nervous. I prepare to fake labor if it will help.

While we wait at a hotel in the capital for our flight to be arranged, I call one of my university colleagues to say goodbye. I tell him that it's best if I leave the country for the safety of my unborn child. He didn't know. It's not customary in Guinea to announce pregnancies. I wonder if he thinks I'm a coward—his wife just had a baby last month. No, I think, I'm just lucky.

The nine-seat Cessna safely lands on the runway of Senegal's international airport. In all of its neo-colonial glitter, Senegal represents Guinea's potential. Even the remotest villages have regular electricity and running water. Private enterprise thrives, inviting wealth and comfort. Hundreds of new housing developments are under construction as suburban communities sprout up, encircling the city. A maze of highway projects is underway, visions of the progressive president, Abdoulaye Wade.

I am always amazed by African hospitality. In Senegal they have a word for it–"Teranga." Chaïkou's uncle picks us up from the airport. On short notice, the uncle has arranged for us to stay at his house in the suburbs. I feel like a refugee, but I am in good hands. The uncle and his wife have eight children who will all sleep together on two beds in one room so Chaïkou and I can have the extra bedroom to ourselves. When we arrive, we are served a hefty platter of lamb meat with sautéed onions on a bed of salad. I pass the days lazing around the house.

Clinique de la Madeleine in downtown Dakar has come highly recommended as one of the best places in town to give birth. The clinic is welcoming. The patient rooms look more like hotel chambers. For dessert, the rooftop restaurant overlooking the Atlantic Ocean serves hunks of double chocolate cake and foamy cappuccinos. I am told that some new mothers pay extra to luxury lounge long after their babies are born. Dr. Zayat, the French-Lebanese obstetrician, is frustratingly disappointed by my scant prenatal care in Guinea. He predicts that I will give birth in early April, a full week after the date set by other doctors I had seen. After all, a lot of pregnancies go a little past 40 weeks, he explains.

Mine would not.

It is 6 o'clock in the morning when I feel the first ache–three weeks early. The pain doesn't come as a heavy knock, dropping me to my knees like in the movies. Rather, it feels more like an annoying menstrual cramp, so I'm not really sure that it's time. I reach for my copy of *What to Expect When You're Expecting*, my pregnancy Bible. I anxiously flip to Chapter 14–Labor and Delivery. I skim. Early labor. Active labor. Advanced active labor. False labor. False labor?

I close the book and decide to wake up my host mother. After eight pregnancies of her own, she will know exactly what to do. Chaïkou and I nervously knock on her bedroom door. I'm feeling the

pain in my lower abdomen, not really in my back the way they say you should if the labor is real, Chaïkou translates for me. Like many Senegalese, my host mother speaks ethnic languages, not French. Should I go to the doctor or could this be a false alarm? Her response stuns me. In her last pregnancy, she had unexplained pains for two months, and she never once called the doctor.

The typical West African woman–suffering is the mark of strength and womanhood. Most African women I know, although they never said much, raised their eyebrows about the fuss I was making over my pregnancy. Every woman needs to feel the pain of her birth, my female obstetrician back in Guinea had counseled me.

We call the clinic. My fiancé summons a taxi, and we take off for the two-hour drive to the city through maddeningly heavy traffic. Our driver decides to take some back roads and alleyways to avoid the morning rush. Could he be the most cautious taxi driver ever in Senegal or he is snaking along at a frightenly slow pace, considering I could have this baby in his back seat? I wonder if he understood the urgency of the situation when my fiancé explained it to him. I want to ask Chaïkou to explain it again, but he looks scared enough, and I don't want to alarm him into a panic. The pains are gaining strength and striking every five minutes.

Suddenly we come to a full stop. A big van stuffed with annoyed passengers has turned onto the narrow street, blocking our way. The two drivers argue back and forth. A small crowd of mediators gather. We anxiously wait until our driver concedes and pulls to the side. We're on our slow way again. We are amazed when the driver starts pointing out downtown landmarks. That's the national police station over there, he says, as he slows the car to a crawl. More than two hours pass before we reach the clinic. The driver wants to know if he should wait for us. I struggle out of the car and slam the door, leaving Chaïkou to explain.

We find Hanifé, the midwife, waiting for us inside the clinic. I roll myself onto the examining table and fasten my feet in the stirrups, Hanifé pokes her gloved hand deep inside me, and I pretend that I'm not uncomfortable. "You're two centimeters dilated," she announces. "You're going to have this baby today." Nurses gather, hooking me up to machines and IV tubes. Hanifé asks how we plan to pay.

Her question conjures an image of Linda from the clinic's administration staff. I envision her taunting me with a smoldering copy of my insurance. Linda and I, for at least two weeks, had locked horns over my insurance. Despite warnings that most Senegalese medical facilities accept only cash payments, I had begged Linda to take a guarantee of payment from the global health plan provided by my company. Obligingly, she had scribbled out an estimate of about $3,000, which included a six-day clinic stay and other requests later deemed extravagances by my insurance.

"Is this hospital a spa or something?" asked Michael, the insurance representative who had called me to say that my initial request for payment had been denied. "We only pay a maximum of 48 hours for a normal birth."

Dr. Zayat strolls into the delivery room, with the same calm, reassuring air that had made me like him instantly the first time I met him. Surprised to see me in labor so early, he flashes a big, shy smile and says hello. I'm so relieved that he speaks English. Hanifé tells him that we have a payment problem. Apparently, Linda claims she never received the multiple copies of the revised payment guarantee the insurance company had sent her. I plead, mostly because I can't think of anything else to do.

"The administration here, they're difficult," Dr. Zayat laments as he encourages me to relax. Could he be on my side? I close my eyes to concentrate on another contraction. It feels like somebody is wringing my insides out like a dish rag. I open my eyes to see my stunned fiancé staring down at me. All of the staff, including Dr. Zayat, has left. We are all alone.

The midwife returns to tell us that we have to pay in cash at least $1,000 before they can continue—a little guarantee until my insurance company pays up. I am flat on my back, strapped down by a fetal heart monitor announcing every frantic drumbeat of my baby's heart. I am scared. For the first time, I wish I was back in the States, not because things are more developed but because I think the system is just easier. Or, at least, I have been raised to understand it. I feel defeated. I had defied and ignored the doubting Americans who warned me that it was a bad idea to have this baby in Africa. Could it be they knew better? Suddenly, I am angry.

From the delivery room bed, I dial the insurance company on my cell phone. Courtney answers. I bark out my dilemma, deliberately sounding aggravated. After calling up the history of my insurance case on her computer, Courtney wants to argue. I immediately regret my mistake.

"Yes," I breathlessly acknowledge, changing my tone to tearful desperation. "I understand that you both faxed and e-mailed the guarantee five days ago. But the hospital claims they haven't received it." I beg Courtney to please, please, for the love of Allah, fax it again. I'm in labor. The most powerful contraction yet creeps across my pelvis as I lay waiting. I clinch my fists and prepare for the hit. Chaïkou had gone upstairs to stand over the fax machine and witness the guarantee arriving this time. Suddenly, he bursts through the delivery room doors—the fax is here!

A small army of white coats unceremoniously filter in. I try to relax as their work on me hastily resumes. A Senegalese anesthesiologist is summoned to bring me an epidural for the pain. I coax my nervous fiancé over to massage my left leg. Propped up on the cold metal stirrup, it feels like it wants to tear from my body. I pinch my eyes shut. "Push, push, push," I hear Dr. Zayat coaching. I push, push, and push until tears squirt from my eyes.

Before I even notice what has happened, a wet, wiggly, screaming little figure is slid up to my chest, his big dark eyes wide open. Dr. Zayat coolly pronounces, "Here's your baby."

Some actual names have been changed.

Writing "Here's Your Baby"

Patricia Willingham

Revising is the true art of writing. My final story must have been my tenth draft. I stopped counting after about the fifth one. It was important to rethink my first thoughts, to walk away from the computer and come back with fresh eyes and a fresh perspective. Seeking the constructive feedback of a trusted friend was also crucial. As a result, the final story is a significant improvement over the first draft.

Putting in this much work was a balancing act, figuratively and literally speaking. At one point I was balancing my newborn baby on one knee while typing on my laptop with two fingers. One time, my fiancé threatened to smash my computer into a million tiny little pieces if I didn't stop typing long enough to breastfeed our crying baby. Despite the challenges, my goal in the end was to produce my best work. Here is one example of how I revised.

The original paragraph in Example A was first written in the top half of the story, woven into the part where I talk about returning to Labé after the rushed doctor's visit. In one of my revisions, I reluctantly removed the paragraph because it seemed to slow down the narrative and it didn't quite fit. In a later revision, I realized that the paragraph made perfect sense in another location, juxtaposed with the consular officer telling us to stay in the house if we were safe. I made it more detailed and descriptive to draw out how comfortable the house always made me feel, until I found myself stuck inside of course. It was important,

too, to help the reader imagine the contrasts between life in the more developed Western world and life in Guinea. What do you think about the revision?

The "track changes" feature in Microsoft Word made revising a lot easier. Instead of writing on paper and then typing on computer, I started out typing. The initial draft was written without stopping much to edit myself. In the next draft, I turned on track changes which allowed me to make corrections and strike out unwanted phrases and paragraphs without losing them, in case I wanted to reinstate them in a later draft. Here's an example of what track changes looks like.

Narrative writing is storytelling, and in every story there is a beginning, middle and an end. But you don't always have to compose in that order. I started with the ending. In fact, that's how this whole story came together. I was still smarting from how the clinic handled my insurance situation and decided to write about it because everyone was tired of hearing me fuss about it over and over. I wrote the whole story scene by scene as I remembered it and finally rearranged it mostly in chronological order to build up to the exhilarating, yet anticipated ending. Writing the story was great therapy as it allowed me to really process all that had happened and all that I had experienced. That is another thing to remember—writing doesn't always have to be a chore; often it can be comforting.

EXAMPLE

ORIGINAL: I miss my spacious three-bedroom house, a luxury villa by local's standards. With solar panels, a chateau d'eau, and hot water heaters, the house has all the conveniences of the Western world, plus a large, manicured yard full of flowers. I imagine baby sounds filling the rooms.

REVISION: I liked my house the minute I moved in. In a village just outside of town, it is considered a luxury villa by locals' standards. Spacious with three bedrooms, it has all the amenities of Western life—solar panels that guarantee electricity when the government lines fail, a chateau d'eau that pumps water through the faucets so we don't have to draw it from an outside well and hot water heaters so our showers are always warm. Jasmine, wild flowers and mint leaves bloom inside the property's tall cement gate. Today, it feels like the walls of this house want to squeeze me to death.

Section Six

Challenges and Recovery

Selected Poems

Byron Lindley

ABSORB

I can't even fathom
the lessons
and blessings
showered on me
daily

I can't absorb
is my challenge
to hold
what I'm given today

it flows
off my back
like rain
on a duck
'cause I'm too hard
too cold
too stubborn
behold
I pray
to open
my heart
today

soften my edges
widen the cracks
the love that flows
off my back
may someday
seep in
absorb
within
that I may know
and live
all that I'm given
every day of my life

I take the step
'cause I can't stand still
can't stand the pain
of being away

flow through me
waves of Spirit
move this body
waves of time
transform this mind
that has the key
stop the worry
disabling fear
that enslaves the soul
and just let go

open the door
let in the light
shining daily
that I keep blocking out

someday I'll learn
how to absorb
how to receive
how to give
more than I
could ever believe.

ALCHEMY

Forewarning
she said
when I take flight
you might never see my face again

        never coming back?
        he asked
        with a sinking feeling
        in the pit of his stomach

oh, I'll be back
she replied
assuredly
but the face you see
may not be
the same me
who leaves you now

because I am the river
heading to the sea
and if you stand still
a twig flows on past
out of your sight
just as the tears
roll down these cheeks
as I shed the skin
from these tired old bones

the mask I've worn
is a heavy dam
of brick and stone
blocking the flow
dying to come down

let the fish on through
to their rightful home
as I spread my wings
fly to the sky
leave this lonely town
far behind

but don't you worry
I'll be back again
she said with a wink
and a mischievous grin
just don't expect
the same old cat
to knock on your door
when I fly back in.

BEGGAR

I am a beggar
sleeping in doorways
rooting through dumpsters
hanging out
at restaurant back doors
waiting
for a bag of trash
or maybe
I can snatch
a pot
with cold soup
burnt to the bottom

I'll wash dishes
for a cup of whiskey
or a moldy tomato
but they won't let me in
I stink

for years
I've hidden from the pain
didn't know it was there
but now
I sense it
I feel it
as I wallow in mud
with pigs

while my father's fortune
is abundant
infinite
and mine for the asking
as I keep grasping
for scraps
from the tables of those
who throw their trash
into the alleys
of separation
and desolation
that I am dying
to crawl out of.

FREEDOM STEP

I've been in this box
like a toy doll
eight sharp corners
blocking the sight
plastic thoughts
can't escape these walls
until a loving hand
opens a flap
my compulsion
to jump higher
see over the lip
perception expands

dogma
that means so much
to separate
you from you
melts away
dissolves
when everything falls up
out of an open box
plastic thoughts
finally see
where they've been held
in a plastic skull prison
no longer serves

no limits and laws
can hold the truth
break out of the walls
imposed by humans
shackled by confusion
so convinced
of right and wrong
who's wrong and who's right
us and them
who's in heaven
and not so much

programming
pulls you away
from clear sight
throws you in a box
where all you can see
is eight sharp corners
and the walls
where we write
what we want to believe

it's time to jump out
time to be free
the times are changing
old ways of being
dissolve
no longer serve
the depth and breadth
of human needs

the human compulsion
is to be free
and a new day
fills with sight
like a sunrise
of expanding light
paints my face
with living colors
when I peek
over the lip
climb out of the box
of tired bones
jump the horizon
find a new home.

LET IT FLY

I've got a freak flag
I just can't find it
where the hell did I hide it?
I think I buried it
along with the wind
and a bell that was rung
in the spaciousness
of eternal freedom

but I got scared
threw it in a hole
the resonation
echoing vibration
got soaked up in the dirt
my sonar lost touch
I wandered off
got lost in valleys
of sterile senility

now I keep searching
for an echo
to reach me
that I might find my
buried treasure
where I hid myself
so long ago

I have a feeling
when I find it
I'll uncover the wind
and a flag
that blows in it
I'll find my voice
that I buried along with it
run with the wolves
howl
at the moon
and the stars
sing to the sun
crashing with waves
soaked up
in loving arms

when I push the ball
it just keeps on rolling
maybe it will lead me
right where I want to be
I'll find my flag
wave it with pride
never hide
never deny
all this crazy love
swirling around inside.

PRIZE FIGHT

Let me into the ring
I want to take the punches
deliver the blows
receive the groans
as I exhale
the breath
pent up inside

anger ensues
skirts around
through the maze I impose
shows its face
peeking through curtains
peering at lights
only found outside

I deny its presence
keep trying to hide
shove it back
to the darkness inside
it wants into the ring
I've denied it the right
of a light that shines down
in the arena of faces
crying for justice
through decades of hate

I can hardly stand it
but I won't stand down
merely a spectator
in the span of my life
I'll climb through the ropes
let me into the ring
I'll blow my top
but it's worth every shot

take me down
I'll fall to my knees
love flows through
fills this void
I leave so vacant
from the space it takes
to hold the energy
of anger and hate

but it won't go easy
without a fight
so let me into this ring
and I'll let out the scream
of a man tortured
by his own bright light.

SISTER MOON

Sister Moon
bathe my face in your radiant love
in this, our little corner of the universe

I am yours
and you are mine
as every star is mine

and yet
you are my star
in this, my little world
the world that I know

and you kiss my face
with the reflection of
the source of your love

as the light that shines
through me
a reflection of the Source
of all that is.

SO MANY TIMES

I can see layers of waves
just below the surface
layers of faces
whispering secrets
from days long gone
under the same sun
but from a past
to which I no longer belong

yet they're stuck in my ocean
crashing up against the shore
making me feel
scraping and tickling my edges
a rocky cliff
crumbles to sand
when I release
let the waves
and fire
guide my hand

no longer stuck
in stubborn physicality
such limiting boundaries
banks and beaches of the mind
constructed
by my culturally crippled imagination
dissolve
I learn how to evaporate
and the whole sky opens

already tried right and left
the whispering depths
murky and wild
keep pulling me down
with archaic weight
guilt and shame
no longer mine
it's time to look up
never even knew
the sky
was an open door
unlike all the others
I tried
so many times before.

Untitled

Her greatest fear
was physical dismemberment
but by the time
she manifested
this necessity
she had gained full awareness
of her transcendence
and when her arm was sliced off
she looked and laughed
for it no longer mattered.

UNTITLED

Those who thought
something was terribly wrong
because all she wanted
to do
was sit and stare
were totally unaware
that she was listening
to angels sing.

Byron Lindley is a writer, poet, and a raw vegan chef. He loves warm ocean breezes, dancing barefoot, and especially writing poetry. He and his wife Lotus live in Los Angeles, California.

The Dance Lesson

Anne Szeligowski

Simulated walnut brown. Mauve. Tan in various shades. And orange. The orange is jarring in a place designed expressly for silence. I almost feel I have to address the issue of the orange, but I don't. I'm not supposed to. These are the colors of this place.

It is in this room of institutional design that Jesse and I get everyone to stand and line up while the nurse sets up the cassette player. The other "clients" respond with different levels of agreement, ranging from manic joy to muted but active reluctance. We turn off the television and take the hands of the mesmerized few. After some minutes, there are about 20 of us arranged in three rows, side by side. I know this cannot be true but I see everyone dressed in gray and black as I close my eyes for the image of it. All except for Lynn, the nurse, whose attendance at a wedding this weekend initiated this evening's dance lesson. She wears white with an oversized dusty rose cardigan to keep her whiteness clean.

I do not know if I can write about this yet. While I think of the last five years as the most phenomenal time of my life, that is, full of surreal phenomena, I still have a difficult time recollecting it. Re-collecting it. Collecting pieces of time, sharp pieces, dark pieces, oddly colored pieces. Yet all these fragments catch the light, and I should gather them to me again. I want to make sense of the non-sense. I need to make some meaning out of the last five years. I need to recompose my life.

The story I want to tell is about losing my mind. I know that metaphor conjures horrible images and I do wish it wasn't a cliché, but when I was diagnosed with Post Traumatic Stress Disorder and Major Depressive Disorder, what happened was that I lost my mind, my mindfulness, my sense of my self and my place and function in the world. It began one night when, at 38, I stood in the shower, crouched down and screaming because I thought the Dark Man of my childhood, that drunken, smelly neighbor who told me I was his favorite, was outside the curtain and was going to hurt me again. In that moment, the Anne I had known—intelligent, compassionate, active, funny, loved and loving—that Anne was gone and this dysfunctional hybrid had replaced her. I never did come to like that composite.

It is this loss of mind that had placed me in the setting of this story—on the Short Term Unit of a large urban psychiatric facility. I had been here before when my therapist and my family and I had decided that I "was a danger to myself or others". I was never a danger to others. Never. Painful to behold perhaps, but dangerous, never. I have found myself in this kind of setting five times before, but this is the first time I remember feeling happy in a place like this. I have felt rested, relieved, diverted, understood, engaged, sympathetic, empathetic, sad, frightened, confused, enraged, resentful, even dead. But never happy before.

Not that anyone would notice my moods. Staff always like that I read and write while I am with them. Sometimes, I go through a book a day; nurses would bring me in novels that they had read when my stash ran out. Of course I have to be careful that I do not spend too much time reading on my bed because that is seen as "isolating" and that is bad. So I pick up my book and go to the stupid unit meetings, where we are supposed to report on our day, discuss any problems we are having in the "community" and hear the litany of offenses that have been committed that day and should be avoided in the future to ensure harmony in our little enclave.

It is during one of these meetings that I first hear Jesse speak. He has been on the unit for three days, coming in on a Sunday with another man about his age, who also seemed to be my age. I remember Jesse and this man sitting at a table tucked into a corner of the ward, near the dining hall. Jesse looks angrily down at the table while this man speaks quickly and quietly and plaintively at him. Jesse never moves and eventually the man leaves at which point Jesse just walks into his room. He remains silent and apart until the day of that unit meeting. I speak out there and Jesse responds.

Virtually everyone I have ever met on a psych unit smokes. I even started again my second day on one after nine years abstinence. Therefore, the scheduled cigarette breaks at this facility, 15 minutes every 2–3 hours, are for most of us, a high point and a necessity. The metal door is opened to us and we can pass through it. We can breathe real air. We can talk and talk, crowded around the plastic patio tables, chain smoking. We can exchange tips on suicide strategies. Never have more than a half a tank of gas when you pull into the garage. Cut your wrists at "this" angle. Odd advice from people who have obviously failed at their attempts.

On a particular afternoon smoke break, the nurse in attendance has left the lighter on the table and one of the patients inadvertently pockets it. When we come back inside and disperse, the nurse remembers the lighter and no one acknowledges having it. So we are reconvened and scolded while staff quickly checks our rooms. We are threatened with revocation of smoking privileges altogether. How pathetic is our response to that threat.

We all are desperate to be taken from a locked unit out into a cage, literally. One door on this second floor wing led out an enormous concrete terrace. Our movement, however, is limited by a covered page fence that gave the 20 or so residents of our unit an area of approximately 240 square feet—12 × 20 with three plastic patio tables and matching chairs where we huddle in cold and rain to smoke, and in that fog, to tell some secrets we cannot bring ourselves to tell without the smoke.

Threatened with the loss of that opportunity, and watching the panic on my partners' faces, I take the measured risk and speak. "I understand what's at issue here about the lighter," I said. "And it will be found and returned. But I profoundly resent being treated like a naughty seven-year old about it. No one took the lighter as a malicious act. We're smokers and when a smoker is getting ready to move we automatically pocket our cigarettes and lighter. It's a reaction, not a subversion of authority. Treat us with some respect and we'll handle this." While I wait for the condescending dismissal, I hear a deep, resonant voice for the first time, and I am startled by it. "Ditto," says Jesse.

The lighter is found in the pocket of an ashen blonde woman who, heavily medicated, had gone to her room after the break and immediately fallen into a deep sleep. But something important has happened. I have heard Jesse speak. He is unique in my experience in these sorts of places. He is a man, a depressed man. He is about my age. And he is African American. On the breaks, he smokes a pipe. I have watched him read books, as I do, caselessly. And he listens to jazz and Sweet Honey in the Rock. I have been curious about him since I watching him stonewall his companion when he was admitted. His silence had been impenetrable. "Ditto".

At dinner that evening, I sit with Jesse, drop my tray and say "So, he speaks!" Despite himself, Jesse laughs and we quickly launch into a rant on the demeaning way we are treated here. That there is no stratification based on level of depression or exhibited behavior.

The next morning, I answer the pay phone where patients make and receive calls. The caller asked for "Father" Jesse. With a furrowed brow I go down to his room and say "*Father* Jesse? You have a call." As he walks past me, he touches my arm and says "I'll explain when I'm done with the call."

On the next smoke break, after our smoking materials are lit, Jesse and I move away from the group and he explains that he does not want it publicly known that he is a priest. He serves as the pastor, he tells me, of a large urban parish in Washington D.C. About four weeks ago, he had simply refused to get out of bed. For three weeks, he hid in bed, refusing calls and visitors, performing minimal hygiene tasks and accepting little food. Finally another priest, a friend, had managed to gain access to his room and head and asked Jesse to go with him to a retreat house out of state where Jesse could get away from the community pressures that had driven him, finally, down to despair. On retreat, Jesse could regroup, he was told. That retreat house had turned out to be the unit he found himself locked up on now. He was still enraged by the deception.

Afterwards, Jesse and I take our meals together and smoke together, swap books and talk. We avoid the darkness of soul that has put us there. We use each other to remember who we are besides the dangerous, damaged entities our presence in that place signifies.

Jesse joins me when I walk out of a room in tears, having bellowed at a fellow resident during a group session. This young man, who was admitted in the middle of the night before, proclaims himself a drunk, not a nut as the rest of "us" are. I have listened to this young man for too long because when I finally respond, it is with rage. "How dare you, you son of a bitch! How dare you put yourself out there as better than us! There's more fucking courage in this room, it takes more fortitude for some of us to keep breathing than it took to get across the fucking beaches on D-Day." Then I bolt from the room and Jesse follows. It was both a personal stand against this other man and a gesture of concern for me. I stay angry into the evening, even after this drunk but mentally fit man apologizes to me, and everyone else who had been present at that meeting.

The next day, my favorite nurse, Lynn, is on the evening shift. Lynn is young, in her mid-twenties, and fairly new to nursing, so she is not cynical or callused in her dealings with us. When she has free time, she invites us to walk the grounds with her and they are lovely. She extends the time we spend on break when she can. And she sits with us in the living area and talks, rather than stay behind the glassed in nurses' station.

It is during one of her conversations that she mentions she is going to a wedding that weekend. She loves weddings; she loves to dance and play and this promised to be a good time. "I have to figure out a way," she says, "to learn The Electric Slide." "I can teach you!" I say. Because of a rash of weddings and fundraising dances a few years earlier, I have mastered the line dance, and any opportunity to demonstrate mastery over anything in my life is welcomed. Jesse too pipes in, "We did that last month at a community dance. I can show you too." Thus the plan is hatched. That night, we will have a dance lesson; all together, we will dance.

Lynn scrounges around and finds a portable stereo with which to record the music. Next, she calls a local radio station and asks them to play "It's Electric" because, after all, we cannot dance the Electric Slide to anything but its anthem. Within a half hour, the song has been played and successfully recorded on cassette. On the next smoke break, we all decide the dance would begin at 8:00 p.m.; the patients will be done with dinner and any visitors, and Lynn will have completed her after dinner duties. We have a little over three hours to wait.

I'm suddenly afraid of this dancing. I try reading, taking a tranquilizer. I don't want to be on display in this place. I don't. I go out to watch some TV; maybe the news will distract me. But Angel is dancing already on the large, block-like coffee table in the middle of the sitting room. She is singing a Boz Scaggs song and swaying her hips and waving her arms, smiling, eyes half closed. I take her hand, trying to retrieve her from this obviously manic episode so I can watch TV, but she will not have it. One of the nurses comes out and takes her off the table, but Angel continues dancing and singing, looking at me critically from time to time.

We take one more cigarette break and everyone talks about dancing. Lynn revels in the idea of not looking like an idiot at the wedding and being able to participate fully. Other patients whine that they will not dance; they are too tried. Some, like Angel, cannot wait. I smile and stay oddly quiet, as does Jesse.

At 8 o'clock, Lynn runs around and gets everyone into the sitting room where we start moving furniture back against the wall to make room for the chorus lines. My jaw aches from clenching it. I stand back from the furniture and look around me. We are mostly women there, ranging in age from about 20 to 45. The few men were about my age—late thirties, early forties. We are all gathered there. Lynn has mustered everyone from their rooms for this, and everyone comes, each for their own reason. I see things in each of those faces as I stare at them and remember psychic war stories that have been told in the smoke. They want to dance. My breath suddenly comes into my body deeply and quickly; I want to dance too. I suddenly do not care where I am or how my behavior is interpreted. I very much want to dance. I look up and smile at Jesse. He smiles back, and we begin lining up our comrades in three rows. We manage to get everyone on their feet, even the man whose medication has given him severe tremors and facial ticks.

Jesse positions himself in the front row on the left. I am in the back row on the right. From there, we can most effectively manage our lesson. First, Jesse and I will show everyone the steps, without music.

"OK! We're going to step-slide three times to the right" I call out. "Then, we do the same to the left. Then walk back three steps, dip forward, now back, click your feet together and turn left. Repeat!" We all join hands while Jesse and I count the steps aloud. And we laugh. At ourselves and at each other, at the bumping and slipping. Jesse does not step-slide the way I had learned the dance. He does a crossover step that I decide looks

"cooler" and adopt. That quick step-slide hurt my hip anyway. We do several music-free runs, and then Lynn starts the cassette.

We play that song at least 10 times that evening. Jesse and I still call out the steps for a while until we both know that everyone who is going to learn the dance, has. Then we just keep dancing. I call out compliments and friendly taunts to the dancers. Jesse mocks my "dip" that comes right before the turn. And we dance until we are all flushed and breathing a bit more heavily. We dance and dance.

Two days later, Jesse is transferred to a partial hospitalization program. He will be leaving the unit to stay in a hospital-owned apartment while attending a program on the grounds. We return each others' tapes and make one last book exchange. We promise to stay in touch.

We do stay in touch for a time. While we both remain patients at this facility, we call back and forth. When we re-enter our lives, we exchange notes and a few phone calls, but the calls become awkward. Talking to each other while in the world serves as a reminder of our damaged souls and of our shame. I am not surprised when we just stop corresponding. This has become a somewhat regular pattern I have noticed with other veterans of the inner wars whom I have met while hospitalized. As much as we have shared within those alien, dead walls, as close as we had become, those feelings are non-transferable. They remain locked inside, ending when the heavy metal doors clicked shut, putting us on the outside at last.

So many heroes. So many scars. So many thwarted souls. We walk around and no one knows of our courage—the courage it takes sometimes just to keep breathing. And we danced that night. We danced.

Living with Insanity

Alexander R. Garbera

When I saw the tiny stains of blood on the sheets, I knew the problem had gone on too long. "It is just a rash," I kept telling myself. My persistent efforts to resolve this mysterious rash for the last three months had only left me itching and labeled by my Doctor as being 'needy.' The blood stained sheets reminded me of the uncomfortable, sleepless nights that almost drove me mad. At least I don't think it drove me insane. It's so hard to tell these days.

Now don't get me wrong. I think I have one of the best Doctors in the state of Connecticut. Yet it always seems that she is in a rush and has, on occasion, reminded me that she wished her physicians spent as much time with her as she does with me. This, of course, makes me feel grateful and guilty at the same time. It always seems that when we first start our sessions she lets off—shall we say—a lot of hot air. It usually stems from all the phone calls and emails I made trying to get through to her. After this initial harsh lecture about what is acceptable and not, and she sees my intentions and what motivated me in the first place, a sense of calm enters the exam room and we both get to the busy details of trying to manage HIV/AIDS. It is during these times I view her less as state licensed, board certified, YALE Doctor as a sister trying to help me get through all this. By the end of our session, we hug.

HIV/AIDS is a very difficult disease to manage, and I am probably even worse. I suppose it's my tenacity that has kept my alive for the last 12 years. To be honest with you I don't know why I am still alive. It seems I spent so much of my youth and young adulthood wishing I was dead. Growing up gay in an alcoholic household and very homophobic culture left scars that still run deep. Yet, for some strange reason, when I found out I was HIV positive, I also found out that I wanted to live and have been doing everything I can to make that a reality.

I actually met my Yale Physician several years ago at a lecture series on HIV. She was very impressed at my knowledge, determination, and strength to survive. So much so, she was surprised to find out that a rash would have me so rattled and panic stricken. I explained to her that part of it was due to the sleep deprivation and constant itching, both of which seemed maddening. So I made an appointment with a dermatologist and a psychiatrist. The first available appointments were over a month away, and that in and of itself, added to my rage.

The other part to my 'neediness,' which I tried to later explain in an email, was that since she first met me alot has happened. I have been the unfortunate witness to the tragic consequences of what happens to people when they 'fall through the cracks.' When HIV waits at the bottom, however, these cracks open a chasm of nasty nightmares that are only far too real.

One of my nightmares concerned my own lover, Mitchel. We were planning a vacation to Fire Island but he seemed to have all the classic signs and symptoms of Cryptococcal Meningitis, which I discussed with my own provider, and I warned him that going on vacation may not be the best thing. He reported his Dr. said it probably wasn't serious. I then tried to convince his best friend, the AIDS coordinator of a hospital, that I didn't think he should be going on vacation, and she reported that his Dr. was very competent and knows what he was doing. Needless to say, my boyfriend found himself in excruciating pain, crawling on the boardwalks of Fire Island. He was later confirmed to have Meningitis, and then took a fast downward spiral. After showing signs of wasting, I once again urged him and his providers, and his own sister (a lesbian) to treat it, which they did not until he was so wasted that there was little left to treat. He died in 1995. After all the arguments I had with his friends and family to advocate better health care, his own lesbian sister asked me not to come to his funeral. She said that they didn't want his mother to know that he was gay.

This experience almost wiped me out, but with the help of my physician, we worked on rebuilding my immunity and physical well being. I met this very hot looking man named Mark. On our first date I found out that he was wearing adult diapers and was suffering from symptoms of medications to treat cryptospoidium, which as it turned out, that he never had. His diarrhea, fevers and night sweats were so bad he went into the hospital, weak and depleted. He was being treated for PCP pneumonia with IV pentamidine. He was a strong and determined individual. Even though he was currently being treated for PCP, the hospital still conducted a bronchoscopy. He died very soon afterwards from collapsed lungs. Of course there is no way of knowing if the PCP caused his lungs to collapse, or if it was a result of the procedure, but it is my understanding that this procedure should not be done to individuals in weakened states, and I wondered why they did it when he was being treated anyway?

When I talk about these unfortunate incidents, people usually agree that the state of health care in the United States is suffering greatly. Some will even go into what they perceive the reasons to be like managed care, HMO'S, the economy, greed, medical malpractice, and the list goes on. Although different causes may be cited, it always seems like the conversation ends up the same—there is a problem and little, if anything, can be done about it.

This academic acceptance of the status quo is little more than tawdry tolerance of a problem that weighs its cost in human suffering, tragedy, and lives. It just doesn't sit well with a person who was told 12 years ago that "you have HIV and you're going to die, and little, if anything, can be done about it."

I don't know why I frustrate myself, and why I should wish that hospitals could be a setting for hope and healing. I recall in the early days of HIV, before they had a name for it, stories about hospitals in NYC disposing bodies into the garbage dumpster. I guess we have made a lot of progress, but a lot of work still needs to be done. One of the nurses at YALE reported that HIV care at the hospital still isn't what it could be, and that it is sometimes hard to get other departments to deal with HIV clients. I shared my own horror story at another New Haven Hospital where a surgeon told me he didn't want to perform a chest tube insertion (to save a collapsing lung) because of my HIV status. He didn't exactly say it with a concern for me. As it turned out, he didn't perform the insertion of the tube anyway but guided a student through it. It was her first time, and she was having difficulty inserting the tube under the skin. It seemed to me to be the equivalent of guiding someone to tie their shoes for the first time by verbal instruction. Except in this case, getting it wrong would puncture the lung and cause a total collapse. Luckily it turned out all right.

I have heard it said that Insanity is doing the same things over and over again, but expecting different results. I guess I am insane. I went back to that hospital for a minor infection in the facial gland called the parotid. I had this problem before. It is not HIV related. For some reason, the little gland in my cheek likes to make little calcium stones that clog up the duct into the mouth. This causes a little back up, and like beavers at a dam, bacteria has a field day. Usually, a dose of oral antibiotics clears it up, which is why I went to the emergency room. The intern, however, probed the infected duct and it started to bleed. The infection quickly spread into my head and neck. As my temperature started to rise, I felt chilled and started to shake. I was admitted to the hospital on IV antibiotics that made me violently ill. While recovering, a Doctor ordered warm hot packs. One clever nurse decided to microwave the packs to get them nice and warm. By the time I left that hospital, I was badly burned, underweight and very weak.

I was so scared. I called some friends at Yale to see if I could get help and switch my health care over there. "Anything would be better," I thought. My friend said she would do what she could, but to be honest with me, things probably weren't going to be any better at Yale.

My Doctor wonders why I am panicky? Even she knew my best friend Eddie, who, after getting radiation therapy for a tumor in his neck, wound up a quadriplegic with little will to fight the disease. Eddie was a body builder, but his health took a serious down turn after going to the March on Washington, DC. He was unaware that taking Bactrim (a drug used to prevent PCP) makes one sensitive to light, and he returned badly burned and blistering. By the time we drove back to CT, his T-shirt was soaked from the blisters. Even as his health started spiraling downward, he fought valiantly but gave up hope after a radiation treatment for a tumor in his neck left him a quadriplegic. I miss Eddy.

I could go on with horror stories, from hospitals and other medical providers, but this would turn out to be more of a Halloween Reader than anything else. It's not the institution that's the problem. It's the attitude, and very often lack of information.

Perhaps outrage is dead, and we have become numb. Not me. Not yet. I want to live. I don't want to be another statistic. I don't want to fall into an acceptable margin of error. I will not be discounted, ignored, categorized and dehumanized. I am alive. I have needs, and if that means being needy, then so be it. It took me almost 30 years to find out that I really wanted to live. It took HIV to kick me in the pants. If I have to kick others to wake them up, well I guess I am not going to be the most popular guy in town, but at least I will probably be the most alive.

The sad truth is that some of the problems in health care and other systems can be solved with some very simple, basic low cost solutions. Because the problems have become so monumental, these simple things like courtesy and common sense, get over looked. Basic human needs are shared by both provider and patient. We are in this all together, and it will take all of us to get out of it. But we all have to decide that we all really want to live and value our lives and life itself. Each and every life becomes the most precious thing in existence. Unfortunately, however, not every one is as lucky as I am. If there is one thing I can thank HIV for, it is, perhaps, this perspective.

Insanity is doing the same things over and over again but expecting different results. Maybe, it is time we do things a little differently. It was very important to de-gay HIV/AIDS in the early days of the epidemic. Now it is time to re-AIDS gay politics. Far too many of us are 'falling through the cracks.' Many have the perception that with the new drugs AIDS is going away. It is not. If anything, the equation for survival has just become more complex, with more variables, and things that can go wrong. Like my friend Gary who almost had total liver and pancreatic failure over the combination therapy he was on. Or Al, whose skin started to fall off from a reaction to a new drug.

I think HIV/AIDS is here to teach us a few lessons. My fear is that unless we learn them, it is not going to go away, and something worse will come along if we keep our heads buried in the sand. My hope is that we will learn from the disease, and we can teach those lessons to those who haven't been infected. I believe that you don't have to contract a fatal illness to appreciate life, and you don't have to lose someone you love to learn compassion. It is time that we do things a little differently.

Proud to Be Me

Tammy N. Bernier

This was the year I chose to confront my father.

I never had a close relationship with my father. I think it started at birth. He never intended to have a girl—he *had* to have a boy. To carry on the name. To play baseball with. Someone to be proud of.

I guess my struggle to prove myself to him started at a very young age. My mother tells me at six months I refused to eat anything that "daddy" was not eating. My mother tried feeding me ahead of time, napping me at dinner time, but nothing worked. I had to eat what he was eating or I would starve.

My mother (still!) tells everyone what a blessing I was. She swears I was walking at nine months and fully self-potty trained by eleven months. Personally, I think she "stretched the truth" just a little. My mother, I believe, is incapable of lying ... but "stretching the truth", as mothers do, was in her boundaries. Whether or not these feats were accomplished at these early ages I am not sure, but I do recall becoming right-handed to please my father (or perhaps it was the slaps on my hand that persuaded me I would become right-handed?).

Anyway, in one way or another, most of my actions were done in the feeble attempt to please my father. I studied to read and write well before kindergarten. I was reading stories to my siblings by the age of four. I even knew my multiplication tables by the first grade! I consistently brought home papers littered with stickers marking "excellent" on all of my homework. Still, he insisted with a grim look, *I could do better*. So, to please him, I did better!

I always had "little warnings" throughout my life to let me know, no matter what I did for him, it would not be good enough. I tried to win him with my love. When that didn't work, I tried to dazzle him with my grades (they wanted to skip me two grades in grammar school—he refused). To him, I was nothing but a useless girl. A "Miss-know-it-all" (what he'd call me after I brought home good grades) right-handed girl at that! I truly believed he would change, though. *He just needed time*, I thought. Things will be different ... later.

I was four years old when I first remember telling my parents that grandpa was "touching me" and "making me feel funny". I was always a "good girl" and my Mommy told me if I ever felt "funny" around someone to Run! Tell! We will believe you, we will help you.

Well, I told my Mommy and she told daddy, but he didn't believe her (or me) because that was his stepfather ... and I'm a liar. My Mommy said she believed me, but there was nothing she could do—that was daddy's stepfather.

So, word got out that I was such a naughty girl, making up such awful stories about grandpa. But that was okay because Mommy believed me and that was all that mattered. She would keep me away from him and she would be there for me.

I truly believed that as long as Mommy believed me everything would be all right. After all, grandpa lived in Maine and the most we would visit him was three timed a year. I was safe in Connecticut for the most part.

It didn't take long before word spread like wildfire that I was "easy" (or at least an easy target at the age of four) and an uncle by marriage started helping himself to me. This time I was hesitant to tell my mother. The only thing that telling did was make us both look like liars. Six months past, and I finally fell apart. My mother knew something was wrong, but she couldn't place her finger on it. I was being defiant and rebellious—not like me at all. She demanded I tell her what was wrong. So, for the second time I told. I told her every detail of what her sister's husband did to me as he was baby-sitting.

This time Mommy didn't ask daddy's permission—she took me straight to the police station. Yes!! Justice would be done! This man would never touch me again ... he could rot in jail, where the bad people go. But when Mommy filed the report, the policeman said we waited too long and there was nothing that they could do except check for me for VD's.

So, the bad man was never put in jail, but they were nice enough to check me for VD's—whatever that was. They brought me to the hospital and explained a doctor was going to look at me. I figured the doctor just wanted to ask some questions, like the policeman did at the station.

*The man with the white coat sat me down and introduced himself. He seemed kind, so I decided I would be nice to him. He asked me to remove my shirt (I guess to look for marks of physical abuse) and proceeded to reach for a **BIG** shot. Wanting to be a doctor as since I was wearing diapers, I asked him if I could please take a closer look at the needle. He said yes and held it out in front of himself as if it were a trophy! The thought of that monstrous needle coming into contact with my body overwhelmed me, and I bolted from the office, topless and all! The eventually found me and brought me back kicking and screaming the whole way. It took four doctors to hold me down.*

*When word got back that my Mommy brought me to the police, the whole family was upset. Daddy beat Mommy and pushed her down the stairs—he wanted to know how she could believe me after all the lies I said about grandpa. Mommy's side of the family wouldn't talk to us for months—they also wanted to know how she could believe me over my uncle's word. As time passed, the family decided to sweep it under the rug, let bygones be bygones; **they** would forgive **me** because I was such a young, confused child; Or—my favorite—"maybe she truly believes it happened, but it was only a dream".*

Well, I'd like to say things got better, but they didn't. Now that the family "forgave me" and everything was

swept under the rug, I was even easier prey for incest by three additional relatives. I guess they figured if no one believed me before, no one believe me now. They were right.

By this time I was winded. I did what I was supposed to do—I ran—I told! It was not them who were punished, but I. I finally decided not to tell anymore. It would only hurt my mother (because she felt powerless to do anything) and tear the family apart. Yes, the best thing to do is to keep silent.

My silence did break, eventually. It was the summer of 1987. I was eleven years old. My father, as usual, wanted to take my mother, me and my three siblings to visit his parents. (Since my mother believed the "accusations", whenever we would visit them my mother would keep a close eye on my grandfather—not leaving him alone with anyone of us for a second. He still got "quick feels" while my parents took family pictures, but that was about it. I wasn't going to tell on him for those—it wasn't worth the hell I'd go through if I did tell.) This particular vacation we were to spend a week and then go home. A week didn't seem like much at all—I could tolerate a week.

Well, a week had passed and I was ready to go home! Grandma's and grandpa's was not my favorite place to be. We all got packed and ready to go home when my father approached me.

"A summer in Maine will do you good," he said flatly.

*That is all he said. He had made arrangements with my grandparents for me to spend the summer and he didn't even warn me! I pleaded with him not to leave me there. Silently I screamed from within ... How could he leave me with him, **alone,** for that long! Doesn't he remember?—This man abused me! How could he not believe his own daughter?! Nonetheless, he left me.*

Grandma and grandpa always slept in separate bedrooms. Since their "shack" only had two bedrooms, I was left to sleep on the living room floor (Easier to get you, my dear ...). Every night, after grandma went to bed (and she would always go to bed early), grandpa would creep out into the living room. He would always take a few minutes to look at me—I could feel his icy gaze through the sheets. Then he would run his fingers up the inside of my thigh and grope me. He would stay there a good amount of time as I closed my eyes tight, pretending I was sleeping. I was paralyzed with fear and decided it would be best to pretend. To pretend to be dead.

Grandpa always had a reason to send grandma to the store. It was during these times that he would make me grope him. Grandpa knew that grandma would be at least an hour, they lived in Maine where every "down the road" means thirty miles.

Three weeks had passed and I was still wondering how I was going to get out of this mess. I wasn't going to be able to take this much longer. Should I run away (so I'm considered a "trouble child" and I'm punished again?)? Commit suicide? ... Was that the only way this was going to end?! I couldn't tell my dad—he'd just call me a liar.

This particular night grandpa decided to push me a little farther. This night, after sending grandma to the store, he forced me to perform oral sex on him. I tried to struggle, to push him away. I wondered why God didn't give me the physical strength to keep him away from me ... how could such an old, dirty man have such power?! (I couldn't believe I didn't have enough sense to bite it off!)

When he was done with me he mumbled some threat if I ever told and pushed me aside. As he went to wash I bolted for the front door. I ran out of there as fast as my feet would carry me! When I reached the nearest phone I dialed feverishly. "O". "Please take the call, please take the call." I prayed as I waited for the operator's assistance. My father never *accepted toll calls, no matter who was calling.*

"Hello?" asked my father.

I yelped out a cry and started sobbing ... I couldn't say anything at all ... I was in complete hysterics.

"Hello?" asked my mother. Oh, thank God he put her on the line! I could talk to her ... she believed me before ... she would believe me again.

"Mom ... he's ... touching ... me ... again," I let out between sobs. She said she'd tell my father and he'd come pick me up (she had a phobia of driving and could never get behind the wheel of a car at the time). She asked me to hold for a second so she could tell my father ... I said okay, I felt better all ready. She believed me and everything was going to be all right. I would be home soon and could put this all behind me.

Something was wrong! She was taking too long on the other end of the line! I heard my father screaming and my mother crying. It was obvious. Once again, he didn't believe me. He was not picking me up and I would have to spend the remaining six weeks in a house that I was being molested.

At that very moment I felt every bit of spirit leave me, as if I had an out of body experience. It was the whole unreality of it all ... how could this keep happening to me? ... how could this be allowed to happen to me? I let out not one whimper, not one cry as I told my mother I loved her and hung up the phone. I was now dead inside.

Not to despair—my cousin, in his early twenties at the time, hitch hiked to Maine to stay with me. Once there, he provided me with food (which we had to steal from the local grocery store, but that's another story) and safety. After a week, he found a wonderful family with a daughter about my age (I remember her name—Sarah).

When my cousin explained the situation, they agreed I could stay with them until the end of the summer (he didn't think it was safe for me to hitch hike back with him, and my father didn't want me back until the end of the summer anyway). God bless them!

My relationship with my father has never been the same since that summer (I guess there was really no relationship anyway). To me, he was only an authoritative figure with control of me until I was sixteen and old enough to move out. Once in a while I tried to get some form of approval out of him ... even in college I called him to tell him I had made the Dean's list (he once told me I could never achieve that and going to school was a waste of time). Once again I was quickly "slapped back into reality" with his grim look and almost respected response ... *you could do better.*

I never blamed my father for the years I doubted myself or the guilt that is accompanied by being sexually aroused as a child. I never blamed my father for the nightmares, the inability to sleep at night, or the incapability to sleep with my head above the covers. I never blamed him for the tight fetal position in which I lay in bed every night, arms and legs crossed tightly while trying to force myself to sleep. Nor do I blame my father for the "nervous breakdown" I suffer just about every year, recalling vivid scenes of past sexual abuse, or worse, I'm only left with broken pictures to leave me assuming the worst. It is not my father's fault that the entire family on *both* sides (besides my mother and one cousin) decided to either sweep it under the rug or ignore it.

It is, however, my father's fault that he was not a "dad." He chose to ignore me, maybe believing that one day I would just disappear. He wouldn't believe me. That, as a result, hurt not only me, but four young girls and four young boys within the family. They never came forward in fear that they would not be believed (because they saw no one believed me).

On Father's Day, June of 1998, I decided to confront my father. I chose to do it by letter so he could think about it instead of me confronting him verbally and having to deal with the initial rage. I kept the letter short, simple and sweet. I asked but one question as straight forward as possible so as not to beat around the bush.

"Why did you leave me in Maine with grandpa when you knew he was sexually molesting me?"

His reply was the typical answer I expected from him. "You made it up ... you're only trying to ruin everything ... even Father's Day!"

If he only knew me. He would know that I didn't try to ruin Father's Day. It was the week of my birthday (which he once again forgot) and I was giving myself a gift. I was, once again trying to prove myself. But this time it was to me. I am strong! I am brave! You are my father, but I am someone too ... you have no power over me now.

I am here to please me.

Death, Love and Life

David C. Berg

As I walked down the darkened hallway of the Hospice, I could hear my Aunt Jean's whiskey and cigarette voice in the distance. I could not make out what she was saying. It was very late in the evening, or early in the morning, depending on your perspective, about 3 a.m. When I had come home from work, I found a message from my Mother telling me that the end was near and I should say good-bye as soon as possible.

Though I loved this woman dearly, I did not want to go. I do not have any fear of the death of others, or discomfort about sickness or hospitals. In fact, the reason I did not want to go was because I had so much experience with all of those things. I wanted to avoid that odd anti-climatic feeling that you sometimes get around Christmas, when you realize that life is not at all like a Christmas movie.

It is also so with death. I did not want to go and feel guilty about being disappointed because our last visit would not meet up with my idea of what a wonderful and meaningful, final few moments should be like. She would not supply me with the missing detail that would clarify all of life's problems. Though she was possibly the most intelligent person I have ever known, she would not be imparting any final words of wisdom. She was too busy dying.

I had been to see her just the day before, and she had slept the sound sleep of someone heavily medicated. I did not want to see her tiny, sick body again. Her white nightgown on the white bed clothes had made her seem even smaller and more frail than she was. I stood there and thought that she looked very much like a baby bird that had been rejected and ejected from the nest. Her fine white hair looked like ruffled downy feathers, all mussed, never to be dressed again.

I went, though. I could not *not* go.

My Father died when I was a small boy, and I had spent several months after his death living with my Aunt Jean in the "Country" (Cheshire), while my Mother made her slow and never altogether complete recovery. During that time my Aunt Jean gave me my very first book, a first edition of "Pudd'nhead Wilson" by Mark Twain.

She explained to me that it was very old and had to be taken care of like a pet. I understood on some level that she was entrusting me with something very special and valuable and felt very important because of it. Over the next month my Aunt Jean, a teacher, taught me to read using the book.

As I sat next to her bed holding her hand, mental pictures of who and what this woman had been overwhelmed my mind. Some were like old grainy films, some were sharp and clear; others were just snapshots of moments I had spent with her.

I have a photograph that she gave me of her and a female friend splashing drunkenly barefoot through a Parisian fountain in the late 1930's. One of her legs is kicking up high, and her skirt is hiked up an immodest amount of thigh for a woman of her age at the time. Her head is thrown back with eyes closed; her mouth wide open in a belly laugh. When I asked her why, she told me without a hint of irony,

"Because I was eighteen."

That eighteen year old has been gone for a long time, but never really dead or forgotten. She was raving in her bed, out of her mind, talking to my Uncle Bill—the self-professed love of her life— who had died twenty-five years before.

"Put another log on the fire, Bill. Come sit over here close to me."

She was the daughter of lace-curtain Irish immigrants, who had done well enough to send her to

Mount Holyoke in the 1930's. After graduation she had married into my family after having met my Uncle in a somewhat scandalous shoreline marina bar,

"Where you had to take your shoes off at the front door, because when the tide came in the floor would be covered with four inches of water."

Before her my Uncle had been:

"Good for singing in his Gregorian Choir, getting drunk, and losing jobs."

They married within weeks of meeting. My Uncle, a rough and tumble born-in-the-old-country Irishman, had left school in the 5th grade. Seven years after marrying my Aunt, he had a Master's Degree in Biology and was teaching it at a local teacher's college.

So she taught English and Literature in the same college.

She would always hit me with lines that would leave me chuckling or at the very least confused. After her retirement her great joy in life was spending Friday nights perched on a stool in a very nice cocktail bar, sipping martinis and calling out song titles to the piano player. She would sing along in her musky contralto and was quite pleased when the management had presented her with her very own tip snifter. One night I took a date to this lounge. My Aunt looked my date over from across the room and motioned me over. In her most vexed voice she said to me,

"Well I guess there is no hope at all that you'll be gay," she looked back at my date, shrugged and said, "well at least she's pretty, but you would be a lot more fun if you were gay." I laughed and made her sing "Danny Boy."

With these thoughts in my head I was now openly weeping. She didn't know where she was, let alone who I was. I decided that I couldn't take anymore as she laughed uproarisly at some joke only she heard. I stood and bent over her, kissed her cheek and whispered into her ear how important she was to me, and that I loved her. Irritably she responded,

"Yes, yes I know you do." She turned towards me and opened her eyes. They were clouded and

out of focus, but my heart leapt for joy when she said,

"David."

"Yes Aunt Jean."

"Have you seen your Uncle Bill? It's pretty cold in here."

I pulled her blanket up to her neck and said,

"No Aunt Jean, I'll go find him if you want."

She was looking up at me with clear eyes and was laughing.

"Now how are you going to do that? He's dead!" I began to laugh too.

"You think I am already gone, but I'm not. Only half way there and anxious to finish the trip."

A couple years before she got sick I had stopped into the cocktail lounge to see her. That night she introduced me to a middle aged man who had been a student of hers. They were "keeping company" she told me and with a little wink said,

"A little of the old Mrs. Robinson."

Her former student told me a story about the first class he had ever taken from my Aunt. His freshman year had an unseasonably hot September, so all the windows in the second floor classroom were open. A one-story wing flowed out below them, and the roof was in the process of being tarpapered. The men doing the work were not happy about the heat and were very vocal, venting their displeasure in an obscene manner.

My Aunt, who was about 26 at the time, rather than closing the window and suffering the heat, rather than be flustered and embarrassed, led the class in a lively discussion about slang and its uses.

She always claimed to not be a fan of Dorothy Parker, and she would often be annoyed by the comparison, but if you knew of them both, you could not ignore the similarities, both physical and personal. She always had a quip or a line ready, sharp and fast. She was natural born philosopher. One saying of hers I will never forget.

"God loves the poor, He must! Why else would He have made so many of them?"

Once when I was young I had tried to climb a bookcase of hers filled with knick-knacks. It crashed over and, thankfully, came to rest on the couch or I would have been squished. My Aunt pulled me out from under it and held me tightly. Years later I discovered that the "knick-knacks" had actually been an extensive collection of Waterford Crystal inherited from her Grandmother. I called my aunt immediately to apologize. She laughed at me and said,

"Just things, honey. They come and go. I have many lovely memories of my Grandmother, that's enough." It was never mentioned again.

"Well, you think I've gone around the bend, she said, you must think I'm high from all the drugs."

I tried to disagree, and she shook her head.

"Don't patronize me, you know better."

She then explained to me that the closer she came to the end the thinner the wall between "here" and "there" became. She told me that for several nights she had been slipping back and forth between the two. She said that each night my Uncle Bill would come and take her out. She was very clear that she was not just reliving memories, but in fact was creating new ones. That "there" she looked as old as she was, but my Uncle looked the same.

"Last night," she said, "he took me dancing. I haven't had so much fun in years. I don't know if it's just in my head or not, but when Bill touches me I can feel him just as I feel you now. It may be just in my head, but who cares? I know it's where I'll stay when it's over. Remember when you were small you asked me about God? I told you that it didn't matter as much if you believed as much as it did that you *lived* as if you believed? This is sort of the same thing, and it's beautiful."

We sat silently holding hands for a bit, and I slowly watched her slide away again. She was gone to me, back to there. Wherever, or whatever it was.

I went home and slept well. The next morning she was there for good, and I was ok. At her funeral her man friend told the roof story. I told the story about the shelf of crystal and the fountain photograph. I left dry eyed with a smile on my face. Sometimes when you are at your most jaded, life will surprise you. Our final moments had not been anti-climatic. I had been surrounded by death and sickness from a very early age, and all my life mortality petrified me. I had been my aunt's very last student and received her most important lesson. I no longer feared my mortality. With her death, my life began.

Behind the Silver Lining

Lorraine Eggeling

I am about to tell a true story that involves racism and discrimination as I have experienced it within my community and family. I will also share the painful realization that I am not fully accepted by my family.

These issues—neither racism nor sexual bias—were ever discussed openly within my family. Instead, I would hear narrow-minded remarks made carelessly about anyone deemed different. Often, I have felt completely out of place within my own family, and did not know why. I have also felt that I could not put my bags down on my mother's kitchen floor and that I was the stranger ringing the doorbell. A few years ago the pieces of the puzzle started to come together for me after I met a childhood acquaintance at the local bus stop. This is where I will begin my story.

It was June, 2006, and just across the street from my family's house, my teen-age niece and I were waiting for the bus to New York City. As we waited, I saw a Black woman crossing the street from the opposite corner, and my niece and I made room for her to sit with us on the bench. The woman said, "thank you," as my niece's cell phone rang. My sister was checking up on us, and we were only across the street! I thought to myself that some things never change.

The constant feeling of being checked up on and the anxiousness of my family leave me exasperated. Can any one person or family really control the world and shut out everything and everyone who is not like oneself? Imagined safety at the price of love and acceptance is beyond my comprehension. Often times, I have thought about the many reasons why I moved away from my childhood town and home.

Joining in the conversation, the woman sitting next to me at the bus stop asked me if I was related to the woman who walks her dog around the neighborhood. I said, "Yes, I'm her sister, and this is her daughter." She recognized my niece, but not me. As I looked at this woman, I began to notice the widow's peak of her hairline, as well as her exquisite nose. She looked familiar to me, but I could not place her. Curiously, I asked her what her name was. She replied, "April," and immediately I responded, ***"Yes! I remember you, we used to play together!"***

I remember playing with April like it was yesterday. What a vivid memory from my childhood! It was the early seventies when April and I played together on a summer day. Unlike the neighborhood kids from my block whom I played with all of the time, she and her two friends came unannounced and uninvited, and only played with us this one time.

I do not remember any of us saying a word but I do remember the excitement of this unexpected encounter. I saw April and the two Black boys walking around the corner past my house coming right towards me and the boys from my block. In fact, I probably looked like one of the boys with my hair cut short and parted to the side. April strode confidently, leading her friends to our side of the block. In a heartbeat, we were all running. Maybe we played hide and seek? If we did, there were no rules, no scores, no taking turns, no calling out each other's names.

What a thrill when April popped out from behind the garbage pails. I remember cautiously moving the cans apart and seeing April hiding behind them, hunched down low. I'd never seen a girl with a widow's peak, nor had I ever played with

Black children before. The next thing I remember is that I was hiding behind my neighbor's boat. My white Keds slipped as I ran through an oily puddle, and I fell down on my knee (squish). How would I explain the dark grease on my pants? Unspoken boundaries were all but forgotten the day the Black kids came to play on my block.

I remember coming out of my neighbor's yard and finding that everyone was gone. April and her friends had left as mysteriously as they had arrived. No "good byes," no "see you tomorrows," no plans for another game.

Running into April in 2006 at the bus stop was such a jolt to my senses; her widow's peak was as powerful as ever. Her presence was once again commanding my full attention. Over the next few weeks and months I would remember forgotten details of my childhood. I had almost forgotten the racism, because by the time I was in public school I didn't feel the boundaries of discrimination. No one told me that I couldn't go to a certain section of the school. I could sit next to anyone, including the Black kids who lived around the block from me.

We all played on sports teams regardless of the color of our skin or our gender. Recently, I spoke with my high school track coach, John Hurley, who is now the principal. He told me that when I was in school the teachers knew that the community was racist, but that it never manifested in the schools. He said that the students did not buy into it—racism.

While growing up in Rutherford, New Jersey, I was allowed to play on Maple Street, but not around the corner on Grove Street. I never asked my parents why. But one day I asked my mom, "Why do people not like Black people? And why are they called Black, because I don't think that they look black? I think their skin looks more like the color brown." I don't remember what she said, if anything. Thinking to myself, I thought white people don't look white. Then I asked, "When I grow up can I marry a Black man?" *Not a word was said.*

As a kid I remember being outraged at the injustice of prejudice and stereotyping. I was especially confused by my mother's racism since she was a foreigner herself. As a child I did not have a word to associate with my own difference; I was just being me.

I grew up wanting to be a carpenter and preferred to play with boys. I had my hair cut short with some of my hair pulled in front of my ears to look like sideburns. Sometimes I would wear a badge, a clip-on tie, and tie clip with my flannel shirt and boy's pants. I still remember my mother's pained look the first time I had my hair cut short. I couldn't have been happier with my new appearance. No more long hair to be painfully brushed out. I looked and acted so much like a boy that I remember being told that the men's room was on the other side of the hall at the local V.F.W.

When my mom entered me in the local "Miss Buddy Poppy Pageant" I told the V.F.W. members that I wanted to be a carpenter when I grew up. My mother quickly explained to her friends that I wanted to be a singer, like Karen Carpenter. I thought that she must be confused, so I corrected her by explaining that I wanted to be a carpenter who used a hammer and nails.

Was I testing the waters by asking my mom if I could marry a Black man? Was I checking to see her reaction to my being different from her expectations of who I should be? As I grew up I had many experiences that showed me that she disapproved of what she may have viewed as non-conformity. Sometimes she feigned tolerance of my preferences with a taut smile. I did not like to wear dresses and fancy shoes. I preferred to follow my dad around and hand him tools for whatever project he was working on. I was just being a kid and didn't understand not being accepted and loved for whom I truly was. I did not understand why some of my possessions were packed up and put out of sight.

One of the most painful experiences of my childhood was when my mother dismantled my shadow box display of model airplanes and cars and put them in the basement. While she was spring cleaning, she packed up the display that my father and I had built together. My dad and I had spent many a Sunday afternoon or early evening building and decorating the models. The culmination of the project came when my dad helped me draw airplane hangars (he taught me perspective drawing) as the backdrop for the display, and he helped me put it all in place on a shelf in my room.

As I walked into my room, after my mother was finished cleaning, I saw the empty shelf. Hesitantly, I asked her where my cars and planes were; they were no where in sight. She told me that she had packed them up and put them downstairs. I discovered that the backdrop panel was thrown on the closet floor. It was obvious to me that I would not be allowed to put the display back together. I screamed and cried to no avail. Eventually, she told me to get a wet cloth to wash away the redness and puffiness underneath my eyes so that I wouldn't look like I had just been crying.

I did not know that I was different (or that it mattered), but I had plenty of examples of how my family treated people who were different. One day while mom was shopping on Park Avenue a Black woman held up a blouse from across the clothes rack. She smiled towards my mom and asked, "Isn't this lovely?" My mom smiled back and answered, "Yes it is." Barely tall enough to see over the rack, I asked my mom, "Why are you talking to that lady, you don't like Black people?" We were the only people in the store besides the salesclerk. Years later, I asked my mom what we did after I had said that. "We left, what else could we do?" she answered.

My mother told that story many times to friends at our kitchen table, and every time she made a point of saying, "I don't know why Lorraine would say that. I've never said that I don't like Black people." She also never told me that she didn't like my looking and acting like a boy, or that I couldn't have boyish looking stuff on display in my room. She shrugged off my appearance by telling her friends that I was going through a phase that I would grow out of. I was just a tomboy.

What could my mom say of racism and hate, and her personal experience of being discriminated against in Northern Ireland? My grandparents worked hard to provide her with an education, yet she was unable to get a secretarial job once the interviewer saw that she had checked Catholic on the application. There is no difference in skin color between Protestants and Catholics. In fact, my grandparents were one of each, and my grandfather converted to Catholicism.

It was as though Catholicism was a disease in my mother's country. She couldn't help what religion she was and she came to America looking for opportunity in a progressive country. She worked hard at trying to lose her Irish accent. Who would she be in this new country, and would she see the irony? Would she realize her own perpetual loss by excluding people based on race, sexuality, marital status, or anything that she deemed different? Would she understand a daughter's hurt at not being accepted by her own mother?

My mother's racism and non-acceptance came to light for me another day when an older Black woman rang our doorbell. As usual my mother checked from her bedroom window to see who was ringing the bell out on the front porch. The woman was wearing a long, dark grey coat and was carrying several bags from her day of shopping. She was probably walking to her home about a block away. Her hands looked worn and tired from carrying her bags; too many bags to shift easily from hand to hand. Her feet looked swollen in her black laced shoes.

My mother answered the door, and the woman asked her if she would call a cab for her. My mother let her come in and the woman sat sideways at the kitchen table. First, my mother looked up the phone number for the local cab company and then stood behind the woman as she dialed the phone that hung on the kitchen wall. The woman sat with her coat still buttoned and with her shopping bags sitting at her feet. She said nothing. I think that the only reason the woman was able to put her bags down at all was due to the force of gravity. It certainly was not due to the force of my mother's smile. Otherwise, I think the woman's bags would have hung in the air. After what seemed like a very long time the cab arrived.

Another day, some years later, mom, grandma and I were driving to the food store through the Black neighborhood around the block from us. Grandma, with her red widow's peak and Belfast accent, commented that while walking, she's noticed that there are coloreds living in this section. She spoke as though the neighborhood had an incurable disease. Did she expect Black people to convert to her color? I felt my blood start to boil as I said, "They have to live somewhere." *Not another word was said.* (I never heard anyone in my family ever say that she didn't like Black people, that part is true.)

In the summer of 2006, I sat next to April at the bus stop; we were two 42 year old women who have shared a lifetime of experiences barely a block apart. She and I talked like old childhood friends who barely knew each other's names. Did April remember me, the girl who looked like a boy?

While talking with me at the bus stop she reminisced about some of her friends from around the block. She told me that one of the young men had died, and she looked sad. Next, April was smiling and told me that her daughter was about to have a baby. I smiled back at April and asked, "When did you graduate high school? I don't remember seeing you there." She said, "1983," and I said, "1982."

I remember the second time that I met April. It was 1976, and it was my first day at the public middle school. Up until then I had attended St. Mary's Catholic Grammar School, protected within the shroud of uniforms and prayers. At school I looked like a girl in the school issued jumper. I would have preferred to wear the boys' uniform but knew that wasn't an option. One time at school, one of the boys was told by our principal, Sister Maria, to get a haircut (his hair was touching his shirt collar). He asked our teacher

why a girl (meaning me) could have her hair short while he couldn't have his long.

I also remember the two older girls who tormented me for two years at the Catholic school, because I had been placed in a higher reading group. Many times they waited outside the school doors. They followed me home only once, stepping on my heels and calling me names. After that, I found a longer route home from a side exit where they hardly ever waited for me. The one day that I did see them waiting by that exit, I snuck back up the stairs and went out another door. I never told my family about my being tormented at school or that I was afraid when I walked home.

As I started my first day at the public middle school I hoped to never run into those girls ever again. Instead, I ran into April as I was leaving school and she offered to walk home with me. As we reached her corner we said good-bye and she kindly offered to walk with me anytime I wanted to. I walked to my house's front porch and I heard my mom ask my sister, "Who was Lorraine walking with?" My sister answered, "That's April, from around the block." *Then, barely a word was said.* Many times I felt like the black sheep of the family.

Back at the bus stop on this sunny June day in 2006 we all stepped on the bus together and we nodded our good byes like old friends. April found a seat up front, and my niece and I sat midway back on the left. I saw April step off the bus near the circle, and I wondered what her life was like. Had the prejudiced community of our childhood changed, or are some of the old boundaries still intact?

Meeting April for the third time in my lifetime reminded me of all the discrimination in our society. It also made me more conscious about why I am aware of it within my own family. I didn't realize how much pain I feel about not being accepted fully for who I am by my own family. My mother's reactions to people of color and difference are all I need to see to know that as a gay woman I am not lovingly embraced. I have never risked having a conversation with my mother about my sexual preference or her prejudice. She has made enough side comments for me to sense her hatred and disapproval.

When I think of my mother's religious discrimination in Northern Ireland I sometimes wonder if she ever felt hatred from either of her parents or her community. As a young girl she snuck out to take dance lessons because her father did not approve. She told me the story of her mother's throwing a wooden hanger at her as she ran out of their house. She did not remember what she had done wrong, but she said that she had probably done something. Did she grow up internalizing hatred and anger? I ask these questions because I cannot comprehend my mom's anger and rage (even if muted) towards people of color, or her lack of understanding and acceptance of me.

I have no expectation of a rational conversation with my mom about my life choices and lifestyle. I dare not bring the topics up. Nor do I expect a warm hug when I arrive with my bags after a long drive. Even though she greets me at the door I still do not feel like I can really put my bags down. I am continually reminded of her anger towards people who don't fit her lifestyle.

Recently, after Barack Obama was elected President I felt my mother's blood boil as she said in an unusually strong Irish accent, "This country has a short memory." Perplexed, I asked her what she meant, and she answered, "It wasn't all that long ago that they were slaves." I had no response. She continued by adding that she did not like Michelle Obama because she is an aggressive woman and may wind up running our country. I pointed out that many aggressive first ladies have been helpful to our country, and I reminded her that she voted for Hillary in the Democratic primary. She continued by telling me that she does not like Michelle because she's tall, and that she doesn't like tall people, because she feels that they are looking down at her. *Not another word was said.*

Shadow Boxing

Lorraine Eggeling

SHADOW BOXING

Misplaced trust
in a brown paper bag

Begging
"with hands as dry and worn as that bag" *
the copper issued the summons

With no time to lie nor to cover up
the container uncapped
openly judged unjust

Badges and baggage
no longer play
by the old rules
from an olden day

These old secret rules no longer apply
to the old wounds that refuse to dry

A price to be paid
if one must

Misplaced hatred
may sound unjust

Clasping
with hands too young to feel
the futility of a mother's steel

But I'll sit with my bags at my feet
if I must
held down by gravity, not by lust

Leaving the force field
of a mother's forced smile

Forged by fortitude
not by style

No longer repackaging
for her world to smile

No Blacks!
  No Gays!
          . . . .
               No Mother's gaze!

Dismantle my planes
while you reframe "Karen Carpenter, the singer"
in my refrain, "I want to be a carpenter"
Is my stammer to blame?

But I will not sit pretty
in the dust of your tattered bags at my feet

For sure, that would be unjust

* borrowed from August 22nd, 2006 NYT article, "Under one roof in Brooklyn-Trial, Penalty, and Civics lesson", by Michael Wilson

Lorraine Eggeling, *a poet and she knows it*
February 2009

Note: 1st version written during a week long poetry workshop in New Haven, CT, facilitated by Sarah Pemberton Strong in 2006. This version was written during the writing of the essay, "Behind the Silver Lining," in 2009.

Questions for "Behind the Silver Lining"

1. What memories and issues does this essay bring up for you?

2. Describe your emotional reaction to reading this essay. Are the feelings that come up for you a strong reaction or weak?

Lorraine Eggeling currently lives in New Haven, CT. She works as a private educator, and is a part-time painter and writer. She has been drawing since she's five years old, and started writing her "100 worst poems" seven years ago. "Poetry, my day job, is in another life."

Lorraine graduated from Rutherford High School, NJ, and went on to receive a BA in mathematics from a small liberal arts college. She also earned her Master's Degree in Education at Fairfield University. She has traveled to Europe, Egypt, and most recently to Guatemala.

First Time

Klara Dannar

"G'mornin' Doodler. Ready for another day of saving lives?" Dad offered me toast, then the weather report, fresh from the gray transistor radio on the pine kitchen table. He poured milk in his coffee, "Mostly sunny, high seventy-two, twenty-percent chance of an afternoon shower. Not bad for October." I felt guilty that the one day he could sleep in, he was up to drive me to work. His morning weather reports, delivered in his quiet, thoughtful manner, were his way to send his four daughters off each day, properly prepared for the outside world.

I hated getting up before dawn, especially on weekends. I hoped the eight hour day shift, on four hours sleep, would be an easy one. Dad dropped me off under the red canopy at the county hospital as the sun scaled the treetops. He pointed to the third floor nursery windows and reminded me I was born there, seventeen years ago.

"Remember Doodler, if it's worth doing, it's worth doing right."

"Thank God the day shift is here! It's been a hell of a night." The nurse's aides, uniforms stained with blood and vomit, were exhausted and eager to leave. I worked the night shift all summer and knew a bad night on the geriatric unit could lead to a challenging day. I crossed my fingers.

The kitchen staff pushed food carts down the wide halls and delivered breakfast—oatmeal and poached eggs. The housekeeping crew mopped the tiled floors and banged trash cans together as they emptied them. Nurses and doctors made rounds.

I was sure everybody wished they were somewhere else. I wanted to turn the clock back twelve hours and be at the Sky-Hi drive in, fooling around with Don in the backseat of his '66 Chevelle, while Bonnie and Clyde robbed banks, then died together on the huge outdoor screen.

"You're going to do special duty today." The charge nurse said. "Only one patient. Just stay with her and try to keep her quiet. She was loud and restless all night. No one near her got enough sleep."

"Should I bathe and feed her?" I asked.

"No, she probably won't live through the shift. Just be there with her." I had never sat with a dying person before and suddenly I wished I had the typical assignment of six patients to bathe, feed and exercise. My stomach grumbled as I entered her room. I longed to be at the breakfast table with Dad. I reviewed everything the charge nurse told me: she is actively dying, her family has been called, and she shouldn't have anything to eat or drink. Just stay with her and keep her as quiet as possible.

"Hello. I'm your aide today. Are you comfortable?" No response. *What a stupid question! She's dying. Of course she is not comfortable.* I realized I had no idea what to say or do. I did not want to look at her damp, pale face, with her gray hair matted across her forehead. The side rails rattled as her small, frail body thrashed. The sound of her head against the metal made me wince and feel nauseous. I snatched flannel blankets from the chair and padded the rails. She grabbed my hands and clutched them to her chest. I recoiled at her rotten breath and eyes staring at something only she could see, as she brought my face close to hers.

"J. E. C. T. N. E. A." In a raspy whisper she was telling me something, by spelling it out. Her dry mouth struggled to produce each sound. "P.L.E.T.", she continued to grip my hands hard. When I managed to pull away, I turned on the call light to summon help.

The charge nurse arrived and jokingly asked me if I had seen a ghost. "She's trying to tell me something. I got scared." The nurse chuckled and told me about her early experiences with death. She checked her pulse and breathing, and whispered, "It won't be long. Call me when she's gone."

I pulled a chair close to the bed and began to listen again, this time with a paper towel in hand to write down the letters as they came. She grabbed my hand again, this time with less intensity. "R. C. O. M. P. L. E. T. I. O. N. P. R. O."

I pulled my hand away and ran to the door. I yelled for the nurse and stood there shaking, holding the paper towel until she appeared. We walked together across the room. She was curled on her side, with her hand resting on the flannel blanket, where my hand had been. No thrashing. No pulse. No respirations. I stood by the window; outside the sun continued to rise, offering warmth and light. Not bad for October.

I looked at the paper towel in my hand and read, PROJECT NEAR COMPLETION.

Klara Dannar, RN, born and raised in Columbia, MO, graduated from the University of Michigan and has practiced nursing for thirty years. Her professional and personal experiences with grief and loss contribute to her passion for exploring life and death. She currently divides her time between a Michigan island in Lake Huron and Tucson, AZ, where she writes stories for Greeting Death. *www.klaradannar.blogspot.com*

Three Letters to Nathan from Tucson

Francis E. Crowley

Monday, January 10, 2011 (after the Tucson tragedy) LETTER #1

AGING

(This is for all the elderly people I met today in my meanderings about town: the old man, frail and alert, at my bus stop whom I saw on the way to Safeway; those with or without walkers, shopping on a Saturday morning at a Safeway on the East side of town at Craycroft and Pima in my neighborhood....; and for those elderly victims earlier at another Safeway on the other side of town....ironically....; for me there is such irony in the situation of elderly people gunned down who just happened to be at another Safeway from the one where I was that same bright, blue sunny morning.)

One true thought for today: always perception before judgment.

Dear Nathan,

I am sorry to begin my "aging" letter to you with such sad news; it is part of today's emotional map for me. So is the humorous and antic side of aging for the past ten days, since I arrived. Tucson's horrific shootings last Saturday, January 8th, at a Safeway market on the other side of town has left my heart filled with a deep and painfull sadness for the victims and for their families and friends. A young, nine-year-old girl who was full of promise and zest for life is gone; a 30 year old man, recently engaged; a beloved Federal Judge; three retirees; bystanders wounded......... For me there is such irony in the range of ages of the victims; the elderly retirees in their 70's happened to be in the right place at the wrong time. Dorwan shielded his wife with his own body; he died and she lives.

I find in these events and ironies of life just how fragile our moments are. Somehow for me at 69 time remaining is much more precious, more valuable by the minute, enjoyable, precarious. Today, it's the juxtaposition of tragedy and comedy, sadness and humor in the conditions of being elderly that I want to describe, as I experience them. Some of grandpa's humorous and self-deprecating moments from the last ten days:

1. First, I've been literally dizzy from a worsening head cold, walking into things.
2. I noticed after coffee, chicken soup, or sweets, sandwiches with "mayo" certain stains like pigeon droppings under my chin on my yellow sweatshirt.
3. My handwriting, once so full and firm with flourishes, has been a little shaky in my blue notebook in these letters I began January 3rd; maybe, from emotional intensity? my cold? the shakes from a glass of red wine the night before?? (ha, ha)
4. My hyper-alertness since this tragedy (along with nightmares, cold sweats, tears) has created in my mind a hurricane of unmanageable impressions, so I begin to sound silly.

Aging for me in the midst of this life-altering tragedy and in gathering impressions to write about it feels like my poet's mind gone mad. Some days my befuddled brain is like a trembling tuning fork out of metronomic synch: wobbling, tipping, speeding up, then slowing, buzzing, moaning. Now that I think about it, this has been gathering for a couple years; moreover, it's not just the big loss of short-term memory, I think. Interesting that I'm having to rely more and more on mnemonic tricks for myself to kick in the fact or name I seek.

Some of these tricks are similar to the strategies I used to suggest to my students of literature who were faced with a fat anthology; **at least I'm able to remember these.** In short, my immediate memory has slipped; long term is still intact.

Ahhh, the ironies in all this self-reflection at 69 and "retired"; I'm both ridiculous at times and very professionally serious as a poet; moreover, my recent success with sonorous alliteration in my verse is increasing. Go figure!

At the same time I notice that, as my short-term memory fogs over, my acute observations this week are spot-on and pitch-perfect in these letters and poems.

Finally, in this misty ambiguity of old age am I playing at being a poor version of the Henry James' gentleman/**observer** (HJ dictum: "try to be one of the few on whom nothing is lost")—the Lambert Strether type from **THE AMBASSADORS, OR,** is it that the mystical poet's truth (RUMI) lives in the hidden world behind logical, rational reality? One thing, Nathan, however, is certain: I am living once again this winter here in Tucson a poet's dream except for this cold/flu which is ironically getting worse as the days this week are in the sunny, dry 70's. I'm in the throes of an inner renewal of creative energies and spirit. I thank God for that at 69!!

One true thought on the writing process in poetry: always seek the rigorous image.

"...**grow old with me, the best is yet to be...**"

"...**to strive, to seek, to find, and not to yield...**" Tennyson's **ULYSSES**

YOUR HAPPY, DITZY, CONFUSED, CREATIVE **GRANDPA FRANK**. OOOOOOPPS

LETTER #2; part one

Dear Nathan,

Living here for a couple of months each each, so close to the Kitt's Peak National Observatory, I have the stars, the moon's and the sun's rituals always on my mind. I can see, amazingly, like this morning the pure white towers like specks in the far distant mountains outside my kitchen window. Star-gazing is part of the desert scene for me. I've loved astronomy since boyhood, and I always note the phases of the moon so that in my imagination I can howl with the coyote at the full.

This brings me to the one true, rigorous, poetic image to describe to you the intense life of the true poet: a supernova or the rare heavenly display of the gigantic explosion of an otherwise small, quiet star near the end of its life cycle. Yes, like us stars have birth, life and death, and I love the image of a poet/star in its transformation to supernova, shedding radiant and overwhelmingly brilliant light; it's sharing its life, so to speak, with the rest of the universe in its last moments of brilliance and illumination from within.

Somehow, mystically, for me this image holds true, also, for the victims of the Tucson tragedy on 1/8/11. In President Obama's speech last night, paying tribute to each person's life, accomplishments and gifts, it was Christina's, age nine, born on 9/11/01 that shone as a supernova for the nation in his peroration at the end of the evening. President Obama's voice rose to climax as he invoked the Biblical, prophetic power of his words to illuminate Christina's life as a star in the heavens to guide America's collective motivation to live up to the promise, to become what our children expect of us as one nation—"a more perfect union"—"a city shining on a hill"—for other nations of the world. He in one salient image transfigured through his invocation one meaning of Christina's life:

"...if there are rainbow puddles in heaven..... then she (Christina) is walking in them."

This was one of Christina's own images from her notebook.

Nathan, I remain in deepest sadness, but I am also feeling peace settle slowly into my soul, after last night's healing ceremonies, prayers and testimony. I loved all the quotations, especially, from the **BOOK OF ISAIAH, JOB, PSALMS,** all profound poetry, really, from **THE BIBLE.** Instead of political references we had poetry! And the last item from President Robert Shelton of the U of A was a poem, too, by W.S. Merwin. More than the instinct in us to turn to poetry for consolation during times of grave national concern, maybe, just maybe, this time poetry could return at last to its rightful place in the cultural life of America—at the top of our moral values, along with kindness, compassion for each other, reverence for our loved ones, respect for our neighbors, tolerance for the "other" person in his/her diversity, and love, spirit, truth and unity. It's my dream, and it seems we made a start. For example, all the buses in Tucson flashed "TOGETHER WE THRIVE", alternately, with the bus # and destination like "#9—Sabino Canyon"; it's true.

Here is a list of some of those killed and injured on 1/8/11, which was memorialized each day in all our Tucson newspapers, so I grew to know them almost as brothers and sisters in tragedy:

U.S. Rep. Gabrielle Giffords: "My first Congress on your corner starts now. Please stop by to let me know what is on your mind or tweet later." This was written moments before..............................

U.S. Judge John M. Roll, age 63, chief judge of the U.S. District Court in Arizona, took his seat on the federal bench in 1991. He was a 1972 graduate of the University of Arizona College of Law.....................

Dorwan Stoddard: he and his wife, Mavanelle, were high school sweethearts who married later in life; she is expected to recover.......................

Christina Taylor Green, age nine, was recently elected to her school's student council and wanted to learn about government. I watched her grieving parents talk about her bright promise on T.V...............................

Gabe Zimmerman, Gifford's constituent services' director, age 30, accompanied his boss to events and worked with people who needed Gifford's help with an issue. He had so much passion for helping people and dedication to his job............

Dear Nathan,

The questions remain, "Why?"; "How?"; "When?" (again?) The victims and mourners, especially, deserve answers, as do the first responders of police, EMT personnel, fire....by-standers who threw themselves in the line of fire to courageously help others. As best we can find under the circumstances of a 22-year old, lone killer, our Nation needs and deserves time-out for reflection and self-examination—not our strong suit, to be sure; for each time something like this seemingly senselessly happens we are bereft of loved ones whom we need to honor with a full attempt at accounting for **this time.** Columbine, Oklahoma, they seem to be occurring with increasing frequency................**now, Tucson!**

Beyond last night's healing ceremonies and coming together I hope a deeper look at possible underlying truths becomes possible this time; otherwise, we grope, again, in the dark like our pioneer forebears on the wild frontier, fearing the coming of the night and acting out "regeneration through violence."

Francis E. Daniel Crowley

THREE LETTERS TO NATHAN FROM TUCSON #2 (part two)

......by the way, Nathan, I snapped some photos of the Presidential motorcade at the cornors of Campbell Ave. and Speedway Blvd. around 4:00 p.m. yesterday. The crowd was both miffed for having to wait to cross and excited to have the close-up. I waved to the Obamas' limousine, a long, blue-black job with the Seal, as it went past on its way to University Medical Center—so much security—lines of motorcycle cops and Secret Service cars. Earlier I had taken photos of the long lines heading to the McKale Center: 13,000 people patiently queuing and snaking around campus for hours. I couldn't handle that with my worsening cold. I had stopped at a student booth, too, where volunteers were stringing together written well-wishes in a long paper ribbon like the ones I made in childhood out of strips of paper and glue, curled into rings for the Christmas tree. This ribbon was an unbroken tribute about a mile long, it seemed, folding back upon itself. What a creative student response and expression of connection in tragedy. I had written that Rumi quote about breathing on my slip of paper as an expression of sympathy and support, one of a thousand or two links in the paper chain.

Another true thought for today: in the poet's life her process becomes her art, i.e., in this sense the process is the payoff in the same way that content and form are inseparable. No one can do the hard work of revision but you! The payoff, sometimes, can be breathless beauty.

Dear Nathan,

Since I arrived in Tucson this trip on January 1, 2011, I have been following my writer's schedule for the most part:

8:00–10:00 a.m. writing to you almost daily one of these letters on the couch in my studio, sipping coffee, looking out at the pigeons lining the telephone wires, watching the sun come up.

10:00–12:00 noon jotting down after-thoughts and residue feelings from the morning's topic in between a shower, breakfast and a second cup at Alice's Restaurant or McDonalds or for the weekend at Beyond Bread and Bookman's (2nd hand).

2:00–4:00 p.m. afternoons, where I am sitting this very moment (2:30 on Monday 1/24) I type up these letters with revisions from notes and spontanious editing here at the Poetry Center of the U of A. When I am too pooped to type from the morning's work, I wander Fourth Avenue in the Arts district in search of the fabulous street musicians. I buy a bagel and coffee, and, sometimes I donate a Ginger Beer or two and curry tempe to the "G-String Band" that warms up around 2:00 in front of the Co-op Food Store on the East side of the Ave. I sit in the sunshine close to the musicians bouncing to the jazzy beat. There I met Matt, the violin-banjo-guitar player who sings his New Orleans original lyrics with his deep, dog-howl longing for love and hope. I love his voice, his mischievous twinkle and his ironic humor. What a gifted star in his repertoire: gypsy (both Romanian and French) and that wonderful Appalachian,

Akshowka melody he bellowed solo *fabuloso* last week on the street!
signing off with the "Shamanic anatomy": the rhythm, the drum beat of poetry,
   your GRANDPA FRANK

3 "Three Letters to Nathan from Tucson"
Humility

On Saturday morning I went back to the Urgent Care Center to retrieve this notebook which had dropped out of my bag. It was around 10:00 a.m. and a whole week since the shootings, so I crossed the street to U.S. Rep. Gabrielle Giffords' main office—1661 N. Swan Rd. A memorial of balloons, cards, candles, flowers, peace lillies, signs and gifts was growing by the hour; parents with small children were approaching the wrap-around space in front of the curved entrance. Passers-by were stopping to pay their respects with a prayerful and mindful attitude; moreover, several T.V. news reporters, one was from KVOA-Channel 4, began to engage the children kneeling at the drawings and pictures made by other children.

I went from message to message of these out-pourings of love. I stood in silence for some time, along with others, as I became flooded with waves of sadness. I remembered the exact time it happened a week ago, shortly after 10:00. Other on-lookers carefully, slowly and with deep reverence in their steps and sadness on their faces seemed to pay special attention to the lines of verse and poetry which had been copied on cardboard for display, along with quotations from the **BIBLE.** Many hand-written notes of sympathy and encouragement were spread out among the photos, pictures, paintings and lists of names of elementary students from Christina's school. I loved the votive candles lit among this make-shift altar in a church without walls, open to the blue sky and bright morning sun.

One true thought: Humility in the face of these events is placing the needs of others first with purity of heart. I am reminded of Kierkegaard's meditation, *PURITY OF HEART,* which I read 45 years ago when I began social work.

Earlier, in times of tragedy and deep misfortune society and civilizations tend to look to their poets for solace and messages of hope:

"Not, I'll not, carrion comfort, Despair, not feast on thee;

Not untwist—slack they may be—these last strands of man

In me or, most weary, cry I can no more. I can;

Can something, hope, wish day come, not choose not to be."

Gerard Manley Hopkins

Grandpa Frank—low energy and flat on my back

The Blue Gate of Paradise

Barbara Peabody

"I'm Tony," he announced. A tall man with sunken, abnormally dilated blue eyes and high cheekbones, he bent his long frame into a chair opposite me at one of the folding tables we painted on in my AIDS art class at the San Diego AIDS Project in August, 1985. He rested his cane against the table, heaved a sigh of relief. He'd been drifting around the Project all morning, bothering the office upstairs with his unending chatter; they must have sent him downstairs to my class.

"Had a seizure in June," he told me, his voice unnaturally loud. "The doctors don't know what the fuck's wrong with me, they don't tell me nuthin'." He unfolded his story without pausing, how he'd been diagnosed with ARC, or AIDS-Related Complex, the limbo of vague, disabling symptoms before graduating into a defined diagnosis of AIDS.

His words gushed from the broken spigot of his loneliness. "Can't remember a damn thing, don't know where I am half the fuckin' time."

"Used to be an *iron*-worker," he said, "not a *steel*-worker. *Iron*-worker. We're the guys in skyscrapers who put iron beams and girders together." Very *macho*. "Been married twice, got five kids. I'm straight." The other students glanced at him skeptically. "But I feel comfortable here at the AIDS Project, been to some support group meetings. These gay men here," he whispered to me, "Y'know what? They're all so nice, they really are."

I started Tony painting wet-on-wet on a large sheet of paper. He was enchanted, daubing blue, yellow and red on the paper and watching the colors run into each other.

"Hey, this is fun!" he yelled, holding his dripping brush in the air as clouds of blue and red fused into jagged yellow lines, creating greens and purples. The other seven students glanced up, irritated. "I really like this, never knew it could be so much fun."

"Say, Barbara, how d'you pay for the paints and stuff?" he asked, curious. "And how come you do this, anyway?"

"Private donations, mostly. People who are interested in the class and want to see it succeed. And I do it because I'm an artist and lost my own son, Peter, to AIDS last year."

"Listen," he yelled, "I'd like to help out. I've got some money and I think this is a worthy cause. Why don't you and me go shopping for art supplies some day? Something like this has to be kept goin', and it's gotta cost a lot of money, the paints and all."

"That'd be great, Tony," I told him. "Sure you can afford it?"

"Yeah, sure. I've got this wonderful insurance and pension, don't have to pay for a damn thing," he assured me. "Got plenty of money, not like some of these poor bastards here." The poor bastards looked up.

"Okay, we'll go," I promised.

***

Tony talked incessantly and loudly through the next class, annoying Steve, whose own volubility had annoyed others when he first started the art class.

"Think I got AIDS years ago, when I worked in the Dominican Republic," he announced. " Went to the whorehouses. Boy, you could get anything there!" As if he'd been walking down the aisles of a Safeway. "Any kind of woman, fat, thin, old, ugly, and even men—men dressed as women, whatever, everything all together. It was sump'n. Of course, *I* didn't do nuthin'"," he assured me, "just looked around and took in the scene." I wondered how doin' nuthin' had infected him.

"Did your son have this diarrhea?" Tony asked me. "It's just shit shit shit all day."

"Yes, he did, and also seizures, like you," I answered.

"I get words mixed up all the time," he jabbed his brush into red paint and slashed the paper, ruffled his rapidly thinning hair with his other hand.

"What about your family, your kids? Do they know what's going on, are they supportive?" I ask.

"Naah," he answered, disgusted. "They know I'm ARC, sent me a thousand dollars when I told 'em. They don't call very often, wish they would. I wish they'd tell me they love me. I told my folks I got this from using drugs, just couldn't tell them I'd been with men. It'd kill my Dad. I've got five kids, all grown up, wasn't a good father, wish I had been. So now they're not here for me now when I need 'em. Fuckers. All I've done for them. Then there's Mary, she was my girlfriend for four years," he said.

"Did you tell her how you got infected?"

"Yeah," he grunted in disgust. "She called me a fag. T'hell with her, the fuckin' bitch."

"Maybe she just needs some time," I suggest.

"Yeah, sure....hmmph," he said. "We lived together four years—I got divorced from my second wife after my divorce five years ago—but I told her to leave, couldn't deal with her drinking and her two crazy dogs. She's pissed at me because I exposed her to AIDS. She tested negative but still afraid she has it—we talk but just end up angry." His voice softened. "She did treat me well, though."

"Do you miss her?"

"Yeah…no…I dunno," he looked out the window, his brush poised mid-air.

Tony was one of the loneliest AIDS patients I'd ever known, isolated in his bubble of bisexuality.

***

The following week, everyone had gone to a "Love and Healing" workshop and Tony and I were alone. Again, he'd been drifting around the build-

ing all day, lost and distracted, interrupting people with his incessant, loud chatter.

"I don't know what to do all day, I'm used to working," he told me. "Would you want to go out to lunch with me some day?"

"Sure, love to," I told him.

"I'm too tired to cook, then too tired to eat, and I don't like to eat out alone. I'd like some company," he said. I smiled; it's hard for a tough guy to admit need.

We sat talking for an hour. With no one else, he opened up and talked fairly coherently. We sat across the table from each other in the Project's dark kitchen because of a meeting in the large room we usually used for the class. The afternoon sun filtered in through the small window, lighting Tony's high cheekbones; he had what I called the "AIDS face," cheeks sucked into gray, the dry wrinkles of premature aging.

"I'm always angry—Mary, my family, my kids. I love 'em all, very much, but I can't talk to them because of my past," he said despondently.

"My Dad don't have legs"—*is he kidding me?*—"my Mom has to lift him and carry him, she's a saint. You should see, she even picks him up and dances with him, it's a crack-up," he grinned; the imagined scene was macabre, I didn't know whether to laugh or cry, if it were even true; I compromised with a small smile. He guffawed, then continued. "She don't need my problems."

"So you think you got infected in the D.R.?" I asked him. We'd already compared notes on the Dominican Republic last class; I'd lived there, too, a year after he'd left. I doubted that was his only exposure.

"Hell, I don't know," he sighed. "My second wife wasn't interested in sex and I wanted to experiment, went to the baths a few times, it was the only place you could lie in the sun to tan, but I never knew the people I was with. Didn't want to get involved in all that gay stuff. Actually, I prefer women to men, there's nuthin' like lyin' next to a woman, though I don't trust 'em. I did like the sex with men. I didn't want to come to the AIDS Project, my social worker suggested it, but there are so many caring people here, they're so kind to me."

"I know what you mean," I said. "The gay community was so good to me last year with my son. I couldn't have done it without them."

"And I love the art class! Never knew I'd like art so much. Hey, I won one hundred dollars last week in a card game and I want to donate it, okay?"

"Oh, Tony, that would be great! We're almost out of supplies," I said.

"Yeah, well, I don't have anything else to spend it on. Glad to do it," he smiled, his cheeks furrowing. His eyes were deep in their dark sockets, the blue pupils surrounded by white, as always. He pulled out his wallet, handed me five twenty-dollar bills.

"I wanna do some painting now," he announced. "I know just what I wanna paint, I had a dream last night and I want to paint it. It felt so good; I dreamt I was entering the gates of paradise, and I was so happy."

"Go for it!" I set out the jars of acrylic paints and lay a large sheet of paper in front of him, then fill a plastic container with water and set it to his side. "Do you want the paper wet?"

"Yeah," he said, pleased, and I dampened a large sheet of paper and laid it in front of him. He chose a fat brush from the rusted coffee can on the table and painted slowly, deliberately, knowing exactly what he wanted to depict: a large, soft orange space to the right, narrower orange swath up the left side. A bright red streak, vertically centered, green to the right. A blue oblong in the middle. Paint flooded the entire sheet of paper.

"That's the gate to paradise," he announced. Content, he leaned back and appraised his work.

"It's beautiful," I said.

"Yeah," he said, leaning back, pleased. "That's where I want to go."

***

We met for breakfast a month later. Tony had stopped coming to class, though we had talked on the phone and met for breakfast several times. The Project wasn't so friendly any more, he said, was

getting too bureaucratic, not as interested in the patients and was too gay for his taste. Probably they had no patience for his unending river of words. He thought a friend in the support group had lied to him; the man had said he wasn't gay yet only had gay friends. I imagined the man was still in the closet, didn't have Tony's frankness about bisexuality. He had stopped calling and Tony felt abandoned. Like my son, he didn't want pity or sympathy but he did want good friends he could trust.

"Do you still like the art class?" I asked.

"Oh, that's different," he said.

"Well, if you come, you don't have to go up to the office, you know," I told him.

He laughed. "Okay, I'll try to go today."

But Tony didn't go to class. He was exhausted, he told me later, and his mental confusion intimidated him. The day before, he'd tried to go to Spring Valley outside the city to sell his guns, but found himself switching lanes constantly, feeling lost, and wondering where he was and why. He finally pulled over, decided to turn around and go home. I didn't like to think of Tony careening around the freeways of southern California.

***

With his fear of driving, Tony stopped going to the art class. He called often, to chat or invite me for breakfast or lunch, which he insisted on paying for. "Got nuthin' else to spend it on," he told me. I'd pick him up and we'd go downtown to a little New Orleans restaurant he liked that had light-as-air beignets, fresh fruit, po' boys and exquisite pastries made by the owner's wife. A small, homey place where he was comfortable.

"Yeah, Mary's still mad at me, fuckin' bitch," he said. "And my kids—they only care about my cars and my money. And I need help, can't take care of the house any more. Burned a whole pot of soup yesterday, burned some pans last week. Forgot about 'em. And not driving—I can't go anywhere."

Do you hear from any friends from work?" I asked.

"Naah, I can't tell them I got AIDS." He drinks coffee, looks out the window. "Ain't got no one I can talk to."

***

I pulled into the parking-lot of Tony's favorite seafood restaurant; I hadn't known where it was and Tony had directed me hither and thither, completely confused, till we found it by accident. "There it is!" he bellowed. The steep stairs to the door were problematic for Tony; he stopped, stumbled, looked down, looked up, unable to cope with steps. How would we descend them later?

Inside, Tony glared down at the carpet, a confusing black, red and yellow composition of curlicues in a pseudo-Spanish design. A slight ramp led to the diningroom and he stumbled, stopped, grabbed the wall. I put my arm through his to give stability and we followed the waitress to a table by the window.

"God, I'm hungry!" Tony yelled as the waitress handed us menus. "I could eat a fuckin' horse!"

"Where the hell is that fuckin' waitress?" Tony yelled after five minutes. The "f-word" was an integral part of his speech; I wondered if he'd always spoken like this, or was it the dementia breaking down inhibitions?

"It's only been a few minutes, Tony," I tried to calm him.

"Well, I'm *starving!*" he mumbled, fidgeting. A waitress hurried over.

"Where the fuck is our lunch?" Two minutes later. His eyes, always abnormally wide, opened even more and flashed.

"I'm goin' to complain to the fucking manager," Tony yelled, fuming. "Goddam, this fuckin' place usually has good service. Dumb fuckin' waitress, bet she's gone home."

"No, no, Tony, it's all right. It'll be here soon," I assured him. He'd already eaten all the bread in the basket. Other diners glanced furtively at us.

"Well, it's about time!" Tony yelled at the waitress when she brought our plates. "Where the hell've you been, for God's sake?"

The waitress apologized, eyed him warily. "The cook had too many orders at once." I tried to act as if nothing were unusual but was tempted to hide out in the bathroom.

"Jesus Christ," mumbled Tony through a mouthful of lettuce. "I'll never come back to this fuckin' place again."

We finished, I stood to leave. Tony tried to stand but suddenly there was a forest of legs entangling him: his own legs, the chair legs, the table legs, his cane. I helped disentangle him and somehow we maneuvered the leg-forest, the red, black and yellow carpet monsters, and the steep flight of stairs outside.

I left him off and went home to collapse, exhausted.

***

"I didn't call to talk to no goddam fuckin' dog!" Tony yelled through my answering machine. I giggled, replayed my outgoing message; yes, my dog was barking at passersby when I'd recorded my words. I laughed again.

***

"Hi," Tony's voice, strangely subdued. "Just thought you might like to do something, go to a movie, maybe. But...well...you're not in, so that's okay."

Click.

***

"Hello...is this Barbara?" A soft woman's voice, unfamiliar.

"Yes," I said. Nine o'clock, Saturday morning.

"I'm Mary, Tony's girlfriend. I thought you'd want to know, Tony tried to kill himself last night."

"My God—no!" I jolted upright. "Is he all right? What happened? He called me last night, a little before nine, wanted to go to the movies."

"Well," she said, "he called me about nine, said he was going down to the beach with his pistol. I freaked out, dashed over—I just knew which beach he meant, the one we always walked on. So I went there and found him wandering around, his gun in his hand."

"Oh, my God," I repeated. "Then what?"

"I persuaded him to go home. Got him into bed, calmed him down, took his gun, gave him some sleeping pills. I stayed with him till about four a.m., then I thought he was okay and went home. I was exhausted." She paused. "I never should have left. I went back about seven, and he'd taken a whole bottle of sleeping pills. He was out, completely. Didn't respond at all, though still breathing. And I thought, what the hell, this is what he wants, why not let him go? What's he got to look forward to?"

"What'd you do?"

"I called my sister, she's a doctor, and told her what had happened, and she told me I had to call an ambulance, I'd be in a lot of legal trouble if I didn't. So I called 911, and he's in ICU at Sharp right now. They said he'll be all right."

"Oh, thank God—" I started to say, but it's not all right, he wanted to die. He knew something was wrong with his brain, he knew what he was facing.

"I wish I hadn't called them," she said.

"I know, I understand. But what could you do? You didn't have a choice." "If only I hadn't come back this morning," she said.

"Yuh, but you did. And you wouldn't want to go to jail," I tried to reassure her. "I wish I'd been here for his call. Can he have visitors?"

"No, no visitors, no calls," she told me.

We talked more; I could see she was torn between anger for his lies about his "other side"—"He must have been going to the baths when he came home late; he lied to me."—and her love for him. "He's the only man I ever felt really good with."

I liked Mary.

***

Michael, another of my art students, and I went to the hospital to visit Tony the next night, but the nurse said he still couldn't have visitors. We watched him on the monitor, an old, hunched man of forty-two, a thin, shadowy figure as he

carefully got out of bed and headed unsteadily for the bedside commode.

***

"Hey, I'm glad you called, I'm so glad," Tony was home again after three days on suicide watch. New medications had quieted his voice. "Let's go out for lunch or sump'n, soon." I agreed, and we resumed our eating-out activities, I picking him up and he choosing the location depending on his appetite and my schedule. He needed friends and the straight community wouldn't contribute them; his homophobia had replaced his former acceptance of gay men and he no longer attended the support group. I decided to take a chance and introduce him to some gay friends who I knew would be compassionate, Tom and Johnny.

"Are they gay?" he asked suspiciously.

"Yeah," I answered nonchalantly.

"Hmmph."

"You're going to like them," I said. "They're really a great couple, have been everything for me this past year.'

"Hmmph."

The dinner, at an Italian restaurant, went well. When we left, Tony accepted a hug from Tom and Johnny.

"Seem like a really nice couple of guys," Tony said. 'I'd like to see them again."

***

I connected Tony with Sam, a one-man mini-AIDS project who filled in patients' needs from rides to groceries to quick cash. A true saint. Sam immediately began taking Tony on errands, to the clinic, out for lunch.

In December, Sam brought Tony back to art class; it was a cold, gray day and no one else had come. Tony was hungry, and Sam invited us to lunch at the chicken pot pie place that Tony loved. I hadn't seen Tony for several days and his eyes stared in their ashen orbits. His eyebrows lifted in the center, furrowing his brow as if he were perpetually bewildered.

Tony's voice was loud again as he fumbled with menu decisions, then tried to butter a roll, the butter-smeared knife swooping like a dove three or four inches from the bread. Like a man adrift in a raging river, he tried to steer himself into the conversation, interrupting often as if trying to grab a log. *This proud man needs attention today,* I thought, *I hope we can convince him.* As we left the restaurant, I trailed Tony as he stumbled and shuffled in a desperate attempt to control his legs and feet. I was frightened by the sudden drop in his condition, wanted to rush him to the hospital, but feared he would resent my usurping his control. Gentle persuasion, as if he decided to seek help, would be the best way to avoid an angry outburst, but anxiety nagged at me.

"Do you want to do some painting today, Tony?" I asked as he fell awkwardly into the chair opposite me back at the Project. I planned to observe him before taking action, though my first impulse was to whisk him over to the Emergency Room. Sam sat down next to me.

"Yeah, sure," he answered loudly with a lopsided grin. I felt like crying as I watched him stab the paints on the palette with his brush, usually missing his target but persevering. No words, just intense concentration on the job.

Tony painted a long, blue, oval shape, then a huge, blood-red cloud behind it. That was all. I watched him struggle to paint the shapes, wondering if he were painting his brain: was it the infection in his blood overwhelming the blueness of his brain? He talked disjointedly as he painted, complaining of his loneliness, his extreme fatigue, his inability to keep his life together, his frustrations. He couldn't concentrate and his manual coordination was erratic, the brush shaky. His uncombed, sparse hair stood up in short spikes.

He wanted to do another painting. This one, even simpler, was of a mass of bright red paint infused with yellow along the upper half of the paper. Below, he painted a blue line waving thickly across the entire page, then yellow up each side corralling the blue and red. With other students, I

had observed yellow grow in importance as their brain infections worsened. Now, I was watching a crumbling brain paint its own self-portrait. Amazing.

"Do you want to name your paintings?" I asked calmly.

"No, no. . . . I'm too tired."

"Tony, how would you feel if I called the hospital to see if someone could see you today?"

"Dunno, I guess that'd be okay," he said hesitantly. "My doctor don't tell me anything, I don't know what's wrong with me." He looked at me, bewildered; he didn't even swear.

"Look—Sam will stay with you while I run upstairs and call a nurse friend of mine at the hospital—she's an AIDS nurse practitioner—see what she says. Okay?" He nodded. I ran upstairs, glad that he hadn't reacted angrily, resenting that I was taking control. My friend, Phyllis, told me to bring him over immediately.

Unexpectedly compliant, Tony agreed to go to the Emergency Room. Despite his confusion, he knew he needed help desperately. And I knew the storm I'd been watching on the horizon had arrived; I felt as if his brain were about to explode.

***

"This'll make you laugh," Phyllis told me two days later, "At AIDS Rounds, your Tony's case was presented. They started with the patient having been referred by the art therapist," she laughed.

"My God, I hope his doctor didn't resent my second-guessing him," I said. But sometimes I could observe symptoms in the art room, through their behavior or art work, that weren't seen in the clinic. Or else they slyly hid the symptoms, fearing hospitalization and the diagnosis of yet one more opportunistic disease, another step down the ladder of AIDS and closer to death.

***

Tony was lying on his side, despondent, staring into space, when I visited him that night.

"How you doing, Tony?" I asked him.

"I dunno," he said, his voice dulled. No more bravado, only an immense sadness.

"Depressed, huh?"

"Yeah....I dunno. I really hate myself, I'm so angry at myself."

"Why, Tony? Because you got AIDS?"

"Yeah....I don't know why I did it. I dunno. I dunno why I had sex with guys...." His voice faded, he looked away. "I hate myself, I can't stand it."

"Tony, I don't understand it, nobody does, but if you hate that part of yourself then you hate all yourself. It just doesn't matter why you did it, or with whom, it just matters that you're sick now and you gotta get better."

"D'you suppose I'm really gay?" he raised his head.

"I don't know, maybe so," I said. "Maybe you'd just kept all that inside, got married, had kids, afraid to come out because people wouldn't like you. So you had to hide that part of you. Must have been hard."

"Hunh," he pondered. "Maybe I really am fuckin' gay," surprised at the idea. "Y'know, I never had a relationship with a gay guy. I didn't even always know their names."

"If you are, don't blame yourself. Gays are born gay, they're not created later."

"Did you always know Peter was gay?" he asked.

"I don't know if I realized it, but I always knew he was different. He was still one of my kids, though; it didn't matter, even when he told me. And now you have gay men as friends—Tom and Johnny—and you know they're good, not bad people."

"Yeah, I know, I do," he sparked up. "That Tom and Johnny, they're some of the nicest—sweetest—people I've ever known. Matter of fact, they seem much more devoted to each other than a lot of regular couples."

That's true," I agreed. "So—you know it isn't the worst thing to be gay, and you needn't hate yourself if you are, or even bisexual. It's just the way you're born, that's all," I shrugged my shoulders.

Yeah...." He mulled that over.

***

"Barbara, this is Mary, Mary this is Barbara," Tony introduced us the next night. So this was "the fuckin' bitch"! She didn't look very bitchy to me, a tall, striking woman with dark brown eyes, sitting next to the bed holding Tony's hand, her face concerned. I was amused to see her here; Tony had told me last night not to tell her he was in the hospital. But later he'd left her an abrupt message: "I'm in the hospital." Nothing more, not even which hospital. She'd called every hospital till she found him; seemed to me like a woman who really loved this man, not a bitch.

Tony was feeling better, more comfortable and less anxious except that the doctors couldn't diagnose the cause of his condition despite multiple tests. He'd be hospitalized a couple more days awaiting more test results.

But there was no final diagnosis for his rapid mental deterioration. Instead, a brain biopsy was scheduled in ten days. He feared the procedure, probably would have refused if his dementia weren't as overwhelming. But he did have enough brain left to put his affairs in order. I helped him pay his bills—he couldn't figure them out any more—and went through his safe deposit box with him. He entrusted a valued bag of old coins his father had given him to me; his paranoia included banks.

One day, I noticed a framed photo on his mantel, a lanky, robust man who could have been a movie star, laughing at the camera, full of life. I drew closer, squinted, about to ask who it was, squinted again, and pulled back in shock, wordless.

***

Six a.m. and still night-dark as we drove to the hospital for his biopsy.

"Y'know," he started, his voice loud again, "I couldn't sleep last night so I called Mom and Dad, must've been about two. Woke 'em up. I was hoping my Dad would say he loved me, I just kept hoping to hear it," he said sadly. "Just once."

"Oh Tony, I know he loves you. It's just hard for a man to say that to his son," I tried to reassure him. He was quiet.

"Finally got to sleep, though," he said lightly. "And Goddam, I had the most beautiful dream, I mean the most beautiful! God! So real it wasn't even a dream. I was floating above myself there on the bed. I was up there, lookin' down, and I just felt so good. Just warm, and soft, and good. I just felt so fuckin' good!" he marveled. "Y'know, I still feel good because of it."

"Some people call that an out-of-body experience," I told him. I'm usually skeptical about psychic assumptions, but Tony wasn't educated enough to have read about it. *I hope he doesn't expect to die during this operation,* I thought.

"I just wished I could've stayed up there forever," he mused. "Whatever it was. I just wish my Dad woulda said he loved me, though."

We parked, went up to his room. Two beds, one occupied by a chubby, gray-haired man of about sixty.

"Hi!" Tony bellowed. The man looked slowly, vacantly at him. "How ya doin'?" No response.

"Guess he don't wanna talk," Tony shrugged. "Why don't he talk?" he asked the male nurse who had just handed him a printed hospital gown and started spoon-feeding breakfast to the old man. Tony changed, got in bed and stared at his roommate.

"He was hit by a car downtown and his brain was damaged," the male nurse replied coldly.

"Oh." Tony stared. "Why're you feedin' him like a baby, can't he feed himself?"

"No." Cold.

"What's his name?"

"Bill." Terse.

"Oh. Pause. "Hiya, Bill!" Tony yelled.

"What's your name?" Tony asked the nurse.

"Harold." Stiff.

Tony glanced slyly at me; *Uh oh,* I thought. "Watch—I'll warm him up, fuckin' sunuva bitch," he promised *sotto voce.* I shivered in dread.

"I'm Dr. Baker," Tony bellowed. "Dr. Baker. I'm a psychiatrist."

"Really?" Harold said with cold skepticism as he wiped the old man's chin.

"Yeah," Tony winked at me. "Hey, Harold, how many kids you got?"

"Two," Harold threw the napkin away and moved the tray to another table.

"Only *two*? Christ, what's the matter with you? I got five. How come you only got two kids?" Another conspiratorial wink. I wanted to slide under the bed. But Harold suddenly blushed, grinned, chuckled burpingly as if he weren't used to laughing.

"I don't really like to fuck very much, y'know," he said confidentially, guy-to-guy, sitting on the foot of Tony's bed. "I just never liked it much," he confessed, blushing like a schoolgirl. Tony's rough charm had worked instantly, and the short, rotund nurse and he were like lifelong buddies. I sat down, relieved I wouldn't need to hit the floor.

With Tony's loud urging, Harold poured out his heart about his two kids, his solid wife, about "getting it up," about his job while Tony interjected his own tidbits, giving Harold advice on how to improve his sex life, winking continually at me. I laughed, too, but at the bizarreness of listening, at seven a.m., to a demented man giving sexual advice to this odd, stiff little man, pulling him out of his tight shell like a snail till they were laughing and joking like two buddies, regular good ole boys. Harold's eyes were wet with laughter.

"Gee, Tony, ole fella, guess I gotta go see my other patients," Harold rose reluctantly, wiping his eyes. "See you later, though, after your surgery." He patted Tony's leg. "Take it easy." I snickered: take it easy? The man's about to have his head drilled open.

"Nice guy, that Harold," commented Tony, pleased that his sandpaper charm had scored again. He folded his arms across his stomach.

Oh, the wondrous world of dementia, I thought, *where you don't care what anyone thinks of you.*

The housekeeper, mop in hand, roused Tony; his eyes lit up. *No, not again!*

"I'm Dr. Baker," Tony started off. The heavy-set black woman glanced up from her mopping.

"Yeah? What kind of doctor are you?" she asked, nearing his bed.

"I'm a chemical biologist," Tony answered proudly.

"Yeah?" A grin teased her lips. "Well, ain't that fine?"

"Yup. Say, how many kids you got?" *Please don't ask her about her sex life, she'll whomp you one.*

"I got three," hands on hips, a grin, daring him.

"I got five," Tony boasts. "How come you don't have more?"

"No, sir, no way, three's enough. No more for me, no sir*ree*."

"How old are they?"

"Twenty, nineteen, seventeen. No, sir, don't want no more," she shook her head.

"You musta been a baby when you had 'em," Tony marveled. "How old are you?"

"Thirty-six. Got married at sixteen, too young."

"Yeah, that's too young. I had my first at nineteen. Too fuckin' young, and they're all no damn good," Tony shook his head. "No damn good."

"Know what you mean," the woman nodded vigorously. "Alla mine turned out rotten. Drugs, daughter's got herself a baby, other'n quit school, out in the streets. No, sir, don't want no more." Friends now, bound by failed children. "Husband up and left, men no damn good, either," she laughed raucously.

"Yeah," Tony stared ahead, eyes wide.

"Well, gotta git goin'. See you tomorrow, okay? Now you take care of yourself, hear?" She shoved her bucket trough the door.

"Okay, see you tomorrow," Tony yelled.

"Good morning, Mr. Vidal," a young doctor, white-coated, entered. Crisp, professional, followed by a nurse with a tray and a resident.

"Who're you?" Tony asked loudly.

"I'm Dr. Smith, your neurosurgeon. I'm going to be doing your surgery today."

"Oh. I thought you were the cleaning-man," Tony winked at me. I ducked my head, again eying the space under the bed. Tony shrugged; you can't win 'em all.

The doctor took a hypodermic from the tray, injected anesthesia into various spots on Tony's head. "This will feel like a bee-sting."

"That's a fuckin' big bee—*ouch!*" Tony winced.

"I'm going to put a round, metal halo around your head and fasten it with screws," the doctor explained. I shuddered. Ouch.

"That's my head, not some goddam piece of wood," Tony exclaimed.

"Those injections should make it painless," the doctor said. He waited a few minutes, then he and the resident placed the halo on Tony's head and started tightening the screws slowly. I flinched in empathetic pain; couldn't they have waited a bit longer?

"God, that *hurts!*" Tony exclaimed loudly, astonished. Attendants came to wheel him to the operating room. I patted his hand, said goodby. He tried to smile, but his eyes were even wider with the fright he'd been trying to hide all morning. He looked as if someone had played a dirty trick on him.

***

I waited the hour of surgery, more time in the recovery room, while anxiety needled my own brain. *What if the biopsy needle hits something it shouldn't? Tony didn't need to lose any more function. And for what? They won't find anything, or if they do, it'll be incurable. Why put him through this?*

***

The biopsied material from Tony's brain indicated he had PML, progressive multifocal leukoencephalopathy, a viral infection that causes paralysis, vision loss, speech problems and mental deterioration. Finally, paralysis stills the lungs and literally takes the patient's breath away. There was no cure. No treatment. They gave Tony one month to live, two at most, and sent him home.

***

In mid-December, we arranged an exhibition of my students' work in the large hall of the Metropolitan Community Church. We matted, framed and hung their paintings on the high, white walls, a complimentary backdrop to the rectangles of vibrant, intense color.

"I can't believe how colorful their work is!" exclaimed one guest at our opening reception. "I expected all grays and blacks."

"No, no, they're still alive, y'know, they're young, they want to live, and color is life," I told her.

I circulated through the crowd, watching for Tony's entrance, afraid he might not be able to come. But finally I saw him hobble through the door, leaning heavily on his cane, assisted by a volunteer. I rushed over.

"Good—you're here!" I told him. "Come see how great your painting looks." I guided him to his framed painting and stood back. He wobbled on his cane, his mouth dropping open.

"Damn…" he sighed. "Look at that! It's beautiful," he said, his face creasing into a wide grin. "Damn! That's *beautiful!*" His chin quivered and a small tear crept slowly out of one eye and made a snail-track down his cheek. "My blue gate…."

***

Tony's twin sister came in December for their birthday; Tony introduced us proudly. The family had finally started to accept his prognosis.

On Christmas Day, his sister, Pat, her husband and daughter brought his mother and father and wanted to meet me. Tony sat on the couch, surrounded by his family. I looked at his legless father (it was true) propped up next to Tony; his mouth smiled happily but his eyes were wetly glazed with pain and sorrow. His mother, the saint, tall and graceful, sat on his other side; as beautiful as Tony had told me despite all that she had already borne. His sister and Mary made coffee and offered food, making jokes while their hearts broke in pieces and their tears flowed over the cookies when they fled to the kitchen.

***

Tony's family mobilized after Christmas. Expecting Tony had a month left, Pat came in January for a

month. She wanted, but also dreaded, being with him at his death. He didn't want his family to suffer the pain of his dying, didn't want them there then. He made me promise to be with him when he took his last breath. I didn't want to be there, either, but promised.

Tony degenerated rapidly after his biopsy though he still talked loudly; his eyes were permanently widened, his memory rotten. He didn't want to die but didn't want to live like this with useless arms and legs, always slumped over in his wheelchair, completely dependent. But he tried to do as much as he could and stay in control.

Tony devised a procedure for re-positioning himself in his wheelchair. Pat and I were to push him smack in front of a corner that had molding he could grab; then, he'd pull himself upright, we pushed the chair against his legs and he hurled himself into the chair, tight against the back. It took several tries to make it work, Tony blasting orders and cuss words into the air. Pat and I doubled over and Tony howled with wild laughter at our feeble awkwardness. Half an hour later, he slid down again and we repeated the process.

With difficulty, we persuaded Tony to accept private nurses through his insurance. The nurse and Pat could overlap while she trained them to deal with Tony. Mary went to his house after work every day but she, too, would need help; Tony was over six feet tall and helpless; a paralyzed body, even emaciated, weighs thrice its weight. His ever-increasing paranoia made him fear the nurses would steal everything. But the plan worked.

His parents wouldn't be back, though, and that hurt. His father, so sick himself, couldn't bear the pain of seeing his son like this. His children visited sporadically, uncomfortably; Sam, Tom and John, the volunteer and I dropped by. But Mary was his lifeline.

***

Tony tried twice more to get himself through the blue gate before resigning himself to a slower death. He persuaded his daughter to bring a bottle of Seconal on one of her rare visits and hid it in his shirt pocket. When Mary found the pills, she and the nurse had to wrestle the bottle from him; determination gave him unexpected strength.

One Sunday when Mary was visiting, he tried to grab a kitchen knife from Pat; Mary and Pat scuffled with him and finally retrieved the knife before he could stab himself.

He was helpless; he couldn't even kill himself. Now it was just a wait until the paralysis gulped down his whole body or a welcome pneumonia overtook him. His anger slipped away and his eyes held the bewilderment of dementia. I'd never known such sad eyes, always dilated and sunk deep into their dark orbits. He couldn't control his arms, legs, brain—even his bladder—nor his own longed-for death. Both life and death were beyond his control.

***

Mary fired one of the nurses; she was bossy, lacking compassion and uncooperative with Mary's wishes. The new nurse put a sling on Tony's left arm; his shoulder hurt from the arm's dead weight. The doctors increased his Tegritol after another seizure and he slept almost all day.

***

April. Three months longer than the doctors' one-month prognosis. Truly macho, this sandpaper man. His painting of the Gate to Paradise hung over his bed, calling silently to him.

"I want it over my bed, makes me feel good," he'd commanded us.

But Mary was starting to crack, feeling very alone. The family lived too far to come visit and help. Tony was living far beyond his prognosis; I suspected they couldn't deal with the prolonged horror. Mary spent all her spare time at his house, supervising the nurses, tending Tony, watching the paralysis envelope his once-beautiful body, like an invisible shroud. All that was left of the man she'd loved so much, tall, handsome, exuberant with life, now weighed one hundred pounds and lay inert all day, staring widely, unable to lift a finger, incontinent. The man with sandpaper charm was a wrinkled shell of weakened ligament, muscle and bone. No resemblance to the proud, laughing man in the photo on his livingroom mantel.

Her Tony had already died.

***

Tony's last act of rebellion: clenching the spoon tightly when the nurse tried to feed him. Mary told the nurses to stop the force-feeding.

***

"He went last night." Tears threaded Mary's words. "It was quick and easy, the way I'd always wanted it to be." She sighed deeply. "The nurse was turning him over and he stopped breathing, just stopped, and he was gone."

Tony had finally passed through his blue gate.

From *The Opposite of Fate*

Amy Tan

a question of fate

This is a true story.

Hours after my twenty-fourth birthday, my life began to change with strangely aligned events that today make me wonder whether they did not spring from the fictional leanings of my mind.

It was the Year of the Dragon, when my life's tide was said by Chinese astrologers to be at its most powerful, when change was inevitable. But all this was nonsense to me, for I was an educated person, a doctoral student in linguistics at UC Berkeley.

I tell you what my major was, because it reveals, I believe, what my mental inclinations were at the time. I was in a field of heady theories, seeking random and fortuitous evidence. As linguists we could not prove much in any terribly convincing scientific way, for instance, that grammar is innate and organized in the brain. But we could convolute ad infinitum on why that was possible and then search for empirical findings that suggested the science. Our methods were descriptive, the everyday use of everyday language by everyday people, the best examples being those that made one ponder such inanities as how the *p* sound came to be in the word *warmth* and what rules led people to innovate words like *hodgepodge*, *hocus-pocus*, and *hanky-panky*. Intricate convolution was also how I liked to occupy my mind when it came to worries about myself and, in particular, about how I showed my ineptitude when compared with other students.

Early that year, I had been married for nearly two years. Although I knew I was with the right person, I had the usual angst of a young woman who felt she had traded her soul's identity for a joint return. Lou and I lived in Danville, California, in a brand-new two-bedroom apartment with gold shag carpeting, a burgundy velour sofa, and a rotating variety of uncuddly pets, including a bull snake that was an escape artist and a tarantula that required a diet of live crickets.

To help us pay the rent, we had a roommate, Pete, a young man who was around our age, a bioengineering student also at Berkeley. He had pale blond air, an amblyopic eye, and a Wisconsin accent. We had met him two years before, when we all worked at a Round Table pizza parlor in San Jose. We continued to work at Round Tables in Berkeley and Danville, where we often took the closing shift and wound up sharing conversations over after-hours pitchers of beer.

Pete liked to argue about what was impossible to know, from conspiracies to eternity. His philosophical meanderings depended on how much beer he had imbibed, and were often related to the intersection of philosophy and science—the physics of infinity, say, or the ecology of ideas. He had a particular fascination with the I Ching, that art of tossing three coins three times and divining a pattern out of heads and tails. Pete would begin with questions: What determined the pattern? Was it random? Was it a higher power? Was it mathematical? Wasn't poker based on mathematical probability and not just luck? Did that mean randomness was actually mathematical? And if the I Ching was governed by mathematics, hey, wouldn't that mean the I Ching was actually predictable, a prescribed answer? And if it was prescribed, did that mean that your life *followed* the I Ching, like some sort of equation? Or did the I Ching simply capture correctly what had already been determined as the next series of events in your life?

And so the circular discussion would go. Somewhere in this mystery, mathematics always held the answer. Don't ask me how. I am only describing what I remember, what I never understood. We had such conversations during backpacking trips, while climbing the backcountry in Yosemite. At night, when we were not arguing over questions of eternity, we read H. P. Lovecraft tales around the campfire, shooed away marauding black bears, and identified the constellations from our sleeping bags, our chilled faces to the sky. Those are elements that strengthen any friendship, I think.

I remember enjoying many long conversations about secular transcendentalism, that motley union of the psychedelic and the physical. We had the sense that we were talking about what really mattered, the hidden universe and our souls. But perhaps that was also the atmosphere of the times, the 1970s, when all things were possible, particularly after eating brownies laced with goodies other than walnuts, when unorthodox speculation could be answered sufficiently with a reverential "Wow."

Pete also talked a lot about his wife. She was a poet, naturally intuitive, a sexy earth-mother type. They were separated, the result of his own immaturity, he said, his predilection for recklessness and his not thinking enough about the consequences. He expressed hope that his wife might understand that he was sorry, and that they'd be together again one day. Several months after we met, while explaining how he had lost his wallet and hence his driver's license, he told us how he had lost his wife.

They had been traveling by car through Nevada on their first trip from Wisconsin to California. A nineteen-year-old hitchhiker offered to spell them from driving, and they gladly let him take the wheel. Just outside Lovelock, while they were speeding through the pitch-black desert, a rear tire blew, and as Pete turned to tell him to let the car drift to a stop, the hitchhiker instinctively slammed on the brakes, and the car began to roll over. It all happened gently enough, Pete told us, that first roll, the kind of flip you experience in an amusement-park ride, with the car landing on its wheels, righting itself. For a moment, it appeared

that they might be able to continue their journey with the only alterations a replaced tire, a slightly dented roof, and one hell of an adrenaline rush. But in the next breath, the car flipped again, this time with the vigor of increased momentum and lift, and when it turned over, it crashed down hard, on its roof, bringing Pete to guess that the car was now totaled. If they were lucky, they might get by with a few injuries, although broken bones seemed likely. And then the car sailed into its third roll, crunched down with the certitude of finality, and slid belly-up into clouds of dust and uprooted sagebrush. When all was quiet, Pete patted himself and found that he was alive and, even more miraculous, uninjured. In the next second, he felt around in the darkness and ascertained that his wife and the hitchhiker were alive as well, breathing hard and fast. But then they let out a final exhale, first the hitchhiker, then Pete's wife, and he was alone. When the police and ambulance crew arrived and asked for his driver's license, he realized that he had lost his wallet.

Two years after the accident, Pete reconciled with his wife in a dream. In fact there were two dreams, a week apart. In the first, which he related to Lou and me, two men, strangers to him, broke into his room, overcame him, and slowly strangled him to death. He described the sensation of absolute terror and the pain of not being able to breathe, and then a tremendous release from struggle. When it was over, he found his wife waiting for him.

Pete went on to say that the dream felt like a premonition. It was scary as hell, but he was at peace with it. His wife would be there. If anything happened to him, he said, he would like Lou and me to distribute his belongings among various friends and family: his guitar to one brother, his camera to another . . .

Stop, I said. Stop being ridiculous. I thought that he, like Lou and me, was nervous about the death threats the three of us had received from a gang whom we had thrown out of the pizza parlor. Two attempts on our lives had already been made, knives and clubs had been drawn, punches exchanged, and my shin nearly broken by a kick with steel-toed boots. Pete had made the mistake of winning one fistfight and breaking his opponent's nose. The gang was now doubly committed to killing us. When we called the Danville police for help, they informed us that our personal thugs had arrest records for dozens of assaults, but there were no convictions, nor were any likely. The best way to deal with future attempts on our lives, someone told us, was to equip ourselves with guns, learn how to use them properly, and make sure that the bodies fell *inside* our door. Outside it was homicide, we were told, inside it was self-defense. Moving to another town was also not a bad idea.

The latter advice was ultimately what we decided to follow. A week after Pete had the disturbing dream he told us about, Lou and I helped him move to Oakland, into a studio apartment in an art deco building. We were placed on a waiting list for a one-bedroom apartment in the same building; for now we kept the apartment in Danville. Pete had few possessions: a bed, a TV set and a stereo, a small table and a chair, his guitar and camera, books, and an expensive calculator that he had purchased with my credit card. There was also a .22 automatic, which he had bought to defend himself in Danville.

Lou and I stayed at Pete's his first night in Oakland, in a sleeping bag on the floor. I recall Pete reiterating his feeling that something bad was going to happen, that someone might break in and kill him. We assured him that there was no way the thugs would know where he had moved. Nor were they industrious enough to want to follow us. Nevertheless, Pete placed the gun between the mattress and the box spring, within easy reaching distance. We kidded him for being paranoid.

The next morning was my twenty-fourth birthday. I can admit now that I was deflated that nothing special was mentioned or offered from the start: no profusion of beautifully beribboned presents, no announcement that plans had been made for going on a lark or winding up at a banquet. But

perhaps this seeming lack of preparation really meant that an even more elaborate scheme was in the works, and I would have to be patient to see what it was. Lou suggested we go for a drive, and Pete declined the invitation. He was going to unpack, settle in, and nurse a cold he had just developed. A ruse, I thought. He would be behind the scenes, getting the surprise party under way. As we left, I mentioned we might stop by later, but we would be unable to call ahead of time, since he did not yet have phone service.

As it turned out, my twenty-fourth birthday was a cobbled assortment of activities, spontaneity being the key and "Why not?" being the answer. Lou and I had an impromptu lunch at a restaurant, a drive through the country later, and then we took up an invitation from a friend in Marin County to have dinner with her parents. We spent the night in their driveway, sleeping in our Volkswagen bus. So there was no grand party. The day had been pleasant, but not as eventful as I had secretly hoped.

The next day, back at the apartment in Danville, an acquaintance called. He lived in the building Pete had moved into—we had learned of the vacancy there from him. I greeted him cheerfully.

"Oh," he said flatly, "then you haven't heard the news."

What news?

"Pete's dead. Two guys broke into his place last night and killed him."

"That is the worst joke I've ever heard," I responded angrily. But later Lou and I learned that, indeed, two men had entered through the bathroom window; according to a witness's report, they did not resemble our thugs from Danville. These men had used Pete's .22 to bash him over the head, then hog-tied him stomach down, the rope lashed around his neck and ankles so that the soles of his feet faced the back of his head. When he could no longer hold his muscles taut, he let go and slowly strangled.

In one imagined version—I've played them a thousand times—the robbers stand and watch as

Pete struggles to stay alive. That's the worst. In another version, they leave him while he is still struggling. The police arrive, but seconds too late. Actually, that is the worst. They are all the worst. As to what happened after Pete was tied up, I have only these facts: The two men ran out of Pete's studio with his gun and went to pound on the door of the apartment manager, demanding to be let in. When the manager refused, they blasted the door with bullets, then ran out of the building toward their car. A man on the sidewalk had the misfortune of being there; they shot and killed him on the spot. A newspaper story identified the man on the sidewalk as a business student from India who attended Armstrong College. I don't remember his name, and I regret that, for no one killed in that manner should be nameless and forgotten.

I've often thought of that young man from India, and of his family, who must think of his death, as I do, every anniversary of that February night in 1976. "Today," I imagine them saying, "our son would have been fifty years old. Can you imagine? That's older than we were when he died."

The next day, Lou and I went to the Oakland Police Department to identify Pete on behalf of his family in Wisconsin. The police showed us only photographs, but what I saw is too obscene to relay in words. Since then, whenever I read stories of wars, or earthquakes, or murders, I have imagined those who have seen what I have, the face of a loved one, not in peaceful slumber as morticians might have devised, but as it appeared at the moment of death, a body unwashed, ungroomed, not prepared, in any conceivable way, to be viewed by another human being, let alone someone who loved that person.

After collecting the Saint Christopher's medal that Pete always wore around his neck, we drove to his apartment to assist detectives in identifying what might have been taken. I remember seeing everything as in a TV documentary filmed in close-up, with no possibility of pulling away: the door, dusted for fingerprints, and the yellow tape; the opening of the door and my recoiling at the

smell. It was the pungent scent of fear, a wild-animal smell of nervous sweat, and it was as potent as if Pete and his assailants had still been in the room, the torment happening in front of me. To the right was further evidence of who had been there, the powdery impressions of fingertips and palms on the doorjamb. Littering the floor were used tissues: so the cold had not been a ruse at all. On the table were the remnants of a dinner—a can of stew (what a poor last meal!)—and a bottle of NyQuil, half empty. Had he been too lethargic to hear the robbers breaking the bathroom window? Was he slow to react? Did he think it was Lou and I who were trying to get back in, looking for a place to stay after a night of birthday-partying? Why didn't he use his gun?

Also on the table was a letter he had written to a friend. I read the page facing up. In it, he described a dream he had had, similar to the one he had recounted the week before: He found himself enmeshed in wads of thick cotton. Soon it became as light as cotton candy, and when he broke free, he saw his wife and others, people whom he did not recognize but who seemed warmly familiar. It was a good dream, the letter said. It felt like a premonition. So that was the second dream. At last, Pete was reconciled with his wife.

When I turned to the left, I saw the rappelling ropes that had been used to strangle him, the bed with a large bloodstain from the blow to his head.

Lou and I listed what had been taken: a stereo; a small television set; a $600 Hewlett-Packard calculator, the prize of any bioengineering student; and a .22 automatic. I wondered whether a birthday present for me must also have been stolen. We were good friends, after all, and so of course he would have bought me something. But whatever it might have been, it was not there, and it pained me that I would never know.

When we returned to Danville that night, we held a wake with a small group of friends. We sat on the floor, on the gold shag carpet, and because we could not talk, we drank. I downed a lot of vodka to block out the images of death, the odor of fear. Soon I vomited, and when my mind became clearer, I heard Pete's voice. By that I mean that it sounded as if he were speaking out loud. It was no doubt grief preying on my imagination, drunken thinking taking voice. Yet I could not help relaying aloud what I had just heard: "The names of the guys who killed him are Ronald and John." My friends stared at me. "Pete just told me," I said. Cracked, their looks implied. She's really cracked.

Four days later, two men were apprehended in a robbery in Oakland. In the backseat of their car were items that had been taken from Pete's apartment, including the calculator that he had purchased on my credit card. The serial number on the receipt matched the one on the calculator. The police told us the names of the men in their custody: Ronald and John.

Lou and I were stunned to hear the names I had blurted the night before. The police guessed that the two had targeted Pete after watching him move into the apartment; robberies often occur around the time of such transitions, they said, as criminals size up victim and possessions. Other than that, the choice of Pete as victim was random, a bit of bad luck. Both men had long arrest records, for robbery, and assault and battery, and they had a nasty penchant for tying up people and beating them. The fingerprints taken at Pete's apartment, however, matched only one of the men arrested. Because of what I had heard or imagined Pete saying, I was certain both men had been in the room. The police were too, but for another, more earthbound reason: A neighbor had heard two men's voices in the hall just before they fired through his door. In the end, only one of the men, John, was charged with Pete's murder.

The police said that I would be called as a witness, because I was the owner of the credit card. They cautioned me that I would have to take the witness stand during the preliminary hearing and the trial itself, and I would be required to look at the morgue photos and once again identify the body. I was sickened even to think of the prospect.

The night before the preliminary hearing, I had a fantastical dream, the first of a series that would occur nightly until Pete's murderer was convicted several months later. The dreams may have been delusional, the result of emotional trauma at having seen the gruesome evidence of a friend's death. Yet even if that is the case, it does not diminish the importance of those dreams to me or what I learned and did as a consequence. While I have always been a prolific dreamer, one who remembers up to a dozen dreams a night, I have never had dreams quite like these before or since. For one thing, these dreams followed a singular convention: I was always aware that Pete was dead and that I was alive, and that where we were meeting was the consciousness called dreams. In addition, each dream consisted of lessons in the form of metaphors that were obvious in their meanings.

In the first dream, I arrived at the place where Pete was now staying. It was—as dreams go—a surreal land with glorious green mountains, flowering meadows, and canyons flowing with waterfalls. Elephants, mastodons, and people flew about, as though a circus had been cast into a gravity-free environment. Only Pete and I were on solid ground.

"Hey," he said, "let's go flying."

"I'm not dead," I reminded him. "I can't fly."

"Oh, right. Well, see over there, that lady at the stand? She can rent you some wings."

He took off, and I turned toward the stand he had mentioned and duly procured a set of plastic wings for the bargain price of a quarter. I slipped them on, walked to the edge of a cliff, and took off soaring, but uncertain as to what I should do next. With the wings I was weightless and could move toward whatever I wished to see. All at once, I had a disturbing thought: How can a pair of cheap wings enable me to fly?

The next instant I was plummeting, the weight of my body pushing down, the wind pressing up, and I knew that soon I would be smashed to pieces. How could this be? Hadn't I been flying a moment ago? In the next instant, I was aloft once more, weightless. Relieved but still puzzled, I wondered again how I could be flying with wings that cost only a quarter—and abruptly, I was falling again. But I was flying a second ago, I said to myself. And immediately, I was aloft. . . . At the instant I realized the meaning of the dream, Pete spoke: "And now you see, it's your belief in yourself that enables you to do what you wish." With that, the dream ended.

The next night, a monster was set on me and I began to run. This was the boogieman I had known since childhood. I ran up a long stairwell, I ran through the dark streets. All the while, Pete was urging me to stop and turn around and look at what was chasing me.

"I can't," I cried. "If he touches me, I'll die."

"Turn around," Pete said firmly.

Finally I did. Before me was a monster, as I had expected, and yes, he was hideous in every respect: a huge, scaly creature with a venomous look. But he was also surprised that I stood there examining him. After a few seconds he started to shrink, and then he disappeared.

"You see," Pete said, "it's your own fears that give them the power to chase you."

And so the dreams went each night, a visceral truth played out to heights of drama. I learned to make money come pouring out of pay phones that had been broken and never connected me to those I was trying to reach. I learned to fly down stairs in huge leaps, rather than being paralyzed with leaden legs and attempting only one small step at a time. I discovered that if I did not like what was before me, I had only to look at my shoes, then look up and walk ahead toward a fresher, more pleasant scene. During this time, my life changed—or rather, I changed my life, in ways I would previously have thought inconceivable. For one thing, I decided to quit my doctoral program.

This drastic decision was clearly born when the idealism of my twenties collided with the shock of tragedy. A valuable life had been lost, and to make up for it, I had to find value in mine. That was the gist of the feeling. The doctorate, I decided, would

be a worthless appendage. Besides, there were no jobs in linguistics, and even if there were, how was I bettering the world by teaching others to examine the intricacies of dead languages and the like?

To leave academia was a terrifying idea, however. It meant abandoning the dream my parents had nurtured in me since the age of six, that I would become a doctor of some sort. Within that doctorate were all the embellishments of my ego, my sense of worth, my place in the world, and hence all my worries as well, the fear that I would never be good enough, that I would forever be struggling to hide that I was a fraud, doomed one day to fail and reveal how inadequate I truly was. But if I left the doctoral program, what could I do instead? What could I do that was worth anything to anyone, including myself? I could see nothing.

I remembered that Pete had once suggested that I apply my linguistics knowledge toward working with disabled children. He had said this a month or so before he died. He himself had intended to make computerized equipment for people with disabilities. At the time, his suggestion held no appeal for me. I was not particularly fond of children, except as objects of research, and I knew nothing about disabilities.

But once I quit my doctoral program, I found a job listing for exactly what he had in mind: a language development specialist for a county program serving children, newborns to five years old, who had developmental disabilities. At the interview, it was as apparent to the administrator as it was to me that I was both overqualified and specifically unqualified for this job. When the interview ended and I stood to leave, I heard Pete telling me that I should simply tell this woman my motivations in applying for a job with exactly these challenges and unknowns. And out came my story of Pete's death and my pledge to do with my life what he had intended to do with his. Ten minutes later, I was hired.

It was my job to observe the children, informally assess their communication skills, and then work with parents and teachers to devise a plan and help them carry it out.

I remember the first talk on language development I gave for the parents. I mustered all my knowledge, prepared a detailed examination of the steps and processes entailed in language acquisition, and delivered an impressive one-hour lecture to a dozen parents, many of whom had just been told their babies had Down's syndrome, cerebral palsy, autism, or some rare congenital disorder that would lead to an early death. At the end of my talk, a mother came up to me and said, "You are _so_ smart." I never felt more stupid. You just have to learn how to learn, I heard Pete say.

After that, I would listen to parents as they discussed their hopes for their children, and then together we would cry before we set out to find new hopes. With the kids themselves, I learned to play, to discover what made them laugh, what they could not resist watching or touching or reaching for. I found myself observing not deficits but the qualities of souls. Over the next five years, I had opportunities to work with more than a thousand families, and from them I sensed the limitlessness of hope within the limits of human beings. I learned to have compassion. It was the best training I could have had for becoming a writer.

Of course, not everything about me had changed for the better. I still worried incessantly about every detail of my life, twisting the permutations of these anxieties into knots. I remember one day, some six months after Pete died, when I was fretting over money, or rather, our profound lack of it. I was driving across the Bay Bridge in our rickety VW bus, coming home from my job, which netted me barely enough for rent, utilities, and food. Lou was in law school, and what little he earned went toward his tuition and books. But now we had a crisis: Our recently adopted cat, Sagwa, had gone into her first throes of heat the night before, and in searching for her Romeo, she jumped out of our fourth-story apartment window. Luckily, she lived, but fixing the resulting broken leg was going to cost us $383. How would we pay for it? We couldn't save that amount in a year. Why the hell did we get the damn cat?

I heard Pete say: "Come on, it was an accident. You worry about things over which you have no control." By then, I had heard his counseling voice many times. In the weeks right after his death, I had believed he was speaking to me across the divide. But now, with the natural waning of grief and shock, I had returned to thinking it was merely my imagination conjuring what he might have said.

"Easy for you to say," I responded. "You're dead. I have real bills."

I heard him laughing. "These things happen by themselves. They'll take care of themselves."

I was about to banter back when I felt something slam the side of the bus, and send me swerving across a lane of traffic on the bridge. I fought to regain control, finally pulled over, and got out of the car with shaky legs. A man rushed up to me.

"Are you all right? I'm so sorry. I don't know what happened. Thank God you're not hurt."

We went around to the side of the VW that he had rammed. At first I could see no sign of damage, but when we bent down and looked at the panel that curved under the bus, we saw it: a long gash, barely noticeable in a vehicle riddled with dings and oxidized paint.

"Get some estimates," the man told me. "Send them to my insurance company and they'll pay."

"It's not worth it," I said. "Even though it's not my fault, this will be reported to my insurance company and my rates will go up."

"I see what you mean," he answered. "Well then, just get one estimate and send it directly to me. Here's my card. I'm the vice-president of this corporation. I'll send a check to you directly."

Fair enough. I drove to the first body shop off the ramp. Ten minutes later, I heard Pete laughing as I stared at the written total for the estimate: $383.

I will relate only one more dream. It was the last.

On Lou's birthday that year, the trial ended, with a conviction on two counts. First-degree robbery. First-degree murder. That night, I dreamt that I met Pete in a garage, a rather prosaic location for a farewell meeting. He told me this was the last dream, now that the trial was over. I protested, "These are *my* dreams. I get to decide when they end." Pete ignored what I said, and went on: "You're going to meet my friend Rose—"

"Rose!" I sneered. "Fat chance. She hates me." When I had called her months before to tell her Pete was dead, she had been curt almost to the point of rudeness. Then again, I had been the same with the messenger who delivered the news to me.

"Rose is going to become very important to you," Pete said. "She's a writer, and she'll be helpful to you when you become a writer."

"Who said I was going to be a writer?"

"That's all I wanted to say," Pete told me, and then, as if going down to the corner store, he left me there.

After that, I still had dreams about him, but they were different, nothing at all like the dream-lessons. The new dreams conveyed the full horror of his death, for in them he was not dead, as I had feared, but alive, as I had hoped. Having survived near-strangling, he was brain-damaged, confused and suspicious, preferring to live as a beer-drinking recluse, unsure of who he was and uninterested in finding out.

Each year for seven years, on the anniversary of Pete's death, I lost my voice. It must have been a psychogenic gesture for the horror I could not talk about. And yes, eventually, Rose and I did connect with each other, tentatively at first, through brief letters, and then in lengthy missives, both of us grasping to understand the transcendental experiences we have had since his death.

If you've followed this story so far, you have already understood that Rose is indeed a writer, and that she was the first person to encourage me to write fiction, suggesting what I might read for inspiration and to which little magazines I might send my first attempts.

Enough time has passed that I can now more reasonably assess that period after Pete died. I have considered that those dreams were the subconscious by-product of trauma and grief, or the delusional thinking that enables a person to cope with horror. The metaphors were ones I have had all along, and through the need to survive, I brought out their meanings. Whatever they sprang from, the dreams were a lot more cost-effective than psychoanalysis. As to the counseling voice of Pete, guiding me toward the job with children, that was my own, pushed by fear of failure to the point that I made myself finally hear it. The coincidence of the $383? Well, that's odd, and hard to explain, except to say that when you are looking for coincidences, you will surely notice them. There are rational answers for everything. Sometimes I think about what they might be.

And yet no matter what these dreams and coincidences were, everything that happened during those months from my birthday to Lou's had a wondrous effect on me, on the shape of my life. It pushed me, enlarged my outlook, and sent me searching for what I should believe in. Does it matter what the origins were?

Today I am neither a believer nor a skeptic. I am a puzzler. I still puzzle over what Pete's story presents: what I fear, what I dream, what I believe. I ask myself: What's real? What's important? What do I gain in believing one reality over another? What do I lose? And if we understand the mysteries of the universe, if they end up being explained entirely by mathematics, as Pete said they could be, will they still bless us with the same amazing joy?

APPENDIX I

General Study Questions

Francis E. Crowley

1. Is time treated in a linear fashion in this story, i.e., chronologically? Do the events recounted unfold in a cause and effect relationship? Are there any flashbacks? Too many? Why, do you suppose, are they used in this story? Do they cause confusion or promote clarity in understanding the overall direction of the plot? Is the use of a linear ("line-ear"), step-by-step, narrative approach always the best strategy for building tension or suspense? Have you personally used an alternative approach?

2. What role does geography, place or space play in the theme of this story? Do you agree with the premise that ". . . geography is destiny . . .!"?

3. Who are the important persons in the story? Are they active or passive within the events/ experiences/ actions of the story? Is the event recounted life-changing in any way?

4. In addition to "time, place and person" in a memoir, there is the element of style and tone. Is the language/diction easy to understand? Is there dialog? Too much? How does the use of dialog clarify and promote the message of the narrative? Is the tone humorous or serious or _____? Is it appropriate to the topic? List the predominantly humorous stories in the book. How well do they work as humor. Do they provide balance for some of the serious narratives?

5. In narration, besides dialog, the use of paragraphing is different from that in an expository essay? Why? How? Is writing a narrative essay for you easier than writing exposition? Why, or why not? Which stories border on exposition in paragraph style? How are transitions handled, i.e., person to person, voice to voice, place to place, one time to another?

6. A memoir combines description with narration that is real, actually happened; it is non-fictional. Are fictional techniques, such as figures of speech and imagery, along with imaginative characters, found in any of our stories? How might you know? (Besides inviting the author into class one day for a guest reading.) What are some of the major distinctions between imaginative literature and non-fiction? How does creative writing (fictional short stories) differ in essence from memoir and narrative essay?

7. How do you like the verse/poems in this book? Can you understand them with ease? Do you prefer the short lyrical poems (as in "lyrics" for a song) or the longer ones that border on telling a little story (narrative poems, as in "narrative painting"). Which topics are talked about in the lyrical poems, besides love and death and loss? Are there any which surprise you?

8. Are there any bilingual writers in this book? How do you know who they are?

9. How would you define a mentor? Do any authors mention a mentor? Name? If so, how would you describe the mentor's role in the author's life and writing life? Are there any non-traditional mentors?

10. How does the subjective vision of our writers, individually, in our book—especially, their ethnic, country-of-origin—or sexual preference—influence their narratives. Slightly? Predominantly? Why?

APPENDIX II

Discussion and Composition Topics for *Stories from the Other Side*

Trans-Mission

Questions and Discussion

1) What does the title signify?
2) Analyze the voice of this narrative. Is his voice serious, humorous, or sarcastic?
3) What do you think about the staff's reaction to Lisa? If you were one of them, would you act differently?

To, and from, Bhutan

Questions and Discussion

1) Why did he decide to go to Bhutan? What made Bhutan very special for him?
2) List the things and landscapes that you would see only in Bhutan. What kind of impact did the author receive from them?
3) The author's aunt said to him, "Perhaps you simply had to go there, to be healed." Do you agree with her? What else did he learn through the experience of going to Bhutan?

Composition

Write about your experiences of traveling and encountering different cultures.

Proud to be Me

Questions and Discussion

1) Why didn't the author's father approve of her? Did he have any reason which made it difficult for him to accept his daughter? Is the answer hidden between the lines?
2) Does this essay represent a stereotypical scenario related to child abuse?

3) The author's father regarded her as a "liar." Do you think she should be blamed?
4) Why do you think sexual abuse causes such deep and long-lasting trauma and pain for the victim?

Excerpt from The Outermost House

1) What does the young swimmer's body signify for the author?

Composition Topic

Write about a moment when you have been inspired by Nature in a short narrative essay or Haiku.

The Language of My Father

1) Analyze the language the author's father used. How did he communicate with his family?
2) Are there any detailed descriptions that imply the father's character in this essay?

My Buddy, Daniel

1) Contrast Daniel's background and the author's. Explain the differences in their characters, too.
2) Why is this author helping Daniel? What kind of feelings does he have toward Daniel when he spends time with him?
3) The author met Daniel through the Buddy Program. Do you think he succeeded in building up a friendship with Daniel? What do you think is the key factor in developing their friendship?
4) How does the author approach Daniel, especially given Daniel's innocence and macho character?

5) The author takes Daniel to different places, including his own house, and buys meals for Daniel. Do you think his generosity has helped Daniel to trust people?

Living with Insanity
1) Why do you think he wrote this essay, revealing his personal situation? What kind of message does he have?
2) Analyze some stereotypical images people might have of those suffering with AIDS.

She Said "Yes" to Life
1) Why does the author's grandmother have such a strong impact on his life? Is there anything special about her character?
2) What does it mean to say "yes" to one's life?

Fear and Uncertainty in Caracas
1) Explain the irony of the title.
2) What do you think about the stereotypical image of the Venezuelan that the author had in the beginning?

Composition
Select one country or one ethnic group and write about some stereotypical images attached to it.

The Story of a Union Soldier
1) What kind of reality of war does this story reveal?
2) Are there any differences or similarities between this union soldier and contemporary American soldiers?

Becoming a Godmother
1) Compare Lilia's life style and Adriana's. Do you agree with the author's view that Lilia tried to "fit their [the students'] image of poverty" to get more donations from them?
2) Read the last section titled "Afterwards" and summarize the author's idea of poverty.
3) According to the author, what kind of attitudes do we need when we participate in charities?

The Dance Lesson
1) Why did the author and Jesse become closer to each other as the story progressed? Why did they accept each other when they were in a difficult situation?
2) After they left the facility, what happened to their friendship?

Haiti
1) What kind of mission does the author have in Haiti? What is her motivation?
2) Find the lines that show the historical background of Haiti.
3) What kind of feelings does the author have when she sees the reality of Haiti?

APPENDIX III

General Inquiry Questions for poems in *Stories from the Other Side*, 6th

1. What are some of the concerns and social issues covered by poets in this book? Can you extrapolate the poet's position and attitude on an issue from the choice of imagery/and/or figures of speech? Can you hear his/her political voice on a social justice topic?

2. Can you infer a set of values, cultural or spiritual, from all the poet's work taken together? How strongly does the poet show his/her beliefs within the lines?

3. Is the speaker in the poem the same voice as the poet's, do you think? If not the same, who is the speaker? Can you describe the voice or the *persona* from any clues: diction, tone, attitude, affect? Why do you think the poet chose to speak in another person's voice for this poem? What effect is gained?

4. Some poets prefer to channel the voice of a famous historical figure for special effect. Can you find such a case of impersonation? Try reading the poem aloud a few times to get the intonation, pitch and timber of the speaker's voice to get a clue.

5. What are your expectations as you approach the poems? Do you expect to be entertained, instructed, amused, challenged....or what? Do you ever feel inspired by new insights in a poem? Do you have a favorite childhood poem or song to compare? Can some be considered light or humorous in tone?

6. Most of the poems in this book are readily accessible in meaning through the use of everyday diction. Do you find any particularly challenging to understand? Among several poems by the same poet, is there one you find opaque or impenetrable? Which one? Why?

7. Do any poems employ conversational language? What's the effect? In contrast, can you find examples of elevated, formal or academic diction in other poems?

8. All poems use a combination of concrete and abstract words. Choose one, longer poem and make parallel lists of each. Do you find that you prefer poems of abstract ideas or sensory description (taste, touch, smell, sight, sound). EXAMPLE: William Carlos Williams advised, "...no ideas but in things."

9. Do any poems have more than one speaker? Does each use distinctive diction? Can you readily tell them apart? How?

10. Who is your favorite, popular, current poet/rapper/performer of spoken word? Have you attended any poetry readings or open-mic performances? Have you read or performed at "spoken word" events? Do you write poetry as a hobby?

11. How important is *THE MUSE* in the life of the poet? How would you define the MUSE? What are her various incarnations and roles in a poet/painter's creative life?

12. Which poets use metaphor in this book? Choose one poem that has appealing imagery for you and that also uses an extended metaphor or symbol. Think about the poet's choice of the figure of speech to illuminate and enhance the poem's meaning. Is the metaphor one that controls the development of the idea or theme?

13. What are some of the topics/themes portrayed in these poems that are common to two or more poets in our book? Does each treat the subject or meaning in a different way? Are there some commonalities between two poets?

14. In modern times some painters/poets have a "beef with the bourgeoisie," so to speak. Why? Are some poets' values and life-styles unalterably at war with the middle class? Is the business-man always the cultural arch-enemy of the bohemian painter or poet? In which societies do you imagine this conflict to be especially sharp? American, Arab, Russian, African, *etc*. Why? Are there any poets in our book that you would call "protest poets" by their choice of theme or message, imagery, diction or strength of conviction?

15. Write a poem for sharing in class on the following phrase and see if you can make it come alive for the listener through your daring use of imagery:
    EXAMPLE: "You never know from one day to the next!!"

16. Which poet in our book do you think clearly seeks spiritual enlightenment; which is the most confessional; which is the "Nature poet" *par excellence*. Are some poets clearly LGBT in point of view?
    Are any poets in the tradition of the "HARLEM RENAISSANCE?"

APPENDIX IV

Poetry: "My Experimental Manifesto"

I want to let go of the normative, ego-based lyrics of my earlier voice for a new community sensitivity: not just imaginative experience through another's feelings and eyes, but much more of a vision of a common humanity with a voice of deep human sympathy and connection.

I'd like to use my poetic gifts in service to others—beyond the single voice of a personal journey and my narrow truth—into the fuller expression of a larger, cultural truth which gives hope. Somehow my creative activity starts with acute observation and the juices of inspiration; this is a taking-in not through "tired eyes" but with fresh eyes and ears to really see and hear what is miraculously, materially there at my feet and in my ears, nose and throat.

I want to put all this analogically together with vibrant imagery for the listener as if it were a gift of gentle touch like a "...slippery tongue in the porches of my ear." But, I must remember to be mindful of how far to ride the metaphor before I fall off, so to speak; otherwise, my verse can quickly revert to self-absorbed, spider webs. In short it takes a "nerve cowboy" to ride the figure for all its worth but a circumspect writer to know when to jump off, so to speak.

Sound is as essential as sense for my own poet's ear and voice. That's a given! It only starts with alliteration for me, but quickly builds with slant rhyme. I find that I'm growing as a poet in my crafting of rhythm much more quickly by attending SLAMS such as at Bentley's Coffee and Tea last Saturday evening on Speedway. I gloriously lose each time; joyously, I listen to new pacing in the Haiku Death Match; uproariously, I celebrate the raucous shouts of the Vagina Warriors of the University of Arizona in their rant and performance. I quickly learn that not everything is worth writing down or recording, even this statement.

Just as we are prisoners in our own sensual bodies, I feel that I am an inmate within our own American conceptions, cultural values and paradigmatic patterns of literary art. For example, let's not have another cop or cowboy screenplay: you know—the Huck and Jim duo on the river, the road, the trail or down mean streets. We're ripe for renewal, thematically maybe, but certainly release from tired, old tropes.

My personal bounded and burdened perceptions and my internal filters of religion, politics and class have occasionally blocked out the daily not-so-minor miracles of human connection, compassion and celebration of Nature, especially here in the desert Southwest. Catastrophic events, such as the recent Haiti earthquake, can shake me out of my old, comfortable shoes, and I open my tired eyes, again, to take in a fresh vision of Hope, which has infused this month's three new poems. My own internal astigmatism of assumptions was realigned by the terrible magnitude of this Haitian tragedy, on top of their agony, and by the spontaneous American response of love and generosity, which continues. To put this another way, as it affects my process of composition, my internal 3-D glasses work much better after a transformative experience.

From 19th Century Romanticism (Wordsworth and the publication of the Lyrical Ballads in 1798), which was my earliest mode to emulate in the first flush of school's enthusiasm, all the way to today in my current, Romantic-Post-Modern poet's emerging voice I have traveled light years in the sound of my true, natural and authentic voice. This feels really good to me in my most recent poems.

Francis E. Crowley, Ph.D., Professor in the Humanities EMERITUS, Gateway Community College, New Haven, CT